Enjoy!

Love,

THE COMPLETE
FAMILY COOKBOOK

EDITORIAL
US Food Editor: Linda Venturoni
Food Editor: Rachel Blackmore
Assistant Editor: Ella Martin
Editorial Assistant: Sheridan Packer
Editorial Coordinator: Margaret Kelly

RECIPE DEVELOPMENT
Jane Ash, Susan Bell, Belinda Clayton, Penny
Cox, Sheryle Eastwood, Sue Geraghty, Joanne
Glynn, Michelle Gorry, Donna Hay, Anneka
Mitchell, Voula Mantzouridis, Meg Thorley

PHOTOGRAPHY
Andrew Elton, Ashley Mackevicius, Harm Mol,
Yanto Noriento, Andrew Payne

STYLING
Lucy Andrews, Wendy Berecry, Rosemary De
Santis, Carolyn Feinberg, Michelle Gorry, Donna
Hay, Jacqui Hing, Anneka Mitchell, Anna Philips,
Susie Smith

DESIGN AND PRODUCTION
Manager: Sheridan Carter
Layout: Lulu Dougherty
Finished Art: Lulu Dougherty, Gavin Murrell

Specially produced for Book Express, Inc.
Airport Business Center,
29 Kripes Road,
East Granby, Connecticut, USA.
By arrangement with
J.B. Fairfax Press Pty Limited
A.C.N. 003 738 430

North American Direct Sales rights in this edition
are exclusive to Book Express, Inc.

Formatted by J.B. Fairfax Press Pty Limited
Printed by Toppan Printing Co, Singapore

Some of the contents of this book have been
previously published in other J.B. Fairfax Press
publications.

JBFP 230 US
The Complete Family Cookbook
Includes Index
ISBN 1 86343 122 5

Printed in Singapore

THE COMPLETE FAMILY COOKBOOK

Book Express
Quality and Value in Every Book...

CONTENTS

INTRODUCTION

Today's family cook is constantly faced with the challenge of what to cook for dinner – and almost every other meal. With an increased number of meals being eaten out and the wide choice of food available for these meals, there is a greater expectation for interesting and tasty meals at home.

Within the pages of The Complete Family Cookbook *you will find recipes and ideas that will not only inspire you as the cook but will also satisfy the tastes and demands of those you are cooking for.*

The wonderful range of recipes, the step-by-step instructions showing special cooking and preparation techniques, and the numerous hints and tips on cooking and food will have you turning to this book time and again for inspiration, advice and help.

For the new cook there is a special section with a guide to the equipment needed to set up a basic kitchen and an explanation of common cooking methods.

With The Complete Family Cookbook *in your kitchen you will never be stuck for interesting family food.*

MEASURING UP

For good results a set of kitchen scales, a set of measuring cups and spoons and a transparent graduated measuring cup for measuring liquids are important items for every cook's kitchen.

In this book you will find that standard United States and metric weights and measures have been given. As it is not practical to give exact conversions, it is important that you do not switch from one set of measures to the other within a recipe. All cup and spoon measures given in this book are level.

Sugar is granulated white unless otherwise stated. Margarine can be used in place of butter if this is your preference. Self-rising flour has been used frequently in recipes however, if it is not available in your area, use 1 cup/125 g all-purpose flour sifted with 1 teaspoon baking powder and a pinch of salt for each 1 cup/125 g self-rising flour called for in the recipe.

Can sizes vary between countries and manufacturers. You may find the quantities in this book are slightly different from what is available. Use the can size nearest to the suggested size in the recipe.

Where microwave instructions occur in this book a microwave oven with a 650 watt output has been used. Wattage on domestic microwave ovens varies between 500 and 800, and it may be necessary to vary the cooking times slightly, depending on your oven.

LIQUID MEASURES

United States Standard	Metric
2 tablespoons/1 fl oz	30 mL
$^1/_4$ cup/2 fl oz	60 mL
$^1/_3$ cup/3 fl oz	90 mL
$^1/_2$ cup/4 fl oz	125 mL
5 fl oz	155 mL
$^2/_3$ cup/5$^1/_2$ fl oz	170 mL
$^3/_4$ cup/6 fl oz	185 mL
7 fl oz	220 mL
1 cup/8 fl oz/$^1/_2$ pint	250 mL
2 cups/16 fl oz/1 pint	500 mL
20 fl oz/1 pint	600 mL
3 cups/24 fl oz	750 mL
4 cups/1 quart	1 liter
5 cups	1.2 liters
6 cups	1.5 liters
7 cups	1.8 liters
8 cups	2 liters
10 cups	2.5 liters

WEIGHT MEASURES

United States Standard	Metric
$^1/_2$ oz	15 g
1 oz	30 g
1$^1/_2$ oz	45 g
2 oz	60 g
2$^1/_2$ oz	75 g
3 oz	90 g
4 oz	125 g
5 oz	155 g
6 oz	185 g
7 oz	220 g
8 oz	250 g
9 oz	280 g
10 oz	315 g
11 oz	350 g
12 oz	375 g
13 oz	410 g
14 oz	440 g
16 oz/1 lb	500 g
1$^1/_2$ lb	750 g
2 lb	1 kg
3 lb	1.5 kg
4 lb	2 kg
5 lb	2.5 kg

OVEN TEMPERATURES

It should be noted that this is offered as a guide only and that different makes and models of ovens can vary slightly.

°F	°C	
250	120	Very cool
275	140	
300	150	Cool
325	160	
350	180	Moderate
375	190	
400	200	Hot
425	220	
475	240	Very hot
500	250	Extremely hot

LINEAR MEASURES

United States Standard	Metric
$^1/_8$ in	3 mm
$^1/_4$ in	5 mm
$^1/_2$ in	1 cm
$^3/_4$ in	2 cm
1 in	2.5 cm
2 in	5 cm
3 in	7.5 cm
4 in	10 cm
6 in	15 cm
7 in	18 cm
8 in	20 cm
9 in	23 cm
10 in	25 cm
12 in	30 cm

THE WELL-STOCKED PANTRY

Setting aside some time each week to plan your family's meals for the week ahead will save you time and money. Drawing up a master grocery list as you go, ensures that you have all the ingredients you need to create delicious meals for family and friends. Use the following checklist as a handy reminder to make your shopping easier and quicker.

TIMESAVING TIPS FOR THE FAMILY COOK

❦ Buy meat prepared for cooking. Ask the butcher to cut, slice or bone-out cuts of meat according to your recipe to help cut down on preparation time.

❦ Buy shredded and grated cheese.

❦ Buy bottled minced garlic, ginger and chilies. These save having to crush, chop and mince when time is short.

❦ A food processor is the ultimate timesaver in the kitchen. This appliance allows you to grate, shred, chop, blend, mix and purée ingredients in a fraction of the time it would take you to do it by hand.

❦ Look for new and interesting convenience products such as sauces and dressings, prepared pastries and pastry shells, canned fruits and vegetables and dessert ideas.

❦ Keep a selection of bread in the freezer. It defrosts quickly and is a good accompaniment to a meal.

❦ Store frozen meals in containers that can go straight from the freezer to the microwave, to the table and then into the dishwasher.

❦ Get to know your supermarket, and write your shopping list according to the layout of the shelves.

❦ Make double quantities of your favorite soups, baked dishes and sauces and freeze half to have on hand for quick meals.

STAPLE ITEMS

- [ ] baking powder
- [ ] baking soda
- [ ] cereal flakes
- [ ] cocoa powder
- [ ] moist coconut: flaked, dry shredded
- [ ] cornstarch
- [ ] cream of tartar
- [ ] dried bread crumbs
- [ ] extract: almond, vanilla
- [ ] flour: all-purpose, self-rising, whole wheat
- [ ] plain gelatin
- [ ] light molasses
- [ ] honey
- [ ] instant coffee
- [ ] bottled minced chilies
- [ ] bottled minced garlic
- [ ] bottled minced ginger
- [ ] prepared stock (chicken, beef, vegetable), or bouillon cubes
- [ ] rolled oats
- [ ] sugar: white granulated, superfine and IOX (confectioners'); brown granulated (raw or demerara) and moist brown (light or dark muscovado)
- [ ] tomato paste
- [ ] tea
- [ ] white and red wine

PERISHABLE GOODS

- [ ] butter or margarine
- [ ] cheese: Parmesan, Cheddar
- [ ] eggs
- [ ] milk
- [ ] plain yogurt

CANNED FOODS

- [ ] apricot halves
- [ ] asparagus spears
- [ ] corn kernels
- [ ] peach halves and slices
- [ ] whole peeled tomatoes
- [ ] puréed tomatoes
- [ ] pineapple chunks
- [ ] salmon
- [ ] tuna

FROZEN FOODS

- [ ] frozen vegetables: peas, beans, sweet corn
- [ ] ice cream
- [ ] pastry: fillo (phyllo), pre-rolled puff and short (flaky) pastry
- [ ] selection of bread rolls, loaves and sliced bread

PASTA AND RICE

- [ ] fettuccine
- [ ] microwavable (instant) lasagne
- [ ] macaroni
- [ ] rice: short and long grain white, quick-cooking brown
- [ ] spaghetti: plain, wholewheat

SAUCES AND MUSTARDS

- [ ] mayonnaise
- [ ] mustard: Dijon, French, coarse grain
- [ ] prepared pasta sauce
- [ ] salad dressing
- [ ] sauces: chili, cranberry, plum, soy, Worcestershire, catsup

HERBS AND SPICES

- [ ] cayenne pepper
- [ ] chili powder
- [ ] cinnamon: ground, sticks
- [ ] curry powder
- [ ] dried herbs: basil, mixed herbs, oregano, sage, tarragon, thyme
- [ ] ground herbs: such as coriander, cumin, paprika, turmeric
- [ ] ground spices: allspice, ginger, pumpkin pie spice, nutmeg
- [ ] rosemary: dried leaves, ground
- [ ] whole black peppercorns
- [ ] whole cloves

OILS AND VINEGARS

- [ ] oils: olive, vegetable, peanut
- [ ] vinegars: white, wine, cider

DRIED FRUITS, NUTS AND SEEDS

- [ ] dried fruits: apricots, currants, golden and seeded raisins
- [ ] ground almonds
- [ ] nuts: such as cashews, pecans, walnuts, chopped mixed nuts
- [ ] poppy seeds
- [ ] sunflower kernels

JAMS AND RELISHES

- [ ] jams: apricot, raspberry, strawberry
- [ ] orange marmalade
- [ ] peanut butter
- [ ] sweet pickle relish
- [ ] sweet fruit chutney

CAKES AND COOKIES

- [ ] plain wafer cookies
- [ ] variety packaged cake mixes
- [ ] crackers and saltines

chapter one

GETTING STARTED

This section has been put together especially to help the new cook. It details the preparation needed to cook a recipe successfully. There is also advice on the equipment required to set up a basic kitchen, and an explanation of some of the most common cooking methods.

RECIPES AND PREPARATION

The first step in preparing a meal, baking a cake or even making a simple snack is to read the recipe and prepare your ingredients. The following simple steps will ensure that cooking is a pleasure rather than a chore.

1 Before you start cooking, look at the recipe and read through the ingredients list and method. This will alert you to any problems, such as not having an ingredient or finding that the recipe is going to take 2 hours to prepare and you need to have it ready in 30 minutes.

2 Following the ingredients list, collect all the foods you will require. This helps to make sure that you have everything you need for the recipe. The ingredients are always listed in their order of use.

3 Next prepare the food to the state it will be required in the recipe. The secret of many recipes is to add the next ingredient at just the right time. If that ingredient is not ready it can mean that a dish is ruined or at least not as good as it should be.

4 The next step is to go through the method and get out the equipment that you will need.

5 As you read through the method, check to see if the oven will be used and, if so, turn it on to preheat.

6 You are now ready to start making your recipe. Remember, being organised and assembling all your ingredients and equipment before you start will save you time in cooking and cleaning up.

Remember to collect and measure your ingredients and to get out the equipment you will need before you start cooking.

COOKING METHODS

The cooking method you choose will depend on what you are cooking and the effect you wish to achieve. The following will help you better understand the different types of cooking methods most often used.

STEAMING

Using this cooking method the food is set over boiling water and cooked in the steam given off. Place the food in a metal basket, on a wire rack, or in a steamer in a saucepan, set 1/2-1 in/1-2.5 cm above the water. Tightly cover the pan and cook for the required time. Steaming is a popular way of cooking vegetables and fish for the diet-conscious. It is one of the best ways to cook food and retain the maximum number of vitamins and minerals.

SIMMERING

This is when liquids are just hot enough for a few bubbles to form slowly and the bubbles burst below the surface. Simmering takes place at a lower temperature than boiling and should not be confused with boiling.

BOILING

This is when liquids are hot enough to form bubbles that rise in a steady pattern and break on the surface. The whole mass of liquid starts to move as the bubbling begins.

Left: Boiling
Below: Pan Frying

PAN FRYING

The food is cooked in a little fat in a skillet or frying pan. The most commonly used fats are butter, margarine or oil. When shallow frying you need to make sure that the fat is hot enough so that the food cooks without absorbing too much fat, but the fat should not be too hot or the food will burn.

DEEP-FRYING

This method of cooking is popular in the cooking of takeout foods. It is an efficient and quick method if done correctly. To deep-fry, it is important that you have a saucepan large enough to hold the food comfortably. For the safest cooking and the best results, the saucepan used should be wide-topped, deep and heavy-based. A wire basket that fits in the saucepan will make it easier and safer to place the food in the oil and to remove it. When deep-frying, the oil must be at the correct temperature before you add the food – too hot and the food will cook on the outside but

remain undercooked or raw in the center, not hot enough and the food will absorb oil and be soggy and greasy. When the oil is at the correct temperature, it should be still, with a slight haze coming from the surface and when a cube of bread is dropped in, it will brown in 50 seconds.

You could also use a thermometer to check the temperature of the oil. The correct temperature for most food is 375°F/190°C.

BROILING

Cooking food by direct dry heat. When broiling meat you should place it on a rack in the broiler pan, to allow the fat to drip through. Broiling can be used to cook foods such as steaks, chops and sausages, as well as for browning or toasting the top of denser foods. The broiler should always be preheated before you start cooking.

Right: Broiling
Below: Baking

BAKING

Cooking food by indirect dry heat. The food can be cooked covered or uncovered, usually in an oven. Cooking meat in this way is called 'roasting'.

When baking cakes, cookies and breads it is important that the oven is preheated before placing the food in it.

STIR-FRYING

This quick method of cooking is usually done in a wok, but a large skillet or frying pan will also give good results. The secret to successful stir-frying is to have all the ingredients prepared before you start cooking. When stir-frying use a large spatula and lift and turn the food quickly so that it comes in frequent contact with the hot cooking surface. Always heat the wok or skillet first, then add the oil and finally the food. One of the great advantages of stir-frying is that only small quantities of oil need be used.

GETTING EQUIPPED

Having the right equipment makes food preparation and cooking easy. Use this as a guide for equipping your kitchen.

Stockpot

Sifter

Grater/Shredder

Soufflé dishes

Casserole dishes

Rolling pin

Potato masher

Mixing bowls

Paring knife

Boning knife

Bread knife

Carving knife

Metal spatula

Meat mallet

Saucepans

Skillets/Frying pans

Colander

Cake pans

Wooden spoon

Cookie (or baking) sheets

Tongs

Measuring spoons

Rubber spatula

Measuring cups, liquid and dry

Hand-held electric mixer

Roasting pan

Wire whisk

COOKIE SHEET

A cookie sheet or baking sheet has a very slightly raised edge and is mainly used for baking cookies and unmolded pastries.

CAKE PANS

These come in many shapes and sizes and it will depend on how much cake baking you intend to do as to how many different types of cake pans you will require. As a start an 8 in/20 cm square pan, a deep 8 in/20 cm round and a loaf pan will satisfy most basic needs. Other useful cake pans to have are a pair of 8 in/20 cm layer pans, a springform pan, a Jelly roll pan and a set of muffin pans.

CASSEROLE (BAKING) DISHES (IN VARIOUS SIZES)

These can be ceramic, pottery, ovenproof glass or metal and are available in a range of sizes and prices. The size and type of dish you decide on will depend on your budget and on how many you are cooking for. It is useful to have several different-sized baking dishes – plus one or two with matching covers – and to have at least one casserole which is flameproof. A flameproof casserole can be used on an element as well as in the oven – useful for pot roasting or when browning meat.

ELECTRIC MIXERS

There are two main types of electric mixers available – hand-held and counter top. Hand-held mixers are useful for mixing small quantities of food. The larger counter top models have heavy-duty motors and are needed for mixing heavier doughs and batters.

FOOD PROCESSORS

There are two types of food processors – the one that stands on the countertop and the hand-held blender.

The hand-held blender is ideal for chopping, mincing and grinding small quantities of food. It comes with its own chopping bowl and beaker and can be used with these accessories or in an ordinary mixing bowl. The hand-held blender is a light, easily managed appliance, particularly suited to disabled and arthritic cooks, as those difficult and fiddly jobs of cutting and chopping are quickly and safely achieved.

The food processor is ideal for larger quantities of food. Cakes, cookies and bars are mixed in seconds and pastry is made in minutes. The food processor will chop, grind, mince and purée. For many recipes, the food processor can take the place of an electric mixer; for example, creaming butter and sugar, mixing cake batter and making one-bowl cookies and bars. Other uses of the food processor include grinding meat, puréeing fruit and vegetables and making pâtés.

FREEZERS

The type of freezer you choose will depend on the size of your family, what you intend to freeze and where you are going to position it. Freezing food preserves its nutritional value and allows you to have a range of cooked and raw foods on hand.

SKILLETS AND FRYING PANS

The best pans are those with heavy bases, as this ensures that the heat spreads evenly and so the food cooks evenly. Nonstick pans mean that you can cook with very little or no fat.

KNIVES

A selection of sharp knives is essential for safe, efficient food preparation. A good set of knives is a cook's best investment and will last you many years. At the very least you will need three knives. A paring knife, which is a small knife with a straight blade, is needed for trimming and peeling vegetables. A chopping or chef's knife, which has a heavy, wide blade is used for chopping and cutting vegetables, herbs, meat, poultry and fish. The blade length ranges from 6-12 in/ 15-30 cm, but for home use a knife with an 8 in/20 cm blade is probably the most useful. A serrated-edged knife is useful for cutting bread, cakes and pastries. The serrated edge cuts through them without tearing. Smaller, serrated-edged knives are used for slicing tomatoes and fruits such as oranges, grapefruit and lemons. The edge on a serrated knife lasts almost indefinitely, but should it need sharpening it must be done professionally.

MEASURING CUPS

For dry ingredients, measuring cups made of plastic or metal are available in nests of four sizes — 1 cup, $\frac{1}{2}$ cup, $\frac{1}{3}$ cup and $\frac{1}{4}$ cup. Spoon ingredient into cup then level off with the straight edge of a knife or spatula. (Pack brown sugar into cup firmly so it keeps the cup shape when turned out.)

Liquid ingredients are measured in a glass or plastic cup with a pour spout and graduated markings for liquid levels. They are available in 1 cup, 2 cup and 4 cup sizes. Be sure to read the desired fill mark at eye level with cup placed on a flat surface.

MEASURING SPOONS

These are available in sets containing a tablespoon, teaspoon, $1/2$ teaspoon and $1/4$ teaspoon. They are a quick and accurate way of measuring small quantities of both dry and liquid ingredients. All measures are level, not rounded.

SCALES

Kitchen scales which provide weight markings in ounces as well as in grams are a useful tool for any cook. They are particularly helpful when using recipes from countries which use the Metric System of measuring.

MIXING BOWLS

These come in many shapes and sizes and can be made from a variety of materials. If you have a microwave oven it is useful to have mixing bowls that are microwave-safe.

PASTRY BRUSH

Use a pastry brush to apply glazes, melted butter and the like to surfaces of food and for brushing dishes with oil or butter.

ROASTING PAN

This rectangular metal pan has low sides and is used for cooking roast meats and vegetables. Once the meat is cooked and removed from the dish, the dish is then placed on an element for making the gravy.

ROLLING PIN

This smooth cylinder is 8-12 in/ 20-50 cm long with a 2-2$1/2$ in/ 5-6 cm diameter. With or without handles a rolling pin can be made from a variety of materials, however the most common is hardwood. A hollow glass rolling pin that can be filled with iced water is useful for pastry making.

SAUCEPANS

One of the most important requirements of a saucepan is that it is the right size for the job. It is therefore necessary to have a range of saucepans in different sizes to suit different jobs. When buying saucepans, don't be tempted by beautiful matching sets, but rather buy a selection of pans to suit your various needs. When choosing your pans they should be heavy-duty with solid bases, insulated handles and tight-fitting lids.

SIFTER

Used for sifting dry ingredients to remove lumps and aerate the ingredients. If you do not have a sifter with a spring mechanism, a simple wire sieve does the job just as well.

SOUFFLE DISHES (LARGE AND SMALL)

A soufflé dish is round with high straight sides, that allows the soufflé to rise vertically as it expands. While obviously used for cooking soufflés, soufflé dishes have many other uses. A large soufflé dish is useful for cooking baked vegetable dishes and can also team as a serving dish. Small soufflé dishes (or ramekins) and custard cups are good for individual baked dishes and individual desserts, such as chocolate mousse.

SPATULAS (METAL AND RUBBER)

Spatulas with flexible metal blades come in a variety of sizes and are used for spreading frostings, fillings and creams. Rubber spatulas are useful for scraping out bowls.

STOCKPOT

This large saucepan should be taller than it is wide and have a handle on either side. The French call this type of saucepan a *fait-tout* which literally means 'do-all'. This pan has a multitude of uses, including stock and soup making and pot roasting. For a domestic kitchen a pan of about 12 quarts/12 liters is a good size as it will easily accommodate bulky bones, but can still be safely lifted when full.

WOODEN SPOONS

As wood does not conduct heat, wooden spoons do not get hot and are therefore ideal for use when cooking foods such as sauces and jams, as the spoon can be left in the mixture during cooking.

chapter two

SEASON TO TASTE

When used correctly, herbs
and spices are a cook's best friend. In
this chapter you will find information on
the various herbs and spices along with a
guide as to which foods they best combine
with. However, be adventurous when
using these exciting seasonings –
you never know what new
combination you may discover.

A–Z OF SPICES

Don't be discouraged by their exotic names or by the (false) idea that spices are expensive or complicated to use; they are the greatest asset of a good cook.

ALLSPICE

The seeds of allspice are just slightly larger than peppercorns and dark brown in color. Allspice is a delicately spicy mingling of cloves, cinnamon and nutmeg, with cloves predominating. Allspice berries are the dried fruit of a tall, aromatic evergreen of the myrtle and clove family, which can grow to over 40 ft/ 12 m. Picked when green and unripe, the seeds are dried in the sun to a rich, deep brown color.

ANISEED

The small, oval grey-green ribbed seeds of anise have a warm, sweet, pungent flavor and can be used in sweet and savory dishes. The aromatic anise annual grows to about 2 ft/60 cm high and is similar to other small members of the parsley family. Anise will grow well in a good summer in light, dry loamy soil in a sunny position. Sow the seeds in mid-spring. The plants produce small white flowers and fern-like leaves.

CARAWAY

A handsome biennial to 2 ft/ 60 cm high with finely cut leaves and clusters of white flowers which produce aromatic seeds with their characteristic flavor. Sow seeds direct in spring or autumn. Needs a sunny, well-drained position protected from wind. Young leaves are used as a garnish for cooked vegetables. The seeds are used in dishes of cabbage, potatoes and parsnips. Also used in some cakes, cookies and apple pies. Leaves and softer stems can be eaten in salads or cooked with other vegetables.

CARDAMOM

The cardamom bush is a herbaceous perennial plant of the ginger family and grows nearly 10 ft/3 m high. Cardamom will only grow in a hot climate. It produces slightly pungent, highly aromatic pods holding seeds which are sweet with a camphor-like flavor.

CASSIA

The bark, unripe seeds and the dried leaves of this plant are all used in cooking. Related to cinnamon, the bark can be used in the same way and has a similar taste but is not as strong. The seeds, also known as Chinese cassia buds, are used in drinks and confections and are often added to potpourris.

CAYENNE PEPPER

Cayenne pepper, paprika and hot red pepper seasoning (Tabasco sauce) are all made from varieties of peppers. Cayenne is derived from a hot, red variety of pepper called 'bird chili'.
Although cayenne is not as hot as some chili powders it is very pungent and should be used sparingly. Store in an airtight container in small quantities and in a dark place.

CELERY SEEDS

These seeds, with a bitter celery flavor, are the tiny light brown seeds of the celery plant. They should be used sparingly in baked dishes and soups. They are a great addition to pickled vegetables and homemade bread, and will add life to any salad dressing.

CHILI

Chilies belong to the pepper family and have an especially hot flavor. All varieties of peppers bear certain common characteristics. The bushy chili shrub prefers tropical or subtropical climates and grows to between 1-6 ft/30 to 180 cm high, depending on the variety. As a general rule, the smaller, narrower and darker the chili, the greater its pungency; unripe fresh chilies are usually less pungent than ripe fresh ones, and these in turn are milder than dried chilies.

CINNAMON

Cinnamon is the bark of a tree which belongs to the laurel family. The cinnamon tree is a tall, thick evergreen tree which prefers tropical climates. The bark is the most important part of the tree – when ground it provides a sweet spice highly valued for both culinary and medical usage. The leaves are pointed, smooth and tough and the small creamy-white flowers are followed by dark blue berries. The dried bark is sold in small quills (usually 3-6 in/7.5-15 cm long) or as powder.

CLOVES

The clove tree is an evergreen which grows abundantly near tropical seashores. Cloves are the highly aromatic flower buds of this tree or shrub which is native to the Moluccas or Spice Islands. Nowadays cloves are mostly imported from Zanzibar and Madagascar.

CORIANDER
Coriander is a member of the parsley family. The plant gives off a strong odor which is replaced by a sweet orange-like aroma when the seeds are dried. The round, light brown seeds are milder than many other spices and can be used in large quantities. The taste is fresh with a hint of bitterness and can be improved by gently roasting before grinding.

CUMIN SEEDS
Like coriander and caraway, cumin seed comes from a plant of the parsley family. Cumin is a small and delicate annual which usually grows to 10 in/25 cm in height. Native to the Middle East, cumin now grows in most hot climates. The small, dark brown, elongated seeds have a rich sweet aroma; their flavor is similarly pungent and they should be used sparingly. Cumin seed is often confused with fennel or anise (both sometimes called 'sweet cumin').

DILL SEEDS
The dill plant is another member of the parsley family and the leaves, stalks and the dried seeds can all be used in cooking. The oval, flattened seeds have a fresh, sweet aroma with a slightly bitter taste similar to that of caraway seeds. Dill seeds are dried and used whole or slightly crushed. Add them to dishes towards the end of cooking or when cooking is over to fully enhance their flavor.

FENNEL SEEDS
Another member of the wonderful parsley family, fennel seeds are like plumper, larger versions of anise seeds with a warm and slightly bitter anise flavor. They are curved, ridged and dullish yellow-green in appearance. Fennel seeds have strong digestive qualities and so are often used with rich meats and oily fish.

FENUGREEK
The fenugreek plant which grows from 1 to 2 ft/30 to 60 cm high, is a member of the bean and pea family. Its flowers and pods resemble those of the pea. Each long, narrow pod contains ten to twenty small, hard yellow-brown seeds. The seeds have a slightly bitter-sweet taste and should be used in moderation. Only when roasted do the seeds give off their pungent aroma. Whole or ground fenugreek is most often used in Indian curries.

GINGER
Ginger is an important spice in both East and West. Like other tropical plants of the same family, such as turmeric, it is the knobbly root of the ginger plant which is used as a spice. Fresh ginger does not keep well, so buy only in small quantities. Dried ginger root can be bruised and ground to a powder (its fibres removed) and used as ground ginger, or bruised and infused in the cooking liquid of savory dishes.

JUNIPER BERRIES
The juniper tree is a small coniferous and prickly evergreen. The round, purple-brown berries are about twice the size of peppercorns with smooth skins. The spicy pine aroma and sweet, resinous flavor varies according to where they are grown. The berries are bought whole and are easy to grind because they are soft. Juniper is commonly used in spice mixtures for meat and are excellent with pork and game.

LAOS POWDER
Laos powder, also known as galangal or galingale, has a peppery ginger taste and is used in the hot and spicy dishes of South-East Asia. Closely related to ginger it is similar in that it is the root of the plant that is powdered. In Europe it is used to flavor liqueurs and bitters.

MACE
Mace and nutmeg are both parts of the fruit of a tropical evergreen tree. Mace blades form the outer casing of the nutmeg and are bright red when harvested, drying to a deep orange.The flavor of mace is similar to nutmeg but more delicate.

MUSTARD SEEDS
Mustard is internationally famous as a condiment and flavoring. The whole seeds are the basis for prepared mustards, and the pungent oil extracted from the seeds and the seeds themselves are also popularly used as culinary spices. There are three main varieties of mustard: black, brown and white. The three plants are very similar in appearance and all bear tiny, spherical, hard seeds. Brown mustard seeds are most commonly used as an Indian cooking spice.

NUTMEG
The small, oval shiny nut, about $1^{1}/_{2}$ in/4 cm long, is dried in its seed coat which is then removed. Nutmeg is slightly milder than mace but has a more nutty flavor – warm and sweetish with a light bitter undertone. Nutmegs can be bought whole or ready-ground. It is best to buy them whole and store in an airtight container. Finely grate as needed.

PAPRIKA

Like cayenne pepper, paprika is a finely ground powder made from the fruit of several different chili plants. The ripe flesh is used for mild, sweet paprika, the seeds are included for more pungent versions. Mild paprika has a light, sweet smell and almost no pungency; the strongest paprika is similar to cayenne pepper.

PEPPER

Pepper comes from the tropical trailing vine of the *Piperaceae* family. The vines grow to heights of 11 ft/3.6 m and bear long strings of 20-30 small berries which ripen from green to reddish-yellow. Black pepper berries are picked when green and dried whole; for white pepper they are allowed to ripen and turn red and the skin is removed before drying. Green peppercorns are picked when still green and usually pickled.

POPPY SEEDS

Poppy seeds, sometimes called maw seeds, come from the opium poppy. The plant is related to both the common field poppy and garden varieties. It grows to anything from 1 to 4 ft/ 30 to 120 cm and bears white, pink or lilac flowers and erect oval seed pods. The tiny, hard seeds are very mild and sweetish and acquire a bitter-sweet nutty flavor when cooked.

SAFFRON

Saffron is the most expensive spice in the world. It is the dried stigmas of the flowers of the saffron crocus. The flowers are extracted from the freshly harvested flowers and dried to become irregular, orange-red threads about $1\frac{1}{2}$ in/4 cm long. It takes about 50 000 stigmas to make up $3\frac{1}{2}$ oz/100 g of saffron! Saffron imparts a distinctive aroma, a bitter honey-like taste and a strong yellow color to food. It's better to buy the threads and store them in an airtight container in a dark place. Ground saffron can vary enormously in quality.

SESAME SEEDS

Sesame is a tropical annual with a pungent smell. The plant grows to anything between 2 and 6 ft/ 60 and 180 cm. The seed pods contain a large number of small, flat oval seeds in a variety of colors. They may be red, light brown or black and have a rich nutty flavor. Dry roast before use or fry lightly until they just color and give off a roasted aroma.

STAR ANISE

Star anise is the star-shaped fruit of an oriental evergreen of the magnolia family which can reach a height of 24 ft/7.3 m. When dried it is a brown color and the flavor is one of pungent aniseed. Whole stars store well in an airtight container, and are preferable to the powdered form.

TAMARIND

Tamarind with its sour flavor is a large pod that grows on the Indian tamarind tree. It is picked, seeded and peeled before being pressed into a dark brown pulp. Tamarind is usually mixed with warm water to give tamarind juice which is then used in chutneys, sauces and curries.

TURMERIC

Turmeric is a typical member of the ginger family and, like ginger, it is the knobbly roots or rhizomes which form the cooking spice. The tropical turmeric has spiky yellow flowers and long, shiny pointed leaves, and can grow to a height of 3 ft/1 m. Turmeric has a strong woody aroma and distinctive, pungent flavor. Because of this it should not be used as a cheap substitute for saffron.

VANILLA

The dark brown pod of vanilla comes from a type of orchid native to South America. It was discovered by the Spaniards in Mexico. When first picked the pod is a yellow green and it is only after curing and drying that it becomes the dark brown we associate with vanilla. Essentially a flavoring used in sweet dishes such as ice cream, custards and rice, it is also popular as a flavoring for wine cups, hot chocolate and coffee drinks. The vanilla pod can be used several times and if kept in a jar of sugar will flavor it to make vanilla sugar.

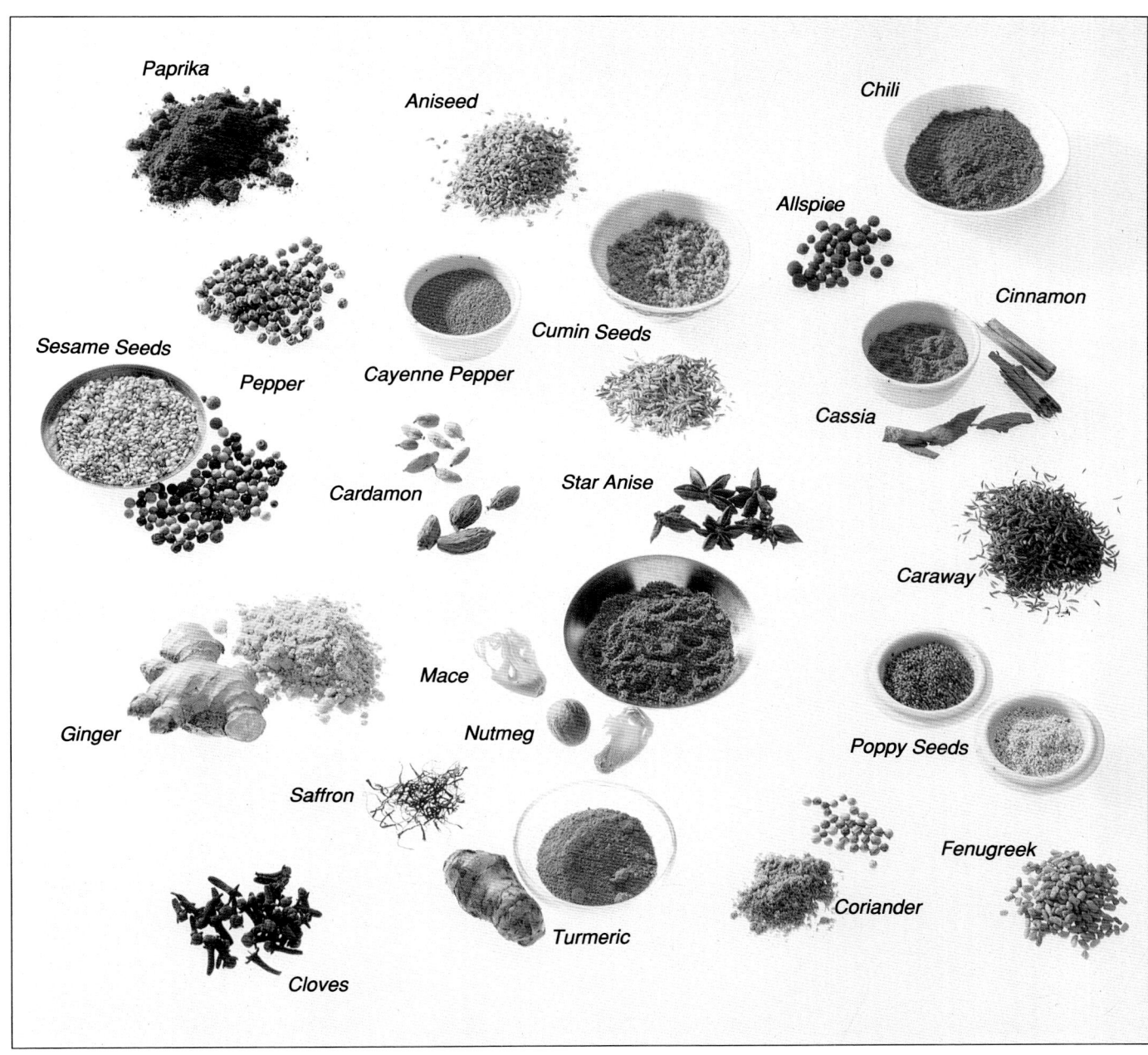

Paprika

Aniseed

Chili

Allspice

Cinnamon

Cumin Seeds

Sesame Seeds

Pepper

Cayenne Pepper

Cassia

Cardamon

Star Anise

Caraway

Mace

Ginger

Nutmeg

Poppy Seeds

Saffron

Fenugreek

Cloves

Turmeric

Coriander

AT-A-GLANCE SPICE GUIDE

SPICE	SOUPS	MAIN DISHES
Allspice	Beef and minestrone soups	Baked ham, meat loaf, spiced meats
Aniseed	Cream soups	Seafood, pork and poultry dishes
Cardamom	Spiced and curried soups	Curries and spicy dishes of Indian and Middle Eastern origin
Cassia		Chinese dishes and curries
Cayenne Pepper	Soups, especially fish and tomato	Curries and spicy dishes, egg dishes
Chili – fresh	Spicy soups	All curries and spicy meat, poultry, fish and egg dishes
Chili – powder	Spicy soups	As for fresh chilies
Coriander – seed	Spicy soups	Curries and spicy meat, poultry, fish dishes
Cumin – seed	Spicy soups	Meat, poultry and fish dishes
Curry Plant	Fish and spicy soups	Casseroles and curries
Dill – seed	Vegetable soups	Lamb, pork and fish dishes
Fennel – seed		Chicken and fish dishes
Fenugreek		Indian and Middle Eastern dishes
Ginger – fresh		Curries
Ginger – ground		Curries, baked ham and fish dishes
Mace		Fish, chicken, beef and veal dishes
Mustard – powder	Leek and celery soups	Broiled meats, ham casseroles
Mustard – seed		Curries, pork, rabbit, veal, some fish dishes
Nutmeg	Cream soups	Fish, chicken, egg and cheese dishes, pasta
Paprika	Most soups	Curries, goulashes, pork, beef, veal and fish dishes
Saffron	Especially fish soups	Chicken, fish, turkey and some egg dishes, paella
Turmeric	Curried and spicy soups	Curries, egg and fish dishes
Vanilla		

VEGETABLE DISHES	DESSERTS AND BAKED PRODUCTS	OTHER USES
Carrot, pea and potato salads	Apple desserts such as pies and crumbles, milk puddings	Pickles, confections, stewed fruit
Salads, carrots and zucchini	Cookies, cakes, fresh fruit, especially good with figs	Cheese dips
Vegetable curries	Breads and yeast cakes, custards, fruit salads	Pickles, stewed fruit, savory and sweet rice dishes
Ground sprinkle over vegetables		Poached and stewed fruit
		Salad dressings
Spicy vegetable dishes		Salad dressings
Spicy vegetable dishes		Salad dressings, dips, pickles, sauces
Spicy vegetable dishes	Cookies, cakes, fruit salad	Yogurt dips, salad dressings, stewed fruit
Cabbage, carrots and legume dishes		Pickles, chutneys, marinades, rice dishes
		Stuffings for veal and game
Cucumber, squash, cabbage and carrots	Cookies, cakes, fruit salad	Pickles
Potatoes	Cookies, sprinkle over breads and coffee cakes	Salad dressings, sauces for fish
Sprouts used in salads		
	Cookies, cakes and cooked apple dishes	Marinades
Vegetable curries and spicy legume dishes	Cakes, cookies, puddings, fruit pies	Pickles, spiced drinks such as mulled wine, stewed fruit
	Cookies, cakes	Flavor whipped cream, stuffings, pâtés
Braised celery and leeks		Salad dressings, stuffings
Cabbage and celery		Stuffings
Cabbage, carrots and root vegetables	Cookies, cakes, milk puddings, pastries, fruit salads, junket, quick breads	Stewed fruits, flavor whipped cream, pâtés
Legume dishes		Rice dishes
	Cookies, cakes, breads	Savory rice dishes
	Coloring for cakes and breads	Rice dishes
	Custards, ice cream, milk puddings	Flavor cream, drinks, sugar

A–Z OF HERBS

Few ingredients are as tasty as fresh herbs plucked from a window box or from a special section of your garden. Many grow with just the slightest encouragement, while others need attention, but either way you'll be amply repaid in flavorsome meals.

ANGELICA

This is a stout biennial or perennial herb which grows to 6½ ft/ 2 m or more. Leaves are soft green and divided into large leaflets. The stems are round, ribbed and hollow with yellow-green flowers which grow in a ball-like cluster. Best suited to cool-climate areas where it can be planted in sun or semi-shade. Shelter from strong wind is desirable because the stems are brittle. Angelica is completely permeated by a unique essence, giving it a delicately sweet and refreshing aroma. Angelica stems can be candied, and can also be used instead of sugar when stewing sour fruits like rhubarb. The roots are edible and can be served as a vegetable. The seeds are used in flavoring gin and some liqueurs.

BASIL

An annual to 2 ft/60 cm high with peppery, clove-scented leaves. There are different types of basil plants but the old favorites sweet basil and bush basil are still the best varieties to grow for the kitchen. Grow from seed in a sunny, moist but well-drained position sheltered from wind. For the best results, sow the seed at the end of spring or at the beginning of summer. Remove the small, white, lipped flower buds to encourage longer life. For a stronger flavor in cooking, use fresh basil leaves as basil loses a lot of its flavor when dried. Excellent with all tomato dishes and torn up in salads. It goes well with carrots, zucchini, pasta sauces and chicken.

BAY

A slow-growing evergreen tree with aromatic leaves, also known as bay laurel or sweet bay. Bay trees make excellent tub specimens and should be grown in a sunny sheltered position. Young plants need protection from frosts. The leaves are large, flat, oval and glossy and can be harvested at any time of the year. Bay leaves have a strong flavor and taste rather bitter when fresh so are most often used dried. A bay leaf is one of the three herbs that make up the classic bouquet garni. Use with tomatoes and beets and to flavor soups, sauces and stews. Add bay leaves to stores of flour, pulses and similar foods to keep weevils away.

BORAGE

This herb is an annual with thick, soft stems, large leaves and branching hairy stems. Height varies from 1 to 3 ft/30 to 90 cm. Leaves are greyish-green, about 4-6 in/10-15 cm long. Star-like summer flowers in white or blue are most attractive. Flowering can continue through winter in mild areas. Flowers and young leaves can be eaten. The leaves have a delicate, cucumber-like flavor. Finely chop and use as a garnish in salads. The flowers can be candied. Both flowers and leaves can be dipped in a light batter and deep-fried.

CHERVIL

A small spreading annual to 20 in/50 cm. Fern-like leaves have a delicate aniseed flavor. The white flowers, which appear in early summer, grow in small, flat umbels. The seeds which follow resemble caraway seeds but are longer and thinner. The seeds should be sown in shallow drills 1 ft/30 cm apart in spring and autumn. Grow in a partially shaded, sheltered position in rich, moist soil. Keep chervil watered at all times. Chervil leaves are delicious with salad greens and spinach. Use in dressings, garnish for soups, and with fish dishes.

CHIVES

A perennial member of the onion family, chives have hollow onion-flavored leaves and attractive edible mauve flowers. Chives like a rich, moist soil in full sun; they also grow well indoors in pots on a sunny window sill. They respond to picking in moderation, but a proportion of fresh leaves must be left. In cold climates, chives die back in winter. Chives should be lifted and divided every two or three years in spring or autumn, or immediately after flowering. Use in fresh salads and to flavor potatoes or any of the squash family. Good in most savory dishes and excellent with eggs and cream.

CORIANDER

Sometimes called Chinese parsley or cilantro, coriander is an attractive annual to 2 ft/60 cm. The lacy foliage has a distinctive, strong aroma quite different from other similar herbs such as anise, caraway, dill and fennel, all of whose leaves have a warm spicy anise-scent. A mixture of lemon peel and sage is one description of the flavor of fresh coriander leaves. Coriander can be grown either in a sunny spot in the garden or indoors in pots on a sunny window sill, by planting the whole coriander seeds. Sow seeds direct in spring and water generously. Harvest seeds in autumn and dry in a light, airy position. When the small oval coriander seeds have hardened and ripened to a pale fawn color, they are one of the most deliciously fragrant of all spices used in cooking. Coriander is used in almost every Thai dish. Leaves are tasty in salads and as a garnish for pea soup. The seeds complement mushrooms, cauliflower, beets and celery and are commonly used in curries, sausage-making and as a flavoring in cakes.

CURRY PLANT

The curry plant is a shrubby perennial plant that grows into a low spreading bush with silvery-grey, green spiky leaves. Although it is not used in authentic curries, the leaves do have a strong curry-like flavor.

CURRY LEAVES

Not to be confused with the silvery-grey leaves of the curry plant. Curry leaves are small, shiny and evergreen and slightly like small bay leaves. The tree is easily grown and decorative, with an exotic spicy fragrance. Curry leaves are usually chopped and fried in oil at the start of making curry. They quickly turn brown and become crisp when the other ingredients are added. The leaves may also be ground to a powder and used in making curry powder and paste.

DILL

A fast-growing, upright annual to 3 ft/90 cm, dill resembles fennel in that both have hollow stems, feathery leaves and clusters of yellow flowers. The flavor of dill is clean and delicate. Sow seeds in a sunny, well-drained soil in spring and autumn. The seeds can be harvested. Dill grows best in a light, medium-rich soil with plenty of moisture. Dill seeds and leaves can both be eaten. Dill seed flavors and helps the digestion of steamed cabbage, coleslaw, sauerkraut, cucumbers, various chutneys and pickles, pastries, breads, sauces and cooked root vegetables. Both the seeds and leaves with their spicy flavor are used, although the foliage does not have the same concentration of oil as the seeds.

FENNEL

Fast-growing tall annual to 5 ft/ 1.5 m. It has bright green, feathery leaves and clusters of yellow flowers followed by aniseed-flavored seeds. Grow in a well-drained, sunny position and provide plenty of water. Both leaves and seeds are traditionally used with fish. If baking a whole fish, branches of the foliage make a fragrant bed for the fish to rest on during cooking. Fennel seeds are used in soups, sauces and with lentils, rice and potatoes. Also used in breads and cakes. The leaves are used in salads, relishes and as garnishes.

GARLIC

A bulbous perennial plant with strap-like leaves measuring approximately 1 in/2.5 cm across and 1 ft/30 cm long. A willowy, round flower-stalk thrusts upwards above the leaves, and the flower that appears is a compact collection of mauve-tinted white petals. Plant separated cloves in early spring in a rich and well-drained soil, preferably in full sun. When the foliage has died down at the end of summer, the bulbs can be carefully lifted. Dig the bulbs, shake them free of dirt and braid several together. Hang the braided garlic in a dry, well-ventilated place. The whole garlic plant has a pungent, lingering odor – it cannot be called scent or aroma due to the essential oil it contains. The oil is antibiotic and contains vitamins A and B, sulphur and iodine.

GINGER

A tall perennial plant to 5 ft/1.5 m high with spikes of white and purple flowers and aromatic rhizomes, ginger prefers a hot, humid climate in a rich, well-drained soil in partial shade. Ginger root has a sweet, hot flavor which goes with meat, fish, vegetables, cakes and sweets. Fresh grated ginger is particularly good with steamed or stir-fried vegetables, especially Chinese cabbage. Ginger is an essential part of many curries, pickles and chutneys.

HORSERADISH

A hardy perennial with long, elliptical dark green leaves. It grows to a height of about 2 ft/60 cm with erect stems and has small, scented, four-petalled white flowers. Often grown for its thick, fleshy, aromatic roots – hot, pungent and full of flavor. Plant in an open sunny position, with a deeply dug, fertile soil. Horseradish sauce uses grated root mixed with cream or some similar viscous liquid. It must be used raw as the cooked roots lose their flavor. Roots can be grated and dried and stored in airtight containers for later use. The leaves are also pungent and tasty and can be chopped and used as a salad ingredient.

LEMON BALM

A perennial to 3 ft/90 cm, lemon balm has dark green, heart-shaped leaves that have a strong lemon scent and flavor. Grow in a rich, well-drained soil in full sun. Pinch back in early summer to encourage new growth. Use only fresh leaves sprinkled over vegetable or fruit salads. Use leaves in fish and poultry dishes, sauces, marinades and stuffings. Lemon balm is sometimes planted in orchards to attract bees to pollinate the fruit blossom.

LEMON GRASS

A grass-like perennial to 10 ft/3 m high, lemon grass has pointed aromatic leaves with a delicious lemon scent. It forms a large clump in a sunny, warm position with plenty of water, but needs good drainage. The fleshy white lower part of the leaves is used in South-East Asian dishes. It adds a tangy taste to salads and is a must for curries.

MARJORAM

A fragrant perennial plant to 2½ ft/75 cm high with small oval leaves and clusters of white or mauve flowers. Grow in full sun in a well-drained soil and keep trimmed to encourage fresh, compact growth. Fresh leaves are used in tomato dishes, with any of the cabbage family and green beans. Marjoram is an excellent addition to spicy meat dishes. It can be included in meat sauces for pasta, meat loaves and rice stuffings for vegetables.

MINT

There are many varieties of mint, but spearmint (*Mentha spicata*) and applemint (*Mentha suaveolens*) are the two most commonly used in cooking. They are fast-growing perennials which prefer a rich, moist soil and light shade. Freshly chopped mint can be used with peas, new potatoes, zucchini and mixed green salad. Also good in fruit salads, cooling drinks, jellies, vinegar and lamb sauce.

OREGANO

A small spreading perennial to around 20 in/50 cm. Small, pungent leaves and tiny white or mauve flowers. Grow in a well-drained soil in a sunny position. The common confusion between marjoram and oregano can be resolved by realising that the cultivated marjoram comes from the wild oregano and that the first has a sweet flavor and the second a strong, peppery one. Fresh marjoram leaves are used to season salads and many tomato dishes, especially tomato sauces used with pasta. It is also used with eggplant, beans, zucchini and cheese.

PARSLEY

A biennial plant to 2 ft/60 cm high with flat or curly leaves. Parsley is grown from seed which should be sown direct in spring and summer. Parsley likes a rich, well-drained soil in partial or full sun, and responds to frequent feeding. It is one of the best herbs of all and can be added to soups, stews, casseroles, sauces and stuffings. Always include the chopped stems as they are full of flavor and nutriment.

ROSEMARY

A Mediterranean evergreen shrub to around 5 ft/1.5 m high. It has thin, dark-green leaves, silver on the underside, highly aromatic; the pale blue flowers grow along the stems as well as at the tips. Choose a sheltered, sunny spot for planting, preferably against a wall, or in a corner, as rosemary needs all the protection it can get. The leaves, used either fresh or dried, are good with meat dishes, particularly lamb. The flavor is strong so they should be used sparingly.

SAGE

A small perennial shrub with soft, grey-green leaves and blue flowers during summer. Grow in a sunny, well-drained position and trim regularly. Give it plenty of water during summer. The leaves, used either fresh or dried, have a strong, clean flavor which cuts the grease of fatty foods. Use chopped fresh leaves sparingly in salads, potato dishes and with cheese. Use with pork and veal and in seasoning.

SAVORY, SUMMER

An annual to 2 ft/60 cm high with tender, narrow leaves of brownish-green and tiny flowers from pink to lavender. Grow in a sunny, well-drained position with plenty of organic matter added. Summer savory grows easily from seed in both warm and temperate climates. It is traditionally served with broad beans, cooked green beans and green bean salad. Also good in stuffings, rice, soups, sauces and stews.

SAVORY, WINTER

A semi-prostrate perennial with narrow green leaves and pale blue flowers. Likes full sun and a well-drained soil with plenty of organic matter added. Particularly good used in stuffings, rice, soups, sauces and stews.

SORREL

A perennial to 3 ft/90 cm tall with large bright green, arrow-shaped leaves that have a sharp lemony, bitter taste. Sorrel prefers a well-drained, rich soil in sun or semi-shade. Young fresh leaves are excellent in a mixed green salad. A few leaves can be added when cooking spinach. Used in the classic French sorrel soup. Use also in sauces and vegetable purées.

TARRAGON

French tarragon is a bushy perennial to around 3 ft/1 m high. It has dark slender leaves with a slight anise flavor. Grow in a moderately rich, well-drained soil in a sunny spot. French tarragon can only be propagated by division. Use with fish, shellfish, poultry, game, veal, liver, kidneys and in egg dishes. Tarragon vinegar is an essential ingredient in Béarnaise sauce.

THYME

A strongly aromatic shrubby perennial to around 18 in/45 cm high. It has tiny, oval leaves and bears pretty pastel-colored flowers. There are many varieties including lemon thyme, caraway thyme and a pretty variegated type. All thymes like a sunny position with a light, well-drained soil. Trim to keep compact. Thyme is one of the most successful herbs for drying. Use fresh leaves sparingly with most vegetables including beets, tomatoes and zucchini. Use in casseroles, meat dishes, pâtés and stuffings.

Basil

Sage

Chives

Parsley

Dill

Rosemary

Coriander

Mint

Oregano

Thyme

AT-A-GLANCE HERB GUIDE

HERB	SOUPS	MAIN DISHES
Angelica		
Basil	Tomato and fish soups	Fish dishes, meat loaves, casseroles
Bay	All soups and stocks	Meat, fish and poultry dishes
Caraway	Vegetable soups	Veal and pork dishes
Chervil	Fish and vegetable soups	Chicken, egg, cheese dishes, casseroles
Chives	Chilled soups, vichysoisse	Egg dishes, meat and chicken dishes
Coriander – fresh	Chilled soups	Oriental and Middle Eastern cooking, seafood, poultry, meat dishes
Curry plant	Fish and spiced soups	Seafood, all curries, casseroles and stews
Dill – fresh	Fish and vegetable soups	Fish, lamb and pork dishes
Fennel – fresh	Fish and vegetable soups	Chicken, fish, pork and egg dishes
Marjoram	Vegetable and meat soups	Casseroles, meat, marinades, meat loaf
Mint	Summer soups	Lamb dishes, trout
Oregano	Minestrone and tomato soups	Italian dishes, pasta and egg dishes, quiches, pizza
Parsley	All soups	All fish, poultry, meat and egg dishes, pasta
Rosemary	Meat stocks, chicken and tomato soups	Lamb and chicken dishes
Sage	Minestrone, chicken, tomato, celery and lentil soups	Meat loaf, pork, cheese and egg dishes
Savory	Vegetable soups	Beef, pork, egg and cheese dishes, pot pies, sausages, dishes made using pulses
Sorrel	Sorrel and vegetable soups	Omelets, chicken and veal dishes
Tarragon	Fish and tomato soups	Fish, chicken and some egg dishes
Thyme	Vegetable and meat soups and stocks	Meat, chicken and pasta dishes

VEGETABLE DISHES	DESSERTS AND BAKED PRODUCTS	OTHER USES
	Stems are candied and used for decoration, cook with fruit	
Tomato and green salads, baked vegetables dishes		Dips, savories, herb sandwiches, pasta sauces, stuffings
Vegetable casseroles	Place a leaf on a baked rice pudding or a baked custard	Flavor pâtés and terrines
Vegetable dishes, especially good with cabbage dishes, coleslaw and salads	Cookies, breads, cakes, pastries	Stewed fruit
Salads, root vegetable dishes	Savory breads and cookies	Herb butters, meat sauces
Salads, potato dishes		Dips, herb butters, garnish
Green salads, oriental dishes		Dips, pickles
		Stuffings for veal and game
Especially good with cucumber and cauliflower		Fish sauces, cheese dips
Salads		Stuffings, salad dressings
Tomato dishes, potato and vegetable baked dishes	Herbed quick breads	Sauces, herb butters, stuffings
New potatoes, peas, carrots, salads	Fruit salads, ice cream	Summer drinks, mint sauce, stuffings
Onions, potatoes, peppers	Herb bread	Pâtés, stuffings
All vegetables and salads	Herb and savory breads	Dressings, stuffings, garnish for most savory dishes
Eggplant, tomatoes, cabbage	Herb and savory breads and scones	Dressings, stuffings, dumplings, pâtés
Salads, vegetarian casseroles	Savory breads	Herbal teas
Broad and green beans		Stuffings for pork and veal
Spinach		Stuffings for veal, chicken and lamb
Mushrooms, carrots, salads		Sauces, stuffings and dressings
Most vegetable dishes		Sauces, stuffings, herbal teas

chapter three

SATISFYING SOUPS

Filling and nutritious
soups, broths and potages
have always been the mainstay
of the family diet. The basis of a
really tasty soup is a good stock
so it is well worth making your own.
In this chapter you will find recipes
for soups that make great first
courses and some that are
meals in themselves.

*Hearty Vegetable Soup,
Creamy Beef and Mushroom Soup,
Red Onion Soup*

MUSHROOM AND BURGUNDY SOUP

This robust mushroom soup is quick and easy to make. It is ideal as a first course or light meal.

Serves 6

- [ ] ¹/₄ cup/¹/₂ stick/2 oz butter
- [ ] 2 onions, chopped
- [ ] 1 lb/500 g open flat mushrooms, sliced
- [ ] 2 large potatoes, diced
- [ ] ¹/₂ cup/125 mL burgundy or red wine
- [ ] 1¹/₂ cups/375 mL beef stock
- [ ] 1 teaspoon ground nutmeg
- [ ] 2 cups/500 mL milk
- [ ] freshly ground black pepper

1   Melt half the butter in a heavy-based saucepan, add onions and three-quarters of the mushrooms and cook over a medium heat, stirring frequently, for 5 minutes.
2   Add potatoes, wine, stock and nutmeg and bring to the boil. Reduce heat and simmer for 15 minutes or until potatoes are tender. Remove pan from heat and set aside to cool slightly.
3   Transfer vegetable mixture to a food processor or blender and process until smooth. Return to a clean pan, stir in milk and season to taste with black pepper. Cook over a low heat, stirring occasionally, until soup is hot.
4   Melt remaining butter in a large skillet, add remaining mushrooms and cook for 4-5 minutes. Stir mushrooms into hot soup and serve immediately.

HEARTY VEGETABLE SOUP

Serves 6

- [ ] ¹/₃ cup/100 g pearl barley
- [ ] 6 cups/1.5 liters water
- [ ] 3 tablespoons/45 g butter
- [ ] 1 large onion, chopped
- [ ] 2 cloves garlic, crushed
- [ ] 1 large carrot, sliced
- [ ] 1 large potato, cubed
- [ ] 3 stalks celery, sliced
- [ ] 1 turnip, diced
- [ ] 1 large parsnip, diced
- [ ] 5 tomatoes, peeled, seeded and chopped
- [ ] ³/₄ cup/185 mL tomato paste
- [ ] ¹/₄ cup/3 tablespoons finely chopped fresh coriander

1   Place barley and water in a large bowl and set aside to soak overnight.
2   Melt butter in a large heavy-based saucepan and cook onion and garlic over a low heat for 5 minutes or until onion is soft.
3   Add carrot, potato, celery, turnip, parsnip, tomatoes, tomato paste, barley and soaking water to pan. Bring to the boil, then reduce heat and simmer, stirring occasionally, for 20 minutes or until vegetables are tender.
4   Ladle soup into bowls, sprinkle with coriander and serve immediately.

RED ONION SOUP

The secret to this wonderful soup is in the slow cooking of the onions and garlic at the beginning.

Serves 6

- [ ] ¹/₄ cup/¹/₂ stick/60 g butter
- [ ] 1 tablespoon olive oil
- [ ] 4 large red onions, sliced
- [ ] 12 whole cloves garlic, peeled
- [ ] 2 tablespoons all-purpose flour
- [ ] 1 teaspoon sugar
- [ ] 2 x 14 oz/440 g cans beef consommé
- [ ] 3 cups/750 mL water
- [ ] ¹/₃ cup/90 mL red wine
- [ ] 1 tablespoon brandy
- [ ] 1 long bread stick, cut into 12 slices
- [ ] ¹/₄ cup/¹/₂ stick/60 g butter, melted
- [ ] 2 cups/250 g shredded Cheddar cheese
- [ ] 1 tablespoon chopped fresh parsley

1   Heat butter and oil in a large, heavy-based saucepan and cook onions and garlic over a low heat for 15-20 minutes or until onions are golden.
2   Add flour and cook over a medium heat, stirring constantly until flour turns a light straw color. Stir in sugar, consommé, water, wine and brandy. Bring to the boil, then reduce heat and simmer, stirring occasionally, for 30 minutes.
3   Brush bread slices on both sides with melted butter. Place under a preheated broiler and toast one side. Sprinkle untoasted side of bread slices with cheese and return to broiler until cheese melts.
4   Place 2 slices of bread into each serving bowl. Ladle soup over bread and sprinkle with parsley. Serve immediately.

POTATO AND BRUSSELS SPROUTS SOUP

Serves 4

- [ ] 8 oz/250 g Brussels sprouts, trimmed
- [ ] 2 large potatoes, diced
- [ ] 4 cups/1 liter chicken or vegetable stock
- [ ] ¹/₂ cup/125 mL milk
- [ ] freshly ground black pepper
- [ ] 2 tablespoons chopped walnuts

1   Place Brussels sprouts, potatoes and stock in a large saucepan and bring to the boil. Reduce heat, cover and simmer for 20-25 minutes or until potatoes are tender. Remove pan from heat and set aside to cool slightly.
2   Place vegetable mixture in a food processor or blender and process until smooth. Return to a clean pan, stir in milk and season to taste with black pepper. Cook over a low heat, stirring occasionally, until soup is hot. To serve, ladle soup into bowls and sprinkle with walnuts.

Nutrition tip: The best vegetables for vitamin C are peppers, chilies, parsley, watercress, broccoli, Brussels sprouts, cauliflower and kohlrabi. These have a higher concentration of vitamin C than citrus fruit but are often overlooked as sources of vitamin C.

CREAMY BEEF AND MUSHROOM SOUP

Serves 6

- [ ] 2 tablespoons vegetable oil
- [ ] 1¹/₂ lb/750 g lean top round steak, cut into ¹/₂ in/1 cm cubes
- [ ] ¹/₄ cup/¹/₂ stick/60 g butter
- [ ] 4 carrots, sliced
- [ ] 2 leeks, sliced
- [ ] 11 oz/350 g button mushrooms, sliced
- [ ] 2 cloves garlic, crushed
- [ ] 3 tablespoons all-purpose flour
- [ ] 8 cups/2 liters beef stock
- [ ] 2 tablespoons sherry
- [ ] 4 potatoes, diced
- [ ] sour cream
- [ ] 2 tablespoons snipped fresh chives

1   Heat oil in a large, heavy-based saucepan and cook meat in batches

over a medium heat until browned on all sides. Remove meat from pan and set aside.

2 Melt butter in pan and cook carrots and leeks over a low heat for 5 minutes or until leeks are soft. Add mushrooms and garlic and cook for 4-5 minutes longer.

3 Stir in flour and cook for 1 minute. Remove pan from heat and gradually blend in stock and sherry. Bring to the boil, then reduce heat. Return meat to pan with potatoes and simmer for 30 minutes or until meat is tender.

4 Ladle soup into serving bowls, top with a spoonful of sour cream and sprinkle with chives.

Potato and Brussels Sprouts Soup, Minestrone Soup

MINESTRONE SOUP

Minestrone is a substantial main meal soup, both tasty and filling. You can vary the vegetables depending on what is available.

Serves 8

- ☐ **2 tablespoons olive oil**
- ☐ **3 cloves garlic, crushed**
- ☐ **1 onion, chopped**
- ☐ **1 large potato, diced**
- ☐ **1 carrot, diced**
- ☐ **2 large zucchini, diced**
- ☐ **4 oz/125 g green beans, trimmed and sliced**
- ☐ **2 tablespoons finely chopped fresh parsley**
- ☐ **1 tablespoon finely chopped fresh basil**
- ☐ **1 teaspoon finely chopped fresh oregano**
- ☐ **¹/₄ cup/60 mL tomato paste**
- ☐ **6 cups/1.5 liters chicken stock**
- ☐ **freshly ground black pepper**
- ☐ **14 oz/440 g canned red kidney beans, drained**
- ☐ **²/₃ cup/100 g macaroni**
- ☐ **¹/₂ small cabbage, finely shredded**

1 Heat oil in a large heavy-based saucepan. Cook garlic and onion for 2-3 minutes. Stir in potato, carrot, zucchini and beans. Cook for 3-4 minutes, stirring frequently.

2 Combine parsley, basil, oregano, tomato paste and stock. Pour over vegetables in pan. Season to taste with black pepper. Cover and simmer for 30 minutes or until vegetables are tender.

3 Add kidney beans. Bring to the boil, drop in macaroni and cook for a further 20 minutes. Add cabbage during last minute of cooking.

CHICKEN AND AVOCADO SOUP

Serves 4

- ☐ 1 tablespoon/15 g butter
- ☐ 1 onion, finely chopped
- ☐ 1 large potato, diced
- ☐ 4 cups/1 liter chicken stock
- ☐ 10 oz/315 g canned corn kernels, drained
- ☐ 1 cooked chicken, flesh removed and chopped
- ☐ freshly ground black pepper
- ☐ $1/4$ cup/90 mL dairy sour cream
- ☐ 1 avocado, pitted, peeled and diced

1 Melt butter in a large saucepan, add onion and cook, stirring frequently, for 4-5 minutes or until onion is soft. Stir in potato and stock, cover and bring to the boil, then reduce heat and simmer for 15-20 minutes or until potato is tender.

2 Add corn, chicken and black pepper to taste and cook for 5-6 minutes longer or until soup is heated through. To serve, spoon soup into bowls and top with sour cream and avocado.

QUICK SEAFOOD SOUP

Serves 4

- ☐ 4 firm white fish fillets, skinned and bones removed
- ☐ 2 tablespoons/30 g butter
- ☐ 2 leeks, sliced
- ☐ 14 oz/440 g canned tomatoes, undrained and mashed
- ☐ 4 cups/1 liter chicken or fish stock
- ☐ 2 tablespoons tomato paste
- ☐ 3 or 4 large oysters, quartered or chopped
- ☐ 8 cooked mussels in shells
- ☐ 1 tablespoon chopped fresh basil
- ☐ $1/2$ teaspoon brown sugar

1 Cut fish fillets into pieces. Melt butter in a large saucepan, add leeks and cook, stirring, for 4-5 minutes or until leeks are soft.

2 Add tomatoes, stock and tomato paste and bring to the boil. Stir in fish, oysters, mussels, basil and sugar and simmer for 5 minutes or until fish is cooked. Serve immediately.

CREAMY ASPARAGUS SOUP

A swirl of unflavored plain yogurt and freshly chopped chives make a wonderful garnish for this flavorsome soup.

Serves 4

- ☐ 14 oz/440 g canned asparagus cuts
- ☐ $1^1/2$ cups/375 mL chicken stock
- ☐ 2 tablespoons snipped fresh chives
- ☐ 1 clove garlic, crushed
- ☐ pinch ground nutmeg
- ☐ 1 cup/250 mL milk
- ☐ freshly ground black pepper

1 Drain asparagus, reserving $1/2$ cup/ 125 mL of liquid. Place asparagus cuts, reserved liquid, stock, chives, garlic and nutmeg in a food processor or blender. Process until smooth.

2 Transfer mixture to a saucepan. Bring to the boil, reduce heat and stir in milk. Heat gently, without boiling. Season to taste with pepper.

Creamy Asparagus Soup

BEEF AND HERB DUMPLING SOUP

A hearty soup that is a meal in itself.

Serves 6

- [ ] ¼ cup/½ stick/60 g butter
- [ ] 2 onions, chopped
- [ ] 4 slices bacon, chopped
- [ ] 1½ lb/750 g lean round steak, cut into thin strips
- [ ] ½ cup/60 g all-purpose flour, sifted
- [ ] 1 tablespoon paprika
- [ ] 8 cups/2 liters beef stock
- [ ] 2 red peppers, halved and roasted
- [ ] ⅓ cup/90 g tomato paste
- [ ] 1 tablespoon caraway seeds
- [ ] freshly ground black pepper
- [ ] 2 tablespoons finely chopped fresh coriander

HERB DUMPLINGS
- [ ] 2 cups/250 g self-rising flour, sifted
- [ ] ¼ cup/½ stick/60 g butter, cut into small pieces
- [ ] 2 eggs, lightly beaten
- [ ] ⅓ cup/90 mL milk
- [ ] 2 tablespoons chopped fresh herbs, such as parsley, coriander, rosemary or thyme

1   Melt butter in a large, heavy-based saucepan and cook onions and bacon over a medium-high heat for 4-5 minutes or until bacon is crisp. Using a slotted spoon remove onions and bacon from pan and set aside.

2   Add beef to pan in small batches and cook over a medium heat to brown all sides. Remove from pan and drain on paper towels.

3   Combine flour and paprika. Add to pan and cook over a medium heat for 1 minute. Remove pan from heat and gradually blend in stock. Return onion mixture and meat to pan. Bring to the boil, then reduce heat and simmer for 1½ hours or until meat is tender.

4   Remove skin from red peppers and chop. Add red peppers, tomato paste and caraway seeds to pan and simmer for 15 minutes longer. Season to taste with black pepper.

5   To make dumplings, place self-rising flour in a large mixing bowl. Rub in butter with fingertips until mixture resembles coarse bread crumbs. Combine eggs, milk and herbs. Pour into flour mixture and mix

to a smooth dough. Shape tablespoons of mixture into small balls. Cook dumplings in boiling water in a large saucepan for 10-12 minutes or until they rise to the surface. Remove dumplings using a slotted spoon. To serve, place a few dumplings in each bowl, ladle soup over and sprinkle with parsley. Serve immediately.

Cook's tip: To roast peppers, place them under a hot broiler and cook until the skin blisters and chars. Place in a paper or freezer bag and leave for 10 minutes or until cool enough to handle. The skins will then slip off.

Beef and Herb Dumpling Soup

SPICY WINTER SQUASH SOUP

A less spicy soup can be made by omitting the coriander, cumin and chili powder. Instead, stir in 2 teaspoons chopped fresh parsley with the cream.

Serves 4

- ☐ **1 tablespoon vegetable oil**
- ☐ **1 onion, chopped**
- ☐ **1 clove garlic, crushed**
- ☐ **$^1/_2$ teaspoon ground coriander**
- ☐ **$^1/_2$ teaspoon ground cumin**
- ☐ **$^1/_2$ teaspoon chili powder**
- ☐ **2 lb/1 kg butternut or Hubbard squash, peeled and chopped**
- ☐ **4 cups/1 liter chicken stock**
- ☐ **$^1/_3$ cup/90 mL thick cream**
- ☐ **freshly ground black pepper**

1   Heat oil in a saucepan and cook onion over a medium heat for 3-4 minutes or until soft. Add garlic, coriander, cumin and chili powder and cook for 1 minute longer.
2   Add squash and stock to pan, bring to the boil, then reduce heat and simmer for 15-20 minutes or until squash is tender. Remove pan from heat and set aside to cool slightly. Place squash and cooking liquid in batches in a food processor or blender and process until smooth.
3   Return soup to a clean saucepan, stir in cream, season to taste with black pepper and cook over a medium heat, without boiling, until heated.

Serving suggestion: Accompany soup with crusty bread and follow with a crisp garden salad.

Cook's tip: Instead of using a food processor to purée the soup, you can remove the cooked squash from the stock and mash it, using a potato masher or fork, then mix in cooking liquid and complete as in recipe.

Spicy Winter Squash Soup, Creamy Broccoli Soup

CHILLED TOMATO SOUP

Serve this delightfully refreshing, low-calorie soup, with Tomato Minted Ice Cubes if desired.

Serves 4

- ☐ **1 tablespoon olive oil**
- ☐ **1 onion, chopped**
- ☐ **1 clove garlic, crushed**
- ☐ **4 cups/1 liter vegetable stock**
- ☐ **2 tablespoons finely chopped fresh mint**
- ☐ **14 oz/440 g canned tomatoes, drained**
- ☐ **2 zucchini, shredded**
- ☐ **freshly ground black pepper**

1   Heat oil in a saucepan and cook onion and garlic over a medium heat for 3-4 minutes or until onion is soft. Add stock and mint, bring to the boil, then reduce heat and simmer for 5 minutes.
2   Place tomatoes and stock mixture in a food processor or blender and process until smooth. Stir in zucchini and season to taste with black pepper. Chill well before serving.

Serving suggestion: Place three Tomato Minted Ice Cubes (see recipe) in a serving bowl and pour chilled soup over.

Freeze it: Half the soup can be frozen in an airtight freezerproof container. Defrost at room temperature for 2-3 hours and then rechill, or defrost in the refrigerator overnight.

TOMATO MINTED ICE CUBES

- ☐ **fresh mint leaves**
- ☐ **$^3/_4$ cup/185 mL tomato juice**
- ☐ **$^3/_4$ cup/185 mL water**

Place a mint leaf in each space of an ice cube tray. Mix together tomato juice and water and pour into ice cube tray. Freeze.

Cook's tip: To store ice cubes, remove from tray and store in a sealed freezer bag.

CREAMY BROCCOLI SOUP

Serves 4

- ☐ **1 tablespoon vegetable oil**
- ☐ **1 onion, chopped**
- ☐ **4 cups/1 liter chicken stock**
- ☐ **1 potato, chopped**
- ☐ **12 oz/375 g broccoli florets**
- ☐ **1 tablespoon chopped fresh parsley**
- ☐ **freshly ground black pepper**

1 Heat oil in a saucepan and cook onion over a medium heat for 3-4 minutes or until soft. Add stock, potato and broccoli, bring to the boil, then reduce heat and simmer for 10-15 minutes or until potato is tender.

2 Transfer mixture to a food processor or blender and process until smooth.

3 Return soup to a clean saucepan, stir in parsley and season to taste with black pepper. Cook over a medium heat until heated.

Serving suggestion: Serve with a swirl of cream and accompany with broiled cheese-topped bagels.

CHICKEN AND CORN SOUP

Serves 4

- ☐ **1 tablespoon vegetable oil**
- ☐ **1 onion, sliced**
- ☐ **pinch ground cumin**
- ☐ **1 potato, diced**
- ☐ **4 cups/1 liter chicken stock**
- ☐ **³/₄ cup/185 g chopped cooked chicken**
- ☐ **7 oz/220 g canned corn kernels, drained**
- ☐ **freshly ground black pepper**
- ☐ **1 tablespoon finely chopped fresh parsley**

1 Heat oil in a saucepan and cook onion and cumin over a medium heat for 3-4 minutes or until soft. Add potato and stock, bring to the boil, then reduce heat and simmer for 10-15 minutes or until potato is tender.

2 Remove onion and potato, using a slotted spoon, and place in a food processor or blender and process until smooth. Return potato purée to stock mixture and whisk to combine. Stir in chicken and corn and cook over a low heat until heated. Season to taste with black pepper.

Serving suggestion: Sprinkle with parsley and serve with a slice of crusty bread.

MEXICAN CORN CHOWDER

For a less spicy but just as delicious soup you can omit the chili.

Serves 6

- ☐ **1 tablespoon/15 g butter**
- ☐ **2 slices bacon, chopped**
- ☐ **1 onion, finely chopped**
- ☐ **2 stalks celery, chopped**
- ☐ **1 small fresh red chili, finely chopped**
- ☐ **2 cups/500 mL chicken stock**
- ☐ **1 teaspoon ground cumin**
- ☐ **1 teaspoon dried thyme**
- ☐ **2 tablespoons all-purpose flour blended with ¹/₄ cup/60 mL milk**
- ☐ **1³/₄ cups/440 mL milk**
- ☐ **14 oz/440 g can corn kernels, drained**
- ☐ **freshly ground black pepper**

1 Melt butter in a large saucepan, add bacon, onion, celery and chili and cook, stirring, for 4-5 minutes or until onion is soft.

2 Add stock, cumin and thyme and bring to the boil, reduce heat and simmer for 10 minutes.

3 Stir flour mixture into stock mixture, then stir in milk and corn kernels. Cook, stirring constantly, until soup comes to the boil, then reduce heat and simmer for 5 minutes. Season to taste with black pepper.

Freeze it: Soups freeze well and can be frozen for up to 3 months. Remember when freezing any liquid to leave a 2 in/ 5 cm space between the liquid and the lid of the container as liquid expands during freezing.

Chilled Tomato Soup,
Chicken and Corn Soup

FRESH TOMATO SOUP

Bursting with flavor, this satisfying soup makes a great winter luncheon served with crusty bread, or try it chilled on hot summer days. If you find the soup is too tart, a teaspoon of sugar stirred into it will sweeten the flavor.

Serves 6

- ☐ **1 tablespoon olive oil**
- ☐ **1 carrot, chopped**
- ☐ **1 onion, chopped**
- ☐ **2 stalks celery, chopped**
- ☐ **1 clove garlic, crushed**
- ☐ **6 tomatoes, peeled, seeded and chopped**
- ☐ **14 oz/440 g can tomatoes, drained and chopped**
- ☐ **4 cups/1 liter chicken stock**
- ☐ **1 teaspoon chopped fresh thyme, or ¹/₄ teaspoon dried thyme**
- ☐ **¹/₂ teaspoon hot red pepper sauce sauce**
- ☐ **1 cup/250 mL thick cream**
- ☐ **2 tablespoons finely chopped fresh basil**
- ☐ **freshly ground black pepper**

1   Heat oil in a large saucepan, add carrot, onion, celery and garlic and cook for 3-4 minutes or until onion softens.

2   Stir in fresh and canned tomatoes, chicken stock, thyme and Tabasco sauce. Bring to the boil and simmer, uncovered, for 30 minutes. Remove from heat.

3   Place in a food processor or blender and process until smooth. Return soup to a clean pan and bring just to a simmer. Remove from heat and stir in cream and basil. Season to taste with black pepper.

Cook's tip: When serving soup as a starter, allow approximately 1 cup/250 mL of soup per person. For soup as a main course, serves may be a little larger.

CONSOMME

Consommé is the French word for a soup based on meat stock that has been enriched, concentrated and then clarified. It is the simplest, yet most sophisticated, soup and you may serve it hot or cold. The perfect garnish for consommé is thin strips of blanched carrot and leek.

Serves 6

- ☐ **4 cups/1 liter cold beef stock**
- ☐ **8 oz/250 g finely ground beef**
- ☐ **1 small onion, chopped**
- ☐ **1 small carrot, chopped**
- ☐ **1 small leek, chopped**
- ☐ **4 whole black peppercorns**
- ☐ **bouquet garni**
- ☐ **2 egg whites, lightly beaten**
- ☐ **1 tablespoon dry sherry**

1   Place stock, beef, onion, carrot, leek, peppercorns, bouquet garni and egg whites in a large saucepan, bring slowly to the boil, whisking continuously. Reduce heat, stir in sherry and simmer gently for 1¹/₂ hours, without stirring.

2   Remove from heat and set aside to stand for 20 minutes. A thick brown scum will have formed on the surface of the stock, skim off scum and strain stock carefully through cheesecloth. Remove fat from surface using paper towels.

Cook's tip: Consommé should be clear. If your consommé is cloudy it may be because the stock was greasy, unstrained or of poor quality. Whisking the stock after it reaches boiling point or not allowing it to stand before straining will also cause the consommé to become cloudy. Remember that the pan and cheesecloth must be very clean when you are making consommé.

CREAM OF MUSHROOM AND HAZELNUT SOUP

A delightfully creamy soup that makes a great starter for a special occasion or is a delicious meal in itself served with crusty French bread and a crispy salad.

Serves 4

- [ ] ¼ cup/½ stick/60 g butter
- [ ] ¼ cup/30 g all-purpose flour
- [ ] 4 cups/1 liter milk
- [ ] 2 teaspoons oil
- [ ] 6 spring onions, chopped
- [ ] 4 oz/125 g button mushrooms, sliced
- [ ] 2 oz/60 g hazelnuts (filberts), toasted, skins removed, and finely chopped
- [ ] 1 teaspoon paprika
- [ ] ½ cup/125 mL thick cream
- [ ] freshly ground black pepper

1 Melt butter in a medium saucepan. Stir in flour and cook for 1 minute. Remove from heat and gradually stir in milk. Return pan to heat and bring slowly to the boil, stirring constantly. Simmer for 3 minutes, remove from heat and set aside.

2 Heat oil in a medium saucepan and cook spring onions for 2 minutes. Add mushrooms, hazelnuts and paprika and cook for 2-3 minutes longer. Stir in milk mixture, bring to the boil, then reduce heat and simmer gently for 10 minutes.

3 Remove from heat, place in a food processor or blender and process until smooth. Return soup to a clean pan and reheat gently. Stir in cream and season to taste with black pepper.

Cook's tip: For a taste variation, replace hazelnuts with toasted, finely chopped almonds.

Consommé, Fresh Tomato Soup, Cream of Mushroom and Hazelnut Soup

CURRIED CHICKEN SOUP

Serves 6

- [ ] ¼ cup/½ stick/60 g butter
- [ ] 2 onions, chopped
- [ ] 2 cloves garlic, crushed
- [ ] 2 large parsnips, chopped
- [ ] 4 stalks celery, chopped
- [ ] ¼ cup/30 g all-purpose flour
- [ ] 1 tablespoon curry powder
- [ ] 6 cups/1.5 liters chicken stock
- [ ] 6 oz/185 g fresh or frozen peas
- [ ] 2 cups/500 g chopped, cooked chicken
- [ ] 1 cup/250 g dairy sour cream
- [ ] 3 tablespoons finely chopped fresh flat leaf parsley
- [ ] 2 tablespoons chopped fresh dill

1 Melt butter in a large saucepan, cook onions, garlic, parsnips and celery over a low heat for 5-6 minutes or until vegetables are soft. Stir in flour and curry powder and cook for 1 minute longer.

2 Remove pan from heat and gradually blend in stock. Cook over a medium heat, stirring constantly until mixture boils and thickens. Reduce heat, and stir in peas and chicken and cook for 10 minutes.

3 Remove pan from heat and whisk in sour cream, then stir in parsley and dill. Cook over a low heat, stirring frequently, for 3-4 minutes or until warmed through. Serve immediately.

PEA AND HAM SOUP

Variations of this soup have been around since the Middle Ages. This one with ham is perfect for a fireside supper.

Serves 6

- [ ] 1½ lb/750 g dried split peas, rinsed
- [ ] 16 cups/4 liters water
- [ ] 1 lb/500 g ham bones
- [ ] 4 onions, finely chopped
- [ ] 4 tablespoons chopped celery leaves
- [ ] 4 stalks celery, chopped
- [ ] 8 oz/250 g smoked ham, cut into ½ in/1 cm cubes
- [ ] freshly ground black pepper

1 Place split peas and water in a large, heavy-based saucepan and set aside to stand overnight.

2 Add ham bones to pan with peas. Bring to the boil, then reduce heat and simmer for 2 hours or until soup thickens.

3 Stir in onion, celery leaves and celery and cook over a low heat for 20 minutes longer.

4 Remove ham bones from soup and discard. Add ham and cook until heated through. Season to taste with black pepper.

5 Ladle soup into serving bowls.

POTATO BACON CHOWDER

Serves 6

- [ ] **8 oz/250 g bacon, chopped**
- [ ] **2 tablespoons/30 g butter**
- [ ] **2 large onions, chopped**
- [ ] **4 stalks celery, chopped**
- [ ] **2 teaspoons dried thyme**
- [ ] **2-3 tablespoons all-purpose flour**
- [ ] **6 cups/1.5 liters chicken stock**
- [ ] **2 large potatoes, cubed**
- [ ] **1¼ cups/300 g dairy sour cream**
- [ ] **3 tablespoons chopped fresh parsley**
- [ ] **2 tablespoons snipped fresh chives**

1 Place bacon in a large, heavy-based saucepan and sauté over a medium heat for 5 minutes or until golden and crisp. Remove from pan and drain on paper towels.

2 Melt butter in pan and cook onions, celery and thyme over a low heat for 4-5 minutes or until onion is soft.

3 Return bacon to pan, then stir in flour and cook for 1 minute. Remove pan from heat and gradually blend in stock. Bring to the boil, then reduce heat. Add potatoes and cook for 10 minutes or until potatoes are tender.

4 Remove pan from heat and stir in sour cream and parsley. Return to heat and cook without boiling, stirring constantly, for 1-2 minutes. Ladle soup into bowls, sprinkle with chives and serve immediately.

Left: Pea and Ham Soup,
Curried Chicken Soup
Right: Potato Bacon Chowder

chapter four

FABULOUS FIRST COURSES

Designed to stimulate the
taste buds, these recipes are the
perfect start to any meal. For a
barbecue you might like to serve
the Bite-sized Kabobs, while the
Smoked Salmon and Watercress
Roulade makes a great first
course for an elegant
dinner party.

*Sesame Shrimp Balls,
Beef and Vegetable Lettuce Cups*

SESAME SHRIMP BALLS

These delicious morsels make a perfect light meal that would be ideal for a luncheon.

Serves 6

- [ ] **2 lb/1 kg medium uncooked shrimp, shelled and deveined**
- [ ] **1 onion, chopped finely**
- [ ] **$1/2$ teaspoon garam masala**
- [ ] **$1/4$ teaspoon ground turmeric**
- [ ] **$1^1/_2$ cups/185 g rice flour**
- [ ] **1 teaspoon sesame oil**
- [ ] **2 tablespoons/15 g finely chopped fresh coriander (cilantro)**
- [ ] **4 tablespoons sesame seeds**
- [ ] **oil for deep-frying**
- [ ] **shredded lettuce**

SAUCE

- [ ] **1 tablespoon cornstarch**
- [ ] **1 cup/250 mL chicken stock**
- [ ] **$1/2$ cup/125 mL prepared tamarind sauce**
- [ ] **2 tablespoons soy sauce**
- [ ] **1 tablespoon lime juice**
- [ ] **1 tablespoon finely chopped coriander**

1   Place shrimp, onion and spices in a food processor or blender and process until smooth. Stir in rice flour, oil and coriander. Cover and refrigerate mixture for 1 hour. Using wet hands, roll mixture into small balls, then roll in seeds. Refrigerate for 1 hour.
2   To make sauce, blend cornstarch with stock in saucepan. Stir in tamarind sauce, soy sauce, lime juice and coriander. Bring to the boil, stirring constantly, reduce heat and simmer, uncovered, for 5 minutes.
3   Heat oil in a large saucepan. Deep-fry balls until golden and cooked through. Serve balls on a bed of shredded lettuce with sauce spooned over.

GARLIC SESAME SHRIMP

Serves 6

- [ ] **1 teaspoon sesame oil**
- [ ] **2 lb/1 kg uncooked shrimp, shelled and deveined, tails left intact**
- [ ] **2 cloves garlic, crushed**
- [ ] **1 teaspoon grated fresh ginger**
- [ ] **2 tablespoons dry sherry**
- [ ] **$3/4$ cup/185 mL fish or chicken stock**

- [ ] **2 teaspoons soy sauce**
- [ ] **$1/4$ cup/60 g finely chopped, canned pimento**
- [ ] **2 tablespoons snipped fresh chives**
- [ ] **1 tablespoon bottled barbecue sauce**
- [ ] **1 tablespoon cornstarch blended with $1/4$ cup/60 mL water**
- [ ] **freshly ground black pepper**
- [ ] **2 tablespoons toasted sesame seeds**

1   Heat oil in a nonstick skillet, add shrimp, garlic and ginger and stir-fry for 3-4 minutes or until shrimp change color.
2   Add sherry, stock, soy sauce, pimento, chives and barbecue sauce and cook for 2-3 minutes longer. Stir in cornstarch mixture and cook, stirring constantly, until sauce boils and thickens. Season to taste with black pepper and serve sprinkled with sesame seeds.

MOZZARELLA PARCELS

This antipasto-style starter also makes a delicious lunch or supper dish, served with crusty bread.

Serves 4

- [ ] **4 spring onions**
- [ ] **6 oz/185 g mozzarella cheese**
- [ ] **4 slices packaged ham**
- [ ] **12 sun-dried tomatoes or 4 tomatoes, sliced**
- [ ] **24 green olives**

LEMON DRESSING

- [ ] **1 clove garlic, crushed**
- [ ] **2 tablespoons olive oil**
- [ ] **1 tablespoon lemon juice**
- [ ] **1 tablespoon chopped fresh basil**
- [ ] **freshly ground black pepper**

1   Cut green tops from spring onions and place tops in a bowl. Reserve spring onion bulbs for another use. Pour boiling water over tops, then drain and cut into long, thin strips. Set aside.
2   Cut mozzarella cheese into four slices. Wrap each slice of mozzarella in a slice of ham and tie with a spring onion strip.
3   To make dressing, place garlic, oil, lemon juice, basil and black pepper to taste in a screwtop jar and shake well to combine. Arrange a Mozzarella Parcel, tomatoes and olives on individual serving plates or on a large platter. Drizzle with dressing and serve immediately.

BEEF AND VEGETABLE LETTUCE CUPS

These tasty lettuce cups make an attractive entertaining dish. The filling can be made up in advance then reheated just before placing in the lettuce cups.

Serves 8

- [ ] **1 tablespoon olive oil**
- [ ] **500 g/1 lb ground beef**
- [ ] **1 teaspoon ground cinnamon**
- [ ] **1 teaspoon ground turmeric**
- [ ] **1 teaspoon ground sweet paprika**
- [ ] **2 tablespoons chopped fresh mint**
- [ ] **2 tablespoons chopped fresh parsley**
- [ ] **$1/4$ cup/60 mL tomato paste**
- [ ] **$1/2$ cup/125 mL red wine**
- [ ] **$1/2$ cup/125 mL beef stock**
- [ ] **13 oz/410 g canned red kidney beans, drained and rinsed**
- [ ] **2 tablespoons chopped pimento**
- [ ] **2 red onions, sliced**
- [ ] **8 oz/250 g baby yellow squash, chopped**
- [ ] **8 oz/250 g snow peas, sliced diagonally**
- [ ] **8 large lettuce cups, washed, drained**

1   Heat oil in a large skillet or wok. Add beef and cook over a high heat for 10 minutes or until meat is well browned and all the liquid has evaporated. Stir in cinnamon, turmeric, paprika, mint, parsley, tomato sauce, wine, stock, beans and pimento, and cook over a medium heat for 5 minutes.
2   Stir in onions, squash and snow peas. Cook until vegetables are crisp but tender, and almost all liquid has evaporated. Spoon beef and vegetables into lettuce cups. Serve immediately.

MUSHROOM AND ZUCCHINI BREAD BASKETS

These delicious bread baskets make wonderful containers for all sorts of different foods. Try filling them with creamy curried vegetables or with salad.

Serves 6
Oven temperature 400°F, 200°C

- [ ] **1 loaf unsliced wholewheat bread**
- [ ] **vegetable oil**

MUSHROOM FILLING
- [ ] **2 tablespoons/30 g butter**
- [ ] **1 clove garlic, crushed**
- [ ] **1 teaspoon ground cumin**
- [ ] **2 small zucchini, cut into 2 in/ 5 cm lengths**
- [ ] **6 oz/185 g small button mushrooms**
- [ ] **3 oz/90 g open flat mushrooms, sliced**
- [ ] **3 oz/90 g oyster mushrooms**
- [ ] **2 tablespoons lemon juice**
- [ ] **6 spring onions, cut into 2 in/5 cm pieces**
- [ ] **2 tablespoons finely chopped fresh mint**
- [ ] **freshly ground black pepper**
- [ ] **fresh mint sprigs**

1 Remove crusts from bread and cut crosswise into six thick slices. Remove center from each slice, leaving base intact to form baskets. Brush all surfaces with oil and bake for 10-15 minutes or until baskets are golden in color.

2 To make filling, melt butter in a skillet. Add garlic and cumin and cook for 1-2 minutes. Toss zucchini and cook for 3-4 minutes. Remove from pan and set aside.

3 Combine mushrooms with lemon juice and add to pan. Cook for 3-4 minutes. Return zucchini with spring onions to the pan and cook for 2-3 minutes longer. Stir in chopped mint and season to taste with pepper.

4 Spoon filling into baskets and garnish with mint sprigs.

Mushroom and Zucchini Bread Baskets

TABBOULEH-FILLED TOMATOES

Serves 4
Oven temperature 400°F, 200°C

- [ ] **4 large tomatoes**

TABBOULEH FILLING
- [ ] **¼ cup/60 g burghul (cracked wheat)**
- [ ] **8 spring onions, chopped**
- [ ] **3 cloves garlic, crushed**
- [ ] **¼ cup/3 tablespoons finely chopped fresh parsley**
- [ ] **2 tablespoons finely chopped fresh mint**
- [ ] **1 tablespoon olive oil**
- [ ] **freshly ground black pepper**

1   Cut tops from tomatoes with a sharp knife. Scoop out pulp using a teaspoon, chop and reserve. Place tomato shells upside down on paper towels to drain.
2   To make filling, place burghul (cracked wheat) in a bowl, cover with boiling water and set aside to soak for 10 minutes. Drain and place in a bowl, add reserved tomato pulp, spring onions, garlic, parsley, mint and oil and mix to combine. Season to taste with black pepper.
3   Spoon filling into tomato shells and place on a lightly greased cookie sheet and bake for 10 minutes or until heated through.

CHEESE CIGARS WITH CORIANDER PESTO

A pesto made of coriander is the perfect accompaniment to these tasty Cheese Cigars – serve as an indulgent snack or as a pre-dinner treat.

Makes 12

- [ ] **12 slices white sandwich bread, crusts removed**
- [ ] **2 teaspoons prepared hot English mustard**
- [ ] **5 tablespoons finely grated fresh Parmesan cheese**
- [ ] **½ cup/60 g shredded mozzarella cheese**
- [ ] **1 tablespoon snipped fresh chives**
- [ ] **cayenne pepper**
- [ ] **1 egg, lightly beaten**
- [ ] **vegetable oil for cooking**

CORIANDER PESTO
- [ ] **3 large bunches/9½ oz/300 g fresh coriander (cilantro)**
- [ ] **2 cloves garlic, crushed**
- [ ] **½ cup/60 g pine nuts (pignola)**
- [ ] **½ cup/125 mL olive oil**
- [ ] **½ cup/60 g grated fresh Parmesan cheese**

1   Roll each slice of bread with a rolling pin, to flatten as much as possible.
2   Combine mustard, Parmesan cheese, mozzarella cheese, chives, and cayenne pepper to taste in a bowl. Divide mixture between bread slices and spread over half of each bread slice. Brush unspread halves of bread slices with egg. Roll each slice up tightly using the egg to seal rolls. Arrange side by side on a tray. Cover and refrigerate until ready to cook.
3   Heat ¾ in/2cm of oil in a skillet. When hot, cook cigars a few at a time until evenly golden all over. Drain on paper towels.
4   To make pesto, place coriander leaves, garlic and pine nuts in a food processor or blender and process until finely chopped. With machine running, slowly pour in oil and process mixture until smooth. Add cheese and process to blend. Serve with hot cigars.

Cheese Cigars with Coriander Pesto

CRUDITES WITH HERB MAYONNAISE

Serves 10

- ☐ **a selection of vegetables such as broccoli and cauliflower florets, carrot sticks and new baby potatoes**

HERB MAYONNAISE
- ☐ **1 oz/30 g fresh parsley sprigs**
- ☐ **1 oz/30 g fresh basil leaves**
- ☐ **¹/₂ cup/125 g mayonnaise**
- ☐ **¹/₃ cup/90 mL dairy sour cream**
- ☐ **2 teaspoons French mustard**
- ☐ **freshly ground black pepper**

1 Steam or microwave vegetables separately until just tender. Drain, refresh under cold running water, drain again and set aside.

2 To make mayonnaise, place parsley and basil in a food processor or blender and process to finely chop. Add mayonnaise, sour cream, mustard and black pepper to taste and process to combine.

To serve: Arrange vegetables on a large platter and accompany with Herb Mayonnaise.

Cook's tip: This mayonnaise is delicious served with any lightly cooked or steamed vegetables. You might like to try serving snow peas, zucchini, asparagus or cucumber on this platter instead of, or as well as, the vegetables that are suggested in the recipe.

CHEESY WALNUT TARTS

Serves 6
Oven temperature 350°F, 180°C

CHEESE PASTRY
- ☐ **5 oz/155 g butter or shortening, softened**
- ☐ **1 tablespoon vegetable oil**
- ☐ **6 oz/185 g Gorgonzola or blue cheese, crumbled**
- ☐ **2 egg yolks**
- ☐ **2 tablespoons water**
- ☐ **2 cups/250 g all-purpose flour, sifted**

WALNUT AND CHEESE FILLING
- ☐ **1 cup/125 g chopped walnuts, lightly toasted**
- ☐ **1¹/₂ cups/375 g ricotta cheese**
- ☐ **¹/₄ cup/30 g grated Parmesan cheese**
- ☐ **3 eggs, lightly beaten**
- ☐ **³/₄ cup/185 mL milk**
- ☐ **¹/₂ teaspoon ground nutmeg**
- ☐ **¹/₂ teaspoon freshly ground black pepper**
- ☐ **1 tablespoon snipped fresh chives**

1 To make pastry, place butter or shortening and oil in bowl and beat until soft and creamy. Stir in cheese, egg yolks and water and mix to combine. Add flour and mix to form a soft dough. Roll dough into a ball, wrap in plastic food wrap and refrigerate for 30 minutes.

2 Roll out pastry between two layers of parchment paper and cut to fit six well-greased 5 in/12 cm fluted tartlet tins. Line pastry shells with parchment paper, fill with uncooked rice and bake for 8 minutes. Remove rice and paper and bake for 5 minutes longer.

3 To make filling, place walnuts, ricotta cheese, Parmesan cheese, eggs, milk, nutmeg, black pepper and chives in a bowl and mix to combine. Spoon filling into pastry shells and bake for 15 minutes or until filling is firm.

Crudités with Herb Mayonnaise

CHEESE AND BACON NACHOS

Serves 6
Oven temperature 350°F, 180°C

- ☐ **6 slices bacon, chopped**
- ☐ **6 spring onions, chopped**
- ☐ **4 jalapeño peppers, finely chopped**
- ☐ **6¹/₂ oz/200 g package corn chips**
- ☐ **1 cup/125 g shredded Cheddar or monterey jackcheese**
- ☐ **1 cup/250 g dairy sour cream**

1   Place bacon, spring onions and peppers in a nonstick skillet and cook over a medium heat for 4-5 minutes or until bacon is crisp. Remove bacon mixture from pan and drain on paper towels.
2   Place corn chips in a shallow baking dish and sprinkle with bacon mixture and cheese. Bake for 5-8 minutes or until heated through and cheese is melted. Serve immediately, accompanied by sour cream for dipping.

Jalapeño peppers: These are the medium-to-dark green peppers that taper to a blunt end and are 2-3 in/5-7.5 cm long and ³/₄-1 in/2-2.5 cm wide. They are medium-to-hot in taste and are also available canned or bottled.

SMOKED SALMON AND WATERCRESS ROULADE

Serves 10
Oven temperature 350°F, 180°C

- ☐ **1 bunch/3 oz/90 g watercress**
- ☐ **1 teaspoon finely chopped fresh parsley**
- ☐ **2 eggs, separated**
- ☐ **2 tablespoons all-purpose flour**
- ☐ **freshly ground black pepper**

SMOKED SALMON FILLING
- ☐ **2 oz/60 g cream cheese**
- ☐ **2 tablespoons dairy sour cream**
- ☐ **3 oz/90 g smoked salmon**
- ☐ **1 teaspoon lemon juice**

- ☐ **1¹/₂ teaspoons plain gelatin dissolved in 2 tablespoons hot water, cooled**

1   Place watercress leaves, parsley, egg yolks, flour and black pepper to taste in a food processor and process until mixture is smooth. Transfer watercress mixture to a bowl. Place egg whites in a bowl and beat until stiff peaks form. Fold egg white mixture into watercress mixture.
2   Spoon roulade mixture into a greased and lined 10¹/₂ x 12³/₄ in/26 x 32 cm Jelly roll tin and bake for 5 minutes or until just cooked. Turn roulade onto a damp teatowel and roll up from short side. Set aside to cool.
3   To make filling, place cream cheese, sour cream, smoked salmon and lemon juice in a food processor and process until mixture is smooth. Stir gelatin mixture into smoked salmon mixture.
4   Unroll cold roulade, spread with filling and reroll. Cover and chill. Cut into slices to serve.

BRUSCHETTA WITH TOMATO AND OLIVES

Bruschetta is the garlic bread of Italy. Delicious cooked on the barbecue, it can be eaten plain or topped with fresh tomatoes or roasted red pepper.

Serves 4

- ☐ ¹/₄ cup/60 mL olive oil
- ☐ 2 cloves garlic, crushed
- ☐ 8 thick slices crusty bread

TOMATO OLIVE TOPPING
- ☐ 3 large ripe tomatoes, peeled and diced
- ☐ 2 tablespoons finely chopped red pepper
- ☐ 6 black olives, finely chopped
- ☐ ¹/₂ red onion, finely chopped
- ☐ 2 tablespoons finely chopped fresh basil
- ☐ 1 tablespoon olive oil
- ☐ 1 tablespoon balsamic or red wine vinegar
- ☐ freshly ground black pepper

1 To make topping, place tomatoes, red pepper, olives, onion, basil, oil, vinegar and black pepper to taste in a bowl and toss to combine.

2 Preheat barbecue or broiler to a medium heat. Combine oil and garlic and brush both sides of each slice of bread. Cook bread on lightly oiled barbecue or under broiler for 2-3 minutes each side or until toasted. Serve immediately, topped with Tomato Olive Topping.

CHICKEN LIVER PATE

Makes 4 x 6 fl oz/185 mL pâté pots

- ☐ 1 lb/500 g chicken livers, chopped
- ☐ ¹/₃ cup/90 mL dry sherry
- ☐ 3 oz/90 g butter
- ☐ 2 spring onions, chopped
- ☐ 1 clove garlic, crushed
- ☐ ¹/₃ cup/90 mL cream
- ☐ ¹/₄ teaspoon pumpkin pie spice
- ☐ ¹/₂ teaspoon ground thyme
- ☐ freshly ground black pepper
- ☐ ¹/₃ cup/90 mL melted butter

1 Place livers in a bowl. Cover with sherry and stand for 2 hours. Drain and reserve liquid.

2 Melt 1¹/₂ oz/45 g of the butter in a skillet. Stir in spring onions, garlic and livers. Cook over a medium heat for 3

minutes, then pour in reserved liquid and cook for 1 minute more. Remove pan from heat.

3 Place liver mixture in a food processor or blender. Melt remaining 1¹/₂ oz/45 g butter and combine with cream, spice and thyme, then blend into liver mixture. Season to taste with black pepper. Pour pâté into individual pâté pots, top with melted butter and refrigerate overnight.

SALMON PATE

Makes 4 x 6 fl oz/185 mL pâté pots

- ☐ 7 oz/220 g can red salmon, drained
- ☐ ¹/₂ cup/125 g ricotta cheese
- ☐ ¹/₂ cup/125 g mayonnaise
- ☐ 2 teaspoons grated lemon rind
- ☐ 2 tablespoons lemon juice
- ☐ 3 spring onions
- ☐ ¹/₂ cup/1 stick/125 g butter, melted

1 Combine salmon, ricotta, mayonnaise, lemon rind, lemon juice and spring onions in a food processor. Add butter and process until smooth.

2 Spoon salmon pâté into individual pâté pots, top with melted butter and refrigerate overnight.

Left: Smoked Salmon and Watercress Roulade
Above: Chicken Liver Pâté, Salmon Pâté

ASPARAGUS GINGER AND CASHEW STIR-FRY

The combination of asparagus and ginger is wonderful, as it allows the true taste of asparagus to come through.

Serves 6

- [ ] **1 tablespoon vegetable oil**
- [ ] **2 teaspoons sesame oil**
- [ ] **1 tablespoon finely chopped fresh ginger**
- [ ] **1½ lb/750 g prepared asparagus spears, cut into 1½ in/4 cm pieces**
- [ ] **½ cup/60 g coarsely chopped roasted cashews**
- [ ] **1 tablespoon soy sauce**

1 Heat vegetable and sesame oils together in a wok or skillet. Stir in ginger and cook for 1 minute.
2 Add asparagus and cook for 4-5 minutes or until tender, crisp and bright green. Stir in cashews and soy sauce. Cook for 1-2 minutes until heated through. Serve immediately.

BAKED ASPARAGUS ROLL-UPS

These roll-ups are delicious as a snack before dinner. To reduce fat content, use light cream cheese.

Makes 28
Oven temperature 400°F, 200°C

- [ ] **28 prepared asparagus spears**
- [ ] **14 slices thin wholewheat bread, crusts removed**
- [ ] **8 oz/250 g cream cheese**
- [ ] **½ teaspoon prepared hot mustard**
- [ ] **⅓ cup/100 g finely chopped sliced packaged ham**
- [ ] **½ cup/1 stick/125 g butter, melted**

1 Boil, steam or microwave asparagus until just tender. Refresh under cold running water. Drain well and set aside.
2 Flatten bread slices using a rolling pin. Combine cream cheese, mustard and ham and spread over each slice of bread.
3 Arrange 2 asparagus spears on each bread slice with tips toward outside edges. Roll up, cut each roll in half and secure with a toothpick. Place seam side down on a baking sheet lined with parchment paper.
4 Brush with butter and bake for 15-20 minutes or until lightly browned.

TUNA PATE

Serves 4

- [ ] **7 oz/220 g can tuna, drained and flaked**
- [ ] **1 small cucumber, peeled, seeded and chopped**
- [ ] **1 cup/250 mL tomato juice**
- [ ] **5 teaspoons plain gelatin dissolved in ½ cup/125 mL hot water**
- [ ] **1 tablespoon chopped fresh dill weed**
- [ ] **1 teaspoon grated lemon rind**
- [ ] **1 teaspoon lemon juice**
- [ ] **2 teaspoons finely chopped capers**
- [ ] **1 teaspoon bottled horseradish**
- [ ] **4 tablespoons plain yogurt**
- [ ] **freshly ground black pepper**

1 Place tuna, cucumber, tomato juice, gelatin mixture, dill, lemon rind, lemon juice, capers, horseradish relish and yogurt in a food processor or blender and process until smooth.
2 Season to taste with black pepper. Spoon tuna mixture into four individual dishes or molds and refrigerate until firm. To serve, turn out and accompany with crackers or Melba toast.

Cook's tip: To make Melba toast, cut bread into slices of a medium thickness and lightly toast. Cut crusts from toast and split each slice of toast horizontally. Cut each slice in half diagonally and bake at 350°F/180°C for 5-7 minutes or until the edges curl and the toast is golden.

Asparagus Orange Hollandaise Pastry Sandwich, Asparagus Ginger and Cashew Stir-Fry, Baked Asparagus Roll-Ups

TIME SAVER
To save time, prepare the Baked Asparagus Roll-ups to final stage earlier, then bake when required.

ASPARAGUS ORANGE HOLLANDAISE PASTRY SANDWICH

These tasty pastry sandwiches make an ideal first course.

Serves 6
Oven temperature 425°F, 220°C

- ☐ **1 sheet/250 g frozen pre-rolled puff pastry, thawed**
- ☐ **1 egg yolk, lightly beaten**
- ☐ **18 prepared asparagus spears**
- ☐ **1 orange, thinly sliced**

ORANGE HOLLANDAISE SAUCE
- ☐ **3 egg yolks**
- ☐ **1 tablespoon lemon juice**
- ☐ **2 tablespoons orange juice**
- ☐ **1/2 cup/1 stick/125 g butter, melted**

1 Cut pastry sheet in half, then each half into six even pieces. Place on a baking sheet lined with parchment paper. Brush each pastry piece with egg yolk. Bake for 10-15 minutes or until pastry is puffed and golden.

2 Boil, steam or microwave asparagus until tender. Drain and keep warm.

3 To make sauce, place egg yolks, lemon juice and orange juice in a food processor or blender and process until light and frothy. With food processor running, slowly pour in melted butter.

4 Place sauce in the top of a double boiler. Cook gently over a low heat until sauce thickens. Arrange 3 asparagus spears on half the pastry pieces and spoon over sauce. Top with remaining pastry and garnish with orange slices.

Microwave it: Hollandaise sauce can be quickly and easily made in a microwave oven. In a glass measuring cup, whisk together egg yolks, lemon and orange juices. Whisk into the melted butter. Cook on MEDIUM (50%) power for 1 1/2 minutes or until sauce thickens, stirring every 30 seconds.

CHAMPAGNE TEMPURA

Serves 4

- [ ] **8 small cauliflower florets**
- [ ] **8 button mushrooms**
- [ ] **12 green beans, trimmed**
- [ ] **1 red pepper, sliced**
- [ ] **1 green apple, cored and sliced**
- [ ] **2 slices pineapple, quartered**
- [ ] **vegetable oil for deep-frying**

CHAMPAGNE BATTER

- [ ] **$^3/_4$ cup/90 g self-rising flour, sifted**
- [ ] **$^1/_2$ cup plus 2 tablespoons/75 g cornstarch, sifted**
- [ ] **1 egg, lightly beaten**
- [ ] **$^1/_2$ cup/125 mL iced water**
- [ ] **$^1/_2$ cup/125 mL chilled champagne**
- [ ] **2 ice cubes**

DIPPING SAUCE

- [ ] **$^1/_4$ cup/60 mL dairy sour cream**
- [ ] **$^1/_4$ cup/60 mL mayonnaise**
- [ ] **1 tablespoon chopped fresh herbs**

1 To make batter, place flour and cornstarch in a bowl. Mix together egg, water and champagne, pour into flour mixture and stir until smooth. Do not overbeat. Place ice cubes in batter.

2 Heat oil in a large deep saucepan until a cube of bread dropped in browns in 50 seconds. Dip cauliflower, mushrooms, beans, red pepper, apple and pineapple pieces into batter and cook a few pieces at a time in oil until golden brown. Using a slotted spoon remove cooked vegetable pieces and drain on paper towels.

3 To make sauce, place sour cream, mayonnaise and herbs in a bowl and mix to combine. Serve as a dipping sauce with hot vegetables.

SALMON SOUFFLES

Serves 4
Oven temperature 400°F, 200°C

- [ ] **7 oz/220 g can red salmon, drained and flaked**
- [ ] **$^1/_2$ cup/125 mL chopped drained fresh or bottled oysters**
- [ ] **2 teaspoons finely chopped capers**
- [ ] **1 teaspoon finely chopped fresh dill weed**
- [ ] **2-3 dashes hot red pepper sauce**
- [ ] **1 cup/250 g cottage cheese**
- [ ] **freshly ground black pepper**
- [ ] **4 egg whites**

1 Combine salmon, oysters, capers, dill, pepper sauce and cottage cheese in a bowl. Season to taste with black pepper.

2 Beat egg whites until stiff peaks form and fold lightly through salmon mixture. Spoon into four lightly greased individual soufflé dishes and bake for 30-35 minutes.

Cook's tip: When incorporating egg whites into a mixture, firstly mix in 1 tablespoon of the beaten egg whites, this loosens the mixture and makes it easier to fold in the remaining egg whites.

MUSHROOMS WITH CHILI BUTTER

Makes 20

- [ ] **20 medium button mushrooms, stalks removed**

CHILI BUTTER

- [ ] **$^1/_4$ cup/$^1/_2$ stick/60 g butter**
- [ ] **$^1/_2$ fresh red chili, finely chopped**
- [ ] **$^1/_2$ teaspoon ground cumin**
- [ ] **1 tablespoon finely chopped fresh parsley**

1 To make Chili Butter, place butter, chili, cumin and parsley in a food processor or blender and process until smooth. Shape butter into a log, wrap in plastic food wrap and chill until required.

2 Cut butter log into twenty pieces, place a piece of butter on each mushroom and cook under a preheated broiler for 4-5 minutes or until butter melts and

mushrooms are cooked. Serve immediately with toothpicks so that your guests can spear a mushroom then eat it.

Cook's tip: When handling fresh chilies do not put your hands near your eyes or allow them to touch your lips. To avoid discomfort and burning, wear rubber gloves. Freshly minced chili is also available in jars from supermarkets.

CAMEMBERT SURPRISE WITH BANANA SAUCE

Serves 4

- [ ] **4 x 4 oz/125 g wheels Camembert cheese**
- [ ] **2 ripe bananas, sliced**
- [ ] **lemon juice**

- [ ] **2 tablespoons flaked coconut**
- [ ] **1 egg, beaten**
- [ ] **¼ cup/60 mL milk**
- [ ] **flour**
- [ ] **3 cups/375 g dried bread crumbs**
- [ ] **vegetable oil for cooking**

BANANA SAUCE
- [ ] **2 ripe bananas**
- [ ] **½ cup/125 mL coconut milk**
- [ ] **2 tablespoons thick cream**
- [ ] **¼ teaspoon pumpkin pie spice**
- [ ] **1 teaspoon lemon juice**

1 Halve Camemberts horizontally. Sprinkle banana slices with lemon juice and arrange on 4 of the Camembert halves. Sprinkle with coconut and top with remaining cheese halves. Press together firmly.

2 Combine egg and milk. Dip each Camembert in flour, egg mixture and bread crumbs. Repeat crumbing process. Chill until firm.

3 Heat oil in a skillet and cook Camemberts until golden. Drain on paper towels and serve with sauce.

4 To prepare sauce, peel and coarsely chop bananas. Place into the bowl of a food processor, add coconut milk, cream, spice and lemon juice. Process until smooth. Serve sauce separately or spooned over Camembert.

Cook's tip: Use a toothpick to hold each Camembert together while preparing and cooking. Remove toothpick before serving.

Left: Salmon Soufflés
Above: Camembert Surprise with Banana Sauce

CARROTS WRAPPED IN SPINACH

A colorful and interesting dish which can be prepared in advance and baked when required. To serve, turn out and top with a fresh herb sauce.

Serves 6
Oven temperature 400°F, 200°C

- [ ] **6 carrots, sliced**
- [ ] **2 tablespoons/30 g butter**
- [ ] **2 egg yolks**
- [ ] **freshly ground black pepper**
- [ ] **spinach leaves**

1 Boil, steam or microwave carrots until tender. Allow to cool. Place in a food processor or blender with butter and egg yolks and process until smooth. Season to taste with black pepper.

2 Lightly grease six individual soufflé dishes or custard cups. Blanch spinach leaves and use to line dishes, leaving some of the leaves to hang over the side. Spoon carrot mixture into the dishes and fold over spinach leaves to cover. Bake for 25-30 minutes or until set.

SALMON AND CRAB AVOCADO

Serves 4

- [ ] **1 large avocado**
- [ ] **2 tablespoons lemon juice**

CRAB AND SALMON FILLING
- [ ] **1 avocado, pitted, peeled and chopped**
- [ ] **$^1/_3$ cup/90 g crab pieces, flaked**
- [ ] **4 slices smoked salmon, chopped**
- [ ] **$^1/_4$ cup/60 mL thick cream**
- [ ] **2 teaspoons mayonnaise**
- [ ] **1 tablespoon tomato catsup**
- [ ] **2-3 dashes hot red pepper sauce**
- [ ] **2 teaspoons lemon juice**

1 To make filling, place avocado, crab, salmon, cream, mayonnaise, tomato sauce, pepper sauce and lemon juice in a bowl and mix to combine

2 Cut avocado into quarters, remove the pit and brush avocado with lemon juice. Spoon filling into cavity of each quarter and serve immediately.

SAVORY CARROT AND CHEESE PARCELS

To prevent the parcel tops from becoming too brown, cover with foil if necessary, and remove for the last few minutes of cooking.

Serves 6
Oven temperature 400°F, 200°C

- [ ] **12 sheets fillo (phyllo) pastry**
- [ ] **$^1/_2$ cup/125 mL olive oil**

FILLING
- [ ] **2 tablespoons/30 g butter**
- [ ] **1 onion, chopped**
- [ ] **2 carrots, coarsely shredded**
- [ ] **1 tablespoon finely chopped fresh dill weed**
- [ ] **1 tablespoon finely snipped fresh chives**
- [ ] **4 tablespoons finely chopped fresh parsley**
- [ ] **8 oz/250 g shredded mozzarella cheese, grated**
- [ ] **freshly ground black pepper**

HERB SAUCE
- [ ] **2 tablespoons/30 g butter**
- [ ] **2 tablespoons all-purpose flour**
- [ ] **$1^1/_2$ cups/375 mL milk**
- [ ] **1 tablespoon finely chopped fresh dill weed**
- [ ] **1 tablespoon finely snipped fresh chives**
- [ ] **2 tablespoons finely chopped fresh parsley**

1 For each parcel, cut 2 sheets of fillo in half. Brush each sheet with olive oil and stack the 4 sheets together.

2 To make filling, melt butter in a small skillet. Add onion and cook for 2-3 minutes or until soft. Mix with carrots, dill, chives and parsley. Place spoonfuls of mixture in the center of each pastry stack. Top with cheese and season to taste with black pepper.

3 Gather up the corners of the pastry over the filling to make a bag. Press together firmly and gently twist just above the filling to seal. Carefully fan out pastry tops attractively and brush each parcel with remaining olive oil. Place on an oiled baking sheet. Bake for 20 minutes or until crisp and golden.

4 To make sauce, melt butter in a saucepan, stir in flour and cook for 1 minute. Slowly mix in milk, dill, chives and parsley, stirring constantly until sauce boils and thickens. Serve immediately.

Microwave it: The sauce can be made quickly and easily in the microwave using a 4 cup/1 liter microwave-safe bowl. Melt butter on HIGH (100%) for 30 seconds, mix in flour, milk, dill, chives and parsley. Cook on HIGH (100%) for 3-4 minutes or until sauce thickens.

SPICY CARROTS WITH CASHEWS

Try this adaptation of an Indian recipe – it is a wonderful way of cooking and serving carrots.

Serves 4

- [ ] **2 tablespoons vegetable oil**
- [ ] **1 lb/500 g carrots, cut lengthwise into thick strips**
- [ ] **1 large onion, sliced**
- [ ] **1 teaspoon grated fresh ginger**
- [ ] **1 teaspoon garam masala**
- [ ] **$^1/_2$ teaspoon chili powder**
- [ ] **1 tablespoon all-purpose flour**
- [ ] **6 oz/185 g cashews**
- [ ] **1 cup/250 mL chicken stock**

1 Heat oil in a heavy-based saucepan. Add carrots and onion and cook for 5 minutes. Stir in ginger, garam masala, chili powder, flour, cashews and stock. Cook over a medium heat, stirring, until mixture thickens. Reduce heat.

2 Simmer over a low heat, stirring frequently, for 15-20 minutes or until carrots are tender.

Spicy Carrots with Cashews, Carrots Wrapped in Spinach, Savory Carrot and Cheese Parcels

MANDARIN AND SMOKED CHICKEN SALAD

Serves 4

- [ ] **8 oz/250 g snow peas, trimmed**
- [ ] **1¹/₂ cups/375 g chopped smoked chicken**
- [ ] **9¹/₂ oz/300 g can mandarin orange segments, drained**
- [ ] **2 oz/60 g bean sprouts**
- [ ] **¹/₂ cup/125 g canned water chestnuts, drained and thinly sliced**

MUSTARD DRESSING
- [ ] **5 tablespoons vegetable oil**
- [ ] **1 tablespoon white wine vinegar**
- [ ] **¹/₂ teaspoon Dijon mustard**
- [ ] **freshly ground black pepper**

1   Boil, steam or microwave snow peas until they just change color. Drain, refresh under cold running water and pat dry with paper towels.
2   Place snow peas, chicken, mandarins, bean sprouts and water chestnuts in a large salad bowl.
3   To make dressing, place oil, vinegar, mustard and black pepper to taste in a screwtop jar and shake well to combine. Spoon dressing over salad and toss. Serve immediately.

PEPPER AND SPINACH SALAD

The sweetness of the peppers mixed with a tangy vinaigrette makes a wonderful starter or part of an anti-pasto platter. Make at least an hour before serving to allow the flavor to develop.

Serves 6

- [ ] **2 red peppers, halved and seeded**
- [ ] **1 yellow pepper, halved and seeded**
- [ ] **1 green pepper, halved and seeded**
- [ ] **1 lb/500 g spinach, thick stalks removed and leaves shredded**
- [ ] **4 oz/125 g button mushrooms**
- [ ] **5 oz/155 g pitted black olives**

BALSAMIC DRESSING
- [ ] **¹/₂ cup/125 mL olive oil**
- [ ] **¹/₄ cup/60 mL balsamic vinegar**

- [ ] **2 teaspoons chopped fresh basil**
- [ ] **1 teaspoon chopped fresh marjoram**
- [ ] **freshly ground black pepper**

1   Place red, yellow and green peppers skin side up under a preheated broiler and cook until skins are black and charred. Place peppers in a plastic food bag, seal and set aside for 5 minutes or until cool enough to handle. Remove peppers from bag, peel away skins and wash under cold water. Pat dry with paper towels and cut into strips. Set aside to cool completely.
2   Arrange spinach on a serving platter, top with peppers, mushrooms and olives.
3   To make dressing, place oil, vinegar, basil, marjoram and black pepper to taste in a screwtop jar and shake well to combine. Spoon dressing over salad.

Balsamic vinegar: This is a dark Italian vinegar. Made by the special processing of wines and musts from the Modena province, it is an interesting addition to any salad dressing and can also be used in sauces for meats or vegetables. Balsamic vinegar is available from supermarkets and delicatessens but if you cannot find it use red wine vinegar in its place.

BITE-SIZED KABOBS

These kabobs make a delicious starter for a barbecue meal, but are just as good when cooked under a broiler. If cooking on a barbecue, make sure that the skewers are long enough so that you do not burn your fingers.

Each recipe is enough for 10 skewers

- [ ] **10 lightly oiled bamboo skewers**

CUCUMBER AND SCALLOPS
- [ ] **1 clove garlic, crushed**
- [ ] **1 spring onion, finely chopped**
- [ ] **1 tablespoon finely chopped fresh basil**
- [ ] **1 tablespoon olive oil**
- [ ] **2 tablespoons white wine vinegar**
- [ ] **freshly ground black pepper**
- [ ] **10 scallops, cleaned or 1 firm white fish fillet cut in 1 in/ 2.5 cm cubes**
- [ ] **10 thin slices cucumber, skin left on**

1   Place garlic, spring onion, basil, oil, vinegar and black pepper to taste in a bowl

and whisk to combine. Add scallops or fish pieces, and cucumber slices and toss to coat, then set aside to marinate for 30 minutes.
2   Preheat a barbecue grill or broiler to a high heat. Drain scallops or fish pieces, and cucumber, reserving marinade. Top each cucumber slice with a scallop or fish piece so that the cucumber folds halfway around the scallop or fish. Brush with reserved marinade and cook on lightly oiled barbecue or under broiler, turning several times, for 2-3 minutes or until scallops or fish pieces are cooked.

CHICKEN AND MUSHROOMS
- [ ] **1 tablespoon lime or lemon juice**
- [ ] **1 tablespoon vegetable oil**
- [ ] **pinch chili powder**
- [ ] **1 chicken breast half, skin and bones removed, cut into 10 cubes**
- [ ] **5 button mushrooms, halved**

1   Place lime or lemon juice, oil and chili powder in a bowl and mix to combine. Add chicken and mushrooms and toss to combine. Set aside to marinate for 30 minutes.
2   Preheat a barbecue grill or broiler to a high heat. Drain chicken and mushrooms, reserving marinade. Thread a chicken cube and a mushroom half onto each bamboo skewer. Brush with reserved marinade and cook on lightly oiled barbecue or under grill, turning several times, for 4-5 minutes or until chicken is cooked.

BACON AND SHRIMP
- [ ] **1 tablespoon Dijon mustard**
- [ ] **1 clove garlic, crushed**
- [ ] **¹/₄ red pepper, finely chopped**
- [ ] **1 tablespoon finely chopped fresh dill weed**
- [ ] **2 tablespoons olive oil**
- [ ] **2 tablespoons lemon juice**
- [ ] **freshly ground black pepper**
- [ ] **10 large cooked shrimp, shelled and deveined, tails left intact**
- [ ] **5 slices bacon, cut into ten 3 in/7.5 cm strips**

1   Place mustard, garlic, red pepper, dill, oil, lemon juice and black pepper to taste in a bowl and mix to combine. Add shrimp and toss to coat. Set aside to marinate for 30 minutes.
2   Preheat a barbecue grill or broiler to a high heat. Drain shrimp and reserve

marinade. Wrap a strip of bacon around each shrimp and thread onto bamboo skewers. Brush with reserved marinade and cook on lightly oiled barbecue or under broiler, turning several times, for 2-3 minutes or until bacon is cooked and crisp.

LETTUCE ROLL-UPS

These roll-ups make an interesting light starter that can be prepared several hours in advance.

Serves 6

- ☐ **6 large lettuce leaves**
- ☐ **2 oz/60 g bean sprouts**
- ☐ **2 mangoes, peeled and chopped**
- ☐ **8 oz/250 g canned water chestnuts, drained and sliced**
- ☐ **2 teaspoons finely chopped preserved ginger in syrup**
- ☐ **2 teaspoons finely chopped fresh mint**
- ☐ **¹⁄₄ cup/60 mL mayonnaise**
- ☐ **1 tablespoon plain yogurt**

1   Tear lettuce leaves in half lengthwise. Place sprouts, mangoes, water chestnuts, ginger and mint in a bowl and toss. Add mayonnaise and yogurt and mix to combine.

2   Place a spoonful of mixture on each lettuce leaf half. Roll up tightly and secure with a toothpick. Chill until ready to serve.

Cook's tip: Canned mangoes can be used in place of the fresh mangoes if you wish.

HOT CHILI SHRIMP

Serves 6

- ☐ **3 lb/1.5 kg uncooked large shrimp, shelled, deveined, tails left intact**

CHILI MARINADE
- ☐ **2 teaspoons cracked black peppercorns**
- ☐ **2 tablespoons sweet chili sauce**
- ☐ **1 tablespoon soy sauce**
- ☐ **1 clove garlic, crushed**
- ☐ **¹⁄₄ cup/60 mL lemon juice**

MANGO CREAM
- ☐ **1 mango, peeled, pitted and roughly chopped**
- ☐ **¹⁄₄ cup/60 mL coconut milk**

1   To make marinade, place black peppercorns, chili sauce, soy sauce, garlic and lemon juice in a bowl and mix to combine. Add shrimp, toss to coat, cover and set aside to marinate for 1 hour. Toss several times during marinating.

2   To make Mango Cream, place mango flesh and coconut milk in a food processor or blender and process until smooth.

3   Preheat a barbecue to a medium heat. Drain shrimp and cook on lightly oiled barbecue for 3-4 minutes or until shrimp change color. Serve immediately with Mango Cream.

Coconut milk: This can be purchased in a number of forms: canned, as a long-life product in cartons, or as a powder to which you add water. Once opened it has a short life and should be used within a day or so. It is available from Asian food stores and some supermarkets, however if you have trouble finding it you can easily make your own. To make coconut milk, place 1 lb/500 g flaked coconut in a bowl and add 3 cups/750 mL boiling water. Set aside to stand for 30 minutes, then strain, squeezing the coconut to extract as much liquid as possible. This will make a thick coconut milk. The coconut can be used again to make a weaker coconut milk.

Hot Chili Shrimp

chapter five

MAIN DISHES WITH FLAIR

In this chapter you will find
dishes to suit all occasions. Recipes
such as Family Chicken Casserole
and Red Currant Lamb Roast make the
perfect family meal, while Honey-glazed
Pork is just the right dish for last-minute
entertaining. Look out for the Masterclass
step-by-step recipes that show you
special techniques and the
secrets to ensure perfect
results everytime.

*Paprika Beef, Tomato and Thyme
Shanks, Lamb Pot Roast*

TOMATO AND THYME SHANKS

Serves 4
Oven temperature 300°F, 150°C

- [ ] **4 lamb shanks**
- [ ] **2 spring onions, chopped**
- [ ] **1 red pepper, chopped**
- [ ] **1 cup/250 mL tomato catsup**
- [ ] **1/2 cup/125 mL cider vinegar**
- [ ] **1 cup/250 mL water**
- [ ] **1 clove garlic, crushed**
- [ ] **1 teaspoon finely chopped fresh thyme**
- [ ] **freshly ground black pepper**

1 Place shanks, spring onions and red pepper in a large casserole dish. Combine tomato catsup, vinegar, water, garlic and thyme and pour over shanks.
2 Cover and bake for 2^1/$_2$ hours or until meat is very tender. Season to taste with black pepper. Serve immediately or allow to cool and serve at room temperature.

PAPRIKA BEEF

Serves 8

- [ ] **2 lb/1 kg chuck steak, cut into1 in/2.5 cm squares**
- [ ] **1/4 cup/60 mL oil**
- [ ] **2 onions, sliced**
- [ ] **1/2 cup/125 mL dry white wine**
- [ ] **1 cup/250 mL water**
- [ ] **3/4 cup/185 g stuffed green olives**
- [ ] **4 tablespoons chopped fresh flat leaf parsley**

YOGURT MARINADE
- [ ] **1 teaspoon ground turmeric**
- [ ] **1^1/$_2$ tablespoons mild paprika**
- [ ] **1/2 teaspoon chili powder**
- [ ] **1 cup/250 mL plain yogurt**
- [ ] **2 teaspoons grated lemon rind**

1 To make marinade, combine turmeric, paprika, chili powder, yogurt and rind in a bowl. Add steak and toss to coat. Cover and refrigerate for 2-4 hours or overnight.
2 Heat oil in a large saucepan. Add onions and cook over a medium heat for about 5 minutes or until onions soften. Add steak and marinade and cook over a high heat for about 10 minutes.
3 Stir in wine and water. Bring to the boil, cover and simmer for about 1^1/$_2$ hours or until steak is tender. Stir in olives and parsley and cook over a medium heat for 3 minutes longer. Season to taste.

LAMB POT ROAST

Serves 6
Oven temperature 350°F, 180°C

- [ ] **4 lb/2 kg leg of lamb**
- [ ] **2 cloves garlic, cut into slivers**
- [ ] **6 small sprigs fresh rosemary**
- [ ] **freshly ground black pepper**
- [ ] **6 potatoes, halved lengthwise**
- [ ] **2 tablespoons lemon juice**
- [ ] **4 tomatoes, peeled and chopped**
- [ ] **2 onions, chopped**
- [ ] **1/2 cup/125 mL chicken stock**
- [ ] **1/4 cup/60 mL dry vermouth**
- [ ] **1/2 in/1 cm piece lemon peel**
- [ ] **small piece cinnamon stick**
- [ ] **2 tablespoons/30 g butter**

1 Cut slits in the surface of the lamb with a sharp knife. Insert garlic slivers and rosemary sprigs. Dust with black pepper, place in a roasting pan and bake for 1 hour. Remove pan from oven and drain off juices.
2 Cut potato halves part way down through rounded side. Brush with lemon juice and arrange around lamb. Top with tomatoes and onions. Combine stock and vermouth and pour over lamb and vegetables. Add the lemon peel and cinnamon stick. Dot with butter and bake for 1^1/$_2$ hours longer.
3 Remove lamb from baking pan. Wrap in aluminum foil and stand for 15 minutes before carving. Skim any excess fat from baking pan contents. To serve, slice meat and accompany with potatoes, and tomato and onion sauce.

CRUSTY INDIVIDUAL LAMB AND KIDNEY PIES

Serves 4
Oven temperature 350°F, 180°C

LAMB AND KIDNEY FILLING
- [ ] **750 g/1^1/$_2$ lb shoulder arm chops**
- [ ] **3 lamb kidneys**
- [ ] **1/4 cup/1/2 stick/60 g butter**
- [ ] **1 onion, chopped**
- [ ] **3 slices bacon, chopped**
- [ ] **2 tablespoons all-purpose flour**
- [ ] **1/4 cup/60 mL red wine**
- [ ] **3/4 cup/185 mL chicken stock**
- [ ] **1 tablespoon tomato paste**
- [ ] **1/2 teaspoon sugar**
- [ ] **1 tablespoon finely chopped fresh thyme**
- [ ] **freshly ground black pepper**

SOUR CREAM CRUST
- [ ] **1/2 cup/1 stick/125 g butter, softened**
- [ ] **1^1/$_4$ cups/300 g dairy sour cream**
- [ ] **1 egg**
- [ ] **1^1/$_2$ cups/185 g self-rising flour**
- [ ] **1 tablespoon finely chopped fresh parsley**

1 To make filling, remove meat from bones and trim of all visible fat. Cut into 1 in/2.5 cm cubes. Trim kidneys of all visible fat and soak in salted water for 10 minutes. Wipe kidneys dry with paper towels, skin and cut into slices.
2 Melt 2 tablespoons/30 g butter in a large saucepan and cook meat in batches until browned on all sides. Remove from pan and set aside. Add kidneys to pan and cook for 1-2 minutes or until kidneys just change color. Remove from pan and set aside. Add onion and bacon to pan and cook, stirring, for 2-3 minutes or until onion is golden. Remove from pan and set aside.
3 Melt remaining butter in pan, add flour and cook, stirring, for 3-4 minutes or until a light straw color. Stir in wine, stock, tomato paste and sugar and cook over a medium heat, stirring constantly, until sauce boils and thickens. Add thyme and season to taste with black pepper. Return meat, kidneys and onion mixture to pan, cover, bring to simmering and simmer for 1^1/$_2$ hours or until meat is tender. Remove pan from heat and set aside to cool slightly.
4 To make crust, place butter, sour cream and egg in a bowl and mix to combine. Stir in 1 cup/125 g self-rising flour and parsley and mix well. Divide two-thirds of the crust mixture into four equal portions. Press each portion over the bottom and sides of four individual dishes, and spoon in filling. Lightly knead remaining self-rising flour into remaining dough. Press out on a lightly floured surface, using palm of hand, to 1^1/$_2$ in/1 cm thick and cut into rounds using a 1^1/$_4$ in/3 cm cookie cutter. Top filling with dough rounds, overlapping them slightly and bake for 30 minutes or until crust is golden and cooked.

Cook's tip: To skin kidneys, nick skin on the rounded side of each kidney and draw it back on each side until it is attached by the core only. Draw out as much core as possible and cut, with skin, close to the kidney.

STEAK WITH FRENCH MUSTARD SAUCE

Serves 4

- [ ] **4 lean rib eye steaks (Delmonico) about 1 in/2.5 cm thick**
- [ ] **2 tablespoons/30 g butter**

FRENCH MUSTARD SAUCE

- [ ] **2 spring onions, finely chopped**
- [ ] **1 tablespoon coarse grain mustard**
- [ ] **2 teaspoons French mustard**
- [ ] **$^1/_2$ cup/125 mL dry white wine**
- [ ] **$^1/_4$ cup/60 mL water**
- [ ] **1 teaspoon honey**
- [ ] **$^1/_4$ teaspoon dried thyme**
- [ ] **2 tablespoons cream or evaporated skim milk**
- [ ] **1$^1/_2$ tablespoons shredded mature Cheddar cheese**

1   Trim meat of all visible fat. Melt butter in a skillet, cook steaks for 4-5 minutes each side. Remove from pan. Keep warm.

2   To make sauce, add spring onion to pan and sauté for 1 minute. Stir in combined mustards, wine, water, honey and thyme. Cook over a medium heat for 3-4 minutes until sauce has reduced slightly.

3   Remove pan from heat and stir in cream or skim milk, and cheese. Spoon sauce over steaks and serve.

MARINATED SATAY CHICKEN WINGS

Satay sauce is available in supermarkets. To make your own, combine 1 tablespoon peanut butter, 1 tablespoon soy sauce, $^1/_2$ teaspoon crushed garlic, 1 teaspoon lemon juice and a pinch of chili powder.

Serves 4

- [ ] **1$^1/_2$ lb/750 g chicken wings**

MARINADE

- [ ] **$^1/_4$ teaspoon five spice powder**
- [ ] **$^1/_4$ teaspoon chili powder**
- [ ] **2 tablespoons satay sauce**
- [ ] **$^1/_2$ teaspoon curry powder**
- [ ] **1 teaspoon cornstarch**
- [ ] **$^1/_2$ teaspoon sugar**
- [ ] **1 teaspoon bottled oyster sauce**
- [ ] **2 tablespoons dry white wine**
- [ ] **$^1/_4$ cup/60 mL oil**
- [ ] **3 onions, cut into eighths**
- [ ] **2 teaspoons grated fresh ginger**

1   Combine chicken wings with five spice powder, chili powder, satay sauce, curry powder, cornstarch, sugar, oyster sauce and white wine. Allow to stand for at least 10-15 minutes to absorb flavor. Drain chicken wings, reserving marinade.

2   Heat 1 tablespoon oil in a skillet or wok. Add onions and ginger and sauté 2-3 minutes until onion is transparent. Remove from pan and set aside.

3   Heat remaining oil. Add chicken wings and cook over a high heat until well browned on both sides. Reduce heat and cook a further 10-15 minutes until tender. Return onions and ginger to pan and pour over reserved marinade. Toss over a high heat for 2-3 minutes or until sauce boils.

Cook's tip: Marinating chicken or meat in a mixture containing wine, soy sauce, fruit juice and herbs or spices will tenderize the meat and add flavor. Marinate the meat or chicken in a glass or plastic bowl for at least 1 hour. But, for really tasty, succulent results, marinate covered overnight in the refrigerator.

Steak with French Mustard Sauce, Marinated Satay Chicken Wings

BEEF WRAPPED IN PASTRY WITH RED WINE SAUCE

Succulent beef surrounded by mushrooms and wrapped in puff pastry, this dish is sure to impress – this Master Class shows you how easy it is.

Serves 6
Oven temperature 425°F, 220°C

- ☐ ¹/₄ **cup/¹/₂ stick/60 g butter**
- ☐ **2 lb/1 kg rib eye (Delmonico) roast, in one piece, trimmed**
- ☐ **1 onion, chopped**
- ☐ **12 oz/375 g button mushrooms, finely chopped**
- ☐ **freshly ground black pepper**
- ☐ **pinch ground nutmeg**
- ☐ **1 tablespoon finely chopped fresh parsley**
- ☐ **1 sheet/250 g frozen pre-rolled puff pastry, thawed**
- ☐ **1 egg, lightly beaten**

RED WINE SAUCE
- ☐ **1 cup/250 mL dry red wine**
- ☐ **1 teaspoon finely chopped fresh thyme, or ¹/₄ teaspoon dried thyme**
- ☐ **1 teaspoon finely chopped fresh parsley**
- ☐ **freshly ground black pepper**
- ☐ **¹/₃ cup/³/₄ stick/90 g butter, cut into eight pieces**
- ☐ **2 teaspoons cornstarch, blended with 1 tablespoon water**

1 Melt half the butter in a heavy-based skillet. When sizzling, add beef and cook over a medium heat for 10 minutes, turning to brown and seal on all sides. Remove pan from heat and set aside to cool completely.

2 Melt remaining butter in pan and cook onion for 5 minutes, or until soft. Add mushrooms and cook over a medium heat for 15 minutes, or until mushrooms give up all their juices, and these evaporate. Stir during cooking to prevent them sticking. Season to taste with black pepper and nutmeg, stir in parsley and set aside to cool completely.

3 Roll out pastry to a length 3 in/7.5 cm longer than roast and wide enough to wrap around meat. Spread half mushroom mixture down center of pastry and place

meat on top. Spread remaining mushroom mixture on top of meat. Cut corners out of pastry. Brush pastry edges with egg. Wrap pastry around meat like a parcel, tucking ends in. Turn pastry-wrapped meat over, place on a lightly greased baking sheet and freeze for 10 minutes.

4 Roll out reserved pastry to a 4 x 12 in/ 10 x 30 cm length and cut into strips ¹/₂ in/ 1 cm wide. Remove meat from freezer and brush pastry all over with egg. Arrange 5 pastry strips diagonally over pastry parcel, then arrange remaining strips diagonally in opposite direction. Brush top of strips only

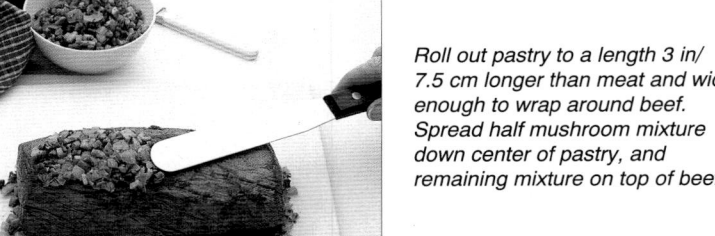

with egg. Bake for 30 minutes for medium-rare beef. Place on a warmed serving platter and set aside to rest in a warm place for 10 minutes.

5 To make sauce, place wine in a small saucepan and cook over a medium heat until reduced by half. Add thyme and parsley and season to taste with black pepper. Remove pan from heat and quickly whisk in 1 piece of butter at a time, ensuring that each piece of butter is completely whisked in and melted before adding next. Pour in cornstarch mixture and stir over a medium heat until sauce thickens. Serve with beef.

Roll out pastry to a length 3 in/ 7.5 cm longer than meat and wide enough to wrap around beef. Spread half mushroom mixture down center of pastry, and remaining mixture on top of beef.

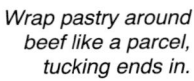

Wrap pastry around beef like a parcel, tucking ends in.

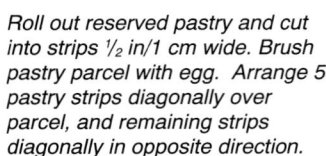

Roll out reserved pastry and cut into strips ¹/₂ in/1 cm wide. Brush pastry parcel with egg. Arrange 5 pastry strips diagonally over parcel, and remaining strips diagonally in opposite direction.

LAMB WITH TANGY APRICOT SAUCE

Serves 4

- [ ] **8 boneless shoulder blade chops or noisettes**

TANGY APRICOT SAUCE
- [ ] **½ cup/125 g apricot jam**
- [ ] **1 tablespoon soy sauce**
- [ ] **1 clove garlic, crushed**
- [ ] **½ teaspoon ground cinnamon**
- [ ] **1 tablespoon white wine vinegar**

1 Broil, pan fry or barbecue chops for 4-5 minutes each side or until cooked to your liking. Set aside and keep warm.
2 To make sauce, place jam, soy sauce, garlic, cinnamon and vinegar in a small saucepan and cook, stirring, over a low heat until jam melts and all ingredients are blended. Spoon sauce over chops.

Cook's tip: Noisettes are rolled, boneless shoulder or loin chops. The meat is rolled up tightly and tied. Most butchers are happy to prepare noisettes for you if you order them in advance.

CHICKEN STIR-FRY

Serves 4

- [ ] **1 lb/500 g boned, skinned chicken breast halves, thinly sliced**
- [ ] **1 red pepper, sliced**
- [ ] **11 oz/350 g broccoli, broken into florets**
- [ ] **2 small zucchini, chopped**
- [ ] **1 carrot, chopped**
- [ ] **2 teaspoons cornstarch blended with 1 tablespoon water**
- [ ] **2 teaspoons grated fresh ginger**
- [ ] **1 tablespoon honey**
- [ ] **2 tablespoons soy sauce**
- [ ] **1 tablespoon sweet chili sauce**
- [ ] **1 tablespoon hoisin sauce**

1 Heat a nonstick skillet and cook chicken for 3-4 minutes or until tender. Remove from pan and set aside.
2 Add red pepper, broccoli, zucchini and carrot to pan and stir-fry for 2-3 minutes.
3 Stir in cornstarch mixture, ginger, honey, soy sauce, chili sauce and hoisin sauce and cook over a medium heat for 2-3 minutes or until sauce boils and thickens.
4 Return chicken to pan and stir-fry for 2-3 minutes longer or until heated through.

QUICK FISH STEAK CRUMBLE

Serves 4

- [ ] **4 x 6 oz/185 g white fish steaks**
- [ ] **2 tablespoons lime juice**

HERB TOPPING
- [ ] **2 cups/125 g wholewheat bread crumbs, made from stale bread**
- [ ] **1½ oz/45 g instant rolled oats**
- [ ] **2 tablespoons finely chopped fresh coriander (cilantro)**
- [ ] **2 tablespoons finely snipped fresh chives**
- [ ] **2 teaspoons olive oil**
- [ ] **1 tablespoon vinegar**
- [ ] **freshly ground black pepper**

1 Brush fish steaks with lime juice and

broil for 5 minutes on one side.

2 To make topping, place bread crumbs, oats, coriander, chives, oil, vinegar and black pepper to taste in a bowl and mix to combine.

3 Turn fish and top each steak with topping and broil for 5 minutes, or until cooked through and topping is golden.

Serving suggestion: Garnish with lemon and accompany with baby new potatoes and a green salad.

TAGLIATELLE WITH TUNA

Serves 4

☐ **12 oz/375 g dried wholewheat tagliatelle or spaghetti**

TUNA SAUCE
☐ **1 onion, finely chopped**
☐ **1 clove garlic, crushed**
☐ **14 oz/440 g canned tomatoes, undrained and mashed**
☐ **1 tablespoon tomato paste**
☐ **1 tablespoon dry red wine**
☐ **2 zucchini, sliced**
☐ **14 oz/440 g canned tuna in water, drained and flaked**
☐ **1 tablespoon finely shredded fresh basil**

1 Cook pasta in a large saucepan of boiling water following packet directions. Drain, set aside and keep warm.

2 To make sauce, heat a nonstick skillet and cook onion, garlic and 1 tablespoon of juice from tomatoes for 4-5 minutes, or until onion is soft. Stir in tomatoes, tomato paste, wine and zucchini and cook over a low heat for 5 minutes.

3 Add tuna and basil to pan and cook gently until heated through.

Serving suggestion: Place pasta on serving plates, spoon sauce over and garnish with basil. Serve with a mixed lettuce and herb salad and crusty bread.

Microwave it: To make Tuna Sauce in a microwave oven, place onion and garlic in a microwave-safe dish and cook on HIGH (100%) for 2 minutes. Stir in tomatoes, tomato paste, wine and zucchini and cook on HIGH (100%) for 3-4 minutes longer. Add tuna and basil and cook on HIGH (100%) for 3-4 minutes, longer.

Left: Chicken Stir-Fry
Above: Quick Fish Steak Crumble, Tagliatelle with Tuna

PORK WITH SAUERKRAUT

Serves 6

- [ ] **2 tablespoons/30 g butter**
- [ ] **1¹/₂ lb/750 g pork tenderloin, sliced**
- [ ] **2 onions, sliced**
- [ ] **2 green apples, cored, peeled and sliced**
- [ ] **2 teaspoons ground paprika**
- [ ] **1 teaspoon caraway seeds**
- [ ] **freshly ground black pepper**
- [ ] **³/₄ cup/185 mL chicken stock**
- [ ] **¹/₄ cup/60 mL dry white wine**
- [ ] **2 tablespoons tomato paste**
- [ ] **14 oz/440 g canned or bottled sauerkraut, drained**
- [ ] **¹/₂ cup/125 g dairy sour cream**

1 Melt butter in a large saucepan and cook pork slices over a medium heat for 3-4 minutes each side, or until meat just changes color. Remove from pan and set aside.

2 Add onions and apples to pan and cook for 4-5 minutes or until onions are soft. Stir in paprika and caraway seeds and cook over a medium heat for 1 minute. Season to taste with black pepper.

3 Combine stock, wine and tomato paste. Pour into pan and cook over a medium heat, stirring constantly to lift sediment from base of pan. Bring to the boil, then reduce heat and simmer for 10 minutes.

4 Return meat to pan, stir in sauerkraut and cook for 2-3 minutes. Remove pan from heat, stir in sour cream and serve immediately.

Sauerkraut: To make sauerkraut, you will require about 6 lb/3 kg cabbage. Trim cabbage, cut into quarters, remove core, and finely shred. Place in a large bowl, sprinkle with 2 oz/60 g salt, mix to combine. Set aside until cabbage wilts. Pack firmly into a sterilized wide-mouthed 4 quart/4 liter crock or glass jar. Cover surface of cabbage with a clean cheesecloth. Choose a china or glass saucer or plate that fits snugly into the top of the container, place on top of cheesecloth and weight heavily. Place in a warm place – around 70°F/21°C is ideal. The cabbage must be covered by liquid.

As the cabbage ferments, bubbles and scum rise to the surface. Each day rinse weight, plate and cloth in warm water. Remove any scum and replace cloth, plate and weight. Fermentation takes 2-4 weeks. Store in glass jars, covered with the brine.

BOILED BEEF DINNER

*Simple and satisfying,
this Boiled Beef Dinner is served
with creamy mashed potatoes and
horseradish cream. There are sure to
be requests for second helpings.*

Serves 6

- ☐ 3 lb/1.5 kg corned boneless beef brisket
- ☐ 2 tablespoons brown sugar
- ☐ 1 tablespoon cider vinegar
- ☐ 2 sprigs fresh mint
- ☐ 1 onion, studded with 4 whole cloves
- ☐ 6 peppercorns
- ☐ 6 small carrots
- ☐ 6 small onions
- ☐ 3 parsnips, halved

REDCURRANT GLAZE
- ☐ $1/2$ cup/125 g redcurrant jelly
- ☐ 2 tablespoons orange juice
- ☐ 1 tablespoon Grand Marnier

1 Place meat in a large heavy-based saucepan. Add brown sugar, vinegar, mint, onion, peppercorns and enough water to cover meat. Bring to the boil, then reduce heat and simmer for $1^1/_4$-$1^1/_2$ hours.

2 Add carrots, onions and parsnips to pan and cook over a low heat for 40 minutes longer or until vegetables are tender.

3 To make glaze, place redcurrant jelly, orange juice and Grand Marnier in a small saucepan and cook over a low heat, stirring occasionally, until well blended. Transfer meat to a serving plate and brush with redcurrant mixture. Slice meat and serve with vegetables and any remaining redcurrant mixture.

Cook's tip: To make horseradish cream, whip $1/2$ cup/125 mL thick cream until soft peaks form then fold through $1/4$ cup/ 60 mL bottled horseradish.

Pork with Sauerkraut, Boiled Beef Dinner

ROAST CHICKEN WITH CURRIED RICE STUFFING

Serves 4
Oven temperature 350°F, 180°C

- [ ] **3 lb/1.5 kg broiler-fryer chicken**
- [ ] **4 slices bacon, chopped**
- [ ] **4 spring onions, chopped**
- [ ] **2 teaspoons curry powder**
- [ ] **³/₄ cup/155 g rice, cooked**
- [ ] **1 cup/60 g soft bread crumbs, made from stale bread**
- [ ] **1 tablespoon olive oil**

TOMATO SAUCE
- [ ] **2 tablespoons/30 g butter**
- [ ] **1 onion, chopped**
- [ ] **1 green pepper, chopped**
- [ ] **4 oz/125 g mushrooms, sliced**
- [ ] **14 oz/440 g canned tomatoes**
- [ ] **2 tablespoons tomato paste**
- [ ] **¹/₄ cup/60 mL red wine**
- [ ] **1 tablespoon sugar**
- [ ] **¹/₂ cup/125 mL water**

1 Wash chicken and pat dry on paper towels. Cook bacon, spring onions and curry powder in a skillet until bacon is crisp. Remove from heat and stir in rice and bread crumbs.
2 Fill chicken with rice mixture, securing opening with a skewer. Place in a baking pan, brush with oil and bake for 1¹/₂ hours, basting frequently with juices from baking pan.
3 To make sauce, melt butter in a saucepan and cook onion, green pepper and mushrooms for 2-3 minutes. Stir in undrained tomatoes, tomato paste, wine, sugar and water and season to taste.
4 Cook over a medium heat, stirring occasionally, for 8-10 minutes until sauce has reduced by a quarter. Break chicken into serving portions, spoon sauce over and serve.

Time saver: Precious time can be saved by keeping cooked rice or pasta in the refrigerator or freezer, it is then ready to use in dishes calling for cooked rice or pasta or can easily be reheated in the microwave oven to accompany a meal.

Below: Roast Chicken with Curried Rice Stuffing
Right: Redcurrant Lamb Roast, Brandied Beef with Horseradish Sauce

REDCURRANT LAMB ROAST

Serves 6
Oven temperature 350°F, 180°C

- [ ] **3 lb/1.5 kg lean leg of lamb**

GINGER BASTE
- [ ] **2 tablespoons/30 g butter**
- [ ] **1 teaspoon grated fresh ginger**
- [ ] **1 clove garlic, crushed**
- [ ] **1 teaspoon soy sauce**
- [ ] **1 tablespoon redcurrant jelly**

REDCURRANT SAUCE
- [ ] **2 tablespoons redcurrant jelly**

COOK'S TIP

Simmering beer, wine or spirits, will cause the alcohol content and most of the calories to evaporate, leaving an excellent flavor.

☐ **1 teaspoon salt**

PINEAPPLE SAUCE

☐ **2¹/₂ tablespoons brown sugar**
☐ **1¹/₂ tablespoons light soy sauce**
☐ **1 cup/250 g canned crushed pineapple**
☐ **2 teaspoons grated fresh ginger**
☐ **2 teaspoons cornstarch blended with 2 tablespoons water**

1   Place pork in an oiled baking pan. Bake for 1³/₄ hours until browned and tender.
2   To make sauce, combine brown sugar, soy sauce, pineapple and ginger and pour over pork during the last 20 minutes of cooking, basting with sauce occasionally.
3   Remove pork from dish and keep warm in a low oven. Skim excess fat from meat juices. Whisk in blended cornstarch and water, stir over heat until sauce boils and thickens. Slice pork and serve with sauce.

BRANDIED BEEF WITH HORSERADISH SAUCE

Serves 6
Oven temperature 350°F, 180°C

☐ **3 lb/1.5 kg boneless rib roast or rib eye roast (Delmonico)**
☐ **freshly ground black pepper**
☐ **2 tablespoons/30 g butter**
☐ **¹/₄ cup/60 mL brandy**

HORSERADISH SAUCE

☐ **¹/₂ cup/125 mL mayonnaise**
☐ **¹/₂ cup/125 mL plain yogurt**
☐ **1 teaspoon lemon juice**
☐ **1 teaspoon bottled horseradish**
☐ **1 avocado, pitted, peeled and chopped**

1   Trim all visible fat from meat and sprinkle with black pepper. Tie with string at even intervals so it will keep its shape during cooking. Heat butter over a high heat in a flameproof casserole and sear meat on all sides until golden brown. Spoon brandy over meat and bake 25-35 minutes until cooked as desired, basting frequently with juices from casserole.
2   To make sauce, combine mayonnaise, yogurt, lemon juice, horseradish and avocado in a food processor or blender. Process until thoroughly combined. Slice beef and serve with sauce.

Cook's tip: Ask the butcher to bone and roll the loin for you, leaving the pork rind attached, if desired. For a pretty effect, have him score the rind in a criss-cross fashion with a very sharp knife.

☐ **1 cup/250 mL chicken stock**
☐ **2 tablespoons chopped fresh mint**
☐ **4 teaspoons cornstarch blended with ¹/₄ cup/60 mL port**

1   Trim meat of excess fat and place in a baking pan. To make baste, combine butter, ginger, garlic, soy sauce and 1 tablespoon redcurrant jelly in a saucepan. Stir over a medium heat until butter melts.
2   Pour over lamb and bake for 1¹/₄-1¹/₂ hours until cooked as desired, basting frequently with liquid from baking pan. Remove meat and keep warm.

3   To make sauce, place baking pan on top of stove. Combine redcurrant jelly, stock and mint. Bring to the boil, whisk in blended cornstarch, stirring until sauce thickens. Slice meat and serve with sauce.

PORK LOIN WITH PINEAPPLE SAUCE

Serves 6
Oven temperature 325°F, 165°C

☐ **3 lb/1.5 kg boned rolled loin pork, sirloin roast with rind on and scored**

MASTERCLASS

CRUSTY CHICKEN GOULASH

Serves 4
Temperature 350°F, 180°C

CHICKEN FILLING
- ☐ **2 tablespoons vegetable oil**
- ☐ **2 large onions, chopped**
- ☐ **500 g/1lb boned skinned chicken breasts, cut into thin strips**
- ☐ **$^1/_2$ tablespoon paprika**
- ☐ **2 tablespoons seasoned flour**
- ☐ **1 tablespoon tomato paste**
- ☐ **$^1/_2$ cup/125 mL red wine**
- ☐ **$^1/_2$ cup/125 mL chicken stock**
- ☐ **$^1/_4$ cup/60 mL plain yogurt**

SOUR CREAM CRUST
- ☐ **$^1/_2$ cup/1 stick/125 g butter, softened**
- ☐ **$1^1/_4$ cups/300 g dairy cream**
- ☐ **1 egg**
- ☐ **1 cup/125 g self-rising flour**
- ☐ **1 tablespoon chopped fresh parsley**

1 To make filling, heat half the oil in a skillet. Cook onions for 2-3 minutes until golden, remove from pan and set aside. Coat chicken in combined paprika and seasoned flour.

2 Heat remaining oil in pan. Cook chicken for 2-3 minutes. Return onions to pan, stir in combined tomato paste, wine and stock. Bring to the boil, stirring constantly, then reduce heat and simmer covered for 6-7 minutes. Remove from heat and stir in yogurt.

3 To make crust, combine butter, sour cream and egg in a bowl. Stir in sifted flour and parsley, mixing until well combined. To assemble, place mixture in an 8 cup/2 liter greased casserole, working mixture up to cover sides and bottom of dish. Spoon in filling, cover and bake for 35 minutes. Uncover and bake a further 10 minutes.

Combine butter, sour cream and egg in a bowl. Stir in sifted flour.

Press crust mixture into an 8 cup/2 liter greased casserole, working mixture up to cover sides and bottom of dish.

Spoon filling into crust, cover and bake.

BASIC MEATLOAF

Serve this meatloaf hot with vegetables as a main dish, or cold cut into slices for sandwiches. Try one of the tasty toppings below to change the flavor completely.

Serves 4
Oven temperature 350°F, 180°C

- ☐ **500 g/1 lb lean ground beef**
- ☐ **1 cup/60 g bread crumbs, made from stale bread**
- ☐ **¼ cup/60 mL beef stock**
- ☐ **1 onion, grated**
- ☐ **1 carrot, shredded**
- ☐ **2 eggs, lightly beaten**
- ☐ **1 teaspoon dried mixed herbs**
- ☐ **1 teaspoon Worcestershire sauce**
- ☐ **freshly ground black pepper**

1 Place meat, bread crumbs, stock, onion, carrot, eggs, mixed herbs and sauce in a bowl. Season to taste with pepper and mix well to combine.
2 Press mixture into a lightly greased 4½ x 8½ in/11 x 21 cm ovenproof loaf pan and bake for 40-45 minutes. Drain off any liquid, cover and allow to stand for 10 minutes before turning out and serving.

HONEY-GLAZED MEATLOAF

Serves 4
Oven temperature 350°F, 180°C

- ☐ **1 quantity Basic Meatloaf mixture**

HONEY-GLAZED TOPPING
- ☐ **1 oz/30 g pepitas (Mexican pumpkin seeds)**
- ☐ **1 oz/30 g sunflower seeds**
- ☐ **2 tablespoons pine nuts (pignola)**
- ☐ **2 tablespoons honey**
- ☐ **1 tablespoon brown sugar**
- ☐ **2 tablespoons lemon juice**
- ☐ **½ teaspoon dry mustard**

1 Prepare and cook Basic Meatloaf as directed in recipe.
2 To make topping, combine pepitas, sunflower seeds and pine nuts. Turn meatloaf onto a shallow baking dish and spread top with seed mixture.
3 Place honey, brown sugar, lemon juice and mustard in a saucepan and heat until honey melts and all ingredients are blended. Pour mixture over meatloaf and bake at 400°F/200°C for 10 minutes.

INDIVIDUAL PASTRY-WRAPPED MEATLOAVES

Serves 4
Oven temperature 350°F, 180°C

- ☐ **1 quantity Basic Meatloaf mixture**
- ☐ **2 sheets/500 g frozen pre-rolled puff pastry, thawed and halved crosswise**
- ☐ **1 egg, lightly beaten**

1 Make up Basic Meatloaf mixture and divide into four equal portions. Press one portion of meat mixture down the center of each pastry piece to form a rectangle.
2 Brush edges of pastry with egg and wrap up like a parcel. Decorate top with leaves cut from pastry scraps. Place rolls on a greased roasting rack in a baking pan. Brush pastry with egg and bake for 25-30 minutes, or until pastry is golden and crisp.

TEX-MEX MEATLOAF

Serves 4
Oven temperature 350°F, 180°C

- ☐ **1 quantity Basic Meatloaf mixture**

TEX-MEX TOPPING
- ☐ **½ cup/125 mL tomato catsup**
- ☐ **1 tablespoon bottled barbecue sauce**
- ☐ **1 teaspoon brown sugar**
- ☐ **1 teaspoon chili sauce**
- ☐ **2 tablespoons finely chopped green pepper**
- ☐ **1 oz/30 g packet corn chips, crushed**
- ☐ **½ cup/60 g shredded Cheddar or monterey jackcheese**

1 Prepare and cook Basic Meatloaf as directed in recipe.
2 To make topping, combine tomato catsup, barbecue sauce, brown sugar, chili sauce and pepper. Turn meatloaf out onto a baking dish. Spread Tex-Mex Topping over surface of meatloaf. Top with corn chips and cheese and bake at 400°F/200°C for 10 minutes or until cheese melts.

Tex-Mex Meatloaf, Individual Pastry-wrapped Meatloaves, Chili Con Carne, Melting Meatballs

SHAPING GROUND MEAT

When shaping ground meat, dampen your hands and work on a lightly floured or dampened surface—this will prevent the meat from sticking to your hands and the surface. You will usually need to add an egg to the meat mixture to bind it and make it easier to shape.

MELTING MEATBALLS

Serves 4

- [ ] **1 quantity Basic Meatloaf mixture**
- [ ] **3 oz/90 g Cheddar cheese, cut into 12 x ³/₄ in/2 cm cubes**
- [ ] **1¹/₂ oz/45 g unprocessed bran**
- [ ] **3 tablespoons finely chopped pistachio nuts**
- [ ] **flour**
- [ ] **1 egg, lightly beaten**
- [ ] **oil for cooking**

1 Make up meatloaf mixture as directed in recipe and divide into twelve equal portions. Wrap one portion of meat around each cheese cube, to make a ball. Repeat with remaining meat and cheese.

2 Combine bran and pistachio nuts. Coat meatballs in flour, dip in egg and roll in bran mixture.

3 Heat oil in a skillet and cook meatballs for 6-8 minutes or until golden brown and cooked through.

CHILI CON CARNE

Serves 4

- [ ] **1 tablespoon vegetable oil**
- [ ] **1 onion, chopped**
- [ ] **2 cloves garlic, crushed**
- [ ] **3 small red chilies, finely chopped**
- [ ] **1 lb/500 g lean ground beef**
- [ ] **¹/₄ teaspoon ground cloves**
- [ ] **¹/₂ teaspoon ground cumin**
- [ ] **1 teaspoon dried oregano leaves**
- [ ] **2 teaspoons paprika**
- [ ] **14 oz/440 g canned tomatoes, undrained and mashed**
- [ ] **1 tablespoon tomato paste**
- [ ] **¹/₂ cup/125 mL beef stock**
- [ ] **10 oz/315 g canned red kidney beans, drained and rinsed**
- [ ] **freshly ground black pepper**

1 Heat oil in a skillet, cook onion, garlic and chilies for 2-3 minutes or until onion is soft.

2 Stir in ground beef, cloves, cumin, oregano and paprika. Cook for 5-6 minutes or until meat browns. Combine tomatoes, tomato paste and stock and pour into pan. Reduce heat and simmer for 20 minutes or until liquid reduces by half.

3 Add kidney beans and cook for 10 minutes longer, or until heated through. Season to taste with black pepper.

SPICY SEAFOOD CAKES

Serves 4

- [ ] 1 lb/500 g potatoes, chopped
- [ ] 1 cup/250 mL water
- [ ] 2 lime leaves, optional
- [ ] 5 oz/155 g uncooked shrimp, shelled and deveined
- [ ] 4 oz/125 g scallops
- [ ] 8 oz/250 g white fish fillets
- [ ] 1/2 cup/60 g shredded Cheddar cheese
- [ ] 2 tablespoons all-purpose flour
- [ ] 2 eggs, lightly beaten
- [ ] 1 tablespoon lemon juice
- [ ] 2 tablespoons lime juice
- [ ] 2 teaspoons grated lemon rind
- [ ] 1 small fresh red chili, seeded and finely chopped
- [ ] 1 tablespoon finely chopped fresh coriander (cilantro)
- [ ] freshly ground black pepper
- [ ] 1 cup/125 g dried bread crumbs
- [ ] oil for shallow-frying

PLUM SAUCE
- [ ] 1/3 cup/90 g fruit chutney, large pieces chopped
- [ ] 1/2 cup/125 g plum jam
- [ ] 1 tablespoon red wine vinegar
- [ ] 1 teaspoon Chinese five spice

1 Boil, steam or microwave potatoes until tender. Drain well and mash.

2 Place water and lime leaves into a skillet and heat over a medium heat until simmering. Reduce heat, add shrimp and scallops and cook for 2-3 minutes or until shrimp just change color. Remove seafood from liquid and drain on paper towels. Place in a food processor or blender and process until smooth.

3 Bring liquid back to the simmer and cook fish for 5-10 minutes, or until it flakes when tested with a fork. Remove pan from heat and allow fish to cool in the liquid. When cool, remove from pan and flake with a fork.

4 Combine potatoes, shrimp mixture, fish, cheese, flour, eggs, lemon and lime juices, lemon rind, chili and coriander in a large bowl and mix well. Season to taste with black pepper. Shape mixture into eight patties, coat with bread crumbs and refrigerate for 30 minutes.

5 Heat oil in a skillet, cook patties until golden brown on each side. Drain on paper towels.

6 To make sauce, place chutney, jam, vinegar and five spice in saucepan. Bring to the boil, stirring constantly, and simmer for 5 minutes. Serve with seafood cakes.

BAKED STUFFED FISH

Bream has been used for this recipe, however any whole fish, such as snapper or emperor, is suitable to use.

Serves 4
Oven temperature 350°F, 180°C

- [ ] 1 tablespoon olive oil
- [ ] 1 small onion, finely chopped
- [ ] 1 clove garlic, crushed
- [ ] 3 spinach leaves, stalks removed and leaves finely shredded
- [ ] 2 slices bacon, finely chopped
- [ ] 2 tablespoons currants
- [ ] 2 tablespoons pine nuts (pignola), toasted
- [ ] 1 cup/60 g soft bread crumbs, made from stale bread
- [ ] 1 egg, lightly beaten
- [ ] 2 teaspoons lemon juice
- [ ] 1 tablespoon chopped fresh parsley
- [ ] 1 tablespoon chopped fresh rosemary
- [ ] freshly ground black pepper
- [ ] 2 whole fish, about 20 oz/600 g each, cleaned and scaled
- [ ] 1 cup/250 mL dry white wine
- [ ] 1/4 cup/1/2 stick/60 g butter, melted

1 Heat oil in a nonstick skillet and cook onion and garlic for 3-4 minutes or until onion is soft. Add spinach and bacon and cook for 5 minutes longer, or until spinach wilts. Remove from heat.

2 Combine spinach mixture, currants, pine nuts, bread crumbs, egg, lemon juice, parsley and rosemary in a large bowl. Season to taste with black pepper and mix well.

3 Divide mixture into two portions and fill the cavities of each fish. Close securely, using skewers or toothpicks. Place in a greased shallow baking dish, pour wine over and brush fish with butter.

4 Bake for 35-40 minutes, or until fish flakes when tested with a fork. Baste frequently during cooking.

Cook's tip: Fish is cooked when it flakes easily when tested with a fork; if it is overcooked it will be dry and tough.

THAI FISH

These broiled fish with their spicy flavor are sure to become a favorite.

Serves 4

- [ ] 4 small whole fish

CHILI MARINADE
- [ ] 2 small fresh red chilies, seeded and finely chopped
- [ ] 1 clove garlic, crushed
- [ ] 2 teaspoons grated fresh ginger
- [ ] 1 1/2 tablespoons chopped fresh coriander (cilantro)
- [ ] 2 tablespoons lime juice
- [ ] 2 tablespoons peanut oil
- [ ] 1 teaspoon ground cumin
- [ ] freshly ground black pepper

1 Rinse fish under cold running water and pat dry with paper towels. Score flesh with a sharp knife to make 2-3 diagonal cuts along the body. Place in a shallow dish.

2 To make marinade, combine chilies, garlic, ginger, coriander, lime juice, oil and cumin in a small bowl. Season to taste with black pepper. Pour over fish and rub well into the flesh. Cover and marinate for 2 hours, or preferably overnight in the refrigerator.

3 Remove fish from marinade and broil under a medium heat for 8-10 minutes, or until fish flakes when tested with a fork. Baste frequently with marinade and turn halfway through cooking.

Cook's tip: These tasty fish are also great barbecued or pan fried.

Spicy Seafood Cakes, Thai Fish, Baked Stuffed Fish

MASTER CLASS

SEAFOOD WITH MANGOES

Squid is also known as cuttlefish or calamari.

Serves 4

- ☐ **8 oz/250 g calamari (squid)**
- ☐ **8 oz/250 g large uncooked shrimp, shelled and deveined**
- ☐ **250 g/8 oz scallops, cleaned**
- ☐ **¹/₄ teaspoon sugar**
- ☐ **1 teaspoon cornstarch**
- ☐ **2 tablespoons vegetable oil**
- ☐ **2 teaspoons grated fresh ginger**
- ☐ **14 oz/440 g canned sliced mangoes or apricots, drained and cut into ³/₄ in/1 cm strips**
- ☐ **6 spring onions, cut into ³/₄ in/1 cm diagonal slices**

SAUCE

- ☐ **2 teaspoons cornstarch blended with ³/₄ cup/185 mL chicken stock**
- ☐ **2 tablespoons dry white wine**
- ☐ **1 tablespoon soy sauce**
- ☐ **1 teaspoon sesame oil**
- ☐ **2 tablespoons white vinegar**
- ☐ **2 teaspoons sugar**

1 Clean squid, cut into halves and spread out flat with inside facing up. Mark in a diamond pattern with a sharp knife, then cut into diagonal pieces. Combine squid, shrimp and scallops with sugar and cornstarch.

2 Heat vegetable oil in skillet or wok. Stir-fry seafood for 2-3 minutes until just tender. Remove and set aside. Add ginger to pan and stir-fry for 1 minute.

3 To make sauce, combine blended cornstarch with wine, soy sauce, sesame oil, vinegar and sugar. Pour into pan and stir until sauce is boiling. Reduce heat and simmer for 3 minutes. Return seafood to pan with mangoes or apricots and spring onions. Toss for 2-3 minutes until heated through.

Cook's tip: To prepare squid, pull away tentacles and intestines from body. Pull feather out of the body and discard. Cut the tentacles from intestines and discard intestines. Rinse the body and tentacles under cold, running water and peel skin away from the body. Drain well and pat dry on paper towels. Halve the bodies

lengthwise and score the surface with a sharp knife in a diamond pattern.

Like all seafood, squid only requires minimal cooking. Overcooking will cause toughness.

Clean squid, cut in halves and spread out flat with inside facing up. Mark in a diamond pattern, then cut into diagonal pieces.

Shell and devein prawns.

Return seafood to pan with mangoes or apricots and spring onions.

ROAST PORK WITH APPLE STUFFING

Serves 6
Oven temperature 500°F, 250°C

- ☐ **3 lb/1.5 kg sirloin or center loin pork roast, bone in and rind scored**
- ☐ **1 tablespoon salt (optional)**

APPLE STUFFING
- ☐ **2 tablespoons/30 g butter**
- ☐ **1 green apple, cored, peeled and finely chopped**
- ☐ **1 cup/60 g bread crumbs, made from stale bread**
- ☐ **1 teaspoon finely grated lemon rind**
- ☐ **1 teaspoon ground allspice**
- ☐ **1 tablespoon apple or mint jelly**
- ☐ **¹/₄ cup/60 g golden raisins**

1 Using a sharp knife, make a pocket in the pork by separating bones from the thickest muscle of the loin, leaving both ends intact.

2 To make stuffing, melt butter in a skillet and cook apple for 2-3 minutes or until soft. Remove pan from heat and stir in bread crumbs, lemon rind, allspice, apple jelly and raisins.

3 Pack mixture into pocket in pork and place on a roasting rack in a baking pan. Rub rind of pork with salt and bake for 20 minutes. Reduce heat to 375°F/190°C and bake for 1 hour longer or until meat is cooked through. Stand for 10 minutes before carving.

Cook's Tip: Ask the butcher to leave the fat and rind attached to the roast if possible, then score the rind into a criss-cross pattern with a very sharp knife. If roasting the loin without rind, omit salt and bake at 375°F/190°C for 1³/₄ hours or until tender.

Roast Pork with Apple Stuffing

TARRAGON PORK WITH VEGETABLES

Serves 6

- [ ] **2 tablespoons/30 g butter**
- [ ] **2 lb/1 kg boned and rolled shoulder of pork**
- [ ] **2 onions, chopped**
- [ ] **1 leek, chopped**
- [ ] **3 cups/750 mL chicken stock**
- [ ] **¼ cup/60 mL lemon juice**
- [ ] **1 teaspoon cracked black pepper**
- [ ] **2 bay leaves**
- [ ] **1 turnip, chopped**
- [ ] **12 new baby potatoes**
- [ ] **2 carrots, chopped**
- [ ] **2 stalks celery, chopped**
- [ ] **¼ cup/60 g redcurrant jelly**
- [ ] **2 tablespoons chopped fresh tarragon**

1   Heat butter in a large saucepan, add pork and cook over a high heat until browned on all sides. Reduce heat to low, add onions and leek and cook for 5 minutes or until onions are soft.

2   Stir in stock, lemon juice, black pepper and bay leaves and bring to the boil. Reduce heat, cover and simmer, turning meat occasionally, for 30 minutes. Add turnip, potatoes, carrots and celery and simmer for 15 minutes longer or until vegetables are tender and meat is cooked.

3   Remove meat and vegetables from pan, set aside and keep warm. Bring juices in pan to the boil and boil, uncovered, for 2 minutes. Stir in redcurrant jelly and tarragon and simmer for 5 minutes. To serve, slice pork and spoon over sauce. Accompany with vegetables.

Cook's tip: There are two types of tarragon – French and Russian. While they look very similar, the Russian tarragon has a coarser leaf and is virtually tasteless.

Tarragon is a herb which is best used fresh, as its essential oils are volatile and are lost in drying. When a recipe calls for tarragon it usually refers to French tarragon.

HOT CHICKEN AND POTATO CURRY

Serves 4

- [ ] **10 new baby potatoes, halved**
- [ ] **2 onions, cut into eighths**
- [ ] **1 clove garlic, crushed**
- [ ] **½ teaspoon curry paste (Vindaloo)**
- [ ] **14 oz/440 g canned tomatoes, undrained and mashed**
- [ ] **1 cup/250 mL chicken stock**
- [ ] **2 tablespoons dry white wine**
- [ ] **2 tablespoons mango chutney**
- [ ] **1 tablespoon curry powder**
- [ ] **2 teaspoons ground cumin**
- [ ] **⅓ cup/90 mL tomato paste**
- [ ] **2 boned, skinned chicken breast halves, cut into ¾ in/2 cm cubes**
- [ ] **1 tablespoon finely chopped fresh coriander (cilantro)**

1   Boil, steam or microwave potatoes until just tender. Set aside to cool.

2   Place onions, garlic, curry paste (Vindaloo) and 1 tablespoon of juice from tomatoes in a saucepan and cook for 2-3 minutes, or until onion is soft.

3   Combine tomatoes, stock, wine, chutney, curry powder, cumin and tomato paste. Stir into onion mixture and cook over a medium heat for 2-3 minutes. Add chicken and potatoes and cook over a low heat for 5 minutes, or until chicken is tender. Just prior to serving, sprinkle with coriander.

Hot Chicken and Potato Curry

FARMHOUSE CHICKEN CASSEROLE

Serves 4
Oven temperature 400°F, 200°C

- [ ] **3 lb/1.5 kg chicken pieces**
- [ ] **¹/₄ cup/30 g seasoned flour**
- [ ] **¹/₄ cup/¹/₂ stick/60 g butter**
- [ ] **2 cloves garlic, crushed**
- [ ] **2¹/₂ cups/600 mL chicken stock**
- [ ] **2 tablespoons tomato paste**
- [ ] **1 tablespoon vegetable oil**
- [ ] **1 turnip, diced**
- [ ] **2 small carrots, diced**
- [ ] **1 parsnip, diced**
- [ ] **8 small onions**
- [ ] **3 slices bacon, trimmed and chopped**
- [ ] **8 new baby potatoes, quartered**
- [ ] **freshly ground black pepper**
- [ ] **3 tablespoons finely chopped fresh parsley**

1 Toss chicken in flour to coat. Shake off excess flour and reserve 1 tablespoon.
2 Melt butter in a large skillet and cook chicken over a medium heat until brown on all sides. Transfer to a large casserole dish.
3 Add garlic and reserved flour to pan and cook over a low heat for 1 minute. Combine stock and tomato paste. Remove pan from heat and gradually blend in stock mixture. Cook over a medium heat, stirring constantly, until mixture boils and thickens. Pour over chicken in dish. Cover and bake chicken for 30 minutes.
4 Heat oil in a large skillet and cook turnip, carrots and parsnip over a medium heat for 3-4 minutes. Remove from pan and set aside. Add onions and bacon to pan and cook for 4-5 minutes or until bacon is crisp.
5 Stir turnip, carrots, parsnip, onion mixture, potatoes, black pepper to taste and parsley into chicken mixture and bake for 40 minutes longer or until vegetables are tender.

LAMB POT ROAST

Pot roasting dates back to prehistoric times when clay pots were filled with game, whole cuts of meat or poultry, and vegetables, then hung over a fire to simmer. Lean meats that need long slow cooking, are ideal for pot roasting.

Serves 6

- [ ] **3 oz/90 g butter**
- [ ] **3-4 lb/1.5-2 kg leg of lamb**
- [ ] **14 oz/440 g canned tomatoes, mashed and undrained**
- [ ] **¹/₂ cup/125 mL red wine**
- [ ] **2 tablespoons tomato paste**
- [ ] **1 tablespoon Worcestershire sauce**
- [ ] **¹/₄ teaspoon mixed dried herbs**
- [ ] **1 teaspoon sugar**
- [ ] **freshly ground black pepper**
- [ ] **vegetable oil**
- [ ] **3 carrots, halved lengthwise**
- [ ] **3 turnips, halved lengthwise**
- [ ] **6 small onions**
- [ ] **3 large potatoes, halved**

1 Melt 2 tablespoons/30 g butter in a large Dutch oven or heavy-based saucepan and cook meat on all sides until well browned.
2 Combine tomatoes, red wine, tomato paste, Worcestershire sauce, herbs, sugar and black pepper to taste. Pour over meat, bring to the boil, then reduce heat, cover, and simmer for 1¹/₂ hours or until meat is tender.
3 About 30 minutes before meat finishes cooking, heat oil and remaining butter in a large heavy-based skillet. Add carrots, turnips, onions and potatoes and cook until vegetables are lightly browned. Reduce heat to low and cook gently for 15-20 minutes or until vegetables are tender.
4 Remove meat from pan, place on a serving platter, set aside and keep warm. Bring sauce that remains in pan to the boil and cook for 10 minutes or until sauce reduces and thickens slightly. Serve sauce with meat and vegetables.

Cook's tip: A boneless veal roast, a whole chicken or a round tip beef roast are also delicious cooked in this way.

*Crusty Steak and Kidney Pie,
Farmhouse Chicken Casserole,
Lamb Pot Roast*

CRUSTY STEAK AND KIDNEY PIE

This modern version of the English steak and kidney pie, is just as tasty as the original, but easier to make .

Serves 4
Oven temperature 350°F, 180°C

- ☐ 1 lb/500 g flank skirt steak
- ☐ 3 lamb kidneys
- ☐ 1/4 cup/1/2 stick/60 g butter
- ☐ 1 onion, chopped
- ☐ 3 slices bacon, chopped
- ☐ 2 tablespoons all-purpose flour
- ☐ 3/4 cup/185 mL beef stock
- ☐ 1/4 cup/60 mL red wine
- ☐ 1 tablespoon tomato paste
- ☐ 1/2 teaspoon sugar
- ☐ 1 tablespoon finely chopped fresh parsley
- ☐ freshly ground black pepper

SOUR CREAM CRUST
- ☐ 1/2 cup/1 stick/125 g butter, softened
- ☐ 1 1/4 cups/300 g dairy sour cream
- ☐ 1 egg
- ☐ 1 1/2 cups/185 g self-rising flour
- ☐ 1 tablespoon finely chopped fresh thyme

1 Trim meat of all visible fat and cut into 1 in/2.5 cm pieces. Trim kidneys of all visible fat and soak in salted water for 10 minutes. Wipe dry with paper towels. Nick skin on rounded side of each kidney and draw it back on each side until it is attached by the core only. Draw out as much core as possible and cut, with skin, close to kidney. Cut each kidney into slices.

2 Melt half the butter in a large saucepan and cook meat in batches until browned on all sides. Remove from pan and set aside. Add kidney to pan and cook for 1-2 minutes to seal. Remove from pan and set aside. Stir in onion and bacon and cook for 2-3 minutes or until onion is golden. Remove from pan and set aside.

3 Melt remaining butter in pan, add flour and cook for 3-4 minutes or until a light straw color. Combine stock, wine, tomato paste and sugar. Remove pan from heat and gradually blend in stock mixture. Cook over a medium heat, stirring constantly, until sauce boils and thickens. Stir in parsley and season to taste with black pepper. Return meat mixture to pan, cover and simmer gently for 1 1/2-2 hours or until meat is tender. Set aside to cool slightly.

4 To make crust, combine butter, sour cream and egg in a bowl. Sift in 1 cup/125 g of the flour and add thyme. Mix until well combined. Spread two-thirds of mixture over bottom and sides of a shallow casserole, then spoon in meat mixture. Lightly knead remaining flour into the remaining dough. Press out on a lightly floured surface, using palm of hand, to 1/2 in/1 cm thick and cut into rounds using a 1 1/4 in/3 cm metal pastry cutter. Top filling with dough rounds, overlapping them slightly. Bake for 30 minutes, or until crust is golden.

MEDITERRANEAN FISH STEW

Serves 6

- ☐ 10 large fresh mussels, scrubbed and beards removed
- ☐ 8 oz/250 g uncooked shrimp
- ☐ 1 1/2 lb/750 g firm white fish fillets, cut into large pieces
- ☐ 8 oz/250 g calamari (squid) rings

TOMATO SAUCE
- ☐ 1 tablespoon olive oil
- ☐ 2 leeks, sliced
- ☐ 2 cloves garlic, crushed
- ☐ 1/2 cup/125 mL dry white wine
- ☐ 1 large red pepper, seeded and chopped
- ☐ 14 oz/440 g canned tomatoes, undrained and mashed
- ☐ 1/2 cup/125 mL chicken stock
- ☐ 1 teaspoon grated lemon rind
- ☐ 1 bay leaf
- ☐ pinch cayenne pepper
- ☐ 3 tablespoons chopped fresh parsley
- ☐ freshly ground black pepper

1 To make sauce, heat oil in a large saucepan, add leeks and garlic and cook for 3-4 minutes or until leeks are tender. Stir in wine and cook over a high heat until wine is nearly evaporated. Mix in red pepper, tomatoes, stock, lemon rind, bay leaf and cayenne pepper and bring to the boil.

2 Add mussels to sauce and cook until shells open. Discard any mussels that do not open after 5 minutes. Remove mussels from pan and set aside. Stir in shrimp, fish and calamari (squid) and cook for 2-3 minutes. Return mussels to pan, stir in parsley and season to taste with black pepper and serve immediately.

MIDDLE EASTERN LAMB WITH BEANS

Serves 6

- ☐ 1 tablespoon vegetable oil
- ☐ 1 large onion, sliced
- ☐ 1 1/2 lb/750 g boneless lamb, cubed
- ☐ 1 1/2 lb/750 g green beans, trimmed
- ☐ 1/4 cup/60 g tomato paste
- ☐ 1/4 teaspoon ground nutmeg
- ☐ 1/2 teaspoon ground cinnamon
- ☐ water

1 Heat oil in a large skillet, add onion and cook, stirring occasionally, for 5 min-utes or until onion is soft. Transfer onion to a casserole dish.

2 Brown lamb in skillet, then add to casserole. Add beans, tomato paste, nutmeg, cinnamon and just enough water to cover the meat.

3 Cover and bake for 1 1/2 hours or until lamb is tender and sauce has thickened.

Serving suggestion: This casserole is delicious served with rice or noodles.

GOLDEN-COATED CHICKEN DRUMSTICKS

Serves 4
Oven temperature 350°F, 180°C

- ☐ 4 chicken drumsticks, skin removed
- ☐ all-purpose flour
- ☐ 1 egg, lightly beaten
- ☐ 1 tablespoon vegetable oil

RICE BRAN COATING
- ☐ 1/2 cup/45 g rice bran
- ☐ 1/2 cup/45 g wholewheat bread crumbs, made from stale bread
- ☐ 1/4 teaspoon dried ground rosemary
- ☐ 1/4 cup/30 g grated Parmesan cheese

1 To make coating, combine rice bran, bread crumbs, rosemary and Parmesan cheese. Coat drumsticks with flour, dip in egg and coat well with crumb mixture.

2 Brush a baking pan with oil, add drumsticks and bake, turning and basting frequently for 1 hour or until chicken is cooked.

LEBANESE PIZZA

Serves 6
Oven temperature 350°F, 180°C

- [ ] **6 oz/185 g cracked wheat (burghul) soaked in 2 cups/500 mL hot water for 10-15 minutes**
- [ ] **1 onion, chopped**
- [ ] **1 clove garlic, crushed**
- [ ] **1 lb/500 g lean ground lamb**
- [ ] **$^1/_2$ teaspoon mixed herbs**
- [ ] **1 tablespoon lemon juice**
- [ ] **1 tablespoon chopped fresh mint**
- [ ] **$^1/_2$ teaspoon chili powder**

TOMATO AND HUMMUS TOPPING
- [ ] **1 cup/250 g hummus**
- [ ] **2 tomatoes, sliced**
- [ ] **8 spinach leaves, blanched and chopped**
- [ ] **3 tablespoons pine nuts (pignola)**
- [ ] **$^1/_2$ cup/60 g shredded Cheddar cheese**

1   Drain cracked wheat and set aside. Cook onion and garlic in a nonstick skillet for 3 minutes or until onion is soft. Transfer cracked wheat and onion mixture to a bowl and combine with lamb, mixed herbs, lemon juice, mint and chili powder.

2   Press meat mixture into a 12 in/30 cm pizza tray and cook for 20 minutes or until base is firm. Drain off any juices.

3   To make topping, spread meat pizza base with hummus then top with tomato slices and spinach. Sprinkle with pine nuts and cheese. Cook under a preheated broiler for 3-4 minutes or until cheese melts.

Serving suggestion: Cut pizza into wedges and serve with crusty bread and a salad.

Cook's Tip: Hummus is a chick pea (garbanzo bean) and sesame seed purée flavored with lemon juice and garlic and used as a dip for pita bread. Look for it at Greek delicatessens.

Lebanese Pizza

BEEF AND MUSHROOM PIE

Homemade puff pastry takes a little time to make but the result is well worth it.

Serves 4
Oven temperature 425°F, 220°C

PUFF PASTRY
- [ ] **3 oz/90 g butter, softened**
- [ ] **3 oz/90 g lard or shortening, softened**
- [ ] **2 cups/250 g flour**
- [ ] **1/2 cup/125 mL cold water**

BEEF AND MUSHROOM FILLING
- [ ] **2 lb/1 kg lean top round beef, cut into 1 in/2.5 cm cubes**
- [ ] **1/2 cup/60 g seasoned flour**
- [ ] **1/4 cup/1/2 stick/60 g butter**
- [ ] **1/4 cup/60 mL olive oil**
- [ ] **2 onions, chopped**
- [ ] **2 cloves garlic, crushed**
- [ ] **8 oz/250 g button mushrooms, sliced**
- [ ] **1/2 cup/125 mL red wine**
- [ ] **1/2 cup/125 mL beef stock**
- [ ] **1 bay leaf**
- [ ] **2 tablespoons finely chopped fresh parsley**
- [ ] **1 tablespoon Worcestershire sauce**
- [ ] **freshly ground black pepper**
- [ ] **1 tablespoon cornstarch blended with 2 tablespoons water**
- [ ] **1 egg, lightly beaten**

1   To make filling, toss meat in flour to coat. Shake off excess flour. Melt butter and oil in a large Dutch oven and cook meat in batches for 3-4 minutes or until browned on all sides. Remove meat from pan and set aside.

2   Add onions and garlic to pan and cook over a medium heat for 3-4 minutes or until onion is soft. Stir in mushrooms and cook for 2 minutes longer. Combine wine and stock, pour into pan and cook for 4-5 minutes, stirring constantly to lift sediment from base of pan. Bring to the boil, then reduce heat. Return meat to pan with bay leaf, parsley, Worcestershire sauce and black pepper to taste. Cover and simmer for 1 1/2 hours or until meat is tender. Stir in cornstarch mixture and cook, stirring, until mixture thickens. Remove pan from heat and set aside to cool.

3   To make pastry, place butter and lard in a bowl and mix until well combined. Cover and refrigerate until firm. Place flour in a large mixing bowl. Cut one-quarter of butter mixture into small pieces and rub into flour using fingertips until mixture resembles coarse bread crumbs. Mix in enough water to form a firm dough.

4   Turn pastry onto a floured surface and knead lightly. Roll pastry out to a 6 x 10 in/ 15 x 25 cm rectangle. Cut another one-quarter of butter mixture into small pieces and place over top two-thirds of pastry. Fold the bottom third of pastry up and top third of pastry down to give three even layers. Half turn pastry to have open end facing you and roll out to a rectangle as before. Repeat folding and rolling twice. Cover pastry and refrigerate for 1 hour.

5   Place cooled filling in a 4 cup/1 liter oval shallow casserole. On a lightly floured surface, roll out pastry 1 1/2 in/4 cm larger than casserole. Cut off a 1/2 in/1 cm strip from pastry edge. Brush rim of dish with water and press pastry strip onto rim. Brush pastry strip with water. Lift pastry top over filling and press gently to seal edges. Trim and press back edges to make a decorative edge. Brush with egg and bake for 30 minutes or until pastry is golden and crisp.

Cut one-quarter of butter mixture into small pieces and place over top two-thirds of pastry.

Fold the bottom third of pastry up and the top third of pastry down to give three even layers.

GLAZED MINTED LAMB RACKS

Serves 4
Oven temperature 350°F, 180°C

- [ ] **2 lean racks of lamb, each containing 6 cutlets**

CRACKED WHEAT SEASONING
- [ ] **$1/3$ cup cracked wheat (burghul)**
- [ ] **$1/2$ cup/30 g bread crumbs, made from stale bread**
- [ ] **3 tablespoons finely chopped fresh parsley**
- [ ] **1 tablespoon finely chopped fresh mint**
- [ ] **1 teaspoon grated lemon rind**
- [ ] **1 tablespoon pine nuts (pignola), toasted**
- [ ] **2 teaspoons mint jelly**
- [ ] **1 apple, cored, peeled and shredded**
- [ ] **1 tablespoon/15 g butter, melted**
- [ ] **freshly ground black pepper**

MINT GLAZE
- [ ] **$1/4$ cup/60 g mint jelly**
- [ ] **2 tablespoons orange juice**
- [ ] **2 tablespoons honey**

1 Using a sharp knife, separate bones from meat, leaving both ends intact, this makes a pocket for the seasoning. Trim excess fat from outside of racks.

2 To make seasoning, cover cracked wheat with boiling water and set aside to soak for 15 minutes. Drain and rinse under cold running water. Dry on paper towels and place in a mixing bowl with bread crumbs, parsley, mint, lemon rind, pine nuts, mint jelly, apple, butter, and black pepper to taste. Pack mixture firmly into pockets. Place racks in a baking dish.

3 To make glaze, place mint jelly in a saucepan and cook over a medium heat until melted. Stir in orange juice and honey. Brush lamb with glaze and bake for 30-35 minutes or until cooked to individual taste. Baste frequently with glaze during cooking.

ROAST VEGETABLES

Serves 4
Oven temperature 350°F,180°C

- [ ] **4 potatoes, halved**
- [ ] **4 pieces butternut squash**
- [ ] **4 brown onions**
- [ ] **1 tablespoon vegetable oil**

1 Boil or steam potatoes for 5 minutes, drain and dry on absorbent paper towels. Set aside until cool enough to handle. Score the upper rounded side of potatoes with a fork. This helps to crisp potatoes during cooking.

2 Brush potatoes, squash and onions with oil, place in a baking pan and bake for 1 hour or until golden and crisp turning once. Remove from baking pan and keep warm.

BEEF WITH SWEET AND SOUR SAUCE

Serves 4

- [ ] **2 tablespoons vegetable oil**
- [ ] **1 lb/500 g lean sirloin steak, cut into thin strips**
- [ ] **1 onion, cut into eighths**
- [ ] **2 cloves garlic, crushed**
- [ ] **1 teaspoon grated fresh ginger**
- [ ] **$3^1/_2$ oz/100 g oyster mushrooms, sliced**
- [ ] **2 stalks celery, sliced diagonally**
- [ ] **2 carrots, sliced diagonally**
- [ ] **$1/_2$ red pepper, chopped**
- [ ] **$1/_2$ green pepper, chopped**
- [ ] **14 oz/440 g canned baby corn, drained**
- [ ] **100 g/$3^1/_2$ oz snow peas, trimmed**

SWEET AND SOUR SAUCE
- [ ] **2 teaspoons chili sauce**
- [ ] **2 tablespoons white vinegar**
- [ ] **2 tablespoons tomato catsup**
- [ ] **2 tablespoons brown sugar**
- [ ] **2 tablespoons dry sherry**
- [ ] **1 tablespoon cornstarch blended with $1/_2$ cup/125 mL pineapple juice**

1 Heat oil in a large skillet or wok, add meat and stir-fry for 2-3 minutes or until it just changes color. Remove meat from pan and set aside.

2 Add onion, garlic and ginger to pan and stir-fry for 1 minute. Stir in mushrooms, celery, carrots, red and green pepper, corn and snow peas and stir-fry for 2-3 minutes. Remove from pan and set aside.

3 To make sauce, place chili sauce, vinegar, catsup, brown sugar, sherry and cornstarch mixture in a small bowl and whisk to combine. Pour into pan and cook for 1 minute or until mixture boils and thickens. Return meat and vegetables to pan and stir-fry for 1-2 minutes or until heated through.

GARLICKY LAMB POT ROAST

Serves 8

- ☐ 3 lb/1.5 kg leg of lamb, tunnel boned
- ☐ ½ teaspoon ground nutmeg
- ☐ ½ teaspoon ground cinnamon
- ☐ ½ teaspoon ground black pepper
- ☐ 2 tablespoons olive oil
- ☐ 2 cups/500 mL chicken stock
- ☐ 2 tablespoons lemon juice
- ☐ 8 oz/250 g sweet potato, cut into matchsticks
- ☐ 8 oz/250 g green beans, trimmed

GARLICKY STUFFING
- ☐ 3 cloves garlic, crushed
- ☐ 1 teaspoon garam masala
- ☐ 2 cups/125 g bread crumbs, made from stale bread
- ☐ 2 tablespoons pine nuts (pignola)
- ☐ 1 tablespoon currants
- ☐ 1 teaspoon finely grated lemon rind

1   To make stuffing, place garlic, garam masala, bread crumbs, pine nuts, currants and lemon rind in a bowl and mix to combine. Spoon stuffing into lamb cavity and secure with string.

2   Place nutmeg, cinnamon and black pepper in a cup and mix to combine. Rub spice mixture over all surfaces of lamb.

3   Heat oil in a Dutch oven, add meat and cook over a high heat until browned on all sides. Add stock, cover and simmer, turning occasionally, for 25 minutes. Stir in lemon juice and simmer for 25 minutes longer.

4   Remove lamb from pan, set aside and keep warm. Add sweet potato to stock in pan and cook for 5 minutes, then add beans and cook for 10 minutes longer or until sweet potato and beans are tender. To serve, slice lamb and accompany with vegetables and pan juices.

Cook's Tip: Ask the butcher to remove the bones without cutting through the meat entirely so that a pocket (shaped like a tunnel) is formed. Refer to Glossary, last pages.

Glazed Minted Lamb Racks with Roast Vegetables

VEAL GOULASH

Makes 4 servings

- ☐ 1lb/500 g lean veal rump steak, cut $1/2$ in/1 cm thick
- ☐ $1^{1}/_{2}$ tablespoons paprika
- ☐ 2 tablespoons all-purpose flour
- ☐ freshly ground black pepper
- ☐ 1 tablespoon vegetable oil
- ☐ 2 onions, chopped
- ☐ 1 clove garlic, crushed
- ☐ 1 tablespoon tomato paste
- ☐ $1/4$ cup/60 mL red wine
- ☐ $1/2$ cup/125 mL beef stock
- ☐ $1/4$ cup/60 g dairy sour cream or plain yogurt

1   Trim meat of all visible fat and cut into $3/4$ in /2 cm cubes. Place paprika, flour and black pepper to taste in a plastic food bag, add meat and shake to coat meat evenly. Shake off excess flour.

2   Heat oil in a large saucepan and cook onion and garlic over a medium heat for 3-4 minutes or until onion is soft. Combine tomato paste, wine and stock. Stir stock mixture and meat into onion mixture. Bring to the boil, then reduce heat and simmer, covered, for 25-30 minutes or until meat is tender.

3   Remove from heat and stir in the sour cream or yogurt. Serve immediately.

Serving suggestion: Serve with fettuccine and boiled, steamed or microwaved vegetables of your choice.

LAMB WITH REDCURRANT SAUCE

Serves 4

- ☐ 4 large, lean, lamb arm chops or leg center slices

REDCURRANT SAUCE
- ☐ 1 tablespoon lime or lemon juice
- ☐ $1/2$ cup/125 g redcurrant jelly
- ☐ 2 tablespoons Dijon mustard

1   Broil, pan fry or barbecue chops for 4-5 minutes each side or until cooked to your liking. Set aside and keep warm.

2   To make sauce, place lime or lemon juice, redcurrant jelly and mustard in small saucepan and cook over a low heat, stirring, for 4-5 minutes or until jelly melts and all ingredients are combined. Spoon sauce over chops and serve.

WHOLE FISH WITH LEEK AND RICE STUFFING

Serves 4
Oven temperature 350°F,180°C,

- ☐ 1 x 3 lb/1.5 kg whole fish, such as snapper or bass, cleaned and skin scored
- ☐ $1/2$ cup/125 mL dry white wine
- ☐ $1/4$ cup/$1/2$ stick/60 g butter, melted

LEEK AND RICE STUFFING
- ☐ 1 cup/185 g rice
- ☐ 2 tablespoons olive oil
- ☐ 2 leeks, sliced
- ☐ 2 cloves garlic, crushed
- ☐ 3 tablespoons pine nuts (pignola)
- ☐ $1/3$ cup golden seedless raisins
- ☐ 1 stalk celery, chopped
- ☐ 3 tablespoons chopped fresh parsley
- ☐ 1 teaspoon lemon juice
- ☐ 1 teaspoon finely grated lemon rind
- ☐ freshly ground black pepper

1   To make stuffing, cook rice following packet directions, then drain and set aside. Heat oil in a large skillet and cook leeks and garlic for 3-4 minutes or until leeks are soft. Remove pan from heat and stir in rice, pine nuts, raisins, celery, parsley, lemon juice, lemon rind and black pepper to taste.

2   Fill cavity of fish with stuffing, close cavity and secure with wooden skewers or toothpicks. Place fish in a lightly greased, shallow baking dish. Pour wine over fish and bake for 35-40 minutes or until fish is cooked. Baste 3-4 times during cooking.

3   Place fish on a serving platter, cover, set aside and keep warm. Pour juices from baking dish into a small saucepan, bring to the boil and boil for 4-5 minutes or until juices are reduced by half. Spoon over fish and serve immediately.

Microwave it: Whole fish cooks well in the microwave oven – but remember the eyes should be removed before cooking as they can explode.

To cook this dish in the microwave oven, prepare the fish and stuffing as described in the recipe, then place in a shallow microwave-safe dish, pour over wine, cover and cook on MEDIUM-HIGH (70%), allowing 5-6 minutes per 1 lb/500 g fish.

STEAK WITH A DEVILED MARINADE

Serves 4

- ☐ 4 boneless rib eye (Delmonico) steaks, trimmed of all visible fat

DEVILED MARINADE
- ☐ 1 teaspoon curry powder
- ☐ 2 tablespoons brown sugar
- ☐ 2 tablespoons tomato catsup
- ☐ 2 teaspoons Worcestershire sauce
- ☐ 1 teaspoon soy sauce
- ☐ 2 teaspoons lime juice

1   To make marinade, place curry powder, sugar, catsup, Worcestershire sauce, soy sauce and lime juice in a small bowl and whisk to combine.

2   Place steak in a shallow glass or ceramic dish, pour over marinade, cover and set aside to marinate for 2-4 hours.

3   Remove meat from marinade and cook under a preheated medium-high broiler for 3-4 minutes each side or until cooked to your liking. Baste frequently with any remaining marinade during cooking.

The perfect steak: Everyone has their own preference on how they like their steak cooked; steak can be cooked to rare, medium-rare and well-done. Rare meat is springy to touch, medium meat less springy and well-done has very little give in it. When testing for doneness do not pierce or cut the meat with a knife as this causes loss of juices and dryness.

BAKED EGGPLANT
WITH LAMB

Serves 8
Oven temperature 350°F, 180°C

- [ ] **8 long thin eggplants, each about 4 oz/125 g**
- [ ] **salt**
- [ ] **¹/₂ cup/125 mL tomato paste**
- [ ] **¹/₂ cup/125 mL chicken stock**
- [ ] **¹/₃ cup/45 g grated Parmesan cheese**
- [ ] **2 tablespoons/30 g butter**

LAMB STUFFING
- [ ] **500 g/1 lb lean ground lamb**
- [ ] **1 onion, finely chopped**
- [ ] **1 clove garlic, crushed**
- [ ] **1 small red pepper, chopped**
- [ ] **2 tablespoons finely chopped fresh basil**
- [ ] **¹/₂ teaspoon dried oregano**
- [ ] **¹/₄ teaspoon chili powder**
- [ ] **freshly ground black pepper**

1   Remove stems from eggplants. Cut almost through each eggplant crosswise at ³/₄ in/2 cm intervals, taking care not to cut right through. Sprinkle cut surfaces liberally with salt and set aside to stand for 30 minutes. Rinse under cold running water and pat dry with paper towels.

2   To make stuffing, place lamb, onion, garlic, red pepper, basil, oregano, chili powder and black pepper to taste in a bowl and mix well to combine. Spoon a generous amount of the meat mixture into each cut of each eggplant and place eggplants in a baking dish.

3   Place tomato paste and stock in a bowl, whisk to combine and pour over eggplants. Sprinkle eggplants with Parmesan cheese, dot with butter and bake, basting frequently with pan juices, for 45 minutes or until eggplants are tender.

Veal Goulash

PORK WITH CABBAGE

Serves 4
Oven temperature 350°F, 180°C

- [ ] 4 large, lean, thick pork loin butterfly chops
- [ ] 1 tablespoon/15 g butter

RICE FILLING
- [ ] ¼ small savoy cabbage, finely shredded
- [ ] 1 stalk celery, finely sliced
- [ ] ½ cup/90 g cup white rice, cooked
- [ ] 1 teaspoon caraway seeds
- [ ] 2 tablespoons dairy sour cream or plain yogurt
- [ ] freshly ground black pepper

WINE SAUCE
- [ ] 2 tablespoons brown sugar
- [ ] 2 tablespoons/30 g butter
- [ ] ¼ cup/60 mL dry white wine
- [ ] ½ cup/125 mL chicken stock
- [ ] ¼ cup/60 mL cider vinegar
- [ ] ½ teaspoon cornstarch blended with 1 teaspoon of water

1 Place each chop between two sheets of plastic food wrap and pound lightly with a rolling pin.
2 To make filling, boil, steam or microwave cabbage and celery, separately, until just tender. Drain and refresh under cold running water. Dry between sheets of paper towels.
3 Combine cabbage, celery, rice, caraway seeds, sour cream or yogurt and black pepper to taste. Divide mixture between chops and spread over one half of each chop. Fold chop over and secure with toothpicks. Melt butter in a skillet, cook chops on both sides until golden brown. Place in a baking pan. Set aside.
4 To make sauce, place sugar and butter in pan and cook until sugar dissolves. Blend in wine, stock and vinegar and simmer for 3 minutes. Pour over chops in baking pan. Bake, uncovered, for 20-30 minutes or until tender. Baste with sauce frequently during cooking. Remove chops from pan, set aside and keep warm.
5 Strain sauce from pan and place in a small saucepan. Stir in cornstarch mixture and heat until sauce thickens slightly. Spoon over chops and serve.

Cook's tip: Butterfly pork chops are cut from the top loin area, boned, cut almost in half and opened out flat. Try placing a fruit or savory filling on one side of the steak, then folding it over and securing with toothpicks. You can then pan fry or bake these chops.

ROASTED PORK LOIN

Serves 8
Oven temperature 500°F, 250°C

- [ ] 3 lb/1.5 kg boned rolled sirloin pork roast, with rind on and scored
- [ ] 1 tablespoon coarse cooking salt (optional)

SEASONING
- [ ] 2 tablespoons/30 g butter
- [ ] 4 spinach leaves, stalks removed and leaves shredded
- [ ] 3 tablespoons pine nuts (pignola)
- [ ] ½ cup/30 g bread crumbs, made from stale bread
- [ ] ¼ teaspoon ground nutmeg
- [ ] freshly ground black pepper

CHUNKY APPLE AND PEAR SAUCE
- [ ] 1 small green apple, cored, peeled and sliced
- [ ] 1 small pear, cored, peeled and sliced
- [ ] 2 teaspoons chopped dried dates
- [ ] ⅓ cup/90 mL apple juice
- [ ] 2 teaspoons honey
- [ ] 1 teaspoon grated lemon rind
- [ ] pinch ground cloves

1 Unroll loin and make a cut in the middle of the fleshy part of the meat, making a space for the seasoning. Score the rind with a sharp knife, cutting down into the fat under the rind.
2 To make seasoning, melt butter in a skillet. Cook spinach and pine nuts for 2-3 minutes. Remove pan from heat and stir in breadcrumbs, nutmeg, and black pepper to taste. Spread spinach mixture over cut flap.
3 Roll up loin firmly and secure with string. Place in a baking dish. Rub all over rind with salt and bake for 20 minutes. Reduce temperature to 350°F/180°C and bake for 1 hour longer or until juices run clear when tested with a skewer in the meatiest part.
4 To make sauce, place apple, pear, dates, apple juice, honey, lemon rind and cloves in a small saucepan. Cover and bring to the boil. Reduce heat and simmer for 5 minutes, or until apple is tender.

Cook's tip: Ask the butcher to leave the fat and rind layer attached to the roast and score the rind into a criss-cross pattern with a very sharp knife. If roasting loin without the rind, omit salt and bake at 350°F/180°C for 1¾ hours or until tender.

MUSTARD SAUCE

Serves 4

- [ ] 2 tablespoons/30 g butter
- [ ] 1½ tablespoons flour
- [ ] 2 teaspoons Dijon-style mustard
- [ ] ¾ cup/185 mL chicken stock
- [ ] 1 teaspoon lime juice
- [ ] freshly ground black pepper
- [ ] ¼ cup/60 mL mayonnaise

1 Melt butter in a saucepan, stir in flour and mustard and cook for 1 minute. Remove pan from heat and blend in stock and lime juice. Season to taste with black pepper.
2 Cook over a medium heat, stirring frequently, until sauce boils and thickens. Remove from heat and stir in mayonnaise.

TOMATO AND PASSION FRUIT SAUCE

Serves 4

- [ ] 1 tomato, peeled, seeded and chopped
- [ ] 1 small apple, cored, peeled and grated
- [ ] 2 tablespoons orange juice
- [ ] 1 tablespoon tomato paste
- [ ] 1½ tablespoons apricot jam
- [ ] ¼ teaspoon yellow mustard seeds
- [ ] pulp 2 passion fruit or ¼ cup/60 mL canned pulp

Place tomato, apple, orange juice, tomato paste, jam, mustard seeds and passion fruit pulp in a saucepan. Cook over a medium heat, stirring frequently, until sauce boils and all ingredients are well blended.

HONEY-GLAZED PORK

Serves 4
Oven temperature 350°F, 180°C

☐ **1 lb/500 g pork tenderloin**

GLAZE
☐ **1 tablespoon honey**
☐ **1 tablespoon orange juice**
☐ **1 teaspoon light soy sauce**

Trim meat of all visible fat and connective tissue. Place in a baking pan. Combine honey, orange juice and soy sauce and brush over tenderloin. Bake for 30 minutes. Halfway through cooking turn and brush with any leftover glaze. Slice pork, spoon over sauce of your choice, and serve.

Cook's tip: Pork tenderloin are lean pieces of meat taken from the loin ribs. Tenderloins are quick and easy to cook and they have no waste. You can roast or pan fry pork tenderloins, then serve, sliced, with a sauce.

BANANA AND APRICOT SAUCE

Serves 4

☐ **1 banana, chopped**
☐ **1 teaspoon lemon juice**
☐ **14 oz/440 g canned apricot halves**
☐ **1/4 teaspoon ground cinnamon**
☐ **2 tablespoons coconut milk**

1 Place banana, lemon juice, undrained apricots, cinnamon and coconut milk in a food processor or blender and process until smooth.
2 Transfer to a small saucepan and cook gently without boiling, until heated through.

Top: Roasted Pork Loin
Center: Honey-glazed Pork with Banana and Apricot Sauce, Mustard Sauce, Tomato and Passion Fruit Sauce
Bottom: Pork with Cabbage and Caraway Seeds

MASTER CLASS

CHICKEN WITH SPINACH RICOTTA AND LEMON FILLING

If chicken marylands are unavailable, you can substitute drumsticks or thighs. If you prefer, substitute cottage cheese for ricotta and fresh spinach in place of frozen.

Serves 4
Oven temperature 350°F, 180°C

- [ ] **4 chicken leg and thigh joints (marylands)**

SPINACH FILLING
- [ ] **4 oz/125 g frozen spinach, thawed**
- [ ] **1 clove garlic, crushed**
- [ ] **$^1/_2$ cup/125 g ricotta cheese**
- [ ] **2 teaspoons grated Parmesan cheese**
- [ ] **1 teaspoon grated lemon rind**
- [ ] **ground nutmeg**
- [ ] **2 tablespoons/30 g butter, melted**

TOMATO SAUCE
- [ ] **10 oz/315 g canned tomato purée**
- [ ] **2 teaspoons Worcestershire sauce**

1 To make filling, squeeze spinach to remove excess liquid and combine with garlic, ricotta cheese, Parmesan cheese, lemon rind and pinch nutmeg.

2 Loosen skin on chicken with fingers. Push spinach filling gently under skin down to the drumstick. Arrange marylands in a baking dish, brush with melted butter and bake for 35-40 minutes.

3 To make sauce, combine tomato purée and Worcestershire sauce in a saucepan and simmer gently for 3-4 minutes. Spoon sauce over chicken and serve.

Squeeze excess liquid from spinach. Combine with other filling ingredients.

Loosen skin on chicken using fingers.

Push spinach filling gently under skin down to the drumstick.

THAI-FLAVORED WHOLE CHILI FISH

For this delicious fish dish baby bream was used, but you might like to use small snapper or similar small fish.

Serves 4

- [ ] **4 small whole fish, such as snapper or trout**
- [ ] **1 fresh red chili, seeded and finely sliced**

SPICY MARINADE
- [ ] **1 tablespoon chopped fresh coriander (including root and stem)**
- [ ] **1 teaspoon grated fresh ginger**
- [ ] **1 clove garlic, crushed**
- [ ] **1/2 teaspoon chili paste (sambal oelek)**
- [ ] **1 teaspoon sugar**
- [ ] **2 teaspoons ground turmeric**
- [ ] **1 tablespoon peanut oil**
- [ ] **1 tablespoon vinegar**
- [ ] **1 tablespoon water**

1   Clean fish and rinse under cold running water. Pat dry with absorbent paper towels and arrange in a deep tray.

2   To make marinade, combine coriander, ginger, garlic, chili paste, sugar, turmeric, oil, vinegar and water. Pour over fish and rub well into the skin and flesh. Cover and refrigerate for 2 hours.

3   Barbecue or broil fish for 3-4 minutes each side or until flesh flakes when tested with a fork. Serve fish with any remaining marinade. Top with chili slices.

Salmon Steaks with Basil Sauce, Thai-flavored Whole Chili Fish, Fish and Basil Vermicelli Soup

SALMON STEAKS WITH BASIL SAUCE

Serves 4

- ☐ **4 x 4 oz/125 g salmon steaks**
- ☐ **freshly ground black pepper**

BASIL SAUCE
- ☐ **1 bunch fresh basil, leaves removed**
- ☐ **2 tablespoons lemon juice**
- ☐ **1 tablespoon olive oil**
- ☐ **1 clove garlic, crushed**
- ☐ **¹/₃ cup/45 g grated Parmesan cheese**
- ☐ **¹/₃ cup/30 g pine nuts (pignola), toasted**

1   Place fish steaks in a glass dish and season to taste with black pepper.
2   To make sauce, place basil leaves, lemon juice, olive oil, garlic, Parmesan and pine nuts in a food processor or blender and process until smooth.
3   Spoon half the sauce over fish. Cover and refrigerate for 30 minutes. Broil or barbecue fish for 4-5 minutes each side or until flesh flakes when tested with a fork. Serve fish with remaining sauce.

FISH AND BASIL VERMICELLI SOUP

Serves 6

- ☐ **1 tablespoon olive oil**
- ☐ **1 onion, finely chopped**
- ☐ **2 cloves garlic, crushed**
- ☐ **2 x 14 oz/440 g cans tomatoes, undrained and mashed**
- ☐ **¹/₄ cup/60 g tomato paste**
- ☐ **¹/₂ teaspoon sugar**
- ☐ **3 cups/750 mL water**
- ☐ **2 lb/1 kg fish steaks, such as mackerel**
- ☐ **2 teaspoons grated lemon rind**
- ☐ **2 tablespoons finely chopped fresh basil**
- ☐ **100 g/3¹/₂ oz vermicelli pasta**
- ☐ **freshly ground black pepper**

1   Heat oil in a large saucepan. Cook onion and garlic for 2-3 minutes or until onion is soft. Stir in tomatoes, tomato paste, sugar and 1 cup/250 mL water. Bring to the boil, reduce heat and simmer, covered, for 10 minutes.
2   Poach fish steaks in remaining 2 cups/500 mL of water, drain and reserve cooking liquid. Remove skin from fish and flake fish into large pieces.
3   Add lemon rind, basil, vermicelli and reserved liquid. Cover and simmer for 5-6 minutes or until pasta is cooked. Season to taste with black pepper. Stir in fish and cook 2-3 minutes to heat through.

GARLIC AND ROSEMARY MACKEREL STEAKS

Serves 4

- ☐ **1 tablespoon olive oil**
- ☐ **2 tablespoons/30 g butter**
- ☐ **2 cloves garlic, crushed**
- ☐ **4 large mackerel steaks or thick fillets**
- ☐ **¹/₄ cup/60 mL lemon juice**
- ☐ **2 teaspoons fresh rosemary leaves or ¹/₂ teaspoon dried rosemary**
- ☐ **freshly ground black pepper**

1   Heat oil and butter in a large skillet, add garlic and cook for 1 minute. Add fish and cook for 3-4 minutes each side or until browned.
2   Pour over lemon juice, sprinkle with rosemary and season to taste with black pepper. Cover and simmer for 5-8 minutes or until fish flakes when tested with a fork. Serve immediately.

Nutrition tip: Omega-3 fats found in fish reduce the tendency for the blood to clot and so lessen its 'stickness'. They can lower blood pressure and reduce the fatty build-up on blood vessel walls. They occur in all fish, but are particularly rich in oily fish such as herring, salmon, tuna, mackerel, sardines and trout. Try to aim to eat fish at least three times a week.

ORIENTAL LAMB AND SPINACH

Serves 4

- ☐ **1 lb/500 g lean lamb leg center slice, cut into thin slices**
- ☐ **2 tablespoons bottled oyster sauce**
- ☐ **2 tablespoons dry white wine**
- ☐ **1 teaspoon sugar**
- ☐ **$^1/_2$ teaspoon sesame oil**
- ☐ **1 bunch/1 lb/500 g spinach, washed**
- ☐ **2 teaspoons grated fresh ginger**
- ☐ **2 tablespoons vegetable oil**
- ☐ **$^1/_2$ teaspoon cornstarch blended with $^1/_4$ cup/60 mL chicken stock**

1   Combine meat with oyster sauce, wine, sugar and sesame oil. Wash spinach, remove any thick white stalks and cut into 1 in/2.5 cm slices, then cut leaves into large pieces.

2   Heat oil in skillet or wok. Stir-fry meat in two batches for 2-3 minutes each batch until meat browns. Remove and set aside. Add spinach stalks and ginger to pan and cook gently for 3 minutes. Return meat to pan and stir in spinach leaves.

3   Pour in blended cornstarch and toss over high heat for 3-4 minutes until spinach has softened.

Cook's tip: Substituting boned skinned chicken breasts or pork tenderloin for the lamb makes a change.

RED PEPPERED BEEF

This recipe is delicious served with rice or noodles.

Serves 4

- ☐ **1 lb/500 g sirloin steak, cut into thin strips**
- ☐ **2 teaspoons cornstarch**
- ☐ **$^1/_3$ cup/90 mL soy sauce**
- ☐ **$^1/_4$ cup/60 mL vegetable oil**
- ☐ **2 red peppers, cut into thin strips**
- ☐ **1 small fresh red chili, finely chopped**
- ☐ **3 spring onions, cut into 2 in/5 cm lengths**
- ☐ **1 clove garlic, crushed**
- ☐ **2 teaspoons grated fresh ginger**
- ☐ **1 teaspoon sugar**
- ☐ **2 tablespoons dry sherry**

Red Peppered Beef, Tangy Lemon Chicken, Oriental Lamb and Spinach

1 Sprinkle meat strips with cornstarch and half the soy sauce. Toss to coat and leave for 5 minutes.

2 Heat half the oil in a skillet or wok, add peppers, chili, spring onions, garlic and ginger and cook for 2-3 minutes. Remove from pan and set aside.

3 Heat remaining oil and stir-fry meat for 2-3 minutes. Return pepper mixture to the pan. Combine remaining soy sauce, sugar and sherry. Pour into pan and stir-fry pepper mixture a further minute to heat through.

Cook's tip: Never scour your wok when washing as this will cause the food to stick the next time you use it.

The best way to clean your wok is to wash it in warm soapy water using a soft cloth. Then rinse thoroghly in plenty of hot running water. Wipe dry with paper towel. It is a good idea to oil your wok lightly before you put it away. This will keep it well seasoned.

TANGY LEMON CHICKEN

Serves 4

- [ ] **1 medium cooked chicken**
- [ ] **2 tablespoons vegetable oil**
- [ ] **2 teaspoons grated fresh ginger**
- [ ] **$^1/_4$ cup/60 mL lemon juice**
- [ ] **1 cup/250 mL chicken stock**
- [ ] **2 tablespoons honey**
- [ ] **2 tablespoons sugar**
- [ ] **1 tablespoon cornstarch blended with 1 tablespoon water**
- [ ] **2 spring onions, chopped**

1 Cut chicken into serving pieces. Heat oil in skillet or wok and stir-fry chicken for 2-3 minutes. Remove, set aside and keep warm.

2 Stir in ginger and cook for 1 minute. Pour in combined lemon juice, stock, honey and sugar. Add blended cornstarch to pan and cook for 1-2 minutes until the sauce thickens.

3 Return chicken to pan and heat through gently. Serve sprinkled with spring onions.

TANGY BROCCOLI AND LAMB

Serves 6

- [ ] **2 tablespoons vegetable oil**
- [ ] **1 lb/500 g boneless lean lamb, cut into strips**
- [ ] **2 teaspoons grated fresh ginger**
- [ ] **1 clove garlic, crushed**
- [ ] **1 lb/500 g broccoli, cut into small florets**
- [ ] **4 stalks celery, sliced diagonally**
- [ ] **4 oz/125 g bean sprouts**
- [ ] **2 tablespoons sesame seeds, toasted**

ORIENTAL SAUCE
- [ ] **1 tablespoon sesame oil**
- [ ] **1 tablespoon soy sauce**
- [ ] **$^1/_4$ cup/60 mL oyster sauce**
- [ ] **2 tablespoons dry sherry**

1 Heat 1 tablespoon oil in a wok or large skillet. Add lamb, ginger and garlic and stir-fry for 3-4 minutes or until lamb changes color. Remove meat mixture from pan, set aside and keep warm.

2 Heat remaining oil in pan, add broccoli and celery and stir-fry until broccoli is bright green. Return meat mixture to pan, add sprouts and stir-fry for 1-2 minutes longer.

3 To make sauce, place sesame oil, soy sauce, oyster sauce and sherry in a small bowl and whisk to combine. Add sauce to meat mixture and cook for 1-2 minutes or until heated. Sprinkle with sesame seeds and serve immediately.

Serving suggestion: For a complete meal accompany with rice or noodles.

BEEF WITH SATAY SAUCE

Serves 6

- [ ] **$1^1/_2$ lb/750 g boneless lean top round or blade steak**

SOY AND GINGER MARINADE
- [ ] **2 tablespoons soy sauce**
- [ ] **2 teaspoons cornstarch**
- [ ] **2 tablespoons honey**
- [ ] **1 teaspoon grated fresh ginger**
- [ ] **1 clove garlic, crushed**
- [ ] **1 teaspoon finely grated lemon rind**
- [ ] **1 tablespoon dry sherry**

SATAY SAUCE
- [ ] **$^1/_2$ cup/125 g peanut butter**
- [ ] **3 tablespoons finely chopped unsalted peanuts**
- [ ] **$^3/_4$ cup/185 mL chicken stock**
- [ ] **$^1/_3$ cup/90 mL dry white wine**
- [ ] **1 tablespoon soy sauce**
- [ ] **1 teaspoon finely grated lemon rind**
- [ ] **1 teaspoon grated fresh ginger root**
- [ ] **1 clove garlic, crushed**
- [ ] **1 teaspoon chili sauce**
- [ ] **$^1/_2$ teaspoon curry paste**

1 Cut meat into 1 in/2.5 cm cubes and thread onto twelve lightly oiled skewers. Place skewers in a shallow glass or ceramic dish.

2 To make marinade, place soy sauce, cornstarch, honey, ginger, garlic, lemon rind and sherry in small bowl and whisk to combine. Pour marinade over meat, cover and set aside to marinate for 2-3 hours or overnight.

3 Remove skewers from marinade and cook under preheated medium-high broiler, turning and basting frequently with any remaining marinade for 5-6 minutes or until cooked to your liking.

4 To make sauce, place peanut butter, peanuts, stock, wine, soy sauce, lemon rind, ginger, garlic, chili sauce and curry paste in a saucepan and cook, stirring, over a low heat for 2-3 minutes or until heated through and all ingredients are blended. Spoon sauce over skewers and serve.

Marinating: This is a clever way of tenderizing and adding flavor to less tender cuts of meat. To make a basic marinade you require oil; flavorings such as herbs and spices; and an acid ingredient such as wine, soy sauce, lemon or wine vinegar to break down tough meat fibers. Place the meat and marinade in a bowl, cover and store in the refrigerator until required. The quantity of marinade should be just sufficient to form a pool to coat the meat. Turn the meat occasionally during marinating to ensure all sides come into contact with the marinade.

MARINATED RABBIT IN RED WINE SAUCE

Serves 6
Oven temperature 350°F, 180°C

- [ ] **3 x 2 lb/1 kg rabbits, cleaned and each sectioned into 4 portions**
- [ ] **$^1/_4$ cup/$^1/_2$ stick/60 g butter**
- [ ] **2 tablespoons olive oil**
- [ ] **6 slices bacon, chopped**
- [ ] **12 baby onions**
- [ ] **3 tablespoons all-purpose flour**
- [ ] **3 cups/750 mL chicken stock**
- [ ] **$^1/_4$ cup/60 mL port**
- [ ] **2 tablespoons French Dijon mustard**
- [ ] **$^1/_4$ cup/60 g tomato paste**
- [ ] **8 oz/250 g button mushrooms**
- [ ] **440 g/14 oz canned butter beans**
- [ ] **2 bay leaves**
- [ ] **1 tablespoon chopped fresh oregano**
- [ ] **freshly ground black pepper**

RED WINE MARINADE
- [ ] **1 large carrot, diced**
- [ ] **2 stalks celery, sliced**
- [ ] **1 large onion, sliced**
- [ ] **3 bay leaves**
- [ ] **2 cloves garlic, crushed**
- [ ] **4 whole cloves**
- [ ] **1 tablespoon finely chopped fresh tarragon**
- [ ] **1 tablespoon finely chopped fresh parsley**
- [ ] **$^1/_2$ cup/125 mL olive oil**
- [ ] **red wine**

1   To make marinade, place carrot, celery, sliced onion, bay leaves, garlic, cloves, tarragon, parsley and oil in a large glass or ceramic bowl. Add rabbit and enough red wine to cover mixture. Cover and set aside to marinate overnight. Strain marinade into a clean bowl and reserve. Discard vegetables.

2   Melt 2 tablespoons 30 g butter with oil in a large flameproof casserole. Add rabbit and bake for 20-25 minutes or until lightly browned. Remove rabbit from casserole, set aside and keep warm. Place casserole with meat juices over a high heat. Stir in bacon and baby onions and cook for 4-5 minutes or until onions are golden. Remove from dish and set aside.

3   Melt remaining butter in casserole, stir in flour and cook over a medium heat until dark brown, taking care not to burn. Combine 3 cups/750 mL reserved marinade, chicken stock and port. Remove casserole from heat and gradually blend in marinade mixture. Cook over a medium heat, stirring constantly, until sauce boils and thickens.

4   Reduce heat and whisk in mustard and tomato paste. Return rabbit, bacon and onions to dish and bake for 30 minutes. Stir in mushrooms, beans, bay leaves and oregano. Season to taste with black pepper and bake for 30 minutes longer, or until rabbit is tender.

RABBIT-FILLED PEPPERS

Serves 4
Oven temperature 350°F, 180°C

- [ ] **4 red or green peppers**
- [ ] **$^1/_4$ cup/$^1/_2$ stick/60 g butter**
- [ ] **1$^1/_2$ lb/750 g rabbit, boned and flesh finely chopped**
- [ ] **2 onions, chopped**
- [ ] **4 oz/125 g mushrooms, chopped**
- [ ] **3 spinach leaves, stalks removed and leaves chopped**
- [ ] **$^1/_2$ cup/125 mL dry white wine**
- [ ] **$^1/_2$ cup/125 mL chicken stock**
- [ ] **1 tablespoon tomato paste**
- [ ] **freshly ground black pepper**
- [ ] **2 tablespoons chopped fresh parsley**
- [ ] **3 teaspoons chopped fresh rosemary**

1   Cut a 1 in/2.5 cm slice from the top of each pepper and set aside. Scrape seeds from peppers. Place pepper shells on a baking sheet and bake for 20 minutes or until shells are tender but still holding their shape.

2   Melt butter in a skillet, add rabbit and onions and cook, stirring, for 5 minutes or until lightly browned. Add mushrooms and spinach and cook, stirring, for 1 minute longer. Stir in wine, bring to the boil and boil until liquid is reduced by half. Stir in stock, tomato paste and black pepper to taste, bring back to the boil, then reduce heat and simmer for 15 minutes. Stir in parsley and rosemary.

3   Fill pepper shells with rabbit mixture, top with reserved pepper tops and bake for 15 minutes.

LAMB AND VEGETABLE HOTPOT

Serves 6

- [ ] **1$^1/_2$ lb/750 g boneless leg of lamb, cut into $^3/_4$ in/2 cm cubes**
- [ ] **2 tablespoons seasoned flour**
- [ ] **1 tablespoon/15 g butter**
- [ ] **2 tablespoons oil**
- [ ] **6 baby onions, peeled and bases left intact**
- [ ] **6 baby new potatoes**
- [ ] **2 cloves garlic, crushed**
- [ ] **3 stalks celery, sliced**
- [ ] **1 red pepper, sliced**
- [ ] **2 slices bacon, chopped**
- [ ] **1 carrot, sliced**
- [ ] **1$^1/_2$ cups/375 mL beef stock**
- [ ] **$^1/_2$ cup/125 mL red wine**
- [ ] **1 tablespoon tomato paste**
- [ ] **2 tablespoons finely chopped fresh rosemary**
- [ ] **8 oz/250 g green beans, trimmed and cut into 1 in/ 2.5 cm lengths**
- [ ] **1 tablespoon cornstarch blended with 2 tablespoons water**
- [ ] **freshly ground black pepper**

1   Toss meat in flour. Heat butter and 1 tablespoon oil in a large heavy-based saucepan and cook meat in batches until brown on all sides. Remove from pan and set aside.

2   Heat remaining oil in pan and cook onions and potatoes until brown on all sides. Remove from pan and set aside. Add garlic, celery, red pepper and bacon and cook for 4-5 minutes. Return meat, onions and potatoes to pan. Mix in carrot, stock, wine, tomato paste and rosemary, bring to the boil, then reduce heat and simmer, covered, for 1 hour or until meat is tender. Stir in beans and cornstarch mixture, season to taste with black pepper and cook for 10 minutes longer.

Lamb and Vegetable Hotpot,
Marinated Rabbit in Red Wine Sauce

ROAST CHICKEN WITH BREAD STUFFING

A stuffing transforms succulent roast chicken into something extra special. For a change, instead of placing the stuffing in the cavity of the bird try placing it between the skin and the flesh.

Serves 4
Oven temperature 350°F, 180°C

- ☐ 1 x 3 lb/1.5 kg chicken
- ☐ 2 tabelspoons/30 g butter, melted
- ☐ 2 cloves garlic, crushed

BASIC BREAD STUFFING
- ☐ 2 cups/125 g bread crumbs, made from stale bread
- ☐ 1 onion, finely chopped
- ☐ ¼ cup/½ stick/60 g butter, melted
- ☐ 1 egg, lightly beaten
- ☐ 3 oz/90 g pine nuts (pignola), toasted
- ☐ 2 teaspoons chopped fresh parsley
- ☐ 1 tablespoon chopped fresh rosemary
- ☐ freshly ground black pepper

1 To make stuffing, combine bread crumbs, onion, butter, egg, pine nuts, parsley and rosemary in a bowl and mix well. Season to taste with black pepper and fill cavity of chicken with stuffing. Secure opening with metal or bamboo skewers.
2 Tuck wings under body of chicken and tie legs together. Place bird breast side up in a baking dish. Combine butter and garlic, brush over chicken and bake, turning several times, for 1-1½ hours or until bird is cooked.

STUFFING VARIATIONS
Fruity Stuffing: Soak ½ cup/125 g chopped dried mixed fruit in ½ cup/125 mL of dry white wine for 30 minutes. Mix into the basic stuffing. Fruits such as apricots, prunes and currants are popular choices. Replace the rosemary with 1 teaspoon ground cinnamon.
Ham and Mushroom Stuffing: Add to the basic stuffing 4 oz/125 g finely chopped ham, 3 oz/90 g sliced button mushrooms that have been cooked in 1 teaspoon olive oil, and 1 tablespoon Dijon mustard.
Hot 'n' Spicy Stuffing: Add ½ teaspoon chili powder to the basic stuffing. Replace pine nuts with the same quantity of sunflower seeds and replace parsley and rosemary with 1 teaspoon ground cumin and 1 teaspoon garam masala.

Cook's tip: To test when a bird is cooked, place a skewer into the thickest part of the bird and when the skewer is removed the juices should run clear. If the juices are tinged pink return the bird to the oven and continue cooking.

On completion of cooking allow whole birds to stand for 10-20 minutes. This tenderizes the meat by allowing the juices to settle into the flesh.

FETA DRUMSTICKS

Serves 6
Oven temperature 350°F,180°C

- ☐ 2 tablespoons/30 g butter
- ☐ 1 clove garlic, crushed
- ☐ 1 bunch/1 lb/500 g spinach, finely shredded
- ☐ 2 slices ham, finely chopped
- ☐ ½ cup/125 g feta cheese, broken into small pieces
- ☐ 1 teaspoon ground coriander
- ☐ 3 teaspoons ground nutmeg
- ☐ freshly ground black pepper
- ☐ 12 chicken drumsticks
- ☐ 2 tablespoons olive oil

1 Melt butter in a skillet, add garlic and cook for 1 minute. Stir in half the spinach and cook for 3-4 minutes, or until spinach is tender. Remove from pan and set aside. Repeat with remaining spinach.
2 Combine spinach mixture, ham, cheese, coriander and 1 teaspoon nutmeg. Season to taste with black pepper. Ease skin carefully away from drumstick to form a pocket. Place a spoonful of mixture into the pocket and pull skin over. Repeat with remaining mixture and drumsticks.
3 Brush drumsticks with oil, sprinkle with remaining nutmeg and place in a baking pan. Bake for 30 minutes, or until drumsticks are cooked through.

CHICKEN DRUMSTICK CASSEROLE

Serves 4

- [ ] **8 chicken drumsticks**
- [ ] **$^1/_2$ cup/60 g all-purpose flour**
- [ ] **$^1/_4$ cup/60 mL olive oil**
- [ ] **1 onion, sliced**
- [ ] **1 clove garlic, crushed**
- [ ] **2 tablespoons/30 g butter**
- [ ] **1 cup/250 mL dry red wine**
- [ ] **$^1/_2$ cup/125 mL chicken stock**
- [ ] **14 oz/440 g canned tomatoes, undrained and mashed**
- [ ] **2 teaspoons finely chopped fresh rosemary**
- [ ] **8 oz/250 g button mushrooms, halved**
- [ ] **$^1/_4$ cup/60 mL cream**
- [ ] **freshly ground black pepper**

1   Coat drumsticks with $^1/_3$ cup/45 g of the flour. Heat half the oil in a large skillet, add drumsticks and brown. Remove from pan and set aside.

2   Add onion and garlic to pan and cook for 3-4 minutes or until onion is soft. Add butter and melt. Stir in remaining flour and cook for 1 minute. Return chicken to pan.

3   Combine wine, stock, tomatoes and rosemary and add to pan. Bring to the boil and simmer for 30 minutes, or until drumsticks are cooked through.

4   Heat remaining oil in a small skillet and cook mushrooms for 3-4 minutes. Stir mushrooms and cream into chicken mixture. Season to taste with black pepper.

Cook's tip: You may wish to use a variety of chicken pieces, such as wings or thighs, with the drumsticks. If you are watching your weight, remove the skin from the chicken before cooking. Most of the fat in the chicken is found in the skin.

Feta Drumsticks, Chicken Drumstick Casserole

MASTER CLASS

WHOLE FISH WITH ORANGE AND TOMATO BUTTER

Serves 2

- ☐ **2 lb/1 kg whole snapper**
- ☐ **2 tablespoons/30 g butter**
- ☐ **3 spring onions, finely chopped**
- ☐ **1 clove garlic, crushed**
- ☐ **1 large orange, segmented**
- ☐ **1 tablespoon chopped fresh parsley**
- ☐ **$^1/_2$ cup/30 g bread crumbs, made from stale bread**

ORANGE AND TOMATO BUTTER
- ☐ **$^1/_2$ cup/1 stick/125 g butter, softened**
- ☐ **1 tablespoon grated orange rind**
- ☐ **1 tablespoon orange juice**
- ☐ **2 teaspoons tomato catsup**
- ☐ **freshly ground black pepper**

1   Run a knife inside fish across bones, starting from head and working down to the tail to remove bones, taking care not to cut through back. Turn fish and repeat with other side. Cut center bone at both ends and gently lift out bone.

2   Melt butter in a skillet. Cook spring onions and garlic for 1-2 minutes. Remove from heat and stir in orange, parsley and bread crumbs, then spread inside fish. Place on a greased sheet of aluminum foil, fold aluminum foil over at top and completely seal ends. Barbecue until fish is tender and flesh flakes when tested.

3   To make Orange and Tomato Butter, combine butter, rind, juice and sauce and mix well. Season to taste with black pepper. Form into a sausage shape on a piece of aluminum foil, wrap and refrigerate until firm. Cut into slices and serve with fish.

Cook's tip: Snapper is a warm water sea fish with a delicate white flesh — if unavailable, substitute any other white-fleshed fish.

Run a knife inside fish across bones, starting from head and working down to the tail to remove bones. Take care not to cut through back.

Segment orange for stuffing.

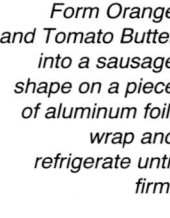

Form Orange and Tomato Butter into a sausage shape on a piece of aluminum foil, wrap and refrigerate until firm.

LAMB CASSEROLE WITH A CHEESY COBBLER TOPPING

Serves 4
Oven temperature 350°F, 180°C

- [ ] 1¹/₂ lb/750 g boneless lean lamb, diced
- [ ] flour
- [ ] 2 tablespoons olive oil

MUSHROOM SAUCE
- [ ] 4 oz/125 g mushrooms, sliced
- [ ] 1 clove garlic, crushed
- [ ] 3 spring onions, chopped
- [ ] 1 teaspoon Dijon mustard
- [ ] 1¹/₄ cups/315 mL chicken stock
- [ ] 2 teaspoons cornstarch blended with ¹/₂ cup/125 mL thick cream or evaporated milk
- [ ] freshly ground black pepper

CHEESY COBBLER TOPPING
- [ ] 2 cups/250 g self-rising flour
- [ ] pinch cayenne pepper
- [ ] pinch chili powder
- [ ] ¹/₂ cup/1 stick/125 g butter
- [ ] 1 egg, lightly beaten
- [ ] ¹/₂ cup/125 mL milk
- [ ] ³/₄ cup/90 g shredded Cheddar cheese
- [ ] ¹/₂ teaspoon dry mustard

1   Toss meat in flour. Heat oil in a large skillet, add meat and cook in batches until browned on all sides. Transfer meat to a shallow casserole dish.
2   To make sauce, add mushrooms, garlic and spring onions to pan and cook, stirring frequently, until mushrooms are soft. Place mushroom mixture on top of meat. Combine Dijon mustard and stock, pour into pan and bring to the boil. Whisk cornstarch mixture into stock mixture and cook over a medium heat, stirring constantly, until sauce boils and thickens. Spoon sauce over meat and mushrooms, cover and bake for 40 minutes or until meat is tender.
3   To make topping, sift flour, cayenne and chili powder together into a large bowl. Rub in three-quarters of the butter until mixture resembles fine bread crumbs. Combine egg and milk and pour into flour mixture all at once. Stir ingredients together to give a soft, sticky dough. Turn dough onto a lightly floured surface and knead briefly. Roll out dough to ¹/₂ in/1 cm thick and cut into 2 in/5 cm rounds.
4   Remove casserole from oven, uncover and quickly top with dough rounds. Melt remaining butter and combine with cheese and mustard. Spread cheese mixture over topping and bake at 425°F/220°C for 12 - 15 minutes or until topping is golden and cooked through.

HAM STEAKS WITH CRANBERRY SAUCE

If you prefer, substitute cream cheese or ricotta cheese for the cottage cheese.

Serves 4

- [ ] 1 tablespoon/15 g butter
- [ ] 4 small smoked ham center slices

CRANBERRY SAUCE
- [ ] ¹/₂ cup/125 mL cranberry sauce
- [ ] ¹/₄ cup/60 g redcurrant jelly
- [ ] 1 tablespoon port (optional)

TOPPING
- [ ] 1 cup/250 g cottage cheese
- [ ] 2 spring onions, finely chopped
- [ ] 2 oz/60 g alfalfa sprouts

1   Melt butter in a skillet and cook ham steaks over medium heat for 1-2 minutes each side. Remove from pan and keep warm.
2   To make sauce, combine cranberry sauce, redcurrant jelly and port, if used, in the pan. Stir over low heat until well mixed.
3   Combine cottage cheese and spring onions. Top each steak with sprouts and cottage cheese mixture and spoon sauce over to serve.

BEEF IN COCONUT MILK

A thick, spicy sauce coats the meat and makes for a satisfying meal.

Serves 4

- [ ] 2 onions, chopped
- [ ] 1 tablespoon chili paste (sambal oelek)
- [ ] ¹/₄ cup/30 g chopped almonds
- [ ] ¹/₂ teaspoon dried shrimp paste
- [ ] 1 cup/250 mL water
- [ ] 2 tablespoons peanut oil
- [ ] 1 lb/500 g lean top round steak, cut into 1 in/2.5 cm cubes
- [ ] 1 cup/250 mL coconut milk
- [ ] 1 tablespoon mango chutney
- [ ] 3 tablespoons lime or lemon juice

1   Place onions, chili paste (sambal oelek), almonds, shrimp paste and 1 tablespoon water in a food processor or blender and process until smooth.
2   Heat oil in a large saucepan, add onion mixture and cook over a low heat, stirring, for 5 minutes. Add meat and cook, stirring, for 2-3 minutes or until meat just changes color.
3   Stir in remaining water, cover, bring to simmering and simmer for 1 hour or until meat is tender.
4   Place coconut milk, chutney and lime or lemon juice in a bowl and mix to combine. Stir into meat mixture, bring back to simmering and simmer, stirring occasionally, for 10-15 minutes longer or until heated through.

Coconut milk: You can make coconut milk using unsweetened shredded or fresh grated coconut and water. To make, place 1 lb/500 g coconut in a bowl, pour over 3 cups/750 mL boiling water and allow to stand for 30 minutes. Strain, squeezing the coconut to extract as much liquid as possible. This will make a thick coconut milk. The coconut can be used again to make a weaker coconut milk.

BRUSSELS SPROUTS AND HAM PIE

This impressive deep pot pie is a meal in itself. You can serve it with a mixed green salad and some crusty bread, and finish the meal with fresh fruit. What could be easier or more delicious for a family meal or for casual entertaining?

Serves 6
Oven temperature 400°F, 200°C

- [ ] 1 sheet/250 g frozen pre-rolled puff pastry, thawed
- [ ] 1 egg, lightly beaten with 1 tablespoon water

BRUSSELS SPROUTS AND HAM FILLING
- [ ] 1 lb/500 g Brussels sprouts, trimmed
- [ ] 2 tablespoons/30 g butter
- [ ] ¹/₄ cup/30 g all-purpose flour
- [ ] ³/₄ cup/375 mL milk
- [ ] 1 cup/125 g shredded Cheddar cheese
- [ ] 8 oz/250 g piece smoked ham, diced
- [ ] freshly ground black pepper

1 To make filling, boil, steam or microwave Brussels sprouts until just tender. Refresh under cold running water, cut into quarters and set aside.

2 Melt butter in saucepan, stir in flour and cook for 1 minute. Gradually stir in milk and cook, stirring constantly, for 4-5 minutes or until sauce boils and thickens. Remove pan from heat, add Brussels sprouts, cheese, ham and black pepper to taste and mix to combine. Set aside to cool completely.

3 Spoon cooled filling into a 4 cup/1 liter capacity casserole. If necessary, roll out pastry to 2 in/5 cm larger than pie dish, Cut off a $^1/_2$ in/1 cm strip from pastry edge. Brush rim of casserole with water and press pastry strip onto rim. Brush pastry strip with water. Lift pastry top over filling and press gently to seal edges. Trim and press back edges to make a decorative edge. Cut slits in top of pie and decorate with pastry leaves made from trimming. Brush pastry with egg mixture and bake for 30 minutes or until pastry is golden and crisp.

STEAKS WITH GARLIC TOMATO CONCASSE

For a change try the concasse with lamb chops or boneless chicken breasts.

Serves 6

☐ **6 x 4 oz/125 g boneless rib eye steaks (Delmonico)**

GARLIC TOMATO CONCASSE
☐ **4 large tomatoes, peeled and chopped**
☐ **2 cloves garlic, crushed**
☐ **2 tablespoons finely chopped chives**
☐ **freshly ground black pepper**

1 To make concasse, place tomatoes, garlic and chives in a saucepan. Cook over a medium heat for 8-10 minutes or until tomatoes are just soft. Season to taste with black pepper.

2 Trim all visible fat from meat. Heat a nonstick skillet and cook steaks over medium-high heat for 4-5 minutes each side. Spoon sauce over steaks and serve immediately.

ATHENIAN LAMB KABOBS

These Mediterranean-flavored kabobs will quickly become a family favorite.

Serves 6

☐ **1$^1/_2$ lb/750 g boneless lean lamb, cubed and trimmed of fat**
☐ **12 bay leaves**
☐ **1 large onion, cut into eighths**
☐ **12 cherry tomatoes**
☐ **1 green pepper, cubed**

LEMON MARINADE
☐ **1 tablespoon olive oil**
☐ **$^1/_4$ cup/60 mL lemon juice**
☐ **1 teaspoon finely chopped fresh rosemary**
☐ **3 tablespoons finely chopped fresh parsley**
☐ **freshly ground black pepper**
☐ **dash hot red pepper sauce**

1 To make marinade, combine oil, lemon juice, rosemary, parsley, black pepper to taste and pepper sauce in a glass bowl. Add meat, toss to coat and marinate for 30 minutes.

2 Remove meat from marinade and thread on to twelve oiled wooden skewers, alternating with bay leaves, onion, tomatoes and pepper.

3 Barbecue or broil kabobs slowly, turning and basting frequently with remaining marinade, until well browned and cooked.

Athenian Lamb Kabobs

CHEESE, SALAMI AND SPINACH STRUDEL

Serves 6
Oven temperature 350°F, 180°C

- [ ] **8 sheets fillo (phyllo) pastry**
- [ ] **¹/₄ cup/60 mL olive oil**

FILLING
- [ ] **4 slices mozzarella cheese**
- [ ] **15 slices soft salami**
- [ ] **¹/₂ cup/125 mL tomato catsup**
- [ ] **¹/₂ teaspoon dried sweet basil leaves**
- [ ] **6 large spinach leaves, shredded**
- [ ] **1 egg, beaten**
- [ ] **10 oz/315 g canned or bottled red peppers, drained and sliced**
- [ ] **4 oz/125 g pepperoni, skin removed and cut into thin slices**
- [ ] **20 stuffed olives, cut in half lengthwise**
- [ ] **2 tablespoons grated Parmesan cheese**

1 Lay pastry sheets on top of each other, brushing between each layer with oil.
2 Place a layer of mozzarella evenly down the long edge of pastry, leaving about 2 in/5 cm at each end, and top with rolled up soft salami. Pour over combined tomato catsup and basil. Arrange spinach over catsup, top evenly with beaten egg. Place peppers over spinach then top with a row each of pepperoni slices and olives.
3 Roll up tightly to enclose filling and tuck ends under. Transfer to a baking sheet, brush with oil, sprinkle with Parmesan cheese and bake for 30 minutes or until lightly browned. Serve sliced.

Cook's tip: When working with fillo pastry, cover any sheets that are not immediately in use with a dampened tea towel, to prevent them from drying out.

PEPPERED ROAST WITH BRANDY CREAM SAUCE

Serves 4
Oven temperature 400°F, 200°C

- [ ] **1 piece boneless sirloin steak, 1¹/₂ in/4 cm thick and about 1¹/₂ lb/750 g in weight**
- [ ] **4 tablespoons cracked black peppercorns**
- [ ] **2 teaspoons vegetable oil**

SAUCE
- [ ] **¹/₂ cup/125 mL beef stock**
- [ ] **¹/₄ cup/60 mL dry white wine**
- [ ] **2 teaspoons brandy**
- [ ] **2 tablespoons cream**

1 Trim all visible fat from meat. Press both sides of steak into peppercorns.
2 Heat oil in a flameproof baking dish. Add meat and brown well on each side. Transfer to oven. Bake for 30-35 minutes or until cooked as desired. Remove meat from dish and cover with aluminum foil. Stand 5 minutes before serving.
3 To make sauce, combine stock, wine and brandy and pour into baking dish. Stir over medium heat for 2-3 minutes lifting sediment from base of dish. Remove from heat and whisk in cream. Slice steak, spoon over sauce and serve.

Microwave it: Prepare ingredients. Preheat browning dish on 100% (HIGH) for 7 minutes. Add oil and steak and cook on MEDIUM/HIGH (70%) 10 minutes, turning after 5 minutes. Remove from dish and stand covered for 10 minutes. Combine stock, wine and brandy. Pour into browning dish. Cook on HIGH (100%) for 2-3 minutes, stirring during cooking.

*Ham Steaks with Cranberry Sauce,
Cheese, Salami and Spinach Strudel,
Peppered Roast with Brandy Cream Sauce*

BEEF AND PICKLED VEGETABLE OMELET

The Chinese mixed vegetables used as the filling for this omelet are available from most Oriental supermarkets.

Serves 4

- ☐ **2 tablespoons peanut oil**
- ☐ **8 oz/250 g lean ground beef**
- ☐ **2 tablespoons bottled Chinese mixed vegetables (tung chai), drained and chopped**
- ☐ **1 teaspoon honey**
- ☐ **2 tablespoons soy sauce**
- ☐ **6 spring onions, finely chopped**
- ☐ **6 eggs, lightly beaten**

1   Heat half the oil in a skillet, add beef, vegetables, honey, soy and spring onions, and stir-fry for 3-4 minutes. Remove from pan, set aside and keep warm.

2   Heat remaining oil in a clean skillet. Pour in a quarter of the beaten eggs. Swirl pan over heat to make a thin omelet.

3   Spoon a quarter of the meat mixture into the center of the omelet and fold over the edges.

4   Remove from pan and keep warm. Repeat with remaining eggs and meat mixture. Cut omelets into slices and serve immediately.

Beef and Pickled Vegetable Omelet

CHICKEN WITH AROMATIC SPICES AND CASHEWS

The addition of coconut milk to aromatic spices gives this quick curry a special touch.

Serves 4

- ☐ **1 onion, finely chopped**
- ☐ **2 cloves garlic, crushed**
- ☐ **$^1/_2$ teaspoon sugar**
- ☐ **$^1/_2$ teaspoon black mustard seeds**
- ☐ **$^1/_2$ teaspoon curry paste**
- ☐ **pinch chili powder**
- ☐ **1 teaspoon fish sauce**
- ☐ **1 tablespoon lime or lemon juice**
- ☐ **1 lb/500 g chicken pieces**
- ☐ **1 tablespoon peanut oil**
- ☐ **1 stalk fresh lemon grass, finely chopped**
- ☐ **1 cup/250 mL coconut milk**
- ☐ **$^1/_2$ cup/125 mL water**
- ☐ **$^1/_4$ cup/45 g chopped roasted cashews**

1 Combine onion, garlic, sugar, mustard seeds, curry paste, chili powder, fish sauce and lime or lemon juice in a glass bowl. Add chicken, toss well and set aside to marinate for 30 minutes.

2 Heat oil in a large skillet and stir-fry lemon grass for a few seconds. Add the chicken mixture to the pan and cook for 4-5 minutes each side.

3 Stir in the coconut milk and water. Simmer for 15-20 minutes or until chicken is tender and sauce thickens. To serve, top with cashews.

Cook's tip: Lemon grass is used extensively in Sri Lankan and Southeast Asian cookery. It is used to flavor curry, meat and fish dishes as well as sweet desserts. Lemon grass is available from Asian supermarkets in both the fresh and dried forms. There is also a powdered form available which is called 'sereh this is strong in flavor and should be used with discretion. If lemon grass is unavailable lemon balm, lemon verbena and lemon rind are possible substitutes.

LAMB WITH GINGER AND HONEY

Lamb, ginger and honey are a wonderful combination in this timesaving treat.

Serves 4

- ☐ **2 tablespoons peanut oil**
- ☐ **3 cloves garlic, crushed**
- ☐ **1 tablespoon grated fresh ginger**
- ☐ **1 lb/500 g lean lamb center slice, cut into thin strips**
- ☐ **1 onion, cut into eighths**
- ☐ **6 oz/185 g oyster mushrooms, sliced**
- ☐ **5 oz/155 g snow peas**
- ☐ **2 tablespoons soy sauce**
- ☐ **1 tablespoon honey**
- ☐ **2 teaspoons lime juice**

1 Heat half the oil in a skillet or wok and stir-fry garlic and ginger for a few seconds. Add meat in batches and stir-fry for 2-3 minutes each batch. Remove from pan and set aside.

2 Heat remaining oil and cook onion, mushrooms and snow peas for 2-3 minutes. Return meat to the pan with vegetables and stir-fry for 1 minute.

3 Combine soy sauce, honey and lime juice and add to the pan. Stir-fry for 1-2 minutes more or until heated through. Serve immediately.

Chicken with Aromatic Spices and Cashews, Lamb with Ginger and Honey

ORIENTAL CHICKEN SALAD

Our light chicken salad is easy to prepare and makes a tasty alternative to heavier, more traditional chicken salads.

Serves 4

- [ ] **4 x 4 oz/125 g boned skinned chicken breast halves**
- [ ] **1 large carrot**
- [ ] **¹/₂ bunch/4 oz/125 g watercress**
- [ ] **¹/₄ small red cabbage, shredded**
- [ ] **3¹/₂ oz/100 g bean sprouts**
- [ ] **¹/₃ cup/90 mL lime juice**

ORIENTAL MARINADE
- [ ] **2 tablespoons dry sherry**
- [ ] **1 tablespoon soy sauce**
- [ ] **2 teaspoons hoisin sauce**
- [ ] **2 teaspoons peanut oil**
- [ ] **2 cloves garlic, crushed**

1   Place chicken breasts between two sheets of plastic food wrap and pound lightly to flatten.
2   To make marinade, combine sherry, soy sauce, hoisin sauce, oil and garlic in a glass bowl. Add chicken and marinate for 1-2 hours.
3   Remove chicken from marinade and barbecue or broil slowly, turning and basting frequently with remaining marinade. Cool and slice thinly.
4   Using a vegetable peeler, slice carrot thinly, lengthwise. Soak slices in iced water for 5-10 minutes. Drain and arrange attractively on individual serving plates with watercress, cabbage and bean sprouts. Sprinkle with lime juice and top with chicken slices. Serve chilled.

CHICKEN AND SPINACH PARCELS

If you are having a dinner party, these chicken parcels make a great main course. Prepare them earlier in the day and cook when required.

Serves 4
Oven temperature 400°F, 200°C

- [ ] **4 x 4 oz/125 g boned skinned chicken breast halves**
- [ ] **¹/₃ cup/90 mL chicken stock**
- [ ] **¹/₃ cup/90 mL dry sherry**
- [ ] **freshly ground black pepper**

SPINACH FILLING
- [ ] **8 large spinach leaves, shredded**
- [ ] **1 large carrot, cut into thin strips**
- [ ] **1 stalk celery, cut into thin strips**
- [ ] **1 leek, cut into thin strips**
- [ ] **pinch ground nutmeg**

1   Place chicken breasts between two sheets of plastic food wrap and pound lightly to flatten.
2   Steam or microwave spinach, carrot, celery and leek until tender. Refresh under cold running water. Pat dry on paper towels. Season to taste with nutmeg and black pepper.
3   Cut four large squares of parchment paper and top each with a chicken breast. Place spinach, carrot, celery and leek over half of each breast. Fold to enclose filling. Sprinkle with stock, sherry and black pepper to taste. Seal the edges of the paper carefully and place parcels on a baking sheet. Bake for 15-20 minutes or until tender. Chill for 1 hour before serving.

Oriental Chicken Salad, Chicken and Spinach Parcels

CREAMY CHICKEN PIE

Serves 6
Oven temperature 400°F, 200°C

CHEESE PASTRY
- ☐ **2 cups/250 g all-purpose flour, sifted**
- ☐ **$^1/_2$ cup/60 g shredded Cheddar cheese**
- ☐ **1 teaspoon dry mustard powder**
- ☐ **$^1/_2$ teaspoon cayenne pepper**
- ☐ **$^3/_4$ cup/1$^1/_2$ sticks/180 g butter, chilled and cut into small cubes**
- ☐ **1 egg yolk, lightly beaten**
- ☐ **4-5 tablespoons water, chilled**

CHICKEN FILLING
- ☐ **1 tablespoon olive oil**
- ☐ **1$^1/_2$ lb/750 g boned skinned chicken breast halves, chopped**
- ☐ **$^1/_4$ cup/$^1/_2$ stick/60 g butter**
- ☐ **1 clove garlic, crushed**
- ☐ **1 stalk celery, chopped**
- ☐ **1 onion, chopped**
- ☐ **$^1/_4$ cup/1 oz all-purpose flour**
- ☐ **1 cup/250 mL chicken stock**
- ☐ **1 cup/250 mL milk**
- ☐ **1 tablespoon chopped fresh parsley**
- ☐ **1 tablespoon chopped fresh rosemary or 1 teaspoon dried rosemary**
- ☐ **freshly ground black pepper**

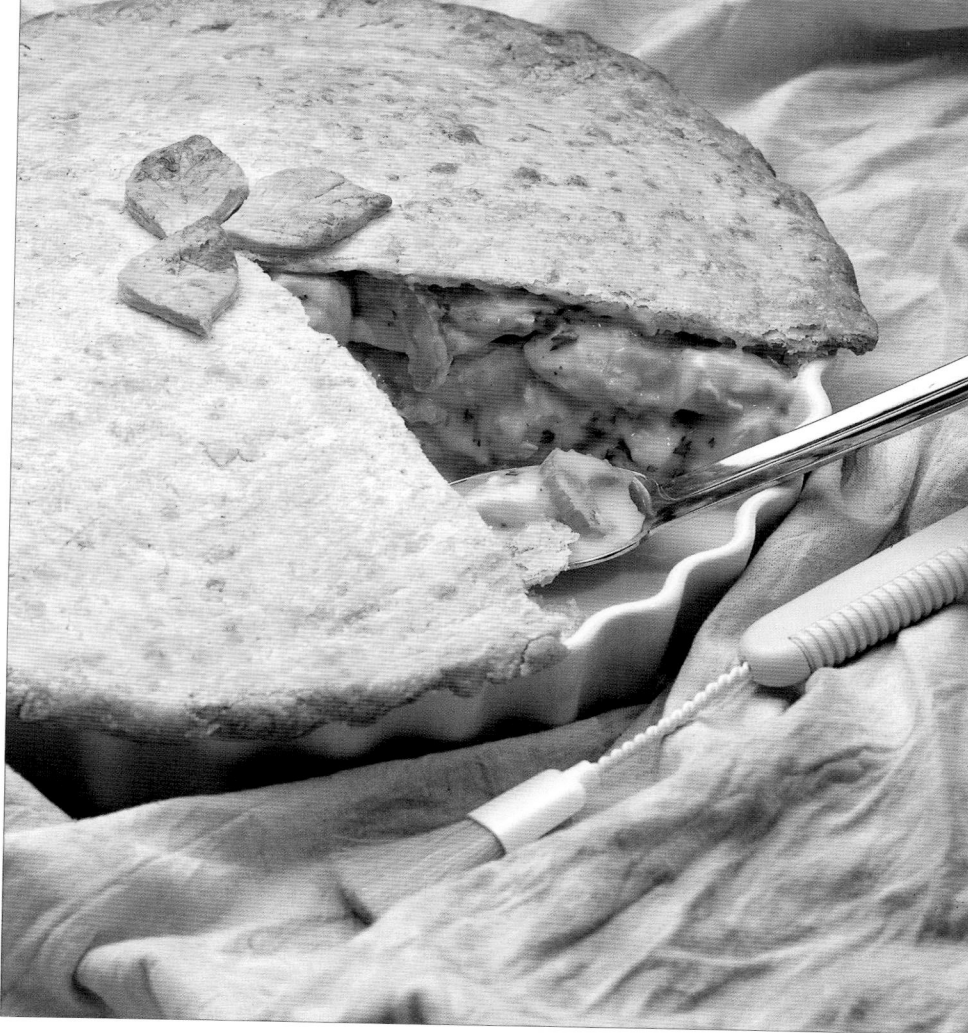

1 To prepare pastry, place flour, cheese, mustard and cayenne pepper in a bowl and mix to combine. Cut in butter cubes with knives or pastry blender until the mixture resembles coarse bread crumbs.
2 Mix in egg yolk and enough water to form a soft dough with a fork. Turn onto a lightly floured surface and knead gently until smooth. Wrap pastry in plastic food wrap and refrigerate for 30 minutes.
3 To make filling, heat oil in a large skillet and cook chicken in batches over a high heat for 3 minutes or until browned. Remove chicken from pan and set aside.
4 Melt butter in a skillet, add garlic, celery and onion and cook, stirring, for 3-4 minutes or until onion is soft. Stir in flour and cook for 1 minute longer. Remove pan from heat and whisk in stock and milk. Return pan to heat and cook, stirring constantly, for 4-5 minutes or until sauce boils and thickens. Add chicken, parsley, rosemary and black pepper to taste to sauce and mix well to combine. Remove pan from heat and set aside to cool completely.
5 Place cooled filling in a 4 cup/1 liter capacity casserole. Roll out pastry to $^1/_4$ in/

5 mm thick. Brush rim of dish with a little water and place pastry over the filling. Trim edges with a knife and decorate as desired. Brush with a little milk and bake for 30-35 minutes or until pastry is golden.

Pastry-making tips: Place your utensils in the refrigerator to chill for 15-20 minutes before making pastry.

The best pastry is made using chilled butter and water.

Always rest the pastry in the refrigerator for 30 minutes before baking; this will minimize shrinkage during cooking.

VEAL ESCALOPES

Serve this easy veal dish with a fresh green salad.

Serves 4

- ☐ **1 lb/500 g veal leg round steak, thinly sliced**
- ☐ **seasoned flour**
- ☐ **1 egg, lightly beaten**
- ☐ **1$^1/_2$ cups/185 g bread crumbs, made from stale bread**
- ☐ **$^1/_4$ cup/$^1/_2$ stick/60 g butter**
- ☐ **8 slices prosciutto ham**
- ☐ **1 cup/125 g shredded mozzarella cheese**
- ☐ **$^1/_4$ cup/30 g grated Parmesan cheese**
- ☐ **$^1/_2$ cup/125 mL thick cream**

1 Cut veal into 8 pieces, pound to $^1/_8$ in/ 3 mm thickness. Coat veal in flour, then dip in egg and coat in bread crumbs.
2 Melt butter in a large skillet until foaming. Add veal and cook for 2 minutes each side or until golden. Wrap each schnitzel in a slice of prosciutto, place in a shallow baking dish, sprinkle with mozzarella and Parmesan cheese and spoon over cream. Cook under a preheated high broiler for 3-4 minutes or until cheese melts and is golden. Serve immediately.

Creamy Chicken Pie

FIERY CHICKEN NOODLE SOUP

Serves 6

- ☐ 3 cups/4 oz/125 g fresh egg noodles
- ☐ 2 tablespoons peanut oil
- ☐ 2 onions, chopped
- ☐ 2 cloves garlic, crushed
- ☐ 1 fresh red chili, finely sliced
- ☐ 1 teaspoon curry paste (Vindaloo)
- ☐ $\frac{1}{2}$ teaspoon powdered saffron
- ☐ 1 tablespoon finely chopped fresh lemon grass
- ☐ 4 cups/1 liter coconut milk
- ☐ $1\frac{1}{2}$ cups/375 mL chicken stock
- ☐ $1\frac{1}{2}$ cups/375 g finely chopped cooked chicken
- ☐ 3 large spinach leaves, finely shredded

1 Cook noodles in a large saucepan of boiling water for 3-4 minutes or until tender. Drain and rinse noodles under cold running water. Drain and place in individual bowls.
2 Heat oil in a large saucepan, cook onions for 2-3 minutes or until golden. Stir in garlic, chili, curry paste (Vindaloo), saffron and lemon grass. Cook for 1 minute over medium heat.
4 Combine coconut milk and chicken stock, add to pan with chicken and spinach. Simmer for 3-4 minutes. Pour over noodles in bowls to serve.

TANDOORI BEEF RIBS

Serves 4

- ☐ 8 beef shortribs
- ☐ 2 tablespoons peanut oil

YOGURT MARINADE

- ☐ 1 cup/250 g plain yogurt
- ☐ $1\frac{1}{2}$ teaspoons grated fresh ginger
- ☐ 2 cloves garlic, crushed
- ☐ 1 tablespoon hot chili sauce
- ☐ 1 teaspoon ground cumin
- ☐ 1 teaspoon ground cardamom
- ☐ 1 tablespoon finely chopped fresh coriander (cilantro)
- ☐ few drops red food coloring
- ☐ 1 tablespoon tamarind paste
- ☐ $\frac{1}{2}$ cup/125 mL water

1 Trim meat of all visible fat and set aside.
2 To make marinade, combine yogurt, ginger, garlic, chili, cumin, cardamom, coriander and food coloring. Blend tamarind paste with water and fold into yogurt mixture.
3 Rub marinade into meat and chill, covered, for at least 3 hours or overnight.
4 Remove meat from marinade and brush with oil. Broil or barbecue over a medium heat for 8-10 minutes, turning and basting frequently with marinade.

DRY BEEF CURRY

Serve this hot curry with plenty of yogurt or our Cucumber Pickle to soothe and cool the palate.

Serves 4

- ☐ ¹/₃ cup/90 mL melted ghee or clarified butter
- ☐ 1 lb/500 g chuck steak, cubed
- ☐ 1 large onion, chopped
- ☐ 2 fresh red chilies, finely sliced
- ☐ 2 cloves garlic, crushed
- ☐ 1 teaspoon ground coriander
- ☐ 1 teaspoon ground saffron
- ☐ 1 teaspoon ground cumin
- ☐ 1 teaspoon black mustard seeds
- ☐ 1 tablespoon ground garam masala
- ☐ ¹/₂ cup/125 mL water
- ☐ 2 large tomatoes, peeled and chopped
- ☐ 2 curry leaves
- ☐ 1 small cinnamon stick
- ☐ ¹/₄ cup/60 mL plain yogurt

1 Heat ¹/₄ cup/60 mL ghee in a large saucepan, cook meat in batches until brown on all sides. Remove from pan and set aside.

2 Heat remaining ghee in pan, add onion and chili, and cook for 2-3 minutes or until onion is soft and golden brown. Stir in garlic, coriander, saffron, cumin, mustard seeds and half the garam masala. Cook for 1 minute longer.

3 Combine water, tomatoes, curry leaves and cinnamon stick. Stir into pan with onion mixture. Bring to the boil, then reduce heat to simmer. Return meat to the pan and simmer for 1¹/₂ hours or until meat is tender.

4 Remove pan from heat and stir in remaining garam masala and yogurt. Simmer gently for 5 minutes.

Cook's tip: The secret of a good curry depends on how well the onions are browned in the first stage of cooking. Heat the oil or ghee first, add the onions and cook until golden brown. Stir gently throughout cooking, being careful not to burn. Once cooked, add the spices and meat, and stir to coat meat well.

Left: Dry Beef Curry, Tandoori Beef Ribs
Far left: Fiery Chicken Noodle Soup

MASTER CLASS

ROAST TURKEY

The Spaniards brought turkeys to Europe from North America in the 1520s. Cooks soon developed wonderful dishes for special occasions with delicious stuffings and accompaniments. Try this Roast Turkey for a Christmas or Thanksgiving dinner.

Serves 10
Oven temperature 350°F, 180°C,

- [ ] **8 lb/4 kg turkey**
- [ ] **¹/₄ cup/¹/₂ stick/60 g butter, melted**
- [ ] **1 cup/250 mL chicken stock**

VEAL FORCEMEAT
- [ ] **2 tablespoons/30 g butter**
- [ ] **1 onion, finely chopped**
- [ ] **1 slice bacon, finely chopped**
- [ ] **8 oz/250 g lean ground veal**
- [ ] **3 cups/185 g bread crumbs, made from stale bread**
- [ ] **¹/₂ teaspoon finely grated lemon rind**
- [ ] **1 tablespoon finely chopped fresh parsley**
- [ ] **¹/₂ teaspoon dried sage**
- [ ] **pinch ground nutmeg**
- [ ] **freshly ground black pepper**
- [ ] **1 egg, lightly beaten**

APPLE AND CHESTNUT STUFFING
- [ ] **14 oz/440 g canned chestnut purée, sieved**
- [ ] **2 cooking apples, cored, peeled and shredded**
- [ ] **3 cups/185 g bread crumbs, made from stale bread**
- [ ] **1 onion, finely chopped**
- [ ] **1 stalk celery, finely chopped**
- [ ] **¹/₃ cup/45 g finely chopped walnuts**
- [ ] **3 tablespoons/45 g butter, melted**
- [ ] **1 tablespoon finely chopped fresh parsley**
- [ ] **pinch ground nutmeg**
- [ ] **1 egg, lightly beaten**

1   To make forcemeat, melt butter in a skillet and cook onion and bacon for 4-5 minutes or until bacon is crisp. Add veal, bread crumbs, lemon rind, parsley, sage, nutmeg, black pepper to taste and egg. Mix well to combine.

2   To make stuffing, combine chestnut purée, apples, bread crumbs, onion, celery, walnuts, parsley, butter, black pepper to taste, nutmeg and egg.

3   Remove giblets and neck from turkey. Wipe turkey inside and out and dry well. Place stuffing in body cavity and lightly fill neck end of turkey with forcemeat. Secure openings with metal skewers and truss legs and wings.

4   Place turkey on a roasting rack in a baking pan. Brush turkey with butter, then pour chicken stock into pan. Bake for 3-3¹/₂ hours or until tender. Baste frequently with pan juices during cooking. Set aside to stand for 20 minutes before carving.

To make forcemeat, melt butter in a skillet and cook onion and bacon for 4-5 minutes.

Place stuffing in body cavity and lightly fill neck end of turkey with forcemeat.

Secure openings of turkey with metal skewers and truss legs and wings.

LAMB WITH EGG SAUCE

It is important when making this recipe that you do not allow the lamb to boil after adding the egg yolks. This dish is wonderful served with fried eggplant and roasted red peppers.

Serves 8

- [ ] **2 lb/1 kg cubed boneless lamb**
- [ ] **$1/4$ cup/60 mL lemon juice**
- [ ] **2 tablespoons olive oil**
- [ ] **2 tablespoons/30 g butter**
- [ ] **1 onion, sliced**
- [ ] **4 slices packaged ham, chopped**
- [ ] **1 tablespoon all-purpose flour**
- [ ] **1 cup/250 mL dry white wine**
- [ ] **$1/4$ cup/60 mL beef stock**
- [ ] **1 tablespoon finely grated lemon rind**
- [ ] **3 egg yolks, beaten**
- [ ] **2 tablespoons chopped fresh parsley**
- [ ] **1 tablespoon chopped fresh marjoram or 1 teaspoon dried marjoram**

1 Place lamb and 1 tablespoon lemon juice in a bowl and toss to combine. Cover and set aside to marinate for 30 minutes. Drain lamb and pat dry with paper towels.

2 Heat oil and butter in a large skillet, add onion and cook for 4-5 minutes or until soft. Add ham and lamb to pan and cook for 4-5 minutes longer.

3 Stir in flour and cook, stirring, for 3-4 minutes, then stir in wine and stock and bring to the boil. Reduce heat, cover and simmer for 30 minutes or until lamb is tender.

4 Stir in lemon rind and remaining lemon juice and cook for 3 minutes longer. Stir in egg yolks and cook, without boiling, for 3-4 minutes or until heated through. Remove pan from heat, stir in parsley and marjoram and serve immediately.

TOMATO AND BEEF BAKE WITH SESAME SEED TOPPING

Serves 4
Oven temperature 350°F, 180°C

BEEF BURGERS
- [ ] **1 lb/500 g lean ground beef**
- [ ] **1 clove garlic, crushed**
- [ ] **1 onion, chopped**
- [ ] **1 egg, beaten**
- [ ] **$1/3$ cup/30 g instant rolled oats**
- [ ] **1 tablespoon bottled oyster sauce**
- [ ] **1 tablespoon tomato catsup**
- [ ] **2 tablespoons olive oil**

TOMATO SAUCE
- [ ] **1 onion, chopped**
- [ ] **14 oz/440 g canned tomatoes, undrained and mashed**
- [ ] **2 tablespoons tomato paste**
- [ ] **$1/2$ teaspoon sugar**
- [ ] **2 teaspoons cornstarch blended with 2 tablespoons water**

SESAME SEED TOPPING
- [ ] **5 slices bread, buttered, crusts removed**
- [ ] **2 tablespoons sesame seeds**

1 To make burgers, place beef, garlic, onion, egg, oats, oyster sauce and catsup in a bowl and mix to combine. Shape meat mixture into eight patties. Heat oil in a large skillet and cook burgers for 2-3 minutes each side or until browned. Transfer burgers to a baking dish. Drain juices from pan.

2 To make sauce, add onion to pan and cook for 2-3 minutes or until soft. Add tomatoes, tomato paste and sugar and bring to the boil. Whisk in cornstarch mixture and cook, stirring constantly, for 4-5 minutes or until sauce thickens. Pour sauce over burgers.

3 To make topping, cut buttered bread into cubes and arrange over sauce, sprinkle with sesame seeds and bake for 35-40 minutes or until topping is golden.

COTTAGE PIE

It's always a problem knowing what to do with leftover roast meat. This simple cottage pie solves all those worries in next to no time.

Serves 4
Oven temperature 400°F, 200°C

- [ ] **$1^1/2$ cups/375 g finely chopped cooked cold meat, such as lamb or beef**
- [ ] **1 onion, grated**
- [ ] **1 tablespoon tomato catsup**
- [ ] **1 tablespoon chopped fresh parsley**
- [ ] **1 teaspoon dried thyme**
- [ ] **$1/2$ teaspoon dried sage**
- [ ] **$1/2$ teaspoon dried oregano**
- [ ] **freshly ground black pepper**
- [ ] **1 tomato, sliced**

INSTANT POTATO TOPPING
- [ ] **4 oz/125 g instant dried potato flakes**
- [ ] **1 cup/250 mL boiling water**
- [ ] **$1/2$ cup/125 mL milk**
- [ ] **2 tablespoons/30 g butter, melted**
- [ ] **$1/2$ cup/30 g crushed potato chips**

1 Place meat, onion, tomato catsup, parsley, thyme, sage, oregano and black pepper to taste in a bowl and mix to combine. Spoon meat mixture into an 8 in/20 cm casserole dish and top with tomato slices.

2 To make topping, place instant potato flakes, water, milk and butter in a bowl, mix to combine and spread over top of meat mixture. Sprinkle with potato chips and bake for 20-25 minutes or until top is golden and pie is heated through. Allow pie to stand for 5 minutes before serving.

Microwave it: For an even faster meal you can easily make the Cottage Pie in the microwave oven. Use an 8 in/20 cm microwave-safe dish and cook on HIGH (100%) for 4-5 minutes. Stand for 5 minutes before serving.

PORK WITH ORANGE AND CRANBERRY SAUCE

Serves 4

- [ ] **4 x 4 oz/125 g thick pork loin butterfly chops**
- [ ] **cracked black peppercorns**
- [ ] **1 tablespoon olive oil**

CRANBERRY MARINADE
- [ ] **1 cup/250 mL orange juice**
- [ ] **2 teaspoons finely grated orange rind**
- [ ] **$1/4$ teaspoon ground cloves**
- [ ] **$1/4$ cup/60 g cranberry sauce**

1 To make marinade, place orange juice, orange rind, cloves and cranberry sauce in a bowl and mix to combine. Place chops in a shallow glass or ceramic dish, pour over marinade, cover and set aside to marinate for 1-2 hours.

2 Remove chops from marinade and reserve marinade. Coat chops with peppercorns. Heat oil in a large skillet, add chops and cook for 4-5 minutes each side or until cooked. Set aside and keep warm.

3 Strain reserved marinade and pour into a saucepan. Bring to the boil and boil until reduced slightly. Spoon sauce over chops and serve immediately.

MEXICAN CHILI PASTA

Serves 4

- ☐ 1¹/₂ lb/750 g fresh tomato fettuccine

MEXICAN CHILI SAUCE
- ☐ 2 onions, chopped
- ☐ 1 clove garlic, crushed
- ☐ 2 fresh red chilies, finely chopped
- ☐ 1 tablespoon water
- ☐ 14 fl oz/440 mL canned tomato purée
- ☐ 14 oz/440 g canned red kidney beans, drained

1 Cook fettuccine in boiling water in a large saucepan following packet directions. Drain, set aside and keep warm.
2 To make sauce, cook onions, garlic, chilies and water in large saucepan for 3-4 minutes, or until onions are soft. Stir in tomato purée and red kidney beans, bring to the boil, then reduce heat and simmer for 4-5 minutes, or until sauce thickens. Spoon sauce over pasta.

HONEY BEEF

Serves 4

- ☐ 1 tablespoon vegetable oil
- ☐ 1 lb/500 g lean sirloin steak, cut into thin strips
- ☐ 1 red pepper, cut into thin strips
- ☐ 4 large spinach leaves, shredded
- ☐ 3 spring onions, cut into 1¹/₄ in/3 cm diagonal lengths
- ☐ 1 parsnip, cut into thin strips
- ☐ 1 clove garlic, crushed
- ☐ 2 teaspoons grated fresh ginger
- ☐ ¹/₃ cup/90 mL soy sauce
- ☐ 2 teaspoons honey
- ☐ 2 teaspoons cornstarch blended with 2 tablespoons dry sherry

1 Heat half the oil in a skillet or wok. Add meat, red pepper, spinach, spring onions and parsnip, and stir-fry for 2-3 minutes, or until meat changes color. Remove mixture from pan and set aside.

2 Heat remaining oil and stir-fry garlic and ginger for 1-2 minutes. Return beef mixture to the pan. Combine soy sauce, honey and cornstarch mixture, pour into pan and cook for 1-2 minutes longer or until heated through. Serve immediately.

Mexican Chili Pasta, Honey Beef

GOLDEN OAT FISH FILLETS

This recipe can be made with any white-fleshed fish. Lemon pepper seasoning is a mixture of pepper, salt, sugar, lemon peel and lemon extract.

Serves 4

- ☐ $^{1}/_{4}$ cup/30 g finely ground oatmeal
- ☐ $^{2}/_{3}$ cup/60 g rolled oats
- ☐ $^{1}/_{2}$ cup/60 g dry bread crumbs, made from stale bread
- ☐ $^{1}/_{2}$ teaspoon lemon pepper seasoning
- ☐ 4 x 4 oz/125 g fish fillets all-purpose flour
- ☐ 1 egg, beaten
- ☐ 2 tablespoons/30 g butter
- ☐ 1 tablespoon vegetable oil

1 Place oatmeal, oats, bread crumbs and lemon pepper in a bowl and mix to combine. Coat fish with flour, then dip in egg and coat with oatmeal mixture.
2 Heat butter and oil in a large skillet, add fish and cook for 2-3 minutes each side or until golden and cooked through.

BLUE CHEESE BEEF BAKE

Serves 4
Oven temperature 350°F, 180°C

- ☐ 2 tablespoons olive oil
- ☐ 1$^{1}/_{2}$ lb/750 g blade steak, cut into 2 in/5 cm cubes
- ☐ 1 cup/250 mL beef stock
- ☐ $^{1}/_{2}$ cup/125 mL tomato paste
- ☐ 2 tablespoons port
- ☐ $^{1}/_{4}$ teaspoon ground cumin
- ☐ 1 cinnamon stick
- ☐ 12 small white onions
- ☐ 3 oz/90 g blue vein cheese, cut into $^{1}/_{2}$ in/1 cm cubes

1 Heat oil in a large skillet, add meat and cook, stirring, for 5 minutes or until browned. Transfer to a casserole dish.
2 Add stock, tomato paste, port, cumin and cinnamon stick to pan and bring to the boil. Pour stock mixture over beef, cover and bake for 1 hour.
3 Boil or microwave onions until just tender. Drain, add to casserole dish with meat and cook for 30 minutes longer. Sprinkle blue cheese over top of casserole, cover and stand for 10 minutes before serving.

CHILI AND CHICKEN PEPPERS

If you can find different-colored peppers, this dish will look spectacular, but using only one variety makes no difference to the delicious flavor. Leftover Christmas turkey is ideal to use in place of the chicken.

Serves 4
Oven temperature 400°F, 200°C

- ☐ 3 red peppers
- ☐ 2 green peppers

CHILI AND CHICKEN FILLING
- ☐ 1 tablespoon vegetable oil
- ☐ 2 spring onions, chopped
- ☐ 1 clove garlic, crushed
- ☐ 1 cooked chicken, skin removed, flesh removed and chopped
- ☐ 8 oz/250 g cream cheese, softened
- ☐ 1 teaspoon chili sauce
- ☐ 2 eggs, lightly beaten
- ☐ $^{1}/_{2}$ cup/60 g shredded Cheddar cheese
- ☐ freshly ground black pepper
- ☐ $^{1}/_{2}$ cup/60 g shredded mozzarella cheese
- ☐ paprika

1 Cut tops from peppers and reserve. Remove seeds and core from peppers. Dice 1 red pepper and reserved tops and reserve. Blanch remaining 4 pepper shells in boiling water or in the microwave until just soft. Place upside down on paper towels to drain.
2 To make filling, heat oil in a large skillet, add reserved diced red and green peppers, spring onions and garlic and cook, stirring, for 5 minutes or until peppers are soft. Place chicken, cream cheese, chili sauce, eggs, Cheddar and black pepper to taste in a bowl, add peppers mixture and mix to combine. Spoon filling into pepper shells, top with mozzarella cheese and sprinkle with paprika.
3 Place filled peppers close together in a lightly greased shallow baking dish and bake for 30-40 minutes or until filling is bubbling hot and cheese is golden.

BEEF POT ROAST

Polenta makes a great accompaniment to this traditional Italian dish.

Serves 4

- ☐ 3 lb/1.5 kg piece top round beef
- ☐ $^{1}/_{4}$ cup/$^{1}/_{2}$ stick/60 g butter
- ☐ 1 onion, chopped
- ☐ 1 cup/250 mL dry white wine

ROSEMARY MARINADE
- ☐ 2 cloves garlic, crushed
- ☐ 2 whole cloves
- ☐ pinch ground cinnamon
- ☐ 2$^{1}/_{2}$ cups/600 mL white wine vinegar
- ☐ 2 stalks celery, chopped
- ☐ sprig fresh rosemary
- ☐ 5 whole black peppercorns

1 To make marinade, place garlic, cloves, cinnamon, vinegar, celery, rosemary and black peppercorns in a large bowl and mix to combine. Add beef and turn to coat. Cover and refrigerate for 12 hours or overnight. Remove beef from marinade. Strain marinade, reserve solids and discard liquid.
2 Melt butter in a large heavy-based saucepan, add meat and brown on all sides. Remove meat from pan and set aside.
3 Add onion and reserved solids to pan and cook over a low heat, stirring, for 5 minutes or until onion is soft. Return meat to pan, pour in wine and bring to the boil. Reduce heat, cover and simmer for 2$^{1}/_{2}$ hours or until meat is very tender. To serve, cut meat into slices and serve with any sauce that has formed during cooking.

Polenta: Simply, this is cooked yellow cornmeal. Serve it by the spoonful on the side of the roast, or spread the cornmeal into a buttered pie plate, and cut into wedges when firm.

BEEF WITH SQUASH AND LEMON GRASS

Serve this unusual and flavorsome dish accompanied by bowls of plain yogurt and topped with freshly chopped coriander.

Serves 4

- ☐ **2 tablespoons vegetable oil**
- ☐ **2 onions, chopped**
- ☐ **1 teaspoon whole allspice**
- ☐ **1 cinnamon stick**
- ☐ **1 teaspoon grated fresh ginger**
- ☐ **2 green peppers, sliced**
- ☐ **1¹/₂ lb/750 g chuck steak, cut into 1¹/₂ in/4 cm cubes**
- ☐ **2 tablespoons chopped fresh lemon grass**
- ☐ **2 cups/500 mL chicken stock**
- ☐ **1 lb/500 g butternut or Hubbard squash, cut into 1¹/₂ in/4 cm cubes**
- ☐ **2 cloves garlic, crushed**

1   Heat oil in a large heavy-based saucepan. Cook onions over a medium heat until golden. Stir in allspice, cinnamon, ginger and peppers.

2   Add meat to pan and cook over a high heat until browned. Stir in lemon grass and chicken stock. Bring to the boil, reduce heat and simmer, covered, for 45 minutes.

3   Stir in squash, cover and simmer for 45 minutes or until beef is tender. Remove from heat and stir in garlic. Season to taste.

SEASONED SAUSAGE RAGOUT

For a complete meal, serve this tasty ragout with a chilled tomato salad and crusty French bread.

Serves 6

- ☐ **1 lb/500 g lean ground beef**
- ☐ **¹/₄ cup/60 g finely chopped fresh parsley**
- ☐ **¹/₄ cup/60 g finely chopped fresh basil**
- ☐ **¹/₄ cup/30 g pine nuts (pignola)**
- ☐ **1 tablespoon olive oil**
- ☐ **2 cloves garlic, crushed**
- ☐ **1 teaspoon cracked black peppercorns**
- ☐ **1¹/₂ cups/185 g bread crumbs, made from stale bread**
- ☐ **¹/₂ cup/60 g grated fresh Parmesan cheese**
- ☐ **seasoned flour**
- ☐ **oil for deep-frying**
- ☐ **12 whole baby potatoes**
- ☐ **12 whole baby onions**
- ☐ **¹/₄ cup/60 mL soy sauce**
- ☐ **¹/₂ cup/125 mL lemon juice**
- ☐ **1 cup/250 mL chicken stock**
- ☐ **1 cup/250 mL dry white wine**
- ☐ **¹/₄ cup/30 g chopped fresh basil**

1   Combine beef, parsley, basil, nuts, olive oil, garlic, black peppercorns, bread crumbs and cheese in large bowl and mix until well combined. Shape into 12 sausages, 4 in/ 10 cm long. Roll in seasoned flour.

2   Heat oil in a deep fryer or saucepan. Cook sausages a few at a time until browned but not cooked through. Remove sausages and drain on paper towels. Repeat with remaining sausages.

3   Arrange sausages, potatoes and onions in a Dutch oven. Combine soy sauce, lemon juice, stock, wine and basil in a bowl and pour into pan. Bring to the boil, reduce heat and simmer, covered, for 20 minutes or until potatoes are tender. Thicken sauce in pan, if desired.

Beef with Squash and Lemon Grass, Seasoned Sausage Ragout

chapter six

THE VEGETARIAN ALTERNATIVE

In today's health-aware society many people are choosing to include vegetarian meals in their general eating plan: in many families one or more members choose vegetarian meals all the time. In this chapter you will find a host of exciting vegetarian meals to suit any occasion.

Mushroom Gougère, Wholewheat Spinach Quiche, Spinach and Basil Risotto

MUSHROOM GOUGERE

Serves 4
Oven temperature 400°F, 200°C

CHOUX PASTRY
- [ ] **1 cup/250 mL water**
- [ ] **¹/₃ cup/90 g butter**
- [ ] **1 cup/125 g all-purpose flour, sifted**
- [ ] **4 eggs**

MUSHROOM FILLING
- [ ] **5 oz/155 g button mushrooms, sliced**
- [ ] **3 eggs, lightly beaten**
- [ ] **²/₃ cup/155 g dairy sour cream**
- [ ] **¹/₂ cup/125 mL thick cream**
- [ ] **1 tablespoon flour**
- [ ] **1 cup/125 g shredded Cheddar cheese**
- [ ] **1 tablespoon chopped fresh parsley**
- [ ] **freshly ground black pepper**
- [ ] **pinch ground nutmeg**

1   To make pastry, place water and butter in a saucepan. Cover and cook over a medium heat until margarine melts and mixture just boils. Remove pan from heat and add flour all at once. Stir vigorously with a wooden spoon, over a low heat, until mixture forms a ball and pulls away from sides of pan. Set aside to cool slightly.
2   Add eggs one at a time, beating well after each addition until mixture is smooth and glossy. Spread mixture around sides of a greased shallow ovenproof dish.
3   To make filling, combine mushrooms, eggs, sour cream, cream, flour, cheese and parsley. Season to taste with black pepper and nutmeg. Spoon filling into center of pastry and bake for 35-40 minutes or until filling is firm and pastry is puffed and golden.

VEGETABLE CHILI

Serves 6
Oven temperature 350°F, 180°C

- [ ] **1 large eggplant cut into ¹/₂ in/ 1 cm cubes**
- [ ] **salt**
- [ ] **¹/₃ cup/90 mL olive oil**
- [ ] **1 large onion, chopped**
- [ ] **1 clove garlic, crushed**
- [ ] **1 green pepper, sliced**
- [ ] **14 oz/440 g canned tomatoes, undrained and mashed**
- [ ] **2 zucchini, sliced**

- [ ] **1 teaspoon chili powder**
- [ ] **¹/₂ teaspoon ground cumin**
- [ ] **¹/₃ cup/60 g finely chopped fresh parsley**
- [ ] **1 lb/500 g canned mixed beans**
- [ ] **freshly ground black pepper**

1   Sprinkle eggplant with salt and set aside to stand for 15-20 minutes. Rinse under cold running water and pat dry with paper towels.
2   Heat oil in a large skillet, add eggplant and cook, stirring frequently, until eggplant is tender. Add more oil during cooking if necessary. Transfer eggplant to a large baking dish.
3   Add onion, garlic and green pepper to pan and cook, stirring, for 5 minutes or until onion is soft. Stir in tomatoes, zucchini, chili powder, cumin, parsley, beans and black pepper to taste and cook for 10 minutes. Transfer to baking dish, cover and bake for 1¹/₂ hours or until skin of eggplant is tender and casserole is bubbling hot.

SPINACH AND BASIL RISOTTO

Risotto is an Italian favorite. Wonderful as a first course, main course or an accompaniment to meat, fish or poultry, it is nutritious and easy to make.

Serves 4

- [ ] **1 bunch/1 lb/500 g spinach, chopped**
- [ ] **1 cup/250 mL water**
- [ ] **¹/₄ cup/60 g butter**
- [ ] **1 large onion, finely chopped**
- [ ] **2 cloves garlic, crushed**
- [ ] **2¹/₄ cups/440 g brown rice**
- [ ] **¹/₂ cup/125 mL white wine**
- [ ] **6 cups/1.2 liters hot chicken stock**
- [ ] **¹/₃ cup/90 g pine nuts (pignola), toasted**
- [ ] **¹/₄ cup/30 g fresh basil leaves**
- [ ] **2 tablespoons olive oil**

1   Place spinach and water in a saucepan and cook over a medium heat for 1-2 minutes. Bring to the boil and cook for 1 minute or until spinach is tender. Remove from heat and set aside to cool.
2   Place spinach mixture in a food processor or blender and process until smooth. Set aside.

3   Melt margarine in a saucepan and cook onion and garlic for 4-5 minutes or until onion is soft. Add rice to pan and stir to coat with butter mixture. Pour in wine and half the chicken stock. Cook over a medium heat, stirring occasionally, until almost all the liquid is absorbed. Stir in remaining stock with reserved spinach mixture and cook until almost all the liquid is absorbed.
4   Place 3 tablespoons of the pine nuts, basil and oil in a food processor or blender and process until smooth. Stir into rice mixture. Sprinkle with remaining pine nuts and serve immediately.

VEGETARIAN PIE

Serves 6
Oven temperature 375°F, 190°C

- [ ] **³/₄ cup/170 g brown rice, cooked**
- [ ] **2 cups/250 g shredded Cheddar cheese**
- [ ] **¹/₃ cup/45 g grated Parmesan cheese**
- [ ] **2 spring onions, chopped**
- [ ] **2 zucchini, shredded**
- [ ] **1 red pepper, diced**
- [ ] **10 oz/315 g canned asparagus cuts, drained**
- [ ] **¹/₄ cup/45 g pine nuts (pignola), toasted**
- [ ] **3 eggs, lightly beaten**
- [ ] **³/₄ cup/200 g plain yogurt**
- [ ] **freshly ground black pepper**

1   Place rice, Cheddar, Parmesan cheese, spring onions, zucchini, red pepper, asparagus, pine nuts, eggs, yogurt and black pepper to taste in a bowl and mix to combine.
2   Spoon rice mixture into a greased, deep-sided 9 in /23 cm springform pan and bake for 40 minutes or until firm. Allow to stand for 5 minutes in pan before serving. Serve cut into wedges.

Microwave it: While you do not really save time cooking rice in the microwave , you are assured of a perfect result and no messy pot. It is also a great way to cook rice that is to be used in a recipe such as this one.

To cook brown rice in the microwave, place 1 cup/220 g rice and 3 cups/750 mL water or stock in a large microwave-safe dish. Cook, uncovered, on HIGH (100%) for 30 minutes or until all the liquid is absorbed and the rice is tender.

THAI VEGETABLE PUFFS WITH DIPPING SAUCE

Spice-laden, savory-filled parcels served with a traditional Thai dipping sauce.

Makes 27

- ☐ **3 sheets/750 g pre-rolled puff pastry, thawed**
- ☐ **oil for deep-frying**

SPICY VEGETABLE FILLING
- ☐ **2 tablespoons/30 g butter**
- ☐ **1 teaspoon curry powder**
- ☐ **$^1/_2$ teaspoon ground cumin**
- ☐ **$^1/_2$ teaspoon garam masala**
- ☐ **1 small onion, finely chopped**
- ☐ **1 large carrot, shredded**
- ☐ **1 zucchini, shredded**
- ☐ **1 tablespoon crunchy peanut butter**
- ☐ **2 large potatoes, cooked and mashed**

DIPPING SAUCE
- ☐ **1 cup/250 mL white vinegar**
- ☐ **$^3/_4$ cup/185 g white sugar**
- ☐ **1 small fresh red chili, finely chopped**
- ☐ **1 small cucumber, peeled, seeded and finely chopped**

1   Using a 3 in/7.5 cm round pastry cutter, cut out 27 rounds from pastry sheets.
2   To make filling, melt butter in a saucepan, stir in curry powder, cumin and garam masala and cook for 1 minute. Add onion, carrot and zucchini and cook, stirring occasionally, for 5 minutes or until vegetables are tender. Stir in peanut butter. Place potatoes in a bowl, add vegetable mixture and mix to combine.
3   Lay a pastry round in the palm of your hand and place a teaspoon of filling in the center. Wet edge of pastry with a little water, fold pastry over filling and pinch edges together. Repeat with remaining pastry rounds and filling.
4   To make sauce, place vinegar and sugar in a small saucepan and cook over a low heat, stirring frequently and without boiling, until sugar dissolves. Mix in chili and cucumber and bring to the boil, then reduce heat and simmer, uncovered, for 5 minutes or until sauce reduces and thickens slightly.
5   Heat oil in a large saucepan until a cube of bread dropped in browns in 50 seconds, then cook a few puffs at a time for 3-4 minutes or until crisp and golden. Drain on paper towels and serve immediately with sauce.

SPINACH PIE

Serve this quick-to-make pie hot or cold. Any leftovers are great to put in school or office lunch boxes.

Serves 8
Oven temperature 400°F, 200°C

- ☐ **12 large spinach leaves, shredded**
- ☐ **2 tablespoons/30 g butter**
- ☐ **1 onion, finely chopped**
- ☐ **$^1/_2$ cup/125 g ricotta cheese**
- ☐ **$^1/_2$ cup/125 g cheese, crumbled**
- ☐ **$^1/_2$ cup/60 g shredded Cheddar cheese**
- ☐ **$^1/_4$ cup/30 g grated Parmesan cheese**
- ☐ **4 eggs, lightly beaten**
- ☐ **$^1/_4$ teaspoon ground nutmeg**
- ☐ **freshly ground black pepper**
- ☐ **8 sheets fillo (phyllo) pastry**
- ☐ **$^1/_4$ cup/60 mL olive oil**

1   Boil, steam or microwave spinach until just tender. Drain and cool completely, then squeeze to remove excess liquid. Chop spinach finely and place in a bowl.
2   Melt butter in a skillet, add onion and cook for 5 minutes or until golden. Add onion, ricotta cheese, feta cheese, Cheddar and Parmesan cheese to spinach and mix to combine. Mix eggs, nutmeg and black pepper to taste into spinach mixture.
3   Layer 4 sheets of pastry together, brushing between each sheet with oil. Repeat with remaining sheets. Line a deep lightly greased 4 cup/1 liter casserole with a pastry layer. Trim edges with scissors about 1 in/2.5 cm from the edge of dish. Spoon in spinach filling, then fold remaining pastry layer in half and place on top of spinach filling. Gently fold edges of pastry together, brush top with oil and bake for 40-45 minutes or until pastry is golden and crisp.

WHOLEWHEAT SPINACH QUICHE

Serves 6
Oven temperature 425°F, 220°C

- ☐ **1$^1/_4$ cups/155 g wholewheat flour, sifted and grits returned**
- ☐ **2 tablespoons vegetable oil**
- ☐ **1 egg, lightly beaten**
- ☐ **1 tablespoon iced water**

SPINACH FILLING
- ☐ **2 tablespoons/30 g butter**
- ☐ **1 onion, finely chopped**
- ☐ **$^1/_2$ bunch/8 oz/250 g spinach, finely shredded**
- ☐ **3 eggs, lightly beaten**
- ☐ **1$^1/_4$ cups/300 g dairy sour cream**
- ☐ **pinch ground nutmeg**
- ☐ **freshly ground black pepper**
- ☐ **$^1/_2$ cup/60 g shredded Cheddar cheese**

1   Place flour in a large mixing bowl. Combine oil, egg and water, add to flour and mix to a firm dough. Turn dough onto a floured surface and knead lightly. Cover and refrigerate for 30 minutes.
2   Roll out pastry and line the bottom and sides of a lightly greased 9 in/23 cm tart pan. Trim edges and line pastry base with parchment paper. Fill with dried beans or rice and blind bake for 15 minutes. Remove beans and paper and bake for 10 minutes longer. Remove from oven and set aside to cool slightly.
3   To make filling, melt butter in a skillet and cook onion over a medium heat for 4-5 minutes or until soft. Stir in spinach and cook for 2-3 minutes or until spinach wilts. Remove pan from heat and set aside.
4   Combine eggs, sour cream, nutmeg, black pepper to taste and cheese. Spread spinach mixture over pastry base, then carefully spoon in egg mixture. Reduce temperature to 350°F/180°C and bake for 30 minutes or until firm.

CORN ROULADE WITH MUSHROOM FILLING

Serves 4
Oven temperature 425°F, 220°C

- [ ] ¼ cup/½ stick/60 g butter
- [ ] ⅓ cup/45 g wholewheat flour
- [ ] ¾ cup/185 mL milk
- [ ] 3 eggs, separated
- [ ] ½ cup/125 g canned creamed sweet corn

MUSHROOM FILLING
- [ ] ¼ cup/90 mL vegetable stock or water
- [ ] ¼ cup/60 mL thick dairy sour cream or plain yogurt
- [ ] 2 tablespoons chopped fresh basil
- [ ] 1 tablespoon/15 g butter
- [ ] 6 oz/185 g mushrooms, finely chopped
- [ ] 1 onion, finely chopped
- [ ] 1 tablespoon all-purpose flour

SAUCE
- [ ] 2 tablespoons/30 g butter
- [ ] 1 onion, chopped
- [ ] 2 teaspoons flour
- [ ] 1 cup/250 mL vegetable stock or water
- [ ] 6½ oz/200 g canned sweet red peppers, drained and chopped

1 Melt butter in a saucepan, stir in flour and cook for 1 minute. Gradually blend in milk and cook over a medium heat, stirring frequently, until mixture boils and thickens. Whisk in egg yolks and corn. Beat egg whites until stiff peaks form and gently fold through corn mixture. Spread mixture into a lightly greased and lined 10½ x 12½ in/ 26 x 32 cm Jelly roll pan. Bake for 15-20 minutes or until puffed and golden.

2 To make filling, whisk together stock, sour cream and basil. Melt butter in a saucepan, add mushrooms and onion and cook for 5 minutes or until onion is soft. Add flour and cook for 1 minute. Gradually stir in stock mixture and cook over a medium heat, stirring constantly, until mixture boils and thickens.

3 To make sauce, melt butter in a saucepan and cook onion for 3 minutes, stir in flour and cook for 1 minute longer. Gradually mix in stock and peppers and cook over a medium heat, stirring frequently, until sauce boils and thickens.

4 Turn roulade onto a wire rack covered with a clean teatowel and remove paper. Quickly spread with warm filling and gently roll up from the short side, with the help of the teatowel. Serve roulade sliced with warm sauce.

GINGERED VEGETABLES IN BREAD BASKETS

Serves 4

- [ ] oil for deep-frying
- [ ] 2 large pita breads, split through the center

FILLING
- [ ] 8 baby new potatoes, cut into bite-sized pieces
- [ ] 1 carrot, chopped
- [ ] 1 zucchini, chopped
- [ ] 8 oz/250 g snow peas
- [ ] 8 oz/250 g green and yellow baby squash, trimmed and quartered
- [ ] 1 tablespoon grated fresh ginger
- [ ] 2 tablespoons honey
- [ ] 2 tablespoons orange juice
- [ ] 2 tablespoons chopped macadamia or brazil nuts, toasted
- [ ] 2 tablespoons finely snipped fresh chives

1 Heat oil in a wok or large saucepan and cook pita breads one at a time. Press with the head of a metal soup ladle to form a basket. Drain on paper towels. Set aside and keep warm.

2 To make filling, boil, steam or microwave potatoes, carrot, zucchini, snow peas and squash separately until tender. Set aside and keep warm.

3 Combine ginger, honey, orange juice, nuts and chives in a large bowl. Add vegetables and toss to coat. Spoon filling into warm baskets and serve immediately.

WARM BASIL SUMMER SALAD

Any small pasta with a good shape for catching the dressing can be used for this salad. You might like to try small shell pasta or small spiral shapes.

Serves 6

- [ ] 8 oz/250 g small pasta shapes
- [ ] 2 tablespoons finely chopped sun-dried tomatoes
- [ ] ½ red pepper, finely sliced
- [ ] ½ green pepper, finely sliced
- [ ] 2 spring onions, chopped
- [ ] 12 black olives
- [ ] 2 tablespoons finely chopped basil
- [ ] 2 tablespoons grated Parmesan cheese

RED WINE VINEGAR DRESSING
- [ ] 1 clove garlic, crushed
- [ ] 1 tablespoon olive oil
- [ ] ¼ cup/60 mL red wine vinegar
- [ ] ¼ teaspoon chili powder
- [ ] freshly ground black pepper

1 Cook pasta in boiling water following packet instructions. Drain, set aside and keep warm.

2 Place tomatoes, red and green pepper, spring onions, olives and basil in a large salad bowl.

3 To make dressing, place garlic, oil, vinegar and chili powder in a screwtop jar and shake well to combine. Season to taste with black pepper.

4 Add warm pasta and dressing to salad bowl and toss lightly to combine. Sprinkle with Parmesan cheese and serve while pasta is still warm.

*Gingered Vegetables in Bread Baskets,
Warm Basil Summer Salad,
Corn Roulade with Mushroom Filling*

MASTERCLASS

CHEESY MUSHROOM SLICE

This recipe is an ideal one to cook ahead. Prepare the whole dish, cover and refrigerate overnight. Bake when you are ready the next day. The flavor develops if allowed to stand before cooking.

Serves 6
Oven temperature 350°F,180°C

- [ ] **¼ cup/½ stick/60 g butter**
- [ ] **12 oz/375 g mushrooms, sliced**
- [ ] **4 spring onions, chopped**
- [ ] **1 small green pepper, chopped**
- [ ] **1 small red pepper, chopped**
- [ ] **6 thick slices white bread, crusts removed**
- [ ] **1 cup/125 g shredded Cheddar cheese**
- [ ] **6 eggs**
- [ ] **2 cups/500 mL milk**
- [ ] **1 tablespoon mayonnaise**
- [ ] **1 teaspoon Dijon mustard**
- [ ] **1 teaspoon Worcestershire sauce**
- [ ] **2 tablespoons chopped fresh parsley**

1   Melt butter in a skillet. Stir in mushrooms, spring onions and peppers and cook until mushrooms are soft.

2   Cut bread slices into 1 in/2.5 cm pieces. Place half the bread in a single layer in a greased 7 x 12 in/18 x 30 cm baking dish. Spoon over mushroom mixture and top with remaining bread. Sprinkle over cheese.

3   Whisk together eggs, milk, mayonnaise, mustard and Worcestershire sauce. Pour over bread mixture, sprinkle top with parsley and bake for 50-60 minutes.

Trim crusts from bread and cut into 1 in/2.5 cm pieces.

Place half the bread in a single layer in a greased baking dish and spoon mushroom mixture over.

Pour eggs, milk, mayonnaise, mustard and sauce over bread mixture.

VEGETABLE AND NUT STIR-FRY

Serves 6

- ☐ **2 tablespoons vegetable oil**
- ☐ **2 onions, cut into eighths**
- ☐ **2 carrots, cut into thin strips**
- ☐ **2 stalks celery, cut into thin strips**
- ☐ **2 teaspoons ground turmeric**
- ☐ **2 cloves garlic, crushed**
- ☐ **6 spring onions, chopped**
- ☐ **2 tablespoons white vinegar**
- ☐ **2 tablespoons sugar**
- ☐ **1 mango, pitted, peeled and chopped**
- ☐ **4 oz/125 g snow peas, trimmed**
- ☐ **³/₄ cup/185 mL vegetable stock**
- ☐ **³/₄ cup/125 g roasted cashews**

1   Heat oil in a wok or skillet. Add onions, carrots and celery and stir-fry for 5 minutes or until lightly browned. Combine turmeric, garlic, spring onions, vinegar and sugar and stir into wok.

2   Add mango, snow peas and stock and stir-fry for 5 minutes, or until vegetables are just tender. Fold through nuts and serve immediately.

WARM RED CABBAGE SALAD

Make this wonderful warm salad in autumn when apples and red cabbage are plentiful and at their best.

Serves 6

- ☐ **1 tablespoon olive oil**
- ☐ **1 clove garlic, crushed**
- ☐ **1 red onion, thinly sliced**
- ☐ **2 tablespoons balsamic vinegar**
- ☐ **¹/₂ small red cabbage, shredded**
- ☐ **2 green apples, cored, peeled and thinly sliced**
- ☐ **1 tablespoon finely snipped fresh chives**
- ☐ **1 tablespoon finely chopped fresh dill weed**
- ☐ **¹/₂ cup/60 g slivered almonds, toasted**
- ☐ **2 oz/60 g feta cheese, crumbled**

1   Heat oil in a large skillet. Add garlic and onion and cook over a medium heat for 2-3 minutes. Stir in vinegar and cook for 1 minute longer.

2   Add cabbage to pan, toss lightly and cook for 4-5 minutes, or until cabbage just starts to wilt and change color. Transfer all contents of the pan to a salad bowl. Toss through apples, chives and dill. Sprinkle top of the salad with almonds and cheese and serve while salad is still warm.

Balsamic vinegar: Balsamic vinegar is a dark Italian vinegar made by the special processing of wines and musts from the Modena province. It is an interesting addition to any salad dressing, and can also be used in sauces for meats or vegetables. Balsamic vinegar is available from delicatessens and some supermarkets.

BLUE CHEESE AND APPLE OMELET

Serves 1

- ☐ **1 tablespoon/15 g butter**
- ☐ **2 eggs**
- ☐ **2 teaspoons water**
- ☐ **freshly ground black pepper**

APPLE FILLING
- ☐ **1 tablespoon/15 g butter**
- ☐ **¹/₂ small green apple, cored and thinly sliced**
- ☐ **1 oz/30 g blue cheese, crumbled**
- ☐ **1 teaspoon finely snipped chives**

1   To make filling, melt butter in a small skillet and cook apple over a gentle heat for 2-3 minutes or until just heated through. Remove from pan and set aside to keep warm.

2   To make omelet, melt butter in another small skillet. Lightly whisk together eggs and water. Season to taste with black pepper and pour into pan. Cook over a medium heat, continually drawing in the edge of the omelet with a fork during cooking, until no liquid remains and the omelet is lightly set.

3   Top omelet with apple slices, blue cheese and chives and fold in half. Slip onto a plate and serve immediately.

Cook's tip: If peeled apples are soaked in cold water with a tablespoon of lemon juice for 15 minutes they remain pale when cooked.

The easiest way to slice apples neatly is to core them first, then peel, halve and finally cut them into even slices.

INDIAN EGG CURRY

A delicious egg curry that combines all the tastes of India.

Serves 6
Oven temperature 350°F, 180°C

☐ **6 hard-boiled eggs, halved lengthwise**

CURRY SAUCE
☐ **1 tablespoon vegetable oil**
☐ **1 large onion, finely chopped**
☐ **1 clove garlic, chopped**
☐ **1 tablespoon finely chopped fresh ginger**
☐ **1 teaspoon ground cumin**
☐ **1 teaspoon ground coriander**
☐ **¹/₂ teaspoon chili powder**
☐ **1 teaspoon ground turmeric**
☐ **14 oz/440 g canned tomatoes, undrained and mashed**
☐ **¹/₂ cup/125 mL coconut milk**
☐ **freshly ground black pepper**

1 To make sauce, heat oil in a skillet, add onion, garlic and ginger and cook, stirring occasionally, for 5 minutes or until onion is soft. Stir in cumin, coriander, chili powder and turmeric and cook for 2 minutes longer.
2 Add tomatoes and coconut milk and bring to the boil, then reduce heat and simmer for 15 minutes or until sauce reduces and thickens. Season to taste with black pepper.
3 Place eggs in a shallow baking dish, spoon sauce over, cover and bake for 20 minutes or until heated through.

Cook's tip: When boiling eggs, to prevent a grey-green ring forming around the yolk, take care not to overcook the eggs, and cool cooked eggs immediately under cold running water.

Warm Red Cabbage Salad,
Blue Cheese and Apple Omelet,
Vegetable and Nut Stir-Fry

EASY VEGETABLE AND RICE PIE

Serves 4
Oven temperature 425°F, 220°C

- [ ] **2 sheets/500 g frozen pre-rolled puff pastry, thawed**
- [ ] **1 egg, lightly beaten with 1 tablespoon water**
- [ ] **1 tablespoon sesame seeds**

VEGETABLE AND RICE FILLING
- [ ] **2 tablespoons/30 g butter**
- [ ] **1 onion, chopped**
- [ ] **1 teaspoon ground turmeric**
- [ ] **1 teaspoon ground cumin**
- [ ] **1 teaspoon ground coriander**
- [ ] **$^1/_2$ red pepper, chopped**
- [ ] **1 carrot, chopped**
- [ ] **1 stalk celery, chopped**
- [ ] **1 zucchini, chopped chopped**
- [ ] **$^2/_3$ cup/125 g white or brown rice, cooked**
- [ ] **2 eggs, lightly beaten**

1 To make filling, melt butter in a large skillet, add onion, turmeric, cumin and coriander and cook for 5 minutes or until onion is soft. Add red pepper, carrot, celery and zucchini and cook, stirring occasionally, for 5 minutes longer. Remove pan from heat, add rice, eggs and black pepper to taste to vegetable mixture and mix to combine.

2 Roll out each pastry to a 10 in/25 cm square and trim off edges to make a 10 in/ 25 cm circle using a dinner plate or cake pan as a guide. Place one pastry circle on a lightly greased baking sheet. Top with filling, spreading out evenly with a fork, leaving a 1 in/2.5 cm border. Moisten border with a little of the egg and water mixture.

3 Top with remaining pastry circle, pressing edges together firmly to seal. Press back edges with finger and knife to make a decorative scalloped edge.

4 Pierce top of round several times with a fork. Brush with remaining egg and water mixture, sprinkle with sesame seeds and bake for 15-20 minutes or until pastry is crisp and golden.

Cook's tip: Any leftover cooked vegetables can be used in this wheel. For a completely different flavor you might like to use fresh or dried mixed herbs in place of the spices.

Vegetables with Almond Curry, Spicy Vegetable Loaf

SPICY VEGETABLE LOAF

Serves 6
Oven temperature 350°F, 180°C

- ☐ 1 tablespoon olive oil
- ☐ 1 clove garlic, crushed
- ☐ 1 onion, finely chopped
- ☐ $^1/_2$ teaspoon chili powder
- ☐ $^1/_2$ teaspoon ground cumin
- ☐ $^1/_2$ teaspoon ground coriander
- ☐ $^1/_2$ teaspoon ground turmeric
- ☐ $1^1/_4$ cups/250 g red lentils
- ☐ 1 carrot, shredded
- ☐ 1 large potato, shredded
- ☐ 14 oz/440 g canned tomatoes, undrained and mashed
- ☐ 2 cups/500 mL vegetable stock
- ☐ 3 egg whites
- ☐ $1^1/_2$ cups/140 g rolled oats
- ☐ freshly ground black pepper

1 Heat oil in a large skillet and cook garlic, onion, chili powder, cumin, coriander and turmeric for 4-5 minutes or until onion is soft.

2 Add lentils, carrot, potato, tomatoes and stock. Bring to the boil, cover and simmer for 30 minutes or until lentils are tender. Remove from heat and set aside to cool slightly. Beat egg whites until stiff peaks form and fold into lentil mixture.

3 Stir in rolled oats and mix well to combine. Season to taste with black pepper. Spoon into a lightly greased and lined 6 x 10 in/15 x 25 cm loaf pan. Bake for 1 hour or until cooked.

VEGETABLES WITH ALMOND CURRY

Serves 4

- ☐ 1 tablespoon olive oil
- ☐ 1 onion, sliced
- ☐ 1 clove garlic, crushed
- ☐ 1 teaspoon ground cumin
- ☐ 1 teaspoon ground coriander
- ☐ 1 teaspoon ground turmeric
- ☐ 2 carrots, peeled and sliced
- ☐ $^2/_3$ cup/125 g red lentils
- ☐ 14 oz/440 g canned peeled tomatoes, undrained and mashed
- ☐ $1^1/_2$ cups/375 mL vegetable stock
- ☐ 1 teaspoon chili sauce, or according to taste
- ☐ 1 lb/500 g butternut or Hubbard squash , cut into $^3/_4$ in/2 cm cubes
- ☐ $^1/_2$ cauliflower, cut into florets
- ☐ 2 tablespoons blanched almonds
- ☐ freshly ground black pepper
- ☐ $^1/_3$ cup/90 mL plain yogurt

1 Heat oil in a large saucepan and cook onion, garlic, cumin, coriander, turmeric and carrots for 5 minutes or until onion is soft.

2 Stir in lentils, tomatoes and stock. Bring to the boil, reduce heat, cover and simmer for 15 minutes.

3 Add chili sauce, squash and cauliflower. Cook for 15-20 minutes longer or until squash is tender. Mix in almonds and season to taste with black pepper. Ladle curry into bowls and top with a spoonful of yogurt.

CORN AND CHILI SOUFFLE

Serves 4

- ☐ $^1/_4$ cup/$^1/_2$ stick/60 g butter
- ☐ 1 onion, finely chopped
- ☐ 1 fresh red chili, seeded and finely chopped
- ☐ $^1/_4$ cup/30 g all-purpose flour
- ☐ $^1/_2$ cup/125 mL milk
- ☐ 10 oz/315 g canned creamed sweet corn
- ☐ 4 egg yolks, lightly beaten
- ☐ freshly ground black pepper
- ☐ 5 egg whites
- ☐ $^1/_4$ cup/30 g bread crumbs made from stale bread

1 Melt butter in a saucepan, add onion and chili and cook over a medium heat, stirring frequently, for 10 minutes, or until onion is soft and golden. Stir in flour and cook for 1 minute. Remove from heat and gradually stir in milk and corn. Return to heat and cook, stirring constantly, until mixture boils and thickens. Remove from heat and beat in egg yolks. Season to taste with black pepper.

2 Place egg whites in a bowl and beat until stiff peaks form. Fold gently into corn mixture.

3 Grease a 7 in/18 cm soufflé dish and sprinkle with bread crumbs. Grease a parchment paper collar, sprinkle with bread crumbs and attach to soufflé dish.

4 Spoon soufflé mixture into prepared dish and bake for 30-35 minutes or until soufflé is puffed and golden. Serve immediately.

CHUNKY HOTPOT

Serves 4

- [ ] 2 tablespoons vegetable oil
- [ ] 1 clove garlic, crushed
- [ ] 1 small fresh red chili, chopped
- [ ] 1 onion, chopped
- [ ] 2 teaspoons curry powder
- [ ] 2 teaspoons ground cumin
- [ ] 1 teaspoon garam masala
- [ ] 2 tablespoons chopped fresh coriander (cilantro)
- [ ] 1 tablespoon chopped fresh ginger
- [ ] 1 head broccoli, broken into small florets
- [ ] 3 carrots, chopped
- [ ] 2 parsnips, chopped
- [ ] 1 large potato, cubed
- [ ] 12 oz/375 g baby squash, halved
- [ ] 1 tablespoon all-purpose flour
- [ ] 1 1/2 cups/375 mL water
- [ ] 3/4 cup/185 mL coconut milk
- [ ] 3/4 cup/125 g roasted cashews, chopped

1 Heat oil in a large saucepan. Cook garlic, chili, onion, curry powder, cumin, garam masala, coriander and ginger over a low heat for 1 minute. Add broccoli, carrots, parsnips, potato and squash. Cook for 5-8 minutes over a medium heat.

2 Stir in flour and cook for 1 minute. Remove pan from heat and gradually blend in water. Cook over a medium heat, stirring constantly, until mixture boils and thickens. Reduce heat, cover and simmer for 10-15 minutes, or until vegetables are tender.

3 Whisk in coconut milk and cook over a low heat for 2-3 minutes. Spoon into individual bowls and sprinkle with cashews to serve.

STIR-FRIED VEGETABLES WITH EGGS

Often called Egg Foo Yung and traditionally made with shrimp, fish or beef, this popular recipe is delicious made just with vegetables.

Serves 2

- [ ] 4 oz/125 g snow peas, trimmed
- [ ] 6 oz/185 g fresh asparagus, cut into 2 in/5 cm pieces
- [ ] 3 eggs
- [ ] 1 teaspoon sesame oil
- [ ] 1/4 cup/60 mL water
- [ ] 1 teaspoon dry sherry
- [ ] 1 teaspoon soy sauce
- [ ] freshly ground black pepper
- [ ] 1 tablespoon vegetable oil
- [ ] 3 spring onions, chopped

1 Boil, steam or microwave snow peas and asparagus separately until just tender. Drain and refresh under cold running water, drain again and set aside.

2 Place eggs, sesame oil, water, sherry and soy sauce in a bowl and whisk to combine. Season to taste with black pepper.

3 Heat oil in a wok or skillet, add egg mixture and stir-fry for 1 minute, or until egg just begins to set. Add snow peas, asparagus and spring onions and stir-fry for 1 minute longer. Serve immediately.

POTATO AND PESTO BAKE

Serves 4
Oven temperature 350°F, 180°C

- [ ] 8 potatoes, thickly sliced

PESTO
- [ ] 2 oz/60 g basil leaves
- [ ] 2 cloves garlic, crushed
- [ ] 2 tablespoons pine nuts (pignola)
- [ ] 1/2 cup/125 mL olive oil
- [ ] 1/3 cup/45 g grated fresh Parmesan cheese

SOUR CREAM TOPPING
- [ ] 1 1/4 cups/300 mL dairy sour cream
- [ ] 1/2 cup/60 g shredded Cheddar cheese
- [ ] freshly ground black pepper

1 Boil, steam or microwave potato slices until almost tender. Drain and layer potatoes in the bottom of a greased baking dish.

2 To make Pesto, place basil, garlic, pine nuts, oil and Parmesan in a food processor or blender and process until smooth. Spread over potatoes.

3 To make topping, spoon sour cream over Pesto and top with Cheddar and black pepper to taste. Bake for 10 minutes or until potatoes are soft and top is golden brown.

Chunky Hotpot, Potato and Pesto Bake, Singapore Noodle Stir-Fry

SINGAPORE NOODLE STIR-FRY

Serves 4

- ☐ **13 oz/410 g rice noodles**
- ☐ **1 tablespoon sesame oil**
- ☐ **1 onion, chopped**
- ☐ **1 tablespoon sesame seeds**
- ☐ **2 fresh red chilies, chopped**
- ☐ **6 oz/185 g sliced bamboo shoots**
- ☐ **4 tablespoons bean sprouts**
- ☐ **¼ small cabbage, finely shredded**
- ☐ **1 carrot, finely chopped**
- ☐ **1 red pepper, diced**

SWEET AND SOUR SAUCE
- ☐ **¼ cup/60 mL bottled plum sauce or sweet and sour sauce**
- ☐ **1 tablespoon sugar**
- ☐ **1 tablespoon white wine vinegar**
- ☐ **¾ cup/185 mL vegetable stock**
- ☐ **2 teaspoons cornstarch blended with 1 tablespoon water**

1   Place noodles in a large saucepan of boiling water and cook until tender. Drain and set aside.
2   Heat oil in pan, add onion and cook 3 minutes or until tender. Stir in sesame seeds and chilies, and cook for 2 minutes.
3   Add bamboo shoots, bean sprouts, cabbage, carrot and red pepper. Cook for 5 minutes, stirring frequently.
4   To make sauce, combine plum sauce, sugar, vinegar and stock. Add to pan with vegetables. Bring to the boil, then reduce heat and simmer for 2 minutes. Pour in cornstarch mixture, and stir until mixture thickens slightly. Toss through noodles and serve immediately.

INDONESIAN COOKED SALAD

Poppadums are the perfect accompaniment to this unusual salad of lightly cooked vegetables topped with eggs and a spicy peanut sauce.

Serves 4

- ☐ **2 potatoes, cut into chunks**
- ☐ **4 carrots, sliced**
- ☐ **8 oz/250 g green beans, sliced**
- ☐ **8 oz/250 g spinach, thick stalks removed**
- ☐ **2 tablespoons vegetable oil**
- ☐ **4 oz/125 g bean sprouts**
- ☐ **1 small cucumber, cut into thicsticks**
- ☐ **2 hard-boiled eggs, quartered**
- ☐ **1 large onion, sliced**

PEANUT SAUCE
- ☐ **1 tablespoon vegetable oil**
- ☐ **1 small onion, chopped**
- ☐ **1 clove garlic, crushed**
- ☐ **1 cup/250 mL coconut milk**
- ☐ **1 tablespoon lemon juice**
- ☐ **⅓ cup/90 g peanut butter**
- ☐ **½ teaspoon chili powder**
- ☐ **1 bay leaf**

1   Boil, steam or microwave potatoes, carrots, beans and spinach, separately, until just tender. Drain and layer in a deep dish.
2   Heat 1 tablespoon oil in a wok or skillet and stir-fry bean sprouts and cucumber for 2-3 minutes. Drain and sprinkle over vegetables in dish. Heat remaining oil in pan and cook onion for 4-5 minutes or until golden. Drain and set aside.
3   To make sauce, heat oil in a saucepan and cook onion and garlic for 4-5 minutes, or until onion is soft. Stir in coconut milk, lemon juice, peanut butter, chili powder and bay leaf. Cook over a medium heat, stirring constantly, until mixture thickens.
4   Arrange eggs over vegetables, pour sauce over and top with sliced onion.

Indonesian Cooked Salad

EGGPLANT LASAGNE

Serves 4
Oven temperature 350°F, 180°C

- ☐ **1 tablespoon olive oil**
- ☐ **¹/₂ teaspoon cracked black peppercorns**
- ☐ **¹/₄ cup/60 mL lemon juice**
- ☐ **1 large eggplant, about 1 lb/500 g, halved lengthwise and cut into ¹/₄ in/5 mm thick slices**
- ☐ **¹/₂ cup/30 g wholewheat bread crumbs, made from stale bread**
- ☐ **¹/₄ cup/30 g grated Parmesan cheese**
- ☐ **1 large onion, chopped**
- ☐ **2 cloves garlic, crushed**
- ☐ **14 oz/440 g canned peeled tomatoes, drained, chopped and 1 tablespoon juice reserved**
- ☐ **³/₄ cup/185 mL tomato purée**
- ☐ **2 tablespoons white wine**
- ☐ **1 teaspoon dried oregano**
- ☐ **1 teaspoon dried basil**
- ☐ **pinch cayenne pepper**
- ☐ **6 plain or wholewheat microwavable lasagne sheets**
- ☐ **³/₄ cup/185 g ricotta cheese**
- ☐ **¹/₄ cup/30 g shredded mozzarella cheese**

1   Combine olive oil, black peppercorns and lemon juice and brush eggplant slices. Cook under a preheated broiler for 3-4 minutes each side or until golden. Combine bread crumbs and Parmesan cheese and set aside.

2   Heat a nonstick skillet and cook onion, garlic and reserved tomato juice over a medium heat for 2-3 minutes. Add tomatoes, tomato purée, wine, oregano, basil and cayenne pepper and cook for 5 minutes longer.

3   Spread one-third of the tomato mixture over base of a 6 x 10 in/15 x 25 cm baking dish. Top with 3 lasagne sheets, half of the bread crumb mixture and cover with a layer of eggplant. Top with half the ricotta cheese. Repeat layers, ending with a layer of tomato mixture. Top with mozzarella cheese and bake for 45 minutes.

PUMPKIN SEED DIP

This dip is delicious served on a platter of raw vegetables as a snack or as part of a light meal.

Serves 6

- ☐ **3¹/₂ oz/100 g pumpkin seeds, toasted**
- ☐ **1 tablespoon lemon juice**
- ☐ **2 tablespoons balsamic vinegar**
- ☐ **1 clove garlic, crushed**
- ☐ **¹/₂ teaspoon Dijon mustard**

Place pumpkin seeds, lemon juice, vinegar, garlic and mustard in a food processor or blender and process until smooth. Chill before serving.

Eggplant Lasagne

chapter seven

RICE AND PASTA TO PLEASE

Rice and pasta are
important staple foods for
much of the world's population.
Quick and easy to prepare and
inexpensive, they are also the perfect
ingredient for the family cook. The
recipes in this chapter show you
exciting ways in which to use
these ever-popular foods.

Hot Pasta and Mushrooms,
Gingered Noodles and Vegetables,
Herby Tomato and Pasta Salad

TUNA-FILLED SHELLS

These shells are fun to eat hot or cold as finger food, or they can be served with a sauce as a first course.

Makes 16 filled shells

- ☐ **16 giant pasta shells**

TUNA FILLING

- ☐ **1 cup/250 g ricotta cheese, drained**
- ☐ **14 oz/440 g canned tuna in brine, drained and flaked**
- ☐ **½ red pepper, diced**
- ☐ **1 tablespoon chopped capers**
- ☐ **1 teaspoon snipped fresh chives**
- ☐ **⅓ cup/45 g shredded Swiss cheese**
- ☐ **pinch ground nutmeg**
- ☐ **freshly ground black pepper**
- ☐ **2 tablespoons grated Parmesan cheese**

1   Cook 8 pasta shells in a large saucepan of boiling water until al dente. Drain, rinse under cold running water and drain again. Set aside in a single layer. Repeat with remaining shells.
2   To make filling, place ricotta cheese and tuna in a bowl and mix to combine. Mix in red pepper, capers, chives half the Swiss cheese, the nutmeg and black pepper to taste.
3   Fill each shell with ricotta mixture, and place in a single layer in a lightly greased, shallow baking dish. Sprinkle with Parmesan cheese and remaining Swiss cheese. Place under a preheated broiler and cook until cheese melts.

GINGERED NOODLES AND VEGETABLES

The flat Oriental noodles that we have used in this recipe are different from egg noodles; they are made from flour and water and are available from Chinese food stores.

Serves 6

- ☐ **1 tablespoon peanut oil**
- ☐ **2 teaspoons grated fresh ginger**
- ☐ **1 clove garlic, crushed**
- ☐ **1 onion, sliced**
- ☐ **1 carrot, sliced diagonally**
- ☐ **2 stalks celery, sliced diagonally**
- ☐ **3½ oz/100 g bean sprouts**
- ☐ **6½ oz/200 g snow peas, trimmed**
- ☐ **1 lb/500 g flat Oriental noodles, cooked**
- ☐ **freshly ground black pepper**

1   Heat oil in a wok or large skillet. Add ginger and garlic, and stir-fry for 1-2 minutes. Stir in onion and carrot, and stir-fry for 4-5 minutes.
2   Add celery, bean sprouts and snow peas, and stir-fry for 2-3 minutes.
3   Stir in noodles, and stir-fry 3-4 minutes or until noodles are heated through. Season to taste with black pepper and serve immediately.

HERBY TOMATO AND PASTA SALAD

As a luncheon, this salad needs only crusty bread to accompany it.

Serves 6

- ☐ **8 oz/250 g fresh spinach tagliatelle**
- ☐ **8 oz/250 g fresh plain tagliatelle**
- ☐ **2 zucchini, cut into matchsticks**
- ☐ **1 small red pepper, sliced**
- ☐ **1 small green pepper, sliced**
- ☐ **6½ oz/200 g green beans, cooked**

TOMATO AND BASIL DRESSING

- ☐ **4 ripe tomatoes, peeled and roughly chopped**
- ☐ **1 clove garlic, crushed**
- ☐ **2 teaspoons olive oil**
- ☐ **2 teaspoons red wine vinegar**
- ☐ **2 tablespoons finely chopped fresh basil**
- ☐ **1 tablespoon finely chopped fresh parsley**
- ☐ **1 tablespoon finely chopped fresh chives**
- ☐ **freshly ground black pepper**

1   Cook both tagliatelles together in boiling water in a large saucepan following packet directions. Rinse under cold running water, drain and set aside to cool completely.
2   Place cold tagliatelles, zucchini, peppers and beans in a large salad bowl.
3   To make dressing, place tomatoes, garlic, oil and vinegar in a food processor or blender. Process until smooth. Stir in basil, parsley and chives, and season to taste with black pepper. Spoon dressing over pasta and vegetables. Toss lightly to coat all ingredients with dressing.

HOT PASTA AND MUSHROOMS

Creamy mushroom sauce and hot pasta – the food that dreams are made of! A green salad and crusty bread will complete your meal.

Serves 4

- ☐ **2 cups/250 g macaroni**
- ☐ **¼ cup finely chopped fresh parsley**
- ☐ **2 tablespoons grated Parmesan cheese**

MUSHROOM SAUCE

- ☐ **2 teaspoons vegetable oil**
- ☐ **1 onion, sliced**
- ☐ **1 lb/500 g mushrooms, sliced**
- ☐ **1 teaspoon paprika**
- ☐ **2 tablespoons tomato paste**
- ☐ **1 cup/250 mL evaporated milk**
- ☐ **freshly ground black pepper**

1   Cook macaroni in boiling water in a large saucepan following packet directions. Drain, set aside and keep warm.
2   To make sauce, heat oil in a nonstick skillet. Cook onion and mushrooms until they are soft. Blend together paprika, tomato paste and milk. Stir into mushroom mixture and cook gently over a low heat for 5 minutes. Season to taste with black pepper.
3   Place pasta in a heated serving dish and spoon over sauce. Toss gently to combine. Sprinkle with parsley and Parmesan to serve.

Perfect pasta: The secret of cooking perfect pasta is to bring a large pot of water to a rolling boil. Add a splash of oil to prevent the pasta from sticking together (do not add salt, as it toughens the pasta). Immerse your pasta, bring back to the boil, then cook 2-3 minutes for fresh or 5-8 minutes for dried. Pasta should taste 'al dente' – just cooked, but with no hard core in the center. Drain and place in bowls, ready for the sauce.

FETTUCCINE WITH BLACK BEAN SAUCE

This East meets West type of dish uses Asian ingredients for the sauce and Italian pasta as the base. If you wish, in place of the fettuccine you could use Asian noodles.

Serves 4

- [ ] **2 teaspoons vegetable oil**
- [ ] **1 clove garlic, crushed**
- [ ] **1 red chili, seeded and finely chopped**
- [ ] **1 tablespoon canned black beans, washed, drained**
- [ ] **1 tablespoon soy sauce**
- [ ] **1 tablespoon vinegar**
- [ ] **1 tablespoon bottled oyster sauce**
- [ ] **2 cups/500 mL vegetable stock**
- [ ] **2 teaspoons brown sugar**
- [ ] **2 tablespoons cornstarch blended with 1/3 cup/90 mL cold water**
- [ ] **1 lb/500 g fettuccine**

1 Heat oil in a saucepan, add garlic and chili and cook for 1 minute. Combine black beans, soy, vinegar, oyster sauce, stock, sugar and cornstarch mixture. Pour black bean mixture into pan, and simmer for 5 minutes, or until sauce thickens.

2 Cook pasta in boiling water in a large saucepan following the packet directions. Drain and place in a serving dish. Toss sauce through and serve.

TORTELLINI WITH SWEET RED PEPPER SAUCE

Serves 4

- [ ] **1 lb/500 g tortellini**

SWEET RED PEPPER SAUCE
- [ ] **1 tablespoon vegetable oil**
- [ ] **1 onion, chopped**
- [ ] **14 oz/440 g canned sweet red peppers, drained and chopped**
- [ ] **1/2 cup/125 mL water**
- [ ] **1 tablespoon honey**
- [ ] **1 tablespoon chopped fresh oregano**

1 Cook tortellini in boiling water in a large saucepan, following packet directions. Drain, set aside and keep warm.

2 To make sauce, heat oil in small pan, add onion and cook for 3 minutes or until tender. Place red peppers, water, honey, oregano and onion in a food processor or blender and process until smooth.

3 Place sweet pepper sauce into a saucepan and heat until simmering. Pour sauce over hot tortellini and serve.

Fettuccine with Black Bean Sauce, Tortellini with Sweet Red Pepper Sauce

CURRIED TUNA LASAGNE

Serves 6
Oven temperature 375°F, 190°C

- [ ] **9 sheets microwavable lasagne noodles**
- [ ] **14 oz/440 g canned tuna, drained and flaked**
- [ ] **1 tablespoon/15 g butter**
- [ ] **2 stalks celery, finely chopped**
- [ ] **1 onion, chopped**

CURRY SAUCE
- [ ] **2 tablespoons/30 g butter**
- [ ] **$^{1}/_{3}$ cup/45 g all-purpose flour**
- [ ] **2 teaspoons curry powder**
- [ ] **2 cups/500 mL milk**
- [ ] **$^{3}/_{4}$ cup/185 mL water**
- [ ] **2 eggs, beaten**
- [ ] **2 tablespoons shredded Cheddar cheese**

CHEESE TOPPING
- [ ] **2 tablespoons shredded Cheddar cheese**
- [ ] **1 teaspoon curry powder**
- [ ] **$^{1}/_{2}$ teaspoon paprika**

SALMON RICE AND SPINACH LOAF

Serves 4
Oven temperature 400°F, 200°C

- [ ] **10-15 large spinach leaves, thick stalks removed**
- [ ] **14 oz/440 g canned salmon, drained**
- [ ] **3 eggs**
- [ ] **$^{1}/_{4}$ cup/60 mL dairy sour cream or plain yogurt**
- [ ] **2 tablespoons mayonnaise**
- [ ] **1 tablespoon lemon juice**
- [ ] **1$^{1}/_{2}$ cups cooked rice**
- [ ] **2 tablespoons grated Parmesan cheese**
- [ ] **freshly ground black pepper**

1   Wet spinach leaves and boil or steam until soft.

2   Line the base and sides of a greased 4 x 9 in/10 x 23 cm loaf pan with half of the spinach leaves, allowing some of the leaves to hang over the sides of the pan.

3   Squeeze excess moisture from remaining leaves, then chop and combine with all the remaining ingredients. Season to taste with black pepper. Spoon salmon mixture into spinach-lined pan. Enclose with the overhanging spinach leaves, cover and bake for 45 minutes or until firm. Stand for 10 minutes before serving.

Microwave it: This loaf cooks quickly in the microwave. Preparation of the loaf is the same, but remember to use a microwave-safe dish. Cover, then cook on HIGH (100%) for 13 minutes. Stand 5 minutes before serving.

1 To make sauce, melt butter in a saucepan. Stir in flour and curry powder and cook for 2-3 minutes. Remove from heat, whisk in combined milk and water. Stir over a medium heat until sauce boils and thickens. Blend in eggs and cheese.

2 Spoon a little sauce over the bottom of a shallow baking dish. Top with 3 lasagne sheets and spread over half the tuna.

3 Melt butter in a skillet and cook celery and onion until onion is soft. Spread half onion mixture over tuna and top with a layer of sauce. Repeat layers, finishing with noodles then sauce.

4 To make topping, combine cheese, curry powder and paprika. Sprinkle over top and bake for 30-35 minutes or until tender.

WHOLEWHEAT SPAGHETTI WITH TOMATOES AND ASPARAGUS

Serves 4

☐ **1 lb/500 g wholewheat spaghetti**

ASPARAGUS SAUCE

☐ **1 tablespoon olive oil**
☐ **1 clove garlic, crushed**
☐ **14 oz/440 g canned tomatoes, drained and chopped**
☐ **9¹/₂ oz/300 g canned asparagus cuts, drained**
☐ **1 tablespoon chopped fresh parsley**
☐ **1 tablespoon brown sugar**
☐ **2 tablespoons red wine**
☐ **freshly ground black pepper**

1 Cook spaghetti in boiling water following the packet instructions. Drain and keep warm.

2 To make sauce, heat oil in a skillet and cook garlic for 1 minute. Stir in tomatoes, asparagus, parsley, sugar and wine and season to taste with black pepper. Cover and simmer for 15-20 minutes. Spoon sauce over hot spaghetti and serve with Parmesan cheese if desired.

Left: Salmon Rice and Spinach Loaf
Below: Curried Tuna Lasagne, Wholewheat Spaghetti with Tomatoes and Asparagus

COATED CHILI RICE BALLS

Makes 16

- [ ] 1 tablespoon olive oil
- [ ] 1 onion, finely chopped
- [ ] 1³/₄ cups/315 g long grain rice
- [ ] ¹/₂ teaspoon ground turmeric
- [ ] 3 cups/750 mL chicken stock
- [ ] ¹/₂ teaspoon chili powder
- [ ] freshly ground black pepper
- [ ] 3 spring onions, finely chopped
- [ ] 1 tablespoon/15 g butter
- [ ] ¹/₄ cup/30 g shredded Cheddar cheese
- [ ] 2 eggs, lightly beaten
- [ ] 4 oz/125 g mozzarella cheese, cut into ³/₄ in/1 cm cubes
- [ ] ³/₄ cup/90 g dried bread crumbs
- [ ] oil for cooking

1 Heat oil in a skillet and cook onion for 2-3 minutes or until soft. Stir in rice and turmeric and cook for 1-2 minutes or until rice is coated with oil.

2 Pour in ³/₄ cup/185 mL stock and bring to the boil. Cook, stirring frequently, until liquid has almost evaporated. Add remaining stock, chili powder and black pepper to taste. Simmer for 10-15 minutes or until liquid has been absorbed and rice is tender. Remove pan from heat and stir through spring onions, butter and Cheddar.

3 Lightly fold eggs through, taking care not to mash rice grains. Divide rice mixture into sixteen equal portions. Take a cheese cube and, with hands, mold one portion of rice around cheese, to form a ball. Repeat with remaining rice and cheese portions.

4 Coat balls in bread crumbs and refrigerate for 30 minutes. Heat oil in a deep saucepan and cook four to five balls at a time, until golden. Remove, drain on paper towels and serve.

MUSHROOM AND BACON SAUCE

This sauce is best used with the long varieties of pasta such as fettuccine, taglierini, spaghetti or linguine.

Serves 4

- [ ] 1 small head broccoli, cut into small florets
- [ ] 2 teaspoons olive oil
- [ ] 4 slices bacon, chopped
- [ ] 4 oz/125 g button mushrooms, sliced
- [ ] 1 clove garlic, crushed
- [ ] 1¹/₄ cups/300 mL thick cream
- [ ] freshly ground black pepper
- [ ] ¹/₄ cup/30 g finely chopped fresh parsley

1 Boil, steam or microwave broccoli until just tender. Drain and refresh under cold running water. Drain and set aside.

2 Heat oil in a skillet and cook bacon for 3-4 minutes or until crisp. Stir in mushrooms and garlic and cook for 2-3 minutes.

3 Pour in cream, bring to the boil, stirring frequently and simmer for 5 minutes or until sauce thickens. Season to taste with black pepper, add broccoli and heat through. Spoon sauce over hot, cooked pasta. Sprinkle with parsley and serve.

SEAFOOD AND TOMATO SAUCE

Any combination of seafood can be used in this sauce.

Serves 4

- [ ] 1 tablespoon olive oil
- [ ] 4 spring onions, finely chopped
- [ ] 1 clove garlic, crushed
- [ ] 1 small fresh red chili, finely chopped
- [ ] 1 lb/500 g cooked shrimp, shelled, deveined and chopped
- [ ] 4 oz/125 g scallops, halved
- [ ] 14 oz/440 g canned tomatoes, undrained and mashed
- [ ] ¹/₄ cup/60 mL red wine
- [ ] ¹/₄ cup/60 mL chicken stock
- [ ] 2 teaspoons tomato paste
- [ ] 1 teaspoon sugar
- [ ] 2 teaspoons chopped fresh basil
- [ ] 1 tablespoon chopped fresh parsley
- [ ] 4-8 oysters in the shell

1 Heat oil in a large saucepan and cook spring onions, garlic and chili for 1 minute. Stir in shrimp and scallops and cook for 2 minutes longer.

2 Combine tomatoes, wine, stock, tomato paste and sugar and pour into pan with shrimp mixture. Bring to the boil, then reduce heat and simmer, uncovered, for 10 minutes.

3 Add basil and parsley. Cook for 2-3 minutes. Spoon sauce over hot, cooked pasta. Garnish with oysters in their shells.

TUNA AND OLIVE SAUCE

Serves 4

- ☐ 2 tablespoons/30 g butter
- ☐ 2 tablespoons all-purpose flour
- ☐ 1/2 cup/125 mL milk
- ☐ 1/4 cup/60 mL chicken stock
- ☐ 14 oz/440 g tuna in brine, drained and liquid reserved
- ☐ 1 tablespoon finely chopped fresh dill weed
- ☐ 12 black olives, pitted and sliced
- ☐ 2 tablespoons capers, finely chopped
- ☐ 2-3 drops hot red pepper sauce
- ☐ 1/4 cup/60 mL thick cream
- ☐ 2 tablespoons lemon juice
- ☐ freshly ground black pepper

1 Melt butter in a saucepan, add flour and cook for 1 minute. Remove from heat.
2 Blend in milk, stock and tuna liquid, stirring over a medium heat until sauce boils and thickens.
3 Reduce heat and add dill, olives, capers, pepper sauce, cream and lemon juice. Season to taste with black pepper and stir well to combine.
4 Break up tuna into smaller chunks and fold through sauce. Cook for 2-3 minutes. Spoon sauce over hot pasta and serve.

PASTA PARCELS WITH BLUE CHEESE SAUCE

Serves 8
Oven temperature 350°F, 180°C

- ☐ 8 fresh spinach lasagne sheets, approximately 6 1/2 in/ 16 cm square, cooked

SPINACH FILLING
- ☐ 1 lb/500 g spinach leaves, blanched and squeezed to remove excess water
- ☐ 4 hard-boiled eggs, chopped
- ☐ 4 oz/125 g prosciutto or lean ham, finely chopped
- ☐ 1 tablespoon finely chopped red onion
- ☐ 1 clove garlic, crushed
- ☐ freshly ground black pepper

BLUE CHEESE SAUCE
- ☐ 3 1/2 oz/100 g soft blue cheese
- ☐ 1 1/2 cups/375 mL thin cream
- ☐ 1 1/2 tablespoons Dijon mustard
- ☐ 4-5 tablespoons lemon juice
- ☐ 2 tablespoons chopped hazelnuts or almonds, toasted

1 To make filling, shred spinach finely. Place spinach, hard-boiled eggs, prosciutto or ham, onion, garlic and black pepper to taste in a bowl and mix to combine.
2 To make sauce, place blue cheese, cream, mustard and lemon juice in a food processor or blender and process until well blended, then stir in hazelnuts or almonds.
3 To assemble parcels, divide filling between lasagne sheets, forming a mound in center of each sheet. Fold in corners of pasta like an envelope to form a parcel. Place parcels in a shallow baking dish, spoon sauce over, cover with aluminum foil and bake for 20 minutes or until heated through.

Left: Coated Chili Rice Balls
Above: Seafood and Tomato Sauce,
Tuna and Olive Sauce,
Pasta with Mushroom and Bacon Sauce

FETTUCCINE WITH VEAL CREAM SAUCE

Serves 4

- [ ] **1 lb/500 g fettuccine**
- [ ] **1 tablespoon olive oil**
- [ ] **1 lb/500 g thinly sliced veal leg, cut into strips**
- [ ] **1 clove garlic, crushed**
- [ ] **1 teaspoon chopped fresh parsley**
- [ ] **2 teaspoons paprika**
- [ ] **2 tablespoons brandy**
- [ ] **2 tablespoons tomato paste**
- [ ] **$1^1/_2$ cups/375 g dairy sour cream**
- [ ] **freshly ground black pepper**

1   Cook fettuccine in boiling water in a large saucepan until al dente. Drain, set aside and keep warm.

2   Heat oil in a large skillet and cook veal for 3-4 minutes or until browned. Add garlic, parsley and paprika and cook for 1-2 minutes longer. Stir in brandy and cook until evaporated. Whisk in tomato paste and sour cream. Season to taste with black pepper and bring to the boil. Reduce heat and simmer until sauce reduces and thickens. Stir in pasta and toss to coat.

CHICKEN LIVERS AND MUSHROOMS ON SPAGHETTI

A variation of a sauce created for the great singer Caruso.

Serves 4

- [ ] **1 lb/500 g spaghetti**
- [ ] **1 tablespoon vegetable oil**
- [ ] **$^3/_4$ cup/90 g grated fresh Parmesan cheese**

TOMATO SAUCE
- [ ] **1 tablespoon vegetable oil**
- [ ] **2 tablespoons/30 g butter**
- [ ] **1 onion, finely diced**
- [ ] **2 cloves garlic, crushed**
- [ ] **12 small button mushrooms, halved**
- [ ] **14 oz/440 g canned tomatoes, undrained and mashed**
- [ ] **1 teaspoon sugar**
- [ ] **$1^1/_4$ cups/300 mL chicken stock**
- [ ] **ground black pepper**

CHICKEN LIVER SAUCE
- [ ] **2 tablespoons/30 g butter**
- [ ] **8 oz/250 g chicken livers, trimmed and sliced**
- [ ] **1 teaspoon finely chopped fresh thyme, or $^1/_4$ teaspoon dried thyme**
- [ ] **$^1/_3$ cup/90 mL Marsala**
- [ ] **1 tablespoon finely chopped fresh parsley**

1   To make Tomato Sauce, heat oil and butter in a saucepan, and cook onion until soft. Add garlic and mushrooms and cook for 2-3 minutes longer. Combine tomatoes and sugar and add to mushrooms. Cook over a low heat for 10 minutes. Stir in stock and simmer for 30 minutes longer or until sauce reduces and thickens. Season to taste with black pepper.

2   To make Chicken Liver Sauce, melt butter in a skillet and cook chicken livers and thyme over a medium heat until livers change color. Increase heat, stir in Marsala and cook for 1-2 minutes. Stir in parsley.

3   Cook spaghetti in boiling water in a large saucepan until al dente. Drain and fold through oil.

4   Arrange half spaghetti on a warm serving platter, top with half chicken liver mixture, then half Tomato Sauce. Sprinkle over half Parmesan cheese, then repeat layers. Serve immediately.

Fettuccine with Veal Cream Sauce,
Spirelli with Ham and Artichokes

PAPPARDELLE WITH PEAS AND BACON

Pappardelle is a strong pasta which goes with rich sauces. It is ideal to serve with game.

Serves 4

- [ ] ¼ cup/½ stick/60 g butter
- [ ] 1 onion, sliced
- [ ] 1 clove garlic, crushed
- [ ] pinch chili flakes, or to taste
- [ ] 3 slices bacon, chopped
- [ ] 3 oz/90 g shelled peas, blanched
- [ ] 1 teaspoon finely chopped fresh mint
- [ ] 1 tablespoon finely chopped fresh parsley
- [ ] freshly ground black pepper
- [ ] 1 lb/500 g pappardelle
- [ ] 2 eggs, lightly beaten
- [ ] ⅓ cup/90 mL cream
- [ ] 1½ tablespoons grated fresh pecorino cheese

1   Melt butter in a large skillet and cook onion, garlic and chili for 6-8 minutes. Add bacon and cook for 5 minutes longer. Stir in peas, mint and 2 teaspoons parsley. Season to taste with black pepper. Set aside and keep warm.

2   Cook pappardelle in boiling water in a large saucepan until al dente. Drain, then add to pea mixture, toss lightly to coat and remove from heat. Combine eggs, cream, pecorino and remaining parsley and stir into pasta mixture. Serve as soon as eggs begin to set and cling to pasta – this will take only a few seconds. The sauce should be slightly runny.

SPIRELLI WITH HAM AND ARTICHOKES

Serves 4

- [ ] 1 lb/500 g spirelli
- [ ] 2 teaspoons olive oil
- [ ] 10 oz/315 g smoked ham, cut into strips
- [ ] 6 canned artichoke hearts, sliced lengthwise
- [ ] 3 eggs, beaten with 1 tablespoon grated fresh Parmesan cheese
- [ ] freshly ground black pepper

1   Cook spirelli in boiling water in a large saucepan following packet directions or until al dente. Drain, set aside and keep warm.

2   Heat oil in a skillet and cook ham and artichoke hearts for 1-2 minutes.

3   Add pasta and toss to combine. Remove from heat and quickly stir in egg mixture. Season to taste with black pepper. Serve as soon as the eggs start to stick to spirelli – this will take only a few seconds.

Pappardelle with Peas and Bacon, Chicken Livers and Mushrooms on Spaghetti

TORTELLINI WITH CREAMY TOMATO SAUCE

Serves 4

- ☐ **1 lb/500 g tortellini**
- ☐ **$1/3$ cup/45 g grated Parmesan cheese**
- ☐ **basil leaves**

CREAMY TOMATO SAUCE
- ☐ **1 tablespoon vegetable oil**
- ☐ **1 onion, finely chopped**
- ☐ **1 clove garlic, crushed**
- ☐ **$1^1/_2$ cups/375 mL canned tomato soup**
- ☐ **2 tablespoons red wine**
- ☐ **1 tablespoon finely chopped fresh basil**
- ☐ **$1/2$ cup/125 mL thick cream**
- ☐ **freshly ground black pepper**

1 Cook tortellini in boiling water in a saucepan following packet directions. Drain, set aside and keep warm.

2 To make sauce, heat oil in a small saucepan and cook onion over a medium heat for 3-4 minutes or until soft. Add garlic, soup, wine and basil, bring to simmering and simmer for 5 minutes. Remove pan from heat, stir in cream and season to taste with black pepper. Spoon sauce over tortellini, top with Parmesan cheese and basil leaves.

Serving suggestion: Accompany with crusty Italian bread.

Fruity Rice Salad, Fast Fried Rice

FAST FRIED RICE

Serves 4

- ☐ **1 tablespoon vegetable oil**
- ☐ **4 spring onions, finely chopped**
- ☐ **2 stalks celery, finely chopped**
- ☐ **2 eggs, lightly beaten**
- ☐ **4 slices packaged ham, finely chopped**
- ☐ **14 oz/440 g canned corn kernels, drained**
- ☐ **1³/₄ cups/300 g rice, cooked**
- ☐ **2 teaspoons soy sauce**

1 Heat oil in a nonstick skillet and cook spring onions and celery over a medium heat for 3-4 minutes or until onion is soft. Remove onion mixture from pan and set aside. Pour egg into pan and cook for 2 minutes or until set. Leaving omelet in pan and using a pancake turner or spatula chop omelet into small pieces.

2 Add onion mixture, ham, corn, rice and soy sauce to pan and stir to combine. Cook for 1 minute longer or until heated.

FRUITY RICE SALAD

This is a great recipe for using leftovers.

Serves 4

- ☐ **1³/₄ cups/300 g rice, cooked**
- ☐ **2 small apples, cored and chopped**
- ☐ **¹/₃ cup/60 g golden raisins**
- ☐ **1 green pepper, chopped**
- ☐ **¹/₃ cup/60 g sunflower seeds**
- ☐ **1 tablespoon finely chopped fresh coriander (cilantro) or parsley**

ORANGE DRESSING
- ☐ **¹/₂ cup/125 mL orange juice**
- ☐ **2 teaspoons finely grated orange rind**
- ☐ **1 teaspoon finely chopped fresh ginger**
- ☐ **2 teaspoons honey, warmed**

1 Place rice, apples, raisins, green pepper, sunflower seeds and coriander or parsley in a bowl and toss to combine.

2 To make dressing, place orange juice, orange rind, ginger and honey in a screwtop jar and shake to combine. Pour dressing over rice salad. Serve immediately.

CHEESY BAKED RICE CUSTARD

Serves 4
Oven temperature 350°F, 180°C

- [ ] **2 tablespoons/30 g butter**
- [ ] **2 leeks, sliced**
- [ ] **3 slices bacon, chopped**
- [ ] **1/2 red pepper, finely chopped**
- [ ] **1/4 cup/60 g short grain rice, cooked**
- [ ] **1 1/2 cups/375 mL milk**
- [ ] **2 eggs, lightly beaten**
- [ ] **1/2 teaspoon dry mustard**
- [ ] **1 teaspoon Worcestershire sauce**
- [ ] **1 tablespoon mayonnaise**
- [ ] **1 cup/125 g shredded Cheddar cheese**
- [ ] **2 tablespoons finely chopped fresh parsley**
- [ ] **1 teaspoon paprika**

1   Melt butter in a skillet. Cook leeks, bacon and pepper for 4-5 minutes, or until leeks are soft and bacon brown. Remove pan from heat and stir rice through. Transfer rice mixture to a deep casserole dish.

2   Place milk in a saucepan and bring almost to the boil. Remove pan from heat and whisk in eggs, mustard, Worcestershire sauce, mayonnaise, cheese and parsley. Pour milk mixture over rice mixture. Sprinkle lightly with paprika.

3   Place casserole in a baking dish. Add hot water to baking dish, so it comes halfway up the side of the casserole. Bake for 25-30 minutes, or until custard is firm.

LASAGNE

Serves 6
Oven temperature 375°F, 190°C,

- [ ] **9 sheets microwavable lasagne pasta**
- [ ] **1/2 cup/60 g shredded Cheddar cheese**
- [ ] **2 tablespoons grated Parmesan cheese**

MEAT AND MUSHROOM SAUCE
- [ ] **2 teaspoons olive oil**
- [ ] **1 onion, chopped**
- [ ] **2 cloves garlic, crushed**
- [ ] **2 slices bacon, chopped**
- [ ] **4 oz/125 g button mushrooms, sliced**
- [ ] **1 lb/500 g lean ground beef**
- [ ] **14 oz/440 g canned tomatoes, undrained and mashed**

EGGPLANT AND RICE PIE

Serves 6
Oven temperature 350°F,180°C

- [ ] **2 large eggplant, cut into 1/4 in/ 5 mm slices**
- [ ] **1/2 cup/125 mL olive oil**
- [ ] **1 onion, chopped**
- [ ] **2 cloves garlic, crushed**
- [ ] **1 lb/500 g lean ground beef**
- [ ] **14 oz/440 g canned tomatoes, undrained and mashed**
- [ ] **1 tablespoon finely chopped fresh oregano**
- [ ] **2 tablespoons tomato paste**
- [ ] **freshly ground black pepper**
- [ ] **1 cup/185 g brown rice, cooked**
- [ ] **8 oz/250 g fresh or frozen peas, cooked**
- [ ] **3/4 cup/90 g shredded Cheddar cheese**
- [ ] **1/4 cup/30 g grated Parmesan cheese**
- [ ] **1/3 cup/45 g dried bread crumbs**

1   Brush eggplant with oil. Heat half the remaining oil in a skillet. Place a single layer of eggplant in pan and cook until golden on each side. Remove and drain on paper towels. Repeat with remaining eggplant.

2   Heat remaining oil in pan, cook onion and garlic for 2-3 minutes or until onion is soft. Stir in meat and cook for 6-8 minutes, or until meat browns.

3   Combine tomatoes, oregano, tomato paste and black pepper to taste. Pour into pan. Simmer for 8-10 minutes, or until liquid reduces by half. Remove pan from heat and add rice, peas, Cheddar and Parmesan cheese.

4   Grease a deep, 9 in/23 cm round cake pan. Sprinkle half the bread crumbs over bottom and sides of pan. Place a layer of overlapping eggplant slices over base and sides of pan. Spoon meat mixture over eggplant. Pack down well using the back of a spoon.

5   Overlap remaining eggplant slices over filling. Sprinkle with remaining bread crumbs. Bake for 25-30 minutes or until golden brown. Stand 5 minutes before turning out and serving.

Eggplant and Rice Pie,
Cheesy Baked Rice Custard

- ☐ ¹/₂ cup/125 mL red wine
- ☐ ¹/₂ teaspoon dried basil
- ☐ ¹/₂ teaspoon dried oregano
- ☐ 1 teaspoon sugar

SPINACH CHEESE SAUCE
- ☐ 2 tablespoons/30 g butter
- ☐ 2 tablespoons all-purpose flour
- ☐ 1 cup/250 mL milk
- ☐ ¹/₂ cup/125mL thick cream
- ☐ ¹/₂ cup/60 g shredded Cheddar cheese
- ☐ 8 oz/250 g frozen spinach, thawed and drained
- ☐ freshly ground black pepper

1   To make meat sauce, heat oil in a skillet and cook onion, garlic, bacon and mushrooms for 2-3 minutes, or until onion is soft.

2   Add beef to pan and cook for 4-5 minutes, or until meat browns. Combine tomatoes, wine, basil, oregano and sugar and pour into pan with meat mixture and bring to the boil. Reduce heat, cover and simmer for 35 minutes, or until sauce thickens.

3   To make cheese sauce, melt butter in a saucepan, add flour and cook for 1-2 minutes. Remove pan from heat and stir in milk and cream. Cook over a medium heat, stirring continuously, until sauce boils and thickens.

4   Remove pan from heat and stir in cheese and spinach. Season with black pepper.

5   To assemble lasagne, spread one-third of cheese sauce over base of a lightly greased 7 x 11 in/18 x 28 cm shallow baking dish. Top with 3 lasagne sheets, spread half the meat sauce over, then another third of spinach cheese sauce. Top with another 3 lasagne sheets and remaining meat sauce. Place remaining lasagne sheets over meat sauce and top with remaining cheese sauce.

6   Combine Cheddar and Parmesan cheese and sprinkle over lasagne. Bake for 40 minutes or until golden.

HAM CHEESE AND LEEK BAKE

Serves 6
Oven temperature 375°F/190°C

- ☐ 1 tablespoon/15 g butter
- ☐ 2 leeks, sliced
- ☐ 1 cup/185 g brown rice, cooked
- ☐ 4 slices leg ham, off the bone, chopped
- ☐ 5 eggs
- ☐ 2 cups/500 mL milk
- ☐ freshly ground black pepper

- ☐ ¹/₂ cup/60 g shredded Cheddar cheese
- ☐ 1 tablespoon chopped fresh parsley

1   Melt butter in a large skillet, add leeks and cook, stirring frequently, for 4-5 minutes or until soft. Remove pan from heat, add rice and ham and mix to combine.

2   Spoon rice mixture into a lightly greased 10 in/25 cm ovenproof dish. Place eggs, milk and black pepper to taste in a bowl and whisk to combine. Pour egg mixture over rice mixture, sprinkle with cheese and parsley and bake for 25 minutes or until firm and golden.

Cook's tip: Precious time can be saved by keeping cooked rice or pasta in the refrigerator or freezer. You will then always have the main ingredient for making a rice or pasta salad or a dish such as this one which requires cooked rice.

RICE FRITTERS

Makes 20

- ☐ ¹/₄ teaspoon chili powder
- ☐ 1 teaspoon garam masala

- ☐ ¹/₂ cup plus 1 tablespoon/75 g wholewheat flour
- ☐ ¹/₂ cup plus 1 tablespoon/75 g besan flour
- ☐ ²/₃ cup/125 g brown rice, cooked
- ☐ 2 eggs, lightly beaten with ³/₄ cup/185 mL milk
- ☐ 4 spring onions, finely chopped
- ☐ ¹/₂ small red pepper, finely choppped
- ☐ oil for shallow-frying

1   Sift chili powder, garam masala and wholewheat and besan flours into a bowl. Mix in rice, then make a well in the center and gradually stir in egg mixture. Mix to a smooth batter and stir in spring onions and red pepper.

2   Heat oil in a large skillet and cook spoonfuls of batter for 3-4 minutes each side or until golden. Drain on paper towels and serve immediately.

Besan flour: Besan flour is made from chickpeas and can be found at Asian specialty food stores. All-purpose plain flour could be used instead if you wish.

Lasagne

ROSE-SCENTED SAFFRON RICE

Serve this fragrant rice accompaniment with chicken or lamb. Rosewater is available from most health food stores.

Serves 6

- [ ] **1 lb/500 g basmati rice, well washed**
- [ ] **¼ cup/60 mL ghee**
- [ ] **1 onion, chopped**
- [ ] **8 oz/250 g ground lamb**
- [ ] **½ teaspoon pumpkin spice**
- [ ] **½ cup/60 g currants**
- [ ] **½ teaspoon powdered saffron**
- [ ] **2 tablespoons rosewater**
- [ ] **4 cups/1 liter chicken stock**
- [ ] **⅓ cup/60 g blanched almonds, toasted**

1 Place rice in a large bowl, cover with cold water and set aside for 30 minutes.
2 Heat ghee in a heavy-based skillet, add onion and cook for 5 minutes or until onion is soft. Increase heat, add lamb and cook until lamb browns. Stir in spice and currants, cook for a further minute, remove pan from heat. Set aside and keep warm.
3 Combine saffron and rosewater. Place chicken stock and 2 teaspoons of rosewater mixture in a large saucepan, bring to the boil. Drain rice and add to the stock. Bring back to the boil, stirring occasionally. Reduce heat, cover and simmer gently for 30 minutes.
4 Fold meat mixture through rice, remove from heat and stand for 5 minutes before serving. To serve, sprinkle with remaining rosewater mixture and top with almonds.

PILAU WITH EGGPLANT

Pilau is a wonderful accompaniment that could easily be a meal on its own. This version with eggplant is particularly tasty and is great served with plain yogurt.

Serves 6

- [ ] **2 eggplant, cut into 1 in/2.5 cm cubes**
- [ ] **salt**
- [ ] **¼ cup/60 mL olive oil**
- [ ] **1 onion, sliced**
- [ ] **14 oz/440 g canned tomatoes, drained and chopped**
- [ ] **2 tablespoons chopped fresh parsley**

- [ ] **1 tablespoon chopped fresh mint**
- [ ] **3 cups/500 g long grain rice, well washed**
- [ ] **3 cups/750 mL chicken stock**

1 Sprinkle eggplant with salt and set aside for 30 minutes. Rinse under cold running water and pat dry with paper towels.
2 Heat oil in a heavy-based skillet. Add eggplant and cook until lightly browned. Remove from pan and set aside.
3 Add onion to pan and cook for 4-5 minutes or until onion is soft. Add tomatoes, parsley, mint and eggplant and cook for a further 5 minutes. Stir in rice and chicken stock. Bring to the boil. Reduce heat, cover and simmer for 30 minutes. Allow to stand for 30 minutes before serving.

LONTONG

Lontong are traditionally wrapped in young banana leaves. If these are not readily available, you can successfully substitute aluminum foil. The fried onion flakes that we have used in this recipe can be purchased from Asian food stores.

Serves 6

- [ ] **young banana leaves or aluminum foil**
- [ ] **2½ cups/500 g short grain white rice, well washed**
- [ ] **2 tablespoons sweet soy sauce**
- [ ] **2 tablespoons fried onion flakes**

1 If using banana leaves, drop in boiling water to clean and soften. Remove leaves from water and pat dry with absorbent kitchen paper. Brush lightly with a little vegetable oil. Cut leaves or foil into 8 in/20 cm squares.
2 Place a large spoonful of rice in the center of each square and fold over to completely enclose, allowing a little room for expansion during cooking. Tie each parcel with string to secure.
3 Bring a large saucepan of water to the boil, drop in rice bundles and simmer for 1 hour. To serve, drain bundles, unwrap and sprinkle with soy sauce and onion flakes.

ARTICHOKE AND WHITE WINE RISOTTO

Try using asparagus as a substitute for artichokes in this aromatic risotto.

Serves 4

- [ ] **¼ cup/½ stick/60 g butter**
- [ ] **1 onion, chopped**
- [ ] **1½ cups/330 g Arborio or risotto rice**
- [ ] **2 cups/500 mL chicken stock**
- [ ] **½ cup/125 mL dry white wine**
- [ ] **14 oz/440 g canned artichoke hearts, drained and liquid reserved**
- [ ] **2 tablespoons chopped fresh parsley**
- [ ] **4 thick slices leg ham, off the bone, cut into strips**
- [ ] **½ cup/60 g grated Parmesan cheese**
- [ ] **4 cherry tomatoes, quartered**
- [ ] **freshly ground black pepper**

1 Melt butter in a large skillet, add onion and cook for 5 minutes or until soft.
2 Add rice to pan and cook, stirring frequently, for 5 minutes. Combine stock, wine and reserved artichoke liquid. The total amount of liquid should equal 3½ cups/875 mL Top up with additional stock, if necessary. Pour one-third of the liquid over the rice and cook over a low heat, stirring, until liquid is absorbed. Continue adding liquid a little at a time and cook, stirring frequently, until all liquid is absorbed.
3 Cut artichokes into quarters. Fold artichokes, parsley, ham, Parmesan cheese and tomatoes into rice. Season to taste with black pepper and serve immediately.

Cook's tip: Arborio rice is an Italian short grain rice from the Po Valley. It is recognisable by the distinctive white spot on each kernel. If it is unavailable, short grain rice can be used instead.

FETTUCCINE WITH WINE AND MUSHROOMS

The perfect way to serve fettuccine – with a magnificent creamy sauce laden with button mushrooms.

Serves 6

- ☐ **1 lb/500 g fettucine**
- ☐ **1 tablespoon olive oil**

CREAMY MUSHROOM SAUCE
- ☐ **1 tablespoon olive oil**
- ☐ **1 large onion, sliced**
- ☐ **2 cloves garlic, crushed**
- ☐ **1 lb/500 g button mushrooms, sliced**
- ☐ **1 tablespoon/15 g butter**
- ☐ **1 tablespoon all-purpose flour**
- ☐ **$^1/_4$ cup/60 mL white wine**
- ☐ **1 cup/250 mL vegetable stock**
- ☐ **$^1/_2$ cup/125 mL thick cream**
- ☐ **2 tablespoons chopped fresh basil**
- ☐ **freshly ground black pepper**
- ☐ **2 tablespoons grated Parmesan cheese**
- ☐ **2 tablespoons snipped fresh chives**

1 Cook fettuccine in boiling water following packet instructions. Drain and toss in oil. Set aside and keep warm.

2 To make sauce, heat oil in a saucepan, add onion and garlic and cook over a medium heat, stirring occasionally, for 10 minutes or until onion is golden. Stir in mushrooms and cook for 2 minutes longer. Remove mushroom mixture from pan and set aside.

3 Melt butter in a clean saucepan, add flour and cook, stirring constantly for 2 minutes. Remove pan from heat and gradually stir in wine and stock. Return pan to heat and cook over a medium heat, stirring constantly, for 5-6 minutes or until sauce boils and thickens. Whisk in cream, then stir in mushroom mixture and basil. Season to taste with black pepper and cook for 3-4 minutes longer or until heated through.

4 To serve, spoon sauce over hot fettuccine and top with Parmesan cheese and chives.

Pilau with Eggplant, Rose-scented Saffron Rice, Lontong

BONBONS FILLED WITH CHICKEN AND HERBS

These look wonderful when made with different-colored pastas. If served as a first course, this recipe will serve six.

Serves 4

BONBONS
- [ ] **6 sheets fresh plain, tomato- or spinach-flavored pasta (9¹/₂ x 11 in/24 x 27 cm)**
- [ ] **1 egg, lightly beaten**
- [ ] **thin cream or melted butter for coating**
- [ ] **grated fresh Parmesan cheese**

CHICKEN AND HERB FILLING
- [ ] **1¹/₃ cups/200 g finely diced cooked chicken,**
- [ ] **¹/₂ cup/60 g finely diced ham**
- [ ] **²/₃ cup/155 g ricotta cheese, drained**
- [ ] **2 tablespoons grated fresh Parmesan cheese**
- [ ] **¹/₂ onion, grated**
- [ ] **¹/₂ teaspoon finely chopped fresh sage**
- [ ] **¹/₂ teaspoon finely chopped fresh oregano**
- [ ] **¹/₂ teaspoon finely chopped fresh parsley**
- [ ] **pinch ground nutmeg**
- [ ] **freshly ground black pepper**

1   Cut each pasta sheet into nine rectangles 3 x 3¹/₂ in/8 x 9 cm. Trim shorter ends of each rectangle using a zigzag pastry wheel. Set pasta aside and cover with a damp cloth.

2   To make filling, combine chicken, ham, ricotta cheese, Parmesan cheese, onion, sage, oregano, parsley and nutmeg. Season to taste with black pepper.

3   To form bonbons, place a teaspoon of filling in center of each pasta rectangle. Brush egg down one long side, and fold over pasta to enclose filling to form a tube. Press to seal, then pinch and twist trimmed ends tightly, like bonbon wrappers. As each bonbon is formed, set aside, uncovered, to rest.

4   Cook bonbons, a few at a time, in a large saucepan of boiling water for 4-5 minutes or until al dente. Remove with a slotted spoon and pile onto a warmed serving platter. To serve, toss in cream or butter and sprinkle with Parmesan cheese.

Cook's tip: These bonbons are best made with homemade pasta thinly rolled.

For something different you might like to make parcels rather than bonbons. To make parcels, cut 2 in/5 cm circles of pasta and place a teaspoon of filling in the center of each circle. Gather up edges to form a pouch and pinch together to seal. Cook and serve as described in the recipe.

TAGLIATELLE WITH SPINACH AND MUSHROOMS

Serves 4

- [ ] **1 lb/500 g fresh tomato tagliatelle**
- [ ] **¹/₄ cup/¹/₂ stick/60 g butter**
- [ ] **1 clove garlic, crushed**
- [ ] **2 tablespoons Marsala**
- [ ] **8 oz/250 g button mushrooms, sliced**
- [ ] **1 cup/250 mL thick cream**
- [ ] **freshly ground black pepper**
- [ ] **1¹/₂ lb/750 g spinach, stalks removed and leaves shredded**
- [ ] **grated Parmesan cheese**

1   Cook tagliatelle in boiling water in a large saucepan following packet directions or until al dente. Drain, set aside and keep warm.

2   Melt butter in a saucepan, add garlic and Marsala and cook over a low heat for 3 minutes or until syrupy. Add mushrooms and cook for 3 minutes longer. Blend in cream and bring to the boil. Season to taste with black pepper.

3   Add pasta to sauce. Toss in spinach and stir to coat. Cook over a low heat for 2-3 minutes or until spinach is heated through. Serve topped with Parmesan cheese.

Tagliatelle with Spinach and Mushrooms, Open Mushroom Ravioli, Bonbons filled with Chicken and Herbs

OPEN MUSHROOM RAVIOLI

A stylish approach for a wonderful first course. A delicious filling is visible between the unjoined sides of pasta.

Serves 4

- [ ] **16 circles fresh plain or tomato fresh pasta, 1¹/₂-2 in/4-5 cm in diameter**
- [ ] **4 dried (porcini) mushrooms**
- [ ] **¹/₃ cup/90 mL hot water**
- [ ] **3 oz/90 g butter**
- [ ] **7 oz/220 g button mushrooms, thinly sliced**
- [ ] **¹/₄ cup/60 mL dry sherry**
- [ ] **¹/₄ cup/60 mL cream**
- [ ] **1¹/₂ tablespoons chicken stock**
- [ ] **pinch ground nutmeg**
- [ ] **freshly ground black pepper**
- [ ] **1 small bunch watercress**
- [ ] **¹/₃ cup/90 g dairy sour cream**

1 Cook pasta circles, a few at a time, in boiling water in a large saucepan for 4-5 minutes or until tender. Remove and lay out in a single layer to dry, on clean teatowels.

2 Place dried mushrooms and hot water in a bowl and set aside to soak for 30 minutes. Drain porcini and chop finely. Reserve liquid.

3 Melt 1 oz/30 g butter in a skillet and gently cook button mushrooms for 2-3 minutes. Stir in soaked mushrooms and reserved liquid. Blend in sherry, cream, stock and nutmeg. Season to taste with black pepper. Cook over a medium heat until mixture reduces and thickens. Stir in remaining butter.

4 Place 2 pasta circles on each serving plate. Top each circle with 1-2 tablespoons mushroom mixture, then a few sprigs of watercress. Partially cover with another circle of pasta. Top each ravioli with a dollop of sour cream and garnish with watercress. Serve immediately.

Cook's tip: Dried mushrooms, known as *porcini* in Italy and *cèpes* in France, have a more intense flavor than fresh mushrooms. Dried mushrooms must be reconstituted in warm water before cooking. If cooked for too long they will lose their flavor. Allow 15-20 minutes cooking and the mushrooms will be perfectly tender.

SPINACH TIMBALES WITH PASTA FILLING

Serves 4
Oven temperature 350°F, 180°C

☐ **12 large spinach leaves, thick stalks removed**

PASTA FILLING
☐ **2 tablespoons olive oil**
☐ **2 small eggplant, chopped**
☐ **1 onion, chopped**
☐ **1 clove garlic, crushed**
☐ **1 red pepper, chopped**
☐ **2 zucchini, chopped**
☐ **1 large ripe tomato, peeled and chopped**
☐ **2 tablespoons tomato paste**
☐ **1 teaspoon hot chili powder**
☐ **¹/₄ cup/60 g finely chopped pitted black olives**
☐ **¹/₃ cup/60 g small pasta shapes, cooked**
☐ **¹/₄ cup/30 g grated Parmesan cheese**
☐ **freshly ground black pepper**

1 Boil, steam or microwave spinach until wilted. Drain well and use to line four greased individual soufflé or custard cups (1 cup/250 mL capacity). Allow some leaves to overhang top.

2 To make filling, heat oil in a saucepan, add eggplant, onion, garlic, red pepper, zucchini and tomato and cook, stirring occasionally, for 15 minutes or until mixture reduces and thickens. Stir in tomato paste, chili powder, olives, pasta, Parmesan cheese and black pepper to taste and mix well to combine.

3 Spoon filling into lined cups, fold overhanging leaves over filling and cover with greased aluminum foil and bake for 20 minutes. Allow to stand for 5-10 minutes before turning out.

BOWS WITH RICH TOMATO BASIL SAUCE

Serves 2

☐ **6 oz/185 g bow pasta**

TOMATO BASIL SAUCE
☐ **2 teaspoons olive oil**
☐ **1 onion, sliced**
☐ **1 clove garlic, crushed**
☐ **3 tomatoes, peeled, seeded and chopped**
☐ **¹/₂ cup/125 mL chicken stock**
☐ **1 tablespoon tomato paste**
☐ **1 tablespoon chopped fresh basil**
☐ **2 teaspoons chopped fresh parsley**
☐ **¹/₂ teaspoon sugar**
☐ **freshly ground black pepper**
☐ **grated Parmeson cheese**

1 Cook pasta in boiling water in a saucepan following packet directions. Drain, set aside and keep warm.

2 To make sauce, heat oil in a saucepan and cook onion and garlic over a medium heat for 3-4 minutes or until onion is soft. Add tomatoes, stock, tomato paste, basil, parsley and sugar and simmer for 10-15 minutes or until reduced and thickened. Season to taste with black pepper. Spoon sauce over pasta. Sprinkle with a little grated fresh Parmesan cheese and extra chopped fresh basil.

Cook's tip: Any leftover sauce can be made into soup. To make, chop 1 small carrot and 1 stalk celery. Place leftover sauce, 1 cup/250 mL chicken stock, carrot and celery in a saucepan. Bring to simmering and simmer for 10-15 minutes or until carrot is tender. Season to taste with black pepper.

Bows with Rich Tomato Basil Sauce, Tomato Soup made from leftover Rich Tomato Basil Sauce

RAVIOLI WITH TUNA SAUCE

Serves 4

- ☐ **12 oz/375 g fresh or frozen ravioli with spinach filling**
- ☐ **2 tablespoons grated Parmesan cheese**
- ☐ **fresh dill weed sprigs**

TUNA SAUCE
- ☐ **2 teaspoons olive oil**
- ☐ **1 onion, finely chopped**
- ☐ **1 clove garlic, crushed**
- ☐ **14 oz/440 g canned tomatoes, undrained and mashed**
- ☐ **1 tablespoon tomato paste**
- ☐ **1 tablespoon dry red wine**
- ☐ **1 teaspoon sugar**
- ☐ **14 oz/440 g canned tuna in brine, drained and flaked**
- ☐ **1 tablespoon finely chopped fresh parsley**
- ☐ **1 tablespoon finely chopped fresh dill weed**
- ☐ **freshly ground black pepper**
- ☐ **dill sprigs**

1 Cook ravioli in boiling water in a large saucepan following packet directions. Drain and keep warm.

2 To make sauce, heat oil in a skillet. Cook onion and garlic for 4-5 minutes or until onion is soft. Stir in tomatoes, tomato paste, wine and sugar. Bring to the boil. Add tuna, parsley and dill, reduce heat and simmer for 10 minutes.

3 Place pasta on a warmed serving platter. Spoon over sauce, sprinkle with Parmesan cheese and garnish with dill sprigs.

SPAGHETTI WITH ASPARAGUS SAUCE

Serves 6

- ☐ **1 lb/500 g spaghetti**
- ☐ **2 tablespoons grated Parmesan cheese**

ASPARAGUS SAUCE
- ☐ **1 lb/500 g fresh asparagus spears, trimmed**
- ☐ **1 tablespoon olive oil**
- ☐ **1 thick slice wholewheat bread, crumbed**
- ☐ **1 cup/250 mL evaporated milk**
- ☐ **1/2 cup/60 g shredded mozzarella cheese**
- ☐ **freshly ground black pepper**

1 Cook spaghetti in boiling water in a large saucepan following packet directions.
2 To make sauce, steam, boil or microwave asparagus until tender. Drain and refresh under cold running water. Cut into 1 1/2 in/3 cm pieces and set aside. Heat oil in a skillet, add bread crumbs and cook over a low heat for 2 minutes, stirring all the time. Stir in milk and asparagus, and cook over medium heat for 5 minutes. Mix in cheese and continue to cook until cheese melts. Season to taste with black pepper.
3 Place spaghetti on a warmed serving platter, spoon over sauce and toss gently to combine. Sprinkle with Parmesan cheese and serve immediately.

Spaghetti with Asparagus Sauce, Ravioli with Tuna Sauce

HOT AND SOUR THAI STIR-FRY

Serves 8

- [ ] 2 tablespoons soy sauce
- [ ] 1 tablespoon dry sherry
- [ ] 1 fresh red chili, seeded and finely chopped
- [ ] 1 clove garlic, crushed
- [ ] 1 lb/500 g tofu, cubed and drained
- [ ] 1 tablespoon vegetable oil
- [ ] 2 onions, sliced
- [ ] 1 red pepper, cut into thin strips
- [ ] 1 green pepper, cut into thin strips
- [ ] 4 oz/125 g snow peas, trimmed
- [ ] 4 oz/125 g egg noodles, cooked and drained
- [ ] 2 spring onions, finely chopped
- [ ] fresh coriander (cilantro) leaves

SPICY PEANUT SAUCE

- [ ] 2 cloves garlic, crushed
- [ ] 1/2 cup/125 g crunchy peanut butter
- [ ] 1/4 cup/60 mL lime or lemon juice
- [ ] 1/4 cup/60 mL soy sauce
- [ ] 1 small fresh red chili, finely chopped
- [ ] 1/2 cup/125 mL vegetable stock or water

1   Preheat barbecue to a high heat. Place soy sauce, sherry, chili and garlic in a bowl, and mix to combine. Add tofu, toss to coat and set aside to marinate for 30 minutes. Drain.

2   To make sauce, place garlic, peanut butter, lime or lemon juice, soy sauce and chili in a food processor or blender and process to combine. With machine running, slowly add vegetable stock or water and process until combined.

3   Heat oil in a wok or frying pan on barbecue and stir-fry onions and red and green pepper for 4-5 minutes. Using a slotted spoon remove onions and peppers and set aside. Add tofu to wok or skillet and stir-fry for 1-2 minutes. Return onions and peppers to wok or frying pan, add snow peas and noodles and stir-fry for 3-4 minutes longer. Add peanut sauce and toss to coat noodles and vegetables evenly with sauce. Transfer to a serving platter, garnish with spring onions and coriander leaves. Serve immediately.

Hot and Sour Thai Stir-fry

VEGETABLE PASTA BAKE

Serves 6
Oven temperature 350°F, 180°C

- [ ] **9 plain or wholewheat microwavable lasagne sheets**
- [ ] **8 oz/250 g soft or silken tofu, beaten until smooth**

VEGETABLE FILLING
- [ ] **1 tablespoon olive oil**
- [ ] **¼ small cabbage, shredded**
- [ ] **1 carrot, finely chopped**
- [ ] **1 large green pepper, finely chopped**
- [ ] **1 large red pepper, finely chopped**
- [ ] **10 oz/315 g canned sweet corn kernels, drained**
- [ ] **14 oz/440 g canned peeled tomatoes, undrained and mashed**
- [ ] **5 tablespoons chopped fresh basil**
- [ ] **freshly ground black pepper**

WALNUT TOPPING
- [ ] **1 cup/125 g shredded grated mozzarella cheese**
- [ ] **½ cup/30 g wholewheat bread crumbs, made from stale bread**
- [ ] **⅓ cup/90 g chopped walnuts**

1 To make filling, heat oil in a saucepan, cook cabbage, carrot, green and red peppers, corn, tomatoes and basil over a medium heat until boiling. Reduce heat and simmer for 15 minutes or until vegetables are soft and mixture reduces and thickens. Season to taste with black pepper.

2 To make topping, combine cheese, bread crumbs and walnuts in a bowl and set aside.

3 Spread one-third of filling over base of lightly greased 8 x 12 in/20 x 30 cm baking dish. Cover with a layer of lasagne sheets, spread with one-third of tofu, then one-third of filling mixture. Repeat layers, finishing with lasagne sheets. Spread with remaining tofu and sprinkle with topping. Bake for 30-35 minutes or until tender.

Vegetable Pasta Bake

chapter eight

VEGETABLES ON THE SIDE

Vegetables as a side dish
are an important part of any meal.
They add variety, texture, flavor
and color and should complement
the main dish. This chapter presents
you with a host of delicious recipes
for vegetable side dishes and
salads that are sure to tempt
even the most reluctant
vegetable eaters.

Tomato and Spinach Stuffed Mushrooms,
Herby Vegetable Salad,
Gipsy Baked Potatoes

TOMATO AND SPINACH STUFFED MUSHROOMS

Serves 6
Oven temperature 400°F, 200°C

- [ ] **6 large open flat mushrooms**
- [ ] **¹/₄ cup/30 g shredded mozzarella cheese**
- [ ] **1 tablespoon grated Parmesan cheese**
- [ ] **1 tablespoon finely snipped fresh chives**

SPINACH FILLING
- [ ] **1 tablespoon olive oil**
- [ ] **1 clove garlic, crushed**
- [ ] **3 spring onions, finely chopped**
- [ ] **4 large spinach leaves, finely shredded**
- [ ] **1 tablespoon tomato paste**
- [ ] **³/₄ cup/45 g bread crumbs, made from stale bread**
- [ ] **freshly ground black pepper**

1 Wipe mushrooms, remove stalks and finely chop.
2 To make filling, heat 1 teaspoon oil in skillet, cook garlic and spring onions for 1-2 minutes. Stir in spinach and tomato paste, cook for 2-3 minutes. Fold through bread crumbs. Season to taste with black pepper.
3 Brush mushroom caps with remaining oil and place on a baking tray. Combine mozzarella and Parmesan cheeses. Spoon filling into mushroom caps, top with cheese mixture, sprinkle with chives and bake for 10-15 minutes.

GIPSY BAKED POTATOES

Serves 4
Oven temperature 350°F, 180°C

- [ ] **2 teaspoons vegetable oil**
- [ ] **1 onion, chopped**
- [ ] **1 clove garlic, crushed**
- [ ] **1 teaspoon finely chopped fresh rosemary**
- [ ] **3 large tomatoes, peeled and chopped**
- [ ] **1 green pepper, diced**
- [ ] **1 teaspoon paprika**
- [ ] **1 cup/250 mL chicken stock**
- [ ] **freshly ground black pepper**
- [ ] **2 large potatoes, cut into thick slices**
- [ ] **2 tablespoons finely snipped fresh chives**

1 Heat oil in a skillet and cook onion, garlic and rosemary for 4-5 minutes or until onion is soft. Add tomatoes, pepper, paprika and chicken stock, bring to the boil and simmer for 10 minutes. Season to taste with black pepper.
2 Arrange potatoes in layers in a lightly greased baking dish, spoon over tomato mixture and bake for 1¹/₂ hours or until cooked through. Sprinkle with chives just prior to serving.

HERBY VEGETABLE SALAD

Serves 4

- [ ] **¹/₄ small cauliflower, broken into florets**
- [ ] **1 head broccoli, broken into florets**
- [ ] **1 large carrot, cut into thin strips**
- [ ] **5 oz/155 g snow peas, trimmed**
- [ ] **1 red pepper, cut into thin strips**
- [ ] **¹/₄ cup/60 mL lemon juice**
- [ ] **2 teaspoons finely chopped fresh coriander (cilantro)**
- [ ] **2 teaspoons finely chopped fresh rosemary**
- [ ] **freshly ground black pepper**

LEMON VINAIGRETTE
- [ ] **2 tablespoons lemon juice**
- [ ] **1 tablespoon olive oil**
- [ ] **1 clove garlic, crushed**
- [ ] **1 teaspoon coarse grain mustard**

1 Boil, steam or microwave cauliflower, broccoli, carrot and snow peas, separately, until just tender. Drain, then refresh under cold water.
2 Drain vegetables well. Toss in a salad bowl with pepper, lemon juice, coriander and rosemary. Season to taste with black pepper. Refrigerate until required.
3 To make vinaigrette, combine all ingredients in a screwtop jar. Shake well to combine. Pour over salad just prior to serving.

COCONUT VEGETABLE SKEWERS

Serves 4

- [ ] **16 button mushrooms**
- [ ] **2 zucchini, cut into 8 pieces**
- [ ] **8 whole baby onions, peeled**
- [ ] **16 cherry tomatoes**
- [ ] **²/₃ cup/30 g shredded coconut, toasted**

MINT MARINADE
- [ ] **1 tablespoon finely chopped fresh mint**
- [ ] **2 tablespoons lime or lemon juice**
- [ ] **2 teaspoons honey**
- [ ] **1 tablespoon chili paste (sambal oelek)**
- [ ] **¹/₃ cup/90 mL coconut milk**

1 To make marinade, place mint, lime or lemon juice, honey, chili paste (sambal oelek) and coconut milk in a bowl and whisk to combine. Add mushrooms, zucchini, onions and tomatoes, toss to coat, cover and set aside to marinate for 1 hour.
2 Drain off marinade and reserve. Thread vegetables onto 8 bamboo skewers, brush with reserved marinade and cook under a medium preheated broiler or on a barbecue grill for 10-15 minutes or until vegetables are cooked. Brush with marinade several times during cooking.
3 Remove skewers from heat, roll in coconut and serve immediately.

SWEET POTATO CHIPS

Serves 4

- [ ] **1 lb/500 g sweet potato**
- [ ] **2 tablespoons lemon juice**
- [ ] **oil for deep-frying**
- [ ] **1 tablespoon salt**
- [ ] **1 teaspoon chili powder or according to taste**
- [ ] **¹/₂ teaspoon superfine sugar**

1 Slice potatoes into paper thin slices. Place potato slices and lemon juice in a large bowl, cover with cold water and refrigerate for 2 hours. Drain on paper towels.
2 Heat oil in a large saucepan until a cube of bread dropped in browns in 50 seconds. Cook a few potato slices at a time for 6 minutes or until golden and almost crisp. Remove potato slices from oil, drain on paper towels, set aside and keep warm. Repeat with remaining potatoes.
3 Return cooked potato slices to hot oil and cook until crisp. Remove from oil and drain on paper towels. Place salt, chili powder and sugar in a small bowl, mix to combine and sprinkle over chips. Serve immediately.

*Alfalfa Potato Salad,
Avocado Salad with Spicy Dressing*

AVOCADO SALAD WITH SPICY DRESSING

Serves 4

- [ ] **2 avocados, pitted, peeled and sliced**
- [ ] **2 small tomatoes, cut into wedges**
- [ ] **4 oz/125 g olives, pitted**
- [ ] **1 lettuce, separated into leaves**

SPICY DRESSING
- [ ] **$^1/_3$ cup/90 mL olive oil**
- [ ] **$^1/_4$ cup/60 mL lemon juice**
- [ ] **2 tablespoons tomato paste**
- [ ] **1 teaspoon chili powder**
- [ ] **$^1/_2$ teaspoon ground cumin**
- [ ] **freshly ground black pepper**

1   To make dressing, place oil, lemon juice, tomato paste, chili powder, cumin, and black pepper to taste in a food processor or blender and process until smooth.

2   Place avocados, tomatoes and olives in a bowl, pour dressing over and toss to combine. Cover and place in the refrigerator to marinate for 30 minutes.

3   Arrange lettuce leaves on a serving platter and top with salad.

ALFALFA POTATO SALAD

Serves 6

- [ ] **1$^1/_2$ lb/750 g potatoes**
- [ ] **1 tablespoon vegetable oil**
- [ ] **2 stalks celery, finely chopped**
- [ ] **1 large cucumber, diced**
- [ ] **2 green peppers, diced**
- [ ] **2 carrots, shredded**
- [ ] **1 raw beet, shredded**
- [ ] **1 small lettuce, leaves torn into bite-sized pieces**
- [ ] **1 oz/30 g alfalfa sprouts**
- [ ] **$^1/_4$ cup/60 g tablespoons mayonnaise**
- [ ] **2 avocados, pitted, peeled and sliced**

1   Boil, steam or microwave washed, unpeeled potatoes until just tender. While still hot, cut into large pieces and place in a bowl. Sprinkle with oil.

2   Add celery, cucumber, green peppers, carrots, beet, lettuce, sprouts and mayonnaise to bowl and toss to combine. Top with avocado slices and serve.

POTATOES FILLED WITH CHILI BEANS

You can substitute butter beans or a canned bean mix for kidney beans.

Serves 4
Oven temperature 425°F, 220°C

- ☐ **4 medium potatoes**
- ☐ **10 oz/315 g canned red kidney beans**
- ☐ **1 tablespoon tomato paste**
- ☐ **1-2 teaspoons chili sauce (according to taste)**
- ☐ **paprika**

CARROT BALLS

Serve 4

- ☐ **3 carrots, shredded**
- ☐ **2 teaspoons orange rind**
- ☐ **¹/₂ cup/60 g shredded Swiss cheese**
- ☐ **¹/₂ cup/60 g grated Parmesan cheese**
- ☐ **1 tablespoon chopped fresh mint**
- ☐ **2 eggs, lightly beaten**
- ☐ **flour**
- ☐ **6 oz/185 g unprocessed bran (about 1¹/₂ cups)**
- ☐ **3 tablespoons finely chopped almonds**
- ☐ **vegetable oil for cooking**

1   Combine carrots, orange rind, cheeses, mint and half the beaten egg. Season to taste. Shape into balls. Coat with flour, dip in remaining beaten egg and roll in combined bran and almonds.

2   Heat oil in a skillet. Cook carrot balls until golden brown. Drain on paper towels. Serve with mango chutney if desired.

Nutrition tip: An alternative low fat cooking method is to lightly oil a baking dish and place the carrot balls in it. Bake the carrot balls on 400°F/200°C for 15-20 minutes, turning frequently during the cooking time for a delicious, crusty texture.

Above: Carrot Balls
Right: Pickled Tomatoes and Beans, Potatoes Filled with Chili Beans

1   Bake scrubbed, unpeeled potatoes for 45 minutes-1hour or until soft but firm. Cool slightly.
2   Cut potatoes in half and scoop out flesh, leaving a thin shell. Mash potato flesh and combine with beans, tomato paste and sauce.
3   Spoon mixture back into potato shells. Dust lightly with paprika and bake at 400°F/200°C until heated through and lightly browned on top.

Microwave it: Potatoes can also be microwaved on HIGH (100%) for 4-5 minutes. Stand for 5 minutes before removing flesh.

PICKLED TOMATOES AND BEANS

This recipe uses canned bean mix which is made up of a mixture of butter beans, kidney beans and lima beans. Any canned mixed beans can be used as a substitute.

Serves 4

- ☐ **2 tablespoons olive oil**
- ☐ **1 clove garlic, crushed**
- ☐ **1 tablespoon chopped fresh basil**
- ☐ **10 oz/315 g canned bean mix, drained**
- ☐ **8 oz/250 g cherry tomatoes, halved**
- ☐ **1 tablespoon white vinegar**
- ☐ **¹/₂ teaspoon sugar**
- ☐ **freshly ground black pepper**

1   Heat oil in a skillet. Cook garlic and basil for 1 minute, stir in beans and tomatoes. Season to taste with black pepper.
2   Cover and simmer for 5-6 minutes. Mix in combined vinegar and sugar. Heat through gently and serve.

GARDEN SALAD WITH CREAMY MAYONNAISE

Serves 4

- ☐ 1 lettuce, leaves separated and torn into pieces
- ☐ 12 cherry tomatoes or tomato wedges
- ☐ 4 hard-boiled eggs, cut into wedges
- ☐ 12 button mushrooms, sliced
- ☐ 2 oz/60 g snow peas or sugar snap peas
- ☐ 1 tablespoon chopped fresh parsley
- ☐ 1 tablespoon chopped fresh basil
- ☐ 1 tablespoon pine nuts (pignola), toasted
- ☐ Croutons (see recipe)

YOGURT DRESSING
- ☐ 1/3 cup/90 mL plain yogurt
- ☐ 1 clove garlic, crushed
- ☐ 1 tablespoon white wine vinegar
- ☐ 1 tablespoon snipped fresh chives
- ☐ freshly ground black pepper

1 Arrange lettuce, tomatoes, eggs, mushrooms and snow peas or sugar snap peas on a serving plate. Sprinkle with parsley, basil, pine nuts and Croutons.
2 To make dressing, place yogurt, garlic, vinegar, chives and black pepper to taste in a bowl and whisk to combine. Spoon a little dressing over the salad and serve immediately.

Croutons: To make Croutons, cut crusts from a slice of bread, then lightly brush slice with oil and cut into cubes. Place cubes on a baking sheet and bake at 400°F/200°C for 10-15 minutes or until Croutons are golden and crisp.

SIMPLE GREEN SALAD

Serves 4

- ☐ 1 small lettuce, leaves separated and torn into pieces
- ☐ 1 small cucumber, sliced
- ☐ 1 green pepper, cut into thin strips
- ☐ 4 spring onions, finely chopped
- ☐ 1 tablespoon snipped fresh chives
- ☐ 1 tablespoon finely chopped fresh parsley

VINAIGRETTE
- ☐ 2 tablespoons olive oil
- ☐ 1 tablespoon cider vinegar
- ☐ 1 teaspoon Dijon mustard
- ☐ freshly ground black pepper

1 Arrange lettuce, cucumber, green pepper and spring onions in a salad bowl. Sprinkle with chives and parsley.
2 Place oil, vinegar, mustard and black pepper to taste in a screwtop jar and shake well to combine. Drizzle Vinaigrette over salad and serve immediately.

JULIENNE VEGETABLE SALAD

Serves 4

- ☐ 2 carrots, cut into thin strips
- ☐ 2 zucchini, cut into thin strips
- ☐ 2 stalks celery, cut into thin strips
- ☐ 1 teaspoon sesame seeds, toasted

GINGER AND SOY DRESSING
- ☐ 1 teaspoon sesame oil
- ☐ 1 teaspoon grated fresh ginger
- ☐ 2 tablespoons soy sauce
- ☐ 2 tablespoons water
- ☐ 1 teaspoon cider vinegar
- ☐ 1 clove garlic, crushed

1 Arrange carrots, zucchini and celery on a serving plate.
2 To make dressing, place oil, ginger, soy sauce, water, vinegar and garlic in a screwtop jar and shake well to combine. Drizzle dressing over salad and sprinkle with sesame seeds.

From left: Waldorf Salad, Garden Salad with Creamy Mayonnaise, Pesto Pasta Salad, Julienne Vegetable Salad, Simple Green Salad

PESTO PASTA SALAD

This salad can be served warm – keep the pasta warm after cooking.

Serves 4

- [ ] **8 oz/250 g spiral pasta**
- [ ] **12 cherry tomatoes, halved**
- [ ] **4 slices leg ham, off the bone cut into thin strips**
- [ ] **4 oz/125 g watercress or snow pea sprouts**

PESTO SAUCE
- [ ] **2 oz/60 g fresh basil leaves**
- [ ] **2 cloves garlic**
- [ ] **2 tablespoons pine nuts (pignola)**
- [ ] **$^1/_3$ cup/90 mL olive oil**
- [ ] **$^1/_2$ cup/60 g grated fresh Parmesan cheese**
- [ ] **freshly ground black pepper**

1 Cook pasta in a saucepan in boiling water following packet directions. Rinse, drain and set aside to cool.

2 To make sauce, place basil, garlic, pine nuts, and 1 tablespoon oil in a food processor or blender and process until smooth. With machine running, gradually add remaining oil. Mix in Parmesan cheese and season to taste with black pepper.

3 Spoon sauce over pasta and toss to combine. Add tomatoes, ham and watercress or snow pea sprouts to salad and toss.

Cook's tip: This is a wonderful main course salad. To serve as a main course, simply increase the pasta quantity to 1 lb/500 g.

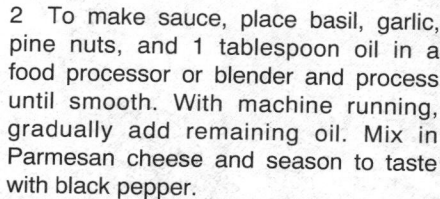

WALDORF SALAD

Serves 4

- [ ] **2 green or red apples, cored and sliced**
- [ ] **2 teaspoons lemon juice**
- [ ] **4 stalks celery, sliced**
- [ ] **2 tablespoons coarsely chopped walnuts**
- [ ] **$^1/_3$ cup/90 g mayonnaise**
- [ ] **freshly ground black pepper**

Place apples in a bowl, pour lemon juice over and toss to coat. Add celery, walnuts and mayonnaise and toss to combine. Season to taste with black pepper.

CANDIED SWEET POTATO

Serve this sweet vegetable with grilled pork chops.

Serves 6

- [ ] **¹/₂ cup/90 g packed brown sugar**
- [ ] **¹/₂ cup/125 mL water**
- [ ] **1 tablespoon/15 g butter**
- [ ] **500 g/1 lb sweet potato, thinly sliced**
- [ ] **2 tablespoons toasted slivered almonds**

1 Combine sugar, water and butter in a nonstick skillet. Cook over a low heat until butter melts. Add sweet potato, cover and continue to cook over a low heat for 15-20 minutes or until sweet potato is tender.
2 Add almonds and toss lightly to combine.

BEET, ORANGE AND HORSERADISH SALAD

Serves 6

- [ ] **4 cooked beets, cut into thin strips**
- [ ] **2 teaspoons grated orange rind**
- [ ] **2 oranges, segmented**

HORSERADISH DRESSING
- [ ] **1¹/₂ tablespoons olive oil**
- [ ] **¹/₄ cup/60 mL cider vinegar**
- [ ] **1 teaspoon dry mustard**
- [ ] **2 teaspoons bottled horseradish**
- [ ] **2 teaspoons sugar**

1 Combine beets, orange rind and orange segments. Arrange attractively in a salad bowl. Cover and refrigerate for 1-2 hours.
2 To make dressing, combine oil, vinegar, mustard, horseradish and sugar in a screwtop jar. Shake well to combine. Pour over salad just prior to serving.

STIR-FRIED BROCCOLI WITH ALMONDS

A colorful stir-fry that is sure to please the whole family.

Serves 4

- [ ] **2 carrots, cut into matchsticks**
- [ ] **1 lb/500 g broccoli, cut into florets**
- [ ] **2 teaspoons peanut oil**
- [ ] **1 onion, sliced**
- [ ] **1 clove garlic, crushed**
- [ ] **2 teaspoons grated fresh ginger**
- [ ] **2 teaspoons soy sauce**
- [ ] **2 tablespoons toasted almonds**

1 Boil, steam or microwave carrots and broccoli until they just change color. Drain and refresh under cold running water.
2 Heat oil in a wok or skillet. Add onion, garlic and ginger and stir-fry for 4-5 minutes. Add carrots, broccoli and soy sauce, and stir-fry for 3-4 minutes longer, or until vegetables are heated through. Just prior to serving toss through almonds.

Nutrition tip: Vegetables of the cabbage family — cabbage, Brussels sprouts, broccoli, cauliflower and turnip — are nutrition 'superstars' and should be included as often as possible. Research has shown that these vegetables contain compounds called indoles and isothiocyanates which can protect against cancer of the bowel. They are also one of the best vegetables for fiber and are high in vitamin C and beta-carotene.

RICOTTA AND HERB ZUCCHINI

Serves 6
Oven temperature 475°F, 240°C

- [ ] **6 large zucchini**
- [ ] **olive oil**

RICOTTA FILLING
- [ ] **$^1/_2$ cup/30 g bread crumbs, made from stale bread**
- [ ] **$^1/_2$ cup/60 g shredded mozzarella cheese**
- [ ] **$^1/_2$ cup/125 g ricotta cheese**
- [ ] **$^1/_4$ cup/30 g grated Parmesan cheese**
- [ ] **1 tablespoon chopped fresh basil**
- [ ] **2 teaspoons chopped fresh oregano**
- [ ] **1 egg white, lightly beaten**

1   Boil, steam or microwave zucchini until just tender. Refresh under cold running water and pat dry with paper towels. Cut almost through each zucchini crosswise at $^3/_4$ in/2 cm intervals, taking care not to cut right through.

2   To make filling, place bread crumbs, mozzarella cheese, ricotta cheese, Parmesan cheese, basil and oregano in a bowl. Stir in egg white and mix well to combine. Place some filling in each zucchini cut. Place zucchini in a lightly oiled baking dish, brush lightly with oil and bake for 15 minutes or until heated through and filling is golden.

Candied Sweet Potato, Stir-fried Broccoli with Almonds, Beet, Orange and Horseradish Salad

HOT COLESLAW WITH BRANDY DRESSING

Serves 4

- ☐ **2 slices bacon, chopped**
- ☐ **¹/₂ small cabbage, shredded**
- ☐ **2 green apples, coarsely chopped**
- ☐ **¹/₂ teaspoon ground nutmeg**

BRANDY DRESSING
- ☐ **1 clove garlic, crushed**
- ☐ **1 tablespoon cider vinegar**
- ☐ **2 tablespoons brandy**
- ☐ **¹/₃ cup/90 mL walnut oil**
- ☐ **freshly ground black pepper**

1   Cook bacon in a heavy-based skillet until just crisp. Add cabbage and apples and toss well. Cook for 3-4 minutes, then mix in nutmeg. Using a slotted spoon transfer to a warmed bowl and toss to combine.

2   To make dressing, combine garlic, vinegar, brandy, oil and black pepper to taste in a screwtop jar and shake well. Pour over coleslaw and serve.

PUNGENT SPINACH CURRY

This quick spinach curry makes a wonderful dish for a vegetarian meal or for use as an accompaniment to a mild meat dish.

Serves 6

- ☐ **¹/₄ cup/60 mL ghee or clarified butter**
- ☐ **1 onion, finely chopped**
- ☐ **2 cloves garlic, crushed**
- ☐ **2 small fresh red chilies, finely sliced**
- ☐ **1 teaspoon grated fresh ginger**
- ☐ **1 lb/500 g fresh spinach, leaves shredded**
- ☐ **freshly ground black pepper**

1   Melt ghee or butter in a skillet. Add onion, garlic, chilies and ginger and cook for 2-3 minutes or until onion is soft.

2   Add spinach, toss to coat with spice mixture and cook for 4-5 minutes or until spinach begins to wilt. Season to taste with black pepper.

CARROT AND GINGER SALAD

Serves 6

- ☐ **3 carrots, shredded**
- ☐ **¹/₂ cup/90 g golden raisins**
- ☐ **2 oz/60 g alfalfa sprouts**
- ☐ **2 tablespoons finely snipped fresh chives**

GREEN GINGER DRESSING
- ☐ **1 tablespoon vegetable oil**
- ☐ **2 tablespoons cider vinegar**
- ☐ **1 tablespoon green ginger wine**
- ☐ **1 teaspoon grated fresh ginger**
- ☐ **freshly ground black pepper**

1   Place carrots and raisins in a bowl and toss to combine.

2   To make dressing, place oil, vinegar, ginger wine, ginger and black pepper to taste in a screwtop jar and shake well to combine. Spoon dressing over carrot mixture and toss to coat with dressing.

3   Line a large serving platter with alfalfa sprouts, top with carrot mixture and sprinkle with chives.

SALAD SUPREMO

Serves 6

- ☐ **1 romaine lettuce, leaves separated and torn into pieces**
- ☐ **8 oz/250 g cherry tomatoes**
- ☐ **1 green pepper, sliced**
- ☐ **4 hard-boiled eggs, quartered**
- ☐ **12 black olives**
- ☐ **2 teaspoons capers**
- ☐ **1 tablespoon olive oil**
- ☐ **4 oz/125 g pepperoni sausage, diced**
- ☐ **2 slices white bread, cut into ¹/₂ in/1 cm cubes**

OREGANO DRESSING
- ☐ **¹/₄ cup/60 mL cider vinegar**
- ☐ **¹/₄ cup/60 mL vegetable oil**
- ☐ **¹/₄ teaspoon sugar**
- ☐ **1 clove garlic, crushed**
- ☐ **1 tablespoon chopped fresh oregano or 1 teaspoon dried oregano**
- ☐ **freshly ground black pepper**

1   Arrange lettuce, tomatoes, green pepper, eggs, olives and capers attractively on a large serving platter.

2   Heat oil in a skillet. Add pepperoni and bread cubes and cook, stirring frequently, for 5 minutes or until bread is crisp and golden. Remove pepperoni and bread from pan and drain on paper towels. Set aside to cool, then sprinkle over salad.

3   To make dressing, place vinegar, oil, sugar, garlic, oregano and black pepper to taste in a screwtop jar and shake well to combine. Drizzle dressing over salad and serve immediately.

CHINESE SESAME SLAW

Serves 6

- ☐ **4 oz/125 g snow peas, trimmed**
- ☐ **¹/₂ Chinese cabbage, finely shredded**
- ☐ **6¹/₂ oz/200 g bean sprouts**
- ☐ **4 spring onions, chopped**
- ☐ **¹/₂ red pepper, cut into strips**
- ☐ **¹/₂ cucumber, diced**
- ☐ **2 tablespoons sesame seeds, toasted**

SESAME DRESSING
- ☐ **2 teaspoons vegetable oil**
- ☐ **1 teaspoon sesame oil**
- ☐ **2 tablespoons white wine vinegar**
- ☐ **1 tablespoon soy sauce**
- ☐ **freshly ground black pepper**

1   Boil, steam or microwave snow peas until they just change color. Drain and refresh under cold running water.

2   Place cabbage, bean sprouts, spring onions, red pepper, cucumber and snow peas in a salad bowl.

3   To make dressing, place vegetable oil, sesame oil, vinegar, soy sauce and black pepper to taste in a screwtop jar and shake well to combine. Spoon dressing over salad and toss to combine. Sprinkle with sesame seeds and serve immediately.

PINEAPPLE AND KIWIFRUIT SLAW

Serves 6

- ☐ ¹/₄ **small red cabbage, shredded**
- ☐ ¹/₂ **Chinese cabbage, shredded**
- ☐ **14 oz/440 g canned pineapple chunks, drained and juice reserved**
- ☐ **2 kiwifruit (Chinese Gooseberries) sliced**
- ☐ **1 red pepper, sliced**
- ☐ **1 green pepper, sliced**

CORIANDER AND MINT DRESSING
- ☐ ¹/₄ **cup/60 mL grapeseed oil**
- ☐ **2 tablespoons reserved pineapple juice**
- ☐ ¹/₄ **cup/30 g finely chopped fresh coriander (cilantro)**
- ☐ ¹/₄ **cup/30 g finely chopped fresh mint**

1 Combine red and Chinese cabbages, pineapple, kiwifruit and red and green peppers in a salad bowl. Toss lightly, cover and refrigerate until required.
2 To make dressing, combine oil, juice, coriander and mint in a screwtop jar. Shake well to combine all ingredients, pour over slaw and serve.

VEGETABLE SLAW WITH PESTO DRESSING

Serves 6

- ☐ ¹/₂ **small savoy cabbage, shredded**
- ☐ **1 large carrot, cut into thin strips**
- ☐ **4 spring onions, chopped**
- ☐ **1 stalk celery, cut into thin strips**
- ☐ **8 radishes, sliced**
- ☐ **1 green pepper, cut into strips**
- ☐ **5 oz/155 g broccoli florets, cooked**

PESTO DRESSING
- ☐ **3 oz/90 g basil leaves**
- ☐ **2 cloves garlic, crushed**
- ☐ **2 tablespoons pine nuts (pignola), toasted**
- ☐ **2 tablespoons grated Parmesan cheese**
- ☐ **7 tablespoons mayonnaise**
- ☐ ¹/₄ **cup/60 mL plain yogurt**

1 Place cabbage, carrot, spring onions, celery, radishes, pepper and broccoli in a salad bowl. Toss lightly, cover and refrigerate until required.
2 To make dressing, place basil, garlic, pine nuts, Parmesan, mayonnaise and yogurt in a food processor or blender and process until smooth. Pour dressing over slaw and toss lightly.

THREE-CABBAGE HOT SLAW

Serves 6

- ☐ **1 tablespoon vegetable oil**
- ☐ **1 tablespoon sesame oil**
- ☐ **1 clove garlic, crushed**
- ☐ **1 teaspoon grated fresh ginger**
- ☐ **1 fresh red chili, seeded and chopped**
- ☐ **1 tablespoon sesame seeds**
- ☐ ¹/₄ **small red cabbage, shredded**
- ☐ ¹/₄ **Chinese cabbage, shredded**
- ☐ ¹/₄ **small savoy cabbage, shredded**

1 Heat vegetable and sesame oils in a wok or skillet until very hot. Add garlic, ginger, chili and sesame seeds and stir-fry for 1 minute.
2 Toss in cabbages and stir-fry for 3-4 minutes or until just cooked. The cabbages should still retain their colors and be crisp. Serve immediately.

Pineapple and Kiwifruit Slaw,
Vegetable Slaw with Pesto Dressing,
Three-Cabbage Hot Slaw,
Hot Coleslaw with Brandy Dressing

SNOW PEA BOATS WITH MINTED CREAM CHEESE

Serves 6

- [ ] **18 snow peas, trimmed**
- [ ] **4 oz/125 g cream cheese**
- [ ] **2 tablespoons/30 g butter**
- [ ] **$\frac{1}{4}$ cup/60 g fresh mint leaves, finely chopped**
- [ ] **1 teaspoon sugar**
- [ ] **1 teaspoon bottled horseradish**

1 Drop snow peas into a saucepan of boiling water and cook for 1 minute. Drain and refresh under cold running water. Pat dry on paper towels.

2 Beat cream cheese and butter together until smooth. Add mint, sugar and horseradish. Slit snow peas along one edge with a sharp knife or scissors. Spoon or pipe cream cheese mixture into snow peas. Refrigerate until firm.

Cook's tip: Snow Peas (mangetout) are edible pea pods. To prepare for cooking, top and tail with a sharp knife and pull away strings from older, larger peas. Snow peas can be steamed, boiled, microwaved or stir-fried.

Drop snow peas into boiling water and cook for 1 minute.

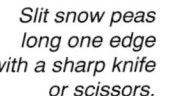

Slit snow peas long one edge with a sharp knife or scissors.

Pipe cream cheese into snow peas.

BAKED POTATO SKINS

Try baking potato skins instead of deep-frying them – they taste just as good!

Serves 4
Oven temperature 400°F, 200°C

- ☐ **4 large potatoes, scrubbed**
- ☐ **vegetable oil**

RED PEPPER HERBED MAYONNAISE
- ☐ **1 fresh red chili, seeds removed and chopped**
- ☐ **2 red peppers, roasted and skinned**
- ☐ **1 clove garlic, crushed**
- ☐ **1 tablespoon tomato paste**
- ☐ **1 cup/250 g mayonnaise**
- ☐ **1 tablespoon finely snipped fresh chives**
- ☐ **1 tablespoon finely chopped fresh basil**
- ☐ **freshly ground black pepper**

1 Bake potatoes for about 1 hour or until tender. Cut a slice from the top of each potato and carefully scoop out the flesh with a teaspoon, leaving a wall approximately 1/4 in/5 mm thick. Brush the inside and skin with oil. Reserve potato flesh for another use.
2 Return potato skins to oven and bake for 15-20 minutes or until crisp and brown.
3 To make mayonnaise, place chili, peppers and garlic in a food processor or blender and process until peppers are chunky. Combine chili mixture with tomato paste, mayonnaise, chives and basil. Season to taste with black pepper. Serve potato skins with the mayonnaise.

Hot tip: When handling fresh chilies do not put your hands near your eyes or allow them to touch your lips. To avoid discomfort and burning, wear rubber gloves. Freshly minced chili is also available from supermarkets.

Cook's tip: Cooked potato flesh can be used to make croquettes, as a topping for a Cottage Pie, or for making Cheesy Potato and Leek Pie.

CHEESY POTATO AND LEEK PIE

Serves 6
Oven temperature 425°F, 220°C

- ☐ **1/2 cup/125 mL milk**
- ☐ **3 leeks, trimmed and thinly sliced**
- ☐ **4 potatoes, peeled and cooked**
- ☐ **1/2 cup/125 g ricotta or cottage cheese**
- ☐ **2 eggs, lightly beaten**
- ☐ **1 slice wholewheat bread, crumbed**
- ☐ **1/3 cup/45 g grated Parmesan cheese**
- ☐ **2 teaspoons chopped fresh parsley**

1 Place milk and leeks in a saucepan. Cook over a low heat for 8-9 minutes. Mash potatoes with leeks and milk. Beat in ricotta or cottage cheese and eggs.
2 Spoon potato mixture into a lightly greased 10 in/25 cm pie plate or into six individual soufflé dishes. Combine bread crumbs, Parmesan and parsley and sprinkle over the potato pie.
3 Bake for 30-35 minutes or until pie is puffy and golden.

Microwave it: Leeks can be cooked in milk in your microwave on HIGH (100%) for 4-5 minutes.

CREAMY SPINACH IN ZUCCHINI

*Fresh spinach may be used in place of
frozen in this recipe if you wish.
Remove any thick stalks from the
spinach, shred the leaves and steam or
microwave until wilted, then
use as in recipe.*

Serves 6
Oven temperature 350°F, 180°C

- [ ] **6 zucchini**
- [ ] **8 oz/250 g frozen spinach,
  thawed**
- [ ] **2 slices bacon, chopped**
- [ ] **¹/₂ cup/60 g shredded Cheddar
  cheese**
- [ ] **paprika**

RICOTTA FILLING
- [ ] **¹/₂ cup/125 g ricotta cheese**
- [ ] **1 egg, beaten**
- [ ] **¹/₄ teaspoon ground nutmeg**
- [ ] **freshly ground black pepper**

1   Trim ends from zucchini and boil, steam
or microwave until just tender. Drain and
cut in half lengthwise. Carefully scoop out
centers leaving shells with a little flesh. Set
aside. Finely chop scooped out zucchini
flesh and place in a bowl.
2   Cook bacon in a skillet for 4-5 minutes
or until crisp. Remove bacon from pan and
drain on paper towels.
3   Squeeze spinach to remove any excess
liquid. Add spinach, ricotta cheese, egg,
nutmeg and black pepper to taste to bowl
with zucchini flesh and mix to combine.
Spoon filling into reserved zucchini shells,
top with bacon and cheese and sprinkle
with paprika. Place filled zucchini on a
greased baking sheet and bake for 15-20
minutes or until cheese melts and is golden.

SWEET POTATO AND ORANGE BAKE

*Serve with pork, ham or poultry in
place of potatoes.*

Serves 6
Oven temperature 400°F, 200°C

- [ ] **3 sweet potatoes, sliced**
- [ ] **2 oranges, peeled and sliced**
- [ ] **2 tablespoons/30 g butter,
  softened**
- [ ] **¹/₄ cup/45 g packed brown sugar**
- [ ] **1 teaspoon cornstarch**
- [ ] **¹/₂ cup/125 mL orange juice**
- [ ] **¹/₂ cup/60 g slivered almonds**

1   Boil, steam or microwave sweet
potatoes until just tender. Drain and arrange
in alternate layers with oranges in a lightly
greased baking dish.
2   Combine butter, brown sugar,
cornstarch and orange juice. Pour over
potatoes and oranges, sprinkle with
almonds and bake for 30 minutes.

*Cheesy Potato and Leek Pie, Sweet Potato
and Orange Bake, Baked Potato Skins*

PERFECT FRENCH FRIES

Serves 4

- [ ] **4 large potatoes, peeled**
- [ ] **oil for deep-frying**

1 Cut potatoes into $1/2$ in/1 cm slices, then into strips. Soak strips in cold water for 10 minutes to remove the excess starch. Drain and dry on paper towels.

2 Heat oil in a deep fryer or saucepan. Drop a strip into the oil and when it rises to the surface surrounded by bubbles the oil is at the correct temperature for cooking. Drop the strips gradually into the hot oil, or lower them in a wire basket and cook for 6 minutes.

3 Remove fries from oil using a slotted spoon, or by lifting the basket, and drain on paper towels. At this point the fries are blanched and can be left for several hours, or frozen before the final cooking stage.

4 Just prior to serving, reheat the oil and test as above. Cook fries quickly for 3-4 minutes or until golden brown and crisp. Remove from pan with a slotted spoon, drain on paper towels. Season to taste and serve immediately.

Cook's tip: Double-cooking fries ensures crisp golden fries every time. The high water content of potatoes initially reduces the temperature of the oil and double-cooking overcomes this problem. A wire fry basket makes it easier to lower and raise a quantity of fries in hot oil. If cooking a large quantity of fries, cook in batches to prevent overcrowding.

PERFECT MASHED POTATO

Serves 4

- [ ] **4 potatoes, peeled and halved**
- [ ] **$1/2$ cup/125 mL milk**
- [ ] **2 tablespoons/30 g butter, softened**

1 Place potatoes in a saucepan of water, cover and bring to the boil. Cook gently for 20 minutes or until tender.

2 Drain potatoes, then return to pan. Shake pan over low heat to dry. Mash potatoes with a potato masher until free of lumps.

3 Stir in milk and butter. Season to taste and beat with a fork until smooth and fluffy.

PERFECT ROAST POTATOES

Serves 4
Oven temperature 350°F, 180°C

- [ ] **4 potatoes, peeled**
- [ ] **1 tablespoon vegetable oil**

1 Boil or steam potatoes for 5 minutes. Drain and dry on paper towels. Set aside until cool enough to handle, then cut in half lengthwise. Score the upper rounded surface with a fork; this helps crisp the potatoes during cooking.

2 Brush potatoes with oil and place in a shallow baking dish and bake for 55-60 minutes, turning occasionally during cooking.

Cook's tip: When roasting vegetables use a shallow baking dish, which will allow the vegetables to brown evenly. Other vegetables can be roasted with the potatoes. Cook butternut squash with or without the skin and cut into a similar size as the potatoes. Brown onions are excellent roasted; peel away 1 or 2 layers of skin, leaving a little of the root end intact to hold onions together during cooking.

POTATO AND BEET TART

This vibrantly colored dish will give any meal a lift. It may be served either hot or cold.

Serves 4
Oven temperature 400°F, 200°C

- [ ] **4 potatoes, cooked and mashed (without milk or butter)**
- [ ] **1 large raw beet, shredded**
- [ ] **1 tablespoon finely chopped fresh dill weed**
- [ ] **1 tablespoon cream**
- [ ] **1 tablespoon mayonnaise**
- [ ] **2 teaspoons bottled horseradish**
- [ ] **freshly ground black pepper**
- [ ] **2 eggs, separated**

1 Combine potatoes, beet, dill, cream, mayonnaise, horseradish, black pepper and egg yolks in a mixing bowl.

2 Beat egg whites until stiff peaks form and fold through potato mixture. Spoon mixture into a well-greased 9 in/ 23 cm tart pan with a removable base. Bake for 25-30 minutes or until firm. Serve warm, or at room temperature, cut into wedges.

JACKET BAKED POTATOES

Serves 4
Oven temperature 350°F, 180°C

- [ ] **4 potatoes**
- [ ] **Dairy sour cream or butter for serving**

Scrub and dry potatoes. Prick with a fork, place on a wire rack in a baking pan or directly on oven shelf and bake for 1 hour or until tender. Serve with sour cream or butter.

Cook's tip: Baked potatoes can be placed in the oven and cooked with other dishes. If the other food you are cooking requires a slightly lower or higher temperature your baked potatoes will happily cook along with it taking just a little shorter or longer time as the case may be.

BACON AND BANANA POTATO CAKES

Serves 4

- [ ] **4 potatoes, cooked and mashed (without milk or butter)**
- [ ] **1 small green apple, shredded**
- [ ] **1 tablespoon mayonnaise**
- [ ] **2 teaspoons chopped fresh mint**
- [ ] **$1/4$ cup/30 g all-purpose flour**

FILLING
- [ ] **4 slices bacon, finely chopped**
- [ ] **1 banana, sliced**

COATING
- [ ] **flour**
- [ ] **1 egg, lightly beaten**
- [ ] **1 cup/125 g dried bread crumbs**
- [ ] **oil for cooking**

1 Combine potato, apple, mayonnaise, mint and flour. Divide potato mixture into sixteen equal portions and form into patties.

2 To make filling, cook bacon in a nonstick skillet for 2-3 minutes or until crisp. Set aside to cool slightly. Place a spoonful of bacon on eight of the patties. Top with banana slices and remaining potato patties. Mold potato patties to completely seal filling.

3 To coat, cover patties lightly with flour, dip in egg then bread crumbs. Refrigerate for 30 minutes.

4 Heat oil in a skillet and cook patties, two at a time, until golden brown on both sides. Remove from pan and drain on paper towels. Set aside and keep warm. Cook remaining patties.

BACON AND CREAMED CORN FILLED POTATOES

You will require only half the potato flesh for this recipe. Reserve the remaining flesh for another use. Leftover potato can be made into potato cakes or croquettes, or can be pan fried.

Serves 4
Oven temperature 350°F,180°C

- ☐ **4 potatoes, baked in their jackeks**
- ☐ **4 slices bacon, chopped**
- ☐ **¹/₂ cup/125 g canned creamed sweet corn**
- ☐ **2 tablespoons dairy sour cream**
- ☐ **pinch chili powder**
- ☐ **¹/₂ cup/60 g shredded Cheddar cheese**

1　Cut potatoes in half, scoop out flesh, leaving a ¹/₂ in/1 cm thick shell. Reserve the flesh and set aside.

2　Cook the bacon in a nonstick skillet for 2-3 minutes or until crisp. Mash half the potato flesh and combine with bacon, corn, sour cream and chili powder. Spoon mixture into potato shells, top with cheese.

3　Place potatoes on a baking sheet and bake for 15 minutes or until cheese melts.

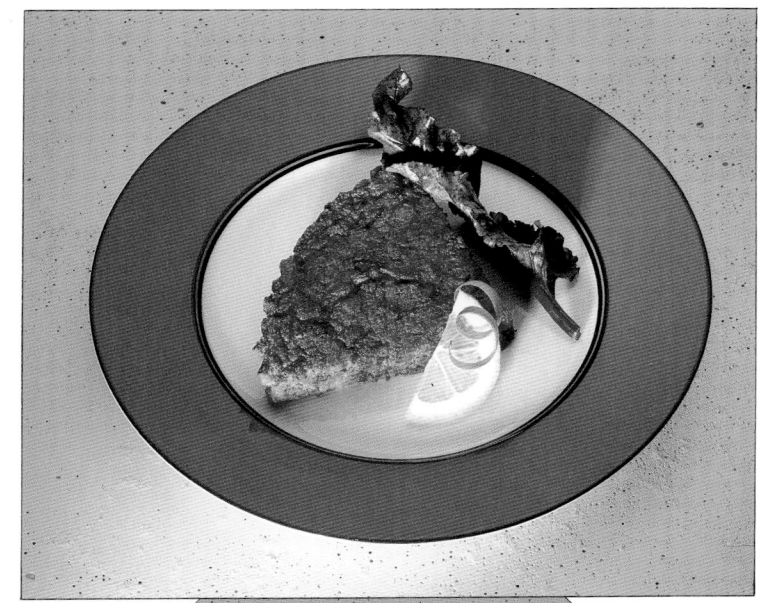

Top: Potato and Beet Tart
Center: Baked Jacket Potatoes, Bacon and Creamed Corn Filled Potatoes
Bottom: Bacon and Banana Potato Cakes

PEAR AND SPINACH SALAD

Serves 6

- [ ] **1 lb/500 g spinach, shredded**
- [ ] **2 spring onions, sliced**
- [ ] **3 slices packaged ham, cut into thin strips**
- [ ] **2 pears, cored, peeled and diced**

LEMON MUSTARD DRESSING
- [ ] **2 tablespoons lemon juice**
- [ ] **1 tablespoon coarse grain mustard**
- [ ] **2 teaspoons sugar**
- [ ] **1 teaspoon dried tarragon leaves**
- [ ] **1/4 cup/60 mL olive oil**
- [ ] **1/2 cup/125 mL vegetable oil**

1 Combine spinach, onions, ham and pears in a large glass serving dish. Toss gently.

2 To make dressing, combine lemon juice, mustard, sugar, tarragon and oils in a screwtop jar and shake until well mixed. Pour dressing over spinach salad and serve.

POTATO NEST WITH CARROT PUREE

For something different try using sweet potatoes in place of the potatoes in this recipe, accompany them with parsnip purée and substitute lemon juice for the orange juice.

Serves 6
Oven temperature 350°F, 180°C

POTATO NEST
- [ ] **4 large potatoes**
- [ ] **2 egg yolks**
- [ ] **1/4 teaspoon nutmeg**
- [ ] **1/4 cup/1/2 stick/60 g butter**
- [ ] **freshly ground black pepper**

CARROT PUREE
- [ ] **6 large carrots**
- [ ] **3/4 cup/185 mL chicken stock**
- [ ] **2 tablespoons orange juice**
- [ ] **1/4 teaspoon ground nutmeg**

1 To make nest, cook potatoes in a saucepan of boiling water until tender. Drain and return to pan. Toss over heat for 2-3 minutes to dry. Remove from heat and mash well. Stir in egg yolks, nutmeg and half the butter. Season to taste with black pepper.

2 Spoon mixture into a pastry bag and pipe a decorative border around the edge of an ovenproof dinner plate. Spoon any leftover potato into the center of plate. Brush with remaining butter, melted, and bake for 20 minutes.

3 To make purée, place carrots and stock in a saucepan, bring to the boil, cover and simmer for 10 minutes or until carrots are tender. Cool slightly. Purée carrot mixture in a food processor until smooth. Return mixture to the pan. Add orange juice and nutmeg. Stir over low heat until heated through. Spoon purée into center of potato nest and serve.

TOMATO AND CHEESE FRITTERS

These fritters are delicious served with pickles or your favorite chutney. Serve hot for a party snack, or as a tasty side dish at your next barbecue.

Serves 6

- ☐ ²/₃ cup/75 g unprocessed bran
- ☐ ¹/₂ cup/60 g shredded Swiss cheese
- ☐ 2 tablespoons chopped fresh basil
- ☐ ¹/₂ 1 teaspoon caraway seeds
- ☐ 3 medium, partially ripe tomatoes
- ☐ ¹/₂ cup/60 g seasoned flour with freshly ground pepper
- ☐ 2 eggs, beaten
- ☐ oil for shallow-frying

1 Combine bran, cheese, basil and caraway seeds. Cut tomatoes into ¹/₄ in/ 5 mm slices. Coat with seasoned flour, dip in egg, then coat with bran mixture.
2 Heat oil in a skillet. Cook tomato slices until golden brown. Drain on paper towels.

Left: Potato Nest with Carrot Purée, Pear and Spinach Salad
Below: Tomato and Cheese Fritters

TWO PEA SALAD

Serves 5

- ☐ 1 lb/500 g frozen peas
- ☐ 5 oz/155 g snow peas, trimmed
- ☐ 1 small onion, thinly sliced

LEMON DRESSING
- ☐ 1 clove garlic, crushed
- ☐ 2 tablespoons vegetable oil
- ☐ 2 teaspoons lemon juice
- ☐ freshly ground black pepper

1 Boil or microwave peas until just cooked. Drain and place in a salad bowl. Boil, steam or microwave snow peas until they just change color. Drain and place in salad bowl with peas. Add onions to bowl.
2 To make dressing, place garlic, oil, lemon juice and black pepper to taste in a screwtop jar and shake well to combine. Spoon dressing over salad and toss to combine. Set aside to cool to room temperature before serving.

ARTICHOKE SALAD WITH PESTO DRESSING

Serves 6

- ☐ 1 lb/500 g watercress, washed
- ☐ 14 oz/440 g canned artichoke hearts, drained
- ☐ 4 tomatoes, peeled and diced
- ☐ 4 oz/125 g mozzarella cheese, sliced

PESTO DRESSING
- ☐ 60 g/2 oz fresh basil leaves
- ☐ 1/4 cup/60 mL olive oil
- ☐ 1 clove garlic, crushed
- ☐ 1/4 cup/30 g grated fresh Parmesan cheese
- ☐ 2 tablespoons pine nuts (pignola), toasted

1 Break watercress into small pieces and place in a bowl. Arrange artichokes, tomatoes and mozzarella cheese over watercress.

2 To make dressing, place basil, oil, garlic, Parmesan cheese and pine nuts in a food processor or blender and process until smooth. Drizzle over salad and toss gently to coat salad ingredients.

SPINACH AND RAISINS ALLA LIGURIA

Serves 4

- ☐ 1 lb/500g spinach, thick stalks removed
- ☐ 2 tablespoons/30 g butter
- ☐ 1 clove garlic, crushed
- ☐ 4 slices prosciutto ham, chopped
- ☐ 1/4 cup/30 g seeded raisins, chopped
- ☐ 1 tablespoon chopped fresh thyme
- ☐ freshly ground black pepper
- ☐ 1/4 cup/60 g pine nuts (pignola), toasted

1 Boil, steam or microwave spinach until just tender. Drain well and chop coarsely

2 Heat butter in a skillet. Cook garlic and prosciutto, stirring, for 1 minute. Add spinach, raisins and thyme and cook, stirring, for 2-3 minutes longer or until heated through. Season to taste with black pepper and transfer to a serving dish. Sprinkle with pine nuts and serve immediately.

MILANESE-STYLE FENNEL

This dish can be made a day ahead of serving then reheated when required.

Serves 6
Oven temperature 400°F, 200°C

- ☐ 2 large fennel bulbs, trimmed and cut into 1/2 in/1 cm strips

WHITE SAUCE
- ☐ 2 tablespoons/30 g butter
- ☐ 2 tablespoons all-purpose flour
- ☐ 1 1/2 cups/375 mL milk
- ☐ 1/4 teaspoon ground nutmeg
- ☐ freshly ground black pepper

CHEESY TOPPING
- ☐ 1cup/60 g bread crumbs, made from stale bread
- ☐ 1/4 cup/30 g grated fresh Parmesan cheese
- ☐ 2 tablespoons/30 g butter, melted
- ☐ paprika

1 Boil, steam or microwave fennel until tender. Drain and set aside.

2 To make sauce, melt butter in a saucepan, add flour and cook, stirring, for 1 minute. Remove from heat and gradually stir in milk. Cook over a medium heat, stirring constantly, until sauce boils and thickens. Add nutmeg and season to taste with black pepper.

3 To make topping, combine breadcrumbs, Parmesan cheese and butter. Arrange fennel in a shallow ovenproof dish, pour sauce over and sprinkle with topping. Dust with paprika and bake for 15-20 minutes or until browned.

Microwave it: To make the sauce in the microwave, melt butter in a microwave-safe pitcher, stir in flour then gradually stir in milk. Cook on HIGH (100%) for 3 minutes, or until sauce boils and thickens. Stir twice during cooking.

ITALIAN BEAN HOTPOT

This recipe is quick and easy to prepare. Served with fresh crusty bread and a salad it makes a perfect luncheon or supper dish.

Serves 6

- ☐ 2 tablespoons olive oil
- ☐ 2 cloves garlic, crushed
- ☐ 1 onion, sliced
- ☐ 1 tablespoon chopped fresh sage, or 1 teaspoon dried sage leaves
- ☐ 2 x 10 oz/315 g cans cannellini beans, drained
- ☐ 14 oz/440 g canned peppers, drained and thinly sliced
- ☐ 14 oz/440 g canned tomatoes, undrained and chopped
- ☐ 14 oz/440 g canned tomato paste
- ☐ 2 zucchini, sliced
- ☐ freshly ground black pepper
- ☐ 1/4 cup/30 g grated fresh Parmesan cheese

1 Heat oil in a skillet and cook garlic, onion and sage for 4-5 minutes or until onion is soft.

2 Stir in beans, peppers, tomatoes, tomato paste and zucchini. Bring to the boil, reduce heat and simmer, uncovered, for 15 minutes or until mixture reduces and thickens. Season to taste with black pepper and sprinkle with Parmesan cheese.

Cook's tip: You can use dried cannellini beans for this recipe if you wish, but you will need to cook them first.

Italian Bean Hotpot, Spinach and Raisins Alla Liguria, Artichoke Salad with Pesto Dressing, Milanese-Style Fennel

CAULIFLOWER
AU GRATIN

Serves 4
Oven temperature 350°F, 180°C

- ☐ **1 small cauliflower, broken into florets**
- ☐ **1¹/₂ cups/375 mL milk**
- ☐ **2 tablespoons cornstarch blended with ¹/₄ cup/60 mL water**
- ☐ **1 teaspoon coarse grain mustard**
- ☐ **¹/₄ cup/60 g plain yogurt**
- ☐ **freshly ground black pepper**
- ☐ **1 cup/60 g crushed corn flakes**
- ☐ **¹/₄ cup/30 g shredded Cheddar cheese**
- ☐ **1 tablespoon/15 g butter, melted**
- ☐ **paprika**

1   Steam, boil or microwave cauliflower until just tender. Drain and set aside.

2   Place milk in a saucepan and cook over a medium heat until almost at boiling point. Remove pan from heat and stir in cornstarch mixture. Return pan to heat and cook over a medium heat until sauce boils and thickens, stirring constantly.

3   Combine mustard and yogurt. Remove sauce from heat and blend in yogurt mixture. Season to taste with black pepper. Spread half the sauce over the bottom of a baking dish. Top with cauliflower and remaining sauce.

4   Combine corn flakes, cheese and butter. Sprinkle on top of cauliflower. Dust lightly with paprika and bake for 15-20 minutes or until golden brown.

Place milk in a saucepan and cook over a medium heat until almost boiling. Remove pan from heat and stir in cornstarch mixture.

Combine corn flakes, cheese and butter and sprinkle over cauliflower.

SPICY ASPARAGUS WITH PINE NUTS

This recipe makes a delicious first course. Use bacon instead of salami for a less spicy flavor.

Serves 4

- ☐ **1 lb/500 g fresh asparagus spears, trimmed and cut into 2 in/5 cm pieces**
- ☐ **1 tablespoon/15 g butter**
- ☐ **¹/₂ cup/60 g pine nuts (pignola)**
- ☐ **4 oz/125 g hot Italian salami, cut into ¹/₄ in/5 mm cubes**
- ☐ **2 tablespoons chopped fresh basil**
- ☐ **¹/₂ cup/30 g grated fresh Parmesan cheese**

1   Steam or microwave asparagus until just tender. Drain and rinse under cold running water to refresh, then drain again and set aside.

2   Heat butter in a skillet and cook pine nuts and salami until lightly browned. Add asparagus and basil and cook, stirring constantly, for 1 minute or until heated through. Sprinkle with Parmesan cheese and serve immediately.

RADICCHIO ANCHOVY SALAD

Serves 6

- ☐ **1 radicchio, washed and leaves separated**
- ☐ **¹/₂ bunch curly endive, washed and leaves separated**
- ☐ **1 Belgian endive (witloof), washed and leaves separated**
- ☐ **8 radishes, washed and sliced**
- ☐ **¹/₄ cup/60 mL chopped fresh Italian flat leaf parsley**

ANCHOVY DRESSING
- ☐ **¹/₄ cup/60 mL olive oil**
- ☐ **¹/₄ cup/60 mL lemon juice**
- ☐ **¹/₄ cup/60 mL dry white wine**
- ☐ **3 anchovy fillets, drained and chopped**
- ☐ **1 clove garlic, crushed**
- ☐ **¹/₂ teaspoon sugar**

1   Arrange radicchio, curly endive and Belgian endive (witloof) attractively on a large platter. Top with radishes and parsley.

2   To make dressing, place oil, lemon juice, wine, anchovies, garlic and sugar in a food processor or blender and process until smooth. Just before serving, drizzle dressing over salad.

FENNEL AND ORANGE SALAD

Serves 6

- ☐ **1 bunch curly endive, leaves separated and washed**
- ☐ **1 small fennel bulb, cut into thin strips**
- ☐ **3 oranges, segmented**
- ☐ **1 onion, sliced**
- ☐ **20 black olives**

ORANGE DRESSING
- ☐ **¹/₃ cup/90 mL olive oil**
- ☐ **¹/₄ cup/60 mL white wine vinegar**
- ☐ **1 tablespoon chopped fresh fennel leaves**
- ☐ **¹/₂ teaspoon grated orange rind**
- ☐ **¹/₂ teaspoon sugar**
- ☐ **freshly ground black pepper**

1   Place endive on a large serving platter. Arrange fennel, oranges, onion and olives attractively over endive.

2   To make dressing, place oil, vinegar, fennel leaves, orange rind, sugar and black pepper to taste in a screwtop jar. Shake well to combine. Pour dressing over salad and serve immediately.

Fennel: The aniseed-flavored fennel – also known as 'Florence fennel' or 'finocchio' – was much esteemed by the Romans, who used it to flavor many of their dishes.

The feathery leaves and aromatic seeds add zing to vegetables, salad dressings, pickles and sauces, and taste delicious as a traditional accompaniment to fish.

Fennel has a strong aniseed flavor but you will find when it is cooked that it loses its aniseed flavor.

SPICY VEGETABLES

Use any vegetables you like for this dish, however you will find this combination perfect. Remember not to overcook your vegetables when stir-frying or they will become soggy and lose many of their valuable vitamins.

Serves 4

- ☐ ¼ **cup/60 mL peanut oil**
- ☐ **2 onions, cut into eighths**
- ☐ **1 teaspoon grated fresh ginger**
- ☐ **6 oz/185 g oyster mushrooms, sliced**
- ☐ **1 small head broccoli, broken into florets**
- ☐ **½ Chinese cabbage, shredded**
- ☐ **1 large carrot, cut into thin strips**
- ☐ **2 stalks celery, sliced diagonally**
- ☐ **8 oz/250 g snow peas**
- ☐ **¼ cup/60 mL chicken stock**

HONEY AND SOY SAUCE
- ☐ **1 tablespoon sesame oil**
- ☐ **1 tablespoon soy sauce**
- ☐ **2 teaspoons honey**
- ☐ **1 teaspoon lemon juice**

1   Heat oil in a wok or large skillet, add onion and stir-fry for 4-5 minutes or until golden. Add ginger and mushrooms and stir-fry for 1 minute longer.

2   Add broccoli, cabbage, carrot, celery, snow peas and stock to pan and stir-fry for 4-5 minutes or until vegetables just change color and are just tender.

3   To make sauce, place sesame oil, soy sauce, honey and lemon juice in a small bowl and whisk to combine. Pour sauce over vegetables in pan and stir-fry for 1-2 minutes longer or until heated through. Serve immediately.

Radicchio Anchovy Salad, Fennel and Orange Salad, Spicy Asparagus with Pine Nuts

MARINATED MUSHROOMS

These mushrooms make an excellent accompaniment to a meal, or a low-calorie (kilojoule) snack.

Serves 4

- ☐ **1 lb/500 g button mushrooms, stems removed**
- ☐ **¹/₂ red pepper, diced**
- ☐ **¹/₂ green pepper, diced**

HERB DRESSING
- ☐ **1 clove garlic, crushed**
- ☐ **1 tablespoon vegetable oil**
- ☐ **¹/₄ cup/60 mL red wine vinegar**
- ☐ **1 tablespoon finely chopped fresh parsley**
- ☐ **1 tablespoon finely snipped fresh chives**
- ☐ **freshly ground black pepper**

1 Place mushrooms and peppers in a bowl.

2 To make dressing, place garlic, oil, vinegar, parsley, chives and black pepper to taste in a screwtop jar. Shake well to combine and pour over mushrooms and peppers. Cover, refrigerate and marinate for about 2 hours before serving.

ITALIAN GREEN BEAN SALAD

Serves 4

- ☐ **1 lb/500 g green beans, topped and tailed**
- ☐ **6 spring onions, finely chopped**
- ☐ **3 tomatoes, peeled and chopped**
- ☐ **8 black olives, pitted**
- ☐ **freshly ground black pepper**

LEMON AND HERB DRESSING
- ☐ **1 tablespoon olive oil**
- ☐ **¹/₄ cup/60 mL lemon juice**
- ☐ **1 clove garlic, crushed**
- ☐ **1 tablespoon chopped fresh parsley**
- ☐ **1 tablespoon finely snipped fresh chives**
- ☐ **1 teaspoon finely chopped fresh rosemary**
- ☐ **1 teaspoon finely chopped fresh thyme**

1 Boil, steam or microwave beans until just tender. Refresh under cold running water.

2 Place beans, spring onions, tomatoes and olives in a salad bowl.

3 To make dressing, place oil, lemon juice, garlic, parsley, chives, rosemary and thyme in a screwtop jar. Shake well to combine and pour over salad. Season with black pepper to taste and toss.

TOMATO AND BASIL SALAD

You might like to try a combination of cherry tomatoes and little yellow teardrop tomatoes to make this aromatic tomato salad look even more attractive.

Serves 6

- ☐ 1¹/₂ lb/750 g ripe tomatoes, peeled and sliced
- ☐ 4 tablespoons finely chopped fresh basil
- ☐ 2 tablespoons grated Parmesan cheese
- ☐ freshly ground black pepper

WHITE WINE VINEGAR DRESSING
- ☐ 1 clove garlic, crushed
- ☐ 1 tablespoon olive oil
- ☐ ¹/₄ cup/60 mL white wine vinegar

1 Arrange overlapping tomato slices on a serving platter and sprinkle with basil leaves.

2 To make dressing, place garlic, oil and vinegar in a screwtop jar. Shake well to combine and sprinkle over tomatoes. Just before serving, sprinkle tomato salad with Parmesan cheese. Season with black pepper to taste.

STIR-FRIED VEGETABLES

Serves 6

- ☐ 1 tablespoon vegetable oil
- ☐ 1 onion, sliced
- ☐ 1 clove garlic, crushed
- ☐ 1 teaspoon finely grated fresh ginger
- ☐ 1 carrot, thinly sliced
- ☐ 1 green pepper, diced
- ☐ 2 stalks celery, sliced
- ☐ 8 oz/250 g mushrooms, sliced
- ☐ 4 oz/125 g snow peas, topped and tailed
- ☐ ¹/₂ small cabbage, shredded
- ☐ 11 oz/350 g canned baby sweet corn
- ☐ 1 tablespoon soy sauce

1 Heat oil until hot in a wok or skillet. Add onion, garlic and ginger and stir-fry for 2-3 minutes. Toss in carrot, green pepper and celery, and cook for 4-5 minutes.

2 To vegetable mixture, add mushrooms and snow peas. Stir-fry for 1-2 minutes, or until snow peas are just tender. Stir in cabbage, sweet corn and soy sauce, and cook for 3-4 minutes. Serve immediately.

TOMATO, ZUCCHINI AND ONION BAKE

Serves 4

- ☐ 1 tablespoon olive oil
- ☐ 2 large onions, sliced into rings
- ☐ 1 clove garlic, crushed
- ☐ 1 green pepper, diced
- ☐ 1 teaspoon dried mixed herbs
- ☐ 4 oz/125 g mushrooms, sliced
- ☐ 14 oz/440 g canned tomatoes, undrained and mashed
- ☐ 1 tablespoon tomato paste
- ☐ 1 tablespoon cornstarch blended with ¹/₂ cup/125 mL water
- ☐ 3 zucchini, thickly sliced

CHEESY TOPPING
- ☐ ¹/₂ cup/30 g bread crumbs, made from stale bread
- ☐ 2 tablespoons shredded Cheddar cheese

1 Heat oil in a saucepan and cook onions, garlic, green pepper and herbs for 2-3 minutes or until onion is soft. Add mushrooms and cook for 5 minutes longer.
2 Stir in tomatoes and tomato paste, and cook until mixture boils. Stir in cornstarch mixture and cook till sauce thickens.
3 Boil, steam or microwave zucchini until just tender. Place zucchini in a shallow baking dish and pour over tomato sauce. Top with bread crumbs and cheese.
4 Place under a preheated broiler and cook for 5 minutes or until top is golden.

*Far left: Italian Green Bean Salad, Tomato and Basil Salad, Marinated Mushrooms
Left: Tomato, Zucchini and Onion Bake, Stir-fried Vegetables*

COOKED AND RAW BEET SALAD

The cooked and raw beet in this salad have quite different textures and make a very interesting combination.

Serves 4

- ☐ **1 large cooked beet, shredded**
- ☐ **1 large raw beet, shredded**
- ☐ **2 green apples, cut into thin strips**
- ☐ **fresh dill weed sprigs**

DILL DRESSING
- ☐ **2 tablespoons lemon juice**
- ☐ **1/3 cup/90 mL vegetable oil**
- ☐ **1 tablespoon finely chopped fresh dill weed**
- ☐ **freshly ground black pepper**

1   Place cooked and raw beets and apples in a salad bowl.
2   To make dressing, place lemon juice, oil, dill and black pepper to taste in a screwtop jar and shake well to combine. Spoon dressing over beet and apples and toss to coat all ingredients with dressing. Top with dill sprigs and serve.

VEGETABLE FRITTERS WITH HERB DRESSING

Serves 4

- ☐ **1/2 small cauliflower, cut into florets**
- ☐ **1 eggplant**
- ☐ **salt**
- ☐ **1 large red pepper, cut into strips**
- ☐ **cornstarch**

BATTER
- ☐ **1/2 cup plus 2 tablespoons/75 g all-purpose flour**
- ☐ **1/4 cup/30 g self-rising flour**
- ☐ **1 cup/250 mL water**
- ☐ **1 egg, lightly beaten**
- ☐ **oil for deep-frying**

HERB DRESSING
- ☐ **1/2 cup/125 mL bottled Italian dressing**
- ☐ **1 tablespoon chopped fresh basil**
- ☐ **1 tablespoon chopped fresh oregano**
- ☐ **1 small fresh red chili, seeded and chopped**

1   Steam, boil or microwave cauliflower until just tender. Drain well and set aside. Cut eggplant in half lengthwise and slice into 1/2 in/1 cm slices. Sprinkle with salt and set aside for 30 minutes. Rinse eggplant under cold running water and pat dry with paper towels. Cut eggplant into strips.
2   Toss cauliflower, eggplant and red pepper in cornstarch. Shake off any excess cornstarch and set aside.
3   To make batter, place all-purpose flour, self-rising flour, water and egg in a food processor or blender and process until smooth. Heat oil in a large saucepan until a cube of bread dropped in browns in 50 seconds. Dip vegetables in batter and cook a few at a time until golden. Remove from oil and drain on paper towels.
4   To make dressing, place Italian dressing, basil, oregano and chili in a screwtop jar and shake well to combine. Serve with hot vegetables.

ROAST PEPPER SALAD

A colorful, strongly flavored salad, this dish is the perfect accompaniment to grilled meats. If yellow peppers are unavailable, make the salad using three green and three red. If possible the salad should stand for 2-3 hours before serving to allow the flavors to develop fully.

Serves 6

- ☐ **2 red peppers**
- ☐ **2 green peppers**
- ☐ **2 yellow peppers**

BASIL DRESSING
- ☐ **12 fresh basil leaves, chopped**
- ☐ **1 clove garlic, crushed**
- ☐ **1/2 cup/125 mL olive oil**
- ☐ **1/4 cup/60 mL red wine vinegar**
- ☐ **freshly ground black pepper**

1   Cut red, green and yellow peppers into quarters, remove seeds and cook, skin side up, under a high preheated broiler for 10 minutes or until skins blister and char. Remove peppers from broiler, place in a plastic food bag, seal and set aside for 10 minutes or until cool enough to handle. Remove skins, cut peppers into strips and place in a salad bowl.
2   To make dressing, place basil, garlic, oil, vinegar and black pepper to taste in a screwtop jar and shake well to combine. Pour dressing over peppers and toss to combine. Cover and refrigerate until ready to serve.

BRUSSELS SPROUTS AND ALMONDS IN TANGY SAUCE

Serves 4

- ☐ **1 lb/500 g Brussels sprouts**
- ☐ **1/4 cup/30 g toasted sliced almonds**

TANGY SAUCE
- ☐ **2 tablespoons/30 g butter, melted**
- ☐ **2 tablespoon brown sugar**
- ☐ **1 tablespoon cornstarch**
- ☐ **1/2 teaspoon prepared mustard**
- ☐ **1 small onion, finely chopped**
- ☐ **1/4 cup/60 mL white vinegar**

1   Boil, steam or microwave Brussels sprouts until tender. Drain and keep warm.
2   Combine butter, sugar, cornstarch, mustard, onion and vinegar in a saucepan. Cook, stirring, until sauce boils and thickens. Pour over Brussels sprouts, with toasted almonds and serve.

Cook's tip: When steaming vegetables of different textures together, place the vegetable that will take longer to cook on the bottom of the steamer where it will cook more rapidly.

MOLDED TOMATO RISOTTO

Serves 6
Oven temperature 400°F, 200°C

- ☐ **1/4 cup/60 mL olive oil**
- ☐ **2 onions, chopped**
- ☐ **1 lb/500 g quick-cook brown rice**
- ☐ **14 oz/440 g canned tomatoes, undrained and mashed**
- ☐ **1/4 cup/60 mL tomato purée**
- ☐ **4 cups/1 liter/60 mL boiling chicken stock**
- ☐ **3 oz/90 g butter**
- ☐ **3/4 cup/100 g grated Parmesan cheese**
- ☐ **freshly ground black pepper**
- ☐ **2 tablespoons chopped fresh basil**
- ☐ **zucchini ribbons for garnish**

1   Heat oil in a skillet and cook onions until golden. Add rice, tossing to coat grains. Pour in combined tomatoes, tomato paste and boiling stock. Stir over heat until rice is cooked and all of the liquid has been absorbed.
2   Fold through butter, Parmesan, black

pepper to taste and basil. Spoon into a well-greased ovenproof bowl. Cover and bake for 10-15 minutes. Turn out onto a serving plate and decorate top with zucchini ribbons.

Cook's tip: To make zucchini ribbons, cut long thin slices from top to base of zucchini using a vegetable peeler.

Right: Molded Tomato Risotto
Above: Brussels Sprouts and Almonds in Tangy Sauce

chapter nine

SWEET REWARDS

Whether as an occasional treat or an everyday occurrence, dessert is the crowning glory of any meal. Next time you are considering what to give the family for dessert , why not try Turkish Syllabub or Orange and Lemon Pudding Cake? The range of recipes in this chapter ensures that you never have to wonder about what to serve for dessert again.

Sour Cream Apple Tart

SOUR CREAM APPLE TART

Serves 8
Oven temperature 400°F,200°C

- [ ] **10 oz/315 g prepared sweet short (flaky) pastry**
- [ ] **3 tablespoons apricot jam**

APPLE FILLING
- [ ] **3 oz/90 g butter**
- [ ] **3 Granny Smith apples, cored, peeled and sliced**
- [ ] **2 tablespoons brown sugar**

CARAMEL SAUCE
- [ ] **¼ cup/60 g sugar**
- [ ] **4 teaspoons water**
- [ ] **¼ cup/60 mL thick cream**
- [ ] **1 oz/30 g butter, cut into small pieces**

SOUR CREAM TOPPING
- [ ] **1 lb/500 g dairy sour cream**
- [ ] **4 teaspoons superfine sugar**
- [ ] **1 teaspoon vanilla extract**

1   Roll pastry out and line a greased, deep 7 in/18 cm fluted tart pan with a removable base. Prick pastry bottom with a fork. Line pastry shell with parchment paper, weigh down with uncooked rice and cook for 10 minutes. Remove rice and paper and bake for 8-10 minutes longer or until pastry is golden. Place jam in a small saucepan and bring to the boil. As soon as the pastry shell is cooked, brush with boiling jam and return to the oven for 3-4 minutes longer. Set pastry shell aside to cool completely.

2   To make filling, melt half the butter in a large skillet and add half the apple slices, sprinkle with half the brown sugar and cook, turning slices until they are tender. Remove apple slices to a plate and repeat with remaining butter, apple slices and brown sugar. Layer apple slices evenly in pastry shell.

3   To make sauce, place sugar and water in a heavy-based saucepan and cook over a low heat, stirring until sugar dissolves. Bring to the boil and boil without stirring for 8 minutes or until mixture is a caramel color. Occasionally brush down sides of pan with a pastry brush dipped in cold water. Reduce heat, stir in cream and continue stirring until sauce is smooth. Mix in butter and set aside to cool slightly. Using a large spoon, drizzle caramel over apples in pastry shell.

4   To make topping, place sour cream, sugar and vanilla extract in a bowl and mix to combine. Spoon sour cream mixture over apples and spread out carefully, using the back of a spoon, taking mixture just to rim of tart. Reduce oven temperature to 350°F/180°C and bake tart for 5-7 minutes. Allow to cool at room temperature, then refrigerate for several hours or overnight before serving.

RASPBERRY MOUSSE TART

Serves 8
Oven temperature 400°F, 200°C

ALMOND PASTRY
- [ ] **1¼ cups/155 g all-purpose flour**
- [ ] **2 tablespoons superfine sugar**
- [ ] **2 tablespoons/15 g ground almonds**
- [ ] **½ cup/1 stick/60 g butter, cut into small pieces**
- [ ] **1 egg yolk, lightly beaten**
- [ ] **3-4 tablespoons water, chilled**

RASPBERRY MOUSSE FILLING
- [ ] **3 oz/90 g raspberries**
- [ ] **2 eggs, separated**
- [ ] **¼ cup/60 g superfine sugar**
- [ ] **½ cup/125 mL thick cream, whipped**
- [ ] **8 teaspoons plain gelatin dissolved in ½ cup/125 mL hot water, cooled to room temperature**
- [ ] **1 lb/500 g mixed berries of your choice**

1   To make pastry, place flour, sugar and almonds in a food processor and process to combine. Add butter and process until mixture resembles fine bread crumbs. With machine running, add egg yolk and enough water to form a soft dough. Turn pastry onto a floured surface and knead lightly until smooth. Wrap in plastic food wrap and refrigerate for 30 minutes.

2   Roll out pastry on a lightly floured surface and line a lightly greased, deep 8 in/20 cm fluted tart pan with a removable base. Refrigerate for 15 minutes. Line pastry shell with parchment paper, weigh down with uncooked rice and bake for 10 minutes. Remove rice and paper and cook for 10 minutes longer or until pastry shell is lightly browned and cooked.

3   To make filling, place raspberries in a food processor or blender and purée. Push purée through a sieve, to remove seeds. Place egg yolks and sugar in a bowl and beat until thick and creamy. Place egg whites in a separate bowl and beat until stiff peaks form.

4   Fold whipped cream and egg whites

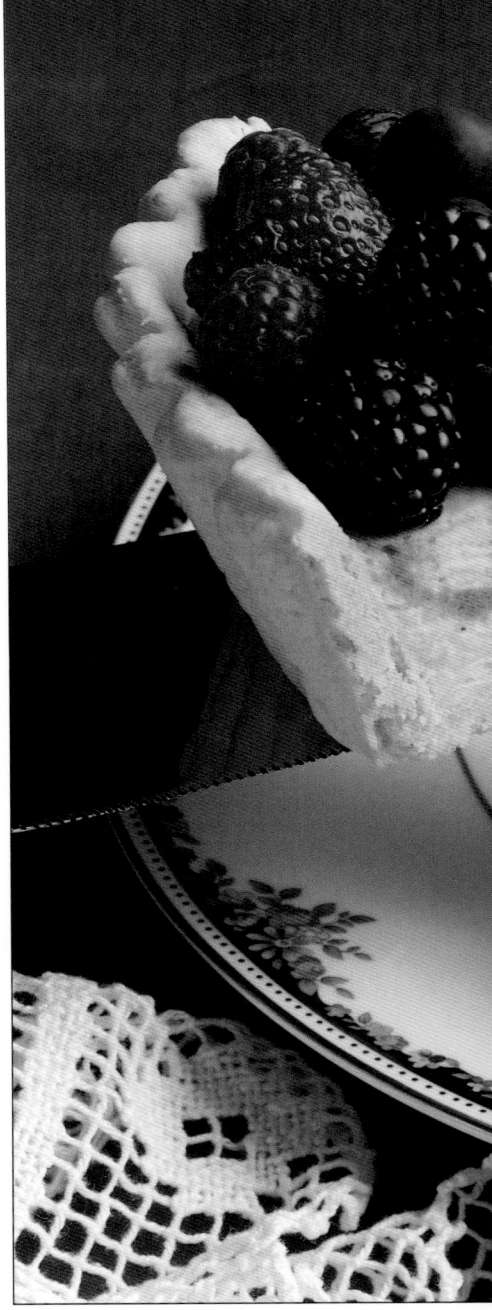

into the egg yolk mixture. Then fold 4 tablespoons of egg mixture into raspberry purée. Fold half the gelatin mixture into the raspberry mixture and the remainder into the egg mixture.

5   Place large spoonfuls of egg mixture into pastry shell, then top with small spoonfuls of raspberry mixture. Repeat until both mixtures are used and pastry shell is two-thirds full. Run a spatula through the mousse to swirl the mixtures. Refrigerate for 2 hours or until mousse is firm. Just prior to serving, top the tart with mixed berries.

STEAMED PEAR PUDDING WITH CARAMEL SAUCE

Serves 8

- ☐ **3 pears, cored, peeled and finely chopped**
- ☐ **$^1/_2$ cup/125 mL water**
- ☐ **2 tablespoons sugar**
- ☐ **3 tablespoons/45 g butter**
- ☐ **$^1/_4$ cup superfine sugar**
- ☐ **2 eggs**
- ☐ **$^3/_4$ cup/90 g self-rising flour, sifted**
- ☐ **$^1/_3$ cup milk**

CARAMEL SAUCE
- ☐ **$^3/_4$ cup/185 g sugar**
- ☐ **$^1/_4$ cup/60 mL water**
- ☐ **3 tablespoons/45 g unsalted (sweet) butter, cut into pieces**
- ☐ **5 fl oz/155 mL thick cream**

1   Place pears, water and sugar in a saucepan and cook over a medium heat for 10 minutes, or until pears are just tender. Remove pan from heat and set aside to cool.

2   Place butter and superfine sugar in a bowl and beat until light and fluffy. Add eggs one at a time, beating well after each addition. Sift flour over mixture and fold in with milk.

3   Strain pears and fold into batter. Pour batter into a greased $1^1/_2$ quart/1.5 liter pudding basin, mold or heatproof mixer bowl. Cover with a round of lightly greased parchment paper, then aluminum foil and pudding basin lid. (If using a mold or bowl securely tie foil to rim with kitchen string.)

4   Place basin in a large saucepan with enough boiling water to come halfway up the side of the basin and bring to the boil. Reduce heat and simmer for $1^1/_2$ hours or until pudding is firm, replacing water if necessary as the pudding cooks. Allow to stand 5 minutes before turning out.

5   To make sauce, place sugar and water in a heavy-based saucepan and cook over a medium heat, stirring, until sugar dissolves and mixture caramelizes and is a deep amber color. Remove pan from heat, add butter a piece at a time, stirring until melted. Return sauce to heat, pour in cream and cook, stirring, for 2 minutes. Remove from heat and set aside to cool. Serve sauce with pudding.

ROCKY ROAD ICE CREAM

Serves 6

- ☐ **1 quart/1 liter vanilla ice cream, softened**
- ☐ **2 oz/60 g semi-sweet dark eating chocolate, coarsely chopped**
- ☐ **15 white marshmallows, chopped**
- ☐ **$^1/_3$ cup/15 g flaked coconut, toasted**
- ☐ **6 red candied cherries, chopped**
- ☐ **6 green candied cherries, chopped**
- ☐ **2 oz/60 g coarsely chopped peanut brittle**

Place ice cream in a large mixing bowl, fold in chocolate, marshmallows, coconut, red and green cherries and peanut brittle. Spoon mixture into a freezerproof container, cover and freeze until firm.

Serving suggestion: Place scoops of ice cream in individual bowls and serve with wafers.

Raspberry Mousse Tart

MASTER CLASS

BRANDY GRAPE TART

Serves 8
Oven temperature 400°F, 200°C

- [ ] **5 oz/155 g prepared short (flaky) pastry, thawed**

GRAPE FILLING
- [ ] **8 oz/250 g cream cheese**
- [ ] **2 tablespoons bottled lemon curd**
- [ ] **1 tablespoon IOX (confectioners') sugar**
- [ ] **1 lb/500 g large green grapes**

APRICOT GLAZE
- [ ] **¼ cup/60 g apricot jam**
- [ ] **2 tablespoons water**
- [ ] **2 teaspoons brandy**

1 Line a lightly greased 8 in/20 cm tart pan with pastry. Line pastry shell with parchment paper, weigh down with uncooked rice and bake for 10 minutes. Remove rice and paper. Reduce temperature to 350°F/180°C and bake 15-20 minutes longer or until pastry is lightly browned. Cool. Set aside to cool.

2 To make filling, place cream cheese in a bowl and beat until soft. Mix in lemon curd and icing sugar. Spread cream cheese mixture over the bottom of pastry shell.

3 Wash grapes and separate from stems. Cut in half and remove seeds. Arrange grapes in a decorative pattern over cream cheese mixture.

4 To make glaze, heat apricot jam and water in a saucepan, stirring until jam melts. Push through a sieve. Stir in brandy and cool slightly. Brush glaze over grapes and chill tart until ready to serve.

Cook's Tip: To make your own fresh Lemon Curd, see the recipe on page 300.

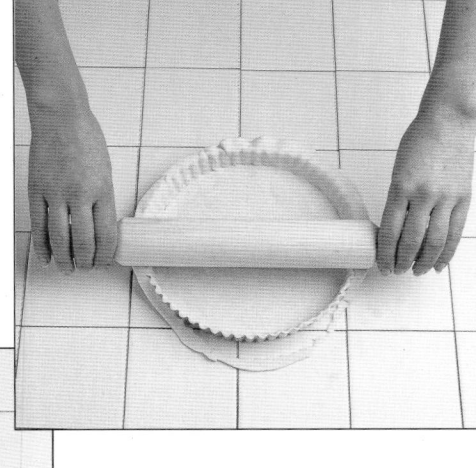

Line a lightly greased 8 in/20 cm tart pan with pastry.

Arrange grapes in a decorative pattern over cream cheese mixture.

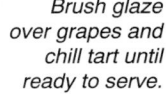
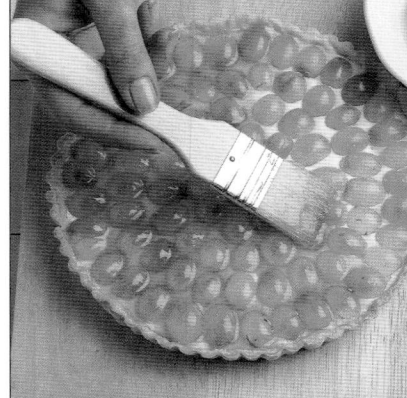

Brush glaze over grapes and chill tart until ready to serve.

RUM BREAD AND BUTTER PUDDING

This is an exotic version of a family favorite. Allowing the mixture to stand for an hour before baking will give a light crusty dessert.

Serves 6
Oven temperature 350°F, 180°C

- ☐ ¹/₄ **cup/45 g golden raisins**
- ☐ ¹/₄ **cup/30 g seeded raisins**
- ☐ **2 tablespoons dark rum**
- ☐ **3 eggs**
- ☐ **3 egg yolks**
- ☐ ²/₃ **cup/170 g superfine sugar**
- ☐ **3 cups/750 mL milk**
- ☐ **1 cup/250 mL thick cream**
- ☐ **2 teaspoons vanilla extract**
- ☐ **1 tablespoon finely grated orange rind**
- ☐ **12 slices buttered bread, crusts removed and slices cut into quarters**
- ☐ **1 teaspoon ground cinnamon**

1 Place both kinds of raisins in a bowl, pour over rum and set aside to soak for 30 minutes.

2 Combine eggs, egg yolks and half the sugar in a mixing bowl and beat until light and fluffy. Place milk and cream in a saucepan and cook over a medium heat, stirring constantly, until almost boiling. Remove pan from heat and set aside to cool slightly. Pour milk mixture into egg mixture and beat until combined. Blend in vanilla extract and orange rind.

3 Place one-third of the bread slices, buttered side up, in a greased 2 quart/ 2 liter capacity baking dish. Top with half raisin mixture. Repeat with remaining bread and raisin mixture, finishing with a layer of bread, buttered side facing up.

4 Pour egg mixture evenly over bread in dish. Combine remaining sugar with cinnamon and sprinkle over pudding. Bake for 1 hour or until a knife inserted in the center comes out clean.

Cook's note: The rum may be omitted from this pudding.

Rum Bread and Butter Pudding

ORANGE AND LEMON PUDDING CAKE

One of those magic puddings – as the pudding cooks it separates to give a layer of fluffy cake over a tangy citrus sauce.

Serves 6
Oven temperature 350°F, 180°C

- [ ] **1 cup/220 g superfine sugar**
- [ ] **¹/₂ cup/1 stick/125 g butter, softened**
- [ ] **¹/₂ cup/60 g self-rising flour**
- [ ] **1 tablespoon finely grated lemon rind**
- [ ] **1 tablespoon finely grated orange rind**
- [ ] **2 tablespoons lemon juice**
- [ ] **2 tablespoons orange juice**
- [ ] **2 eggs, separated**
- [ ] **1 cup/250 mL milk**

1   Place sugar and butter in a bowl and beat until light and fluffy. Mix in flour, lemon rind, orange rind, lemon juice and orange juice.

2   Place egg yolks and milk in a small bowl and whisk to combine. Mix into citrus mixture.

3   Beat egg whites until stiff peaks form then fold into batter. Spoon into a greased 1 quart/1 liter capacity ovenproof dish. Place ovenproof dish in a baking dish with enough boiling water to come halfway up the side of ovenproof dish. Bake for 45 minutes or until pudding is cooked. Serve hot with cream or ice cream.

Orange and Lemon Pudding Cake

LIQUEUR FRUIT SALAD

Serves 4

- [ ] **¹/₂ pineapple, cubed**
- [ ] **14 oz/440 g canned lychees, drained**
- [ ] **8 oz/250 g raspberries**
- [ ] **4 mandarin oranges, segmented**
- [ ] **¹/₂ cup/125 mL champagne or sparkling white wine, chilled**

ORANGE SYRUP
- [ ] **1 tablespoon finely grated orange rind**
- [ ] **1 tablespoon finely grated lemon rind**
- [ ] **¹/₂ cup/125 g superfine sugar**
- [ ] **1 cup/250 mL water**
- [ ] **¹/₂ cup/125 mL fresh orange juice**
- [ ] **¹/₄ cup/60 mL orange-flavored liqueur**
- [ ] **2 tablespoons fresh or canned passion fruit pulp**

1 To make syrup, place orange rind, lemon rind, sugar and water in a saucepan and cook over a low heat until sugar dissolves. Bring to the boil and boil rapidly for 5 minutes. Remove from heat and set aside to cool completely. Strain syrup and discard rinds. Stir in orange juice, liqueur and passion fruit pulp.
2 Place pineapple, lychees, raspberries and mandarin segments in a bowl, pour syrup over fruit, cover and set aside to macerate overnight. To serve, drain fruit, place in a serving bowl and pour champagne over.

COFFEE SPONGE PUFFS

Serves 6
Oven temperature 350°F, 180°C

- [ ] **2 eggs**
- [ ] **¹/₂ cup/125 g superfine sugar**
- [ ] **¹/₃ cup/45 g self-rising flour, sifted**
- [ ] **¹/₃ cup/45 g cornstarch**
- [ ] **IOX (confectioners') sugar**

COFFEE CUSTARD FILLING
- [ ] **1 cup/250 mL milk**
- [ ] **1 tablespoon instant coffee powder**
- [ ] **3 egg yolks**
- [ ] **¹/₄ cup/60 g superfine sugar**
- [ ] **1¹/₂ tablespoons all-purpose flour**
- [ ] **¹/₂ cup/125 mL thick cream, whipped**

1 Place eggs in a mixing bowl and beat until thick and creamy. Add sugar a little at a time, beating well after each addition until mixture thickens and sugar dissolves. This will take about 10 minutes.
2 Sift flour and cornstarch together then fold through egg mixture in two batches. Spoon heaped tablespoons of mixture onto lightly greased cookie sheets, leaving about 2 in/5 cm between each puff. Bake for 8-10 minutes or until puffs are golden. Transfer puffs to a wire rack to cool.
3 To make filling, place milk and coffee in a saucepan and heat until almost boiling. Whisk together egg yolks, sugar and flour until thick and creamy. Gradually whisk milk mixture into egg mixture. Return mixture to saucepan and heat, stirring, until mixture thickens. Remove from heat and set aside to cool. Fold whipped cream through mixture.
4 Spread filling over flat side of half the puffs and top with remaining puffs. Dust tops with IOX (confectioners') sugar and serve immediately.

CASSATA SICILIANA

A simple do-ahead dinner party dessert that looks spectacular when decorated with extra glacé fruit. It is best prepared a day before serving.

Serves 8

- [ ] **1 lb/500 g ricotta cheese**
- [ ] **1 cup/250 g sugar**
- [ ] **2 tablespoons chopped pistachios**
- [ ] **¹/₄ cup/45 g chopped mixed candied fruit**
- [ ] **¹/₄ teaspoon ground cinnamon**
- [ ] **2 oz/60 g semi-sweet dark chocolate, shredded**
- [ ] **2 tablespoons almond-flavored liqueur**
- [ ] **8 in/20 cm round sponge cake layer, cut into ¹/₄ in/1 cm slices**

ALMOND TOPPING
- [ ] **1 cup/250 mL thick cream**
- [ ] **1 tablespoon almond-flavored liqueur**
- [ ] **selection candied fruit**

1 Beat ricotta and sugar together until light and fluffy. Divide mixture in half. Fold pistachios and chopped fruit through half of mixture. Mix cinnamon, chocolate and liqueur into other half. Cover and set aside.
2 Line base and sides of an 8 in/20 cm bowl or mold with plastic food wrap, then with three-quarters of cake slices. Fill with ricotta fruit mixture and cover with remaining cake. Cover and freeze for 2 hours or overnight.
3 When mixture is set pour chocolate mixture over, return to freezer and freeze until set.
4 To make topping, whip cream and liqueur together until soft peaks form. Just prior to serving, turn out cassata, spread completely with cream and decorate with glacé fruit.

SICILIAN ROLL

Serves 8
Oven temperature 350°F, 180°C

- [ ] **3 eggs**
- [ ] **¹/₂ cup/125 g superfine sugar**
- [ ] **³/₄ cup/90 g self-rising flour, sifted**
- [ ] **2 tablespoons hot milk**
- [ ] **¹/₂ cup/125 mL thick cream, whipped**
- [ ] **2 oz/60 g semi-sweet chocolate, shaved**

RICOTTA FILLING
- [ ] **8 oz/250 g ricotta cheese**
- [ ] **¹/₃ cup/60 g IOX (confectioners') sugar**
- [ ] **¹/₂ teaspoon vanilla extract**
- [ ] **1 tablespoon crème de cacao**
- [ ] **1 oz/30 g semi-sweet chocolate, shaved**
- [ ] **1 tablespoon chopped candied fruit**

1 Place eggs in a large mixing bowl and beat until thick and creamy. Add sugar a little at a time, beating well after each addition until sugar dissolves and mixture thickens. Fold in flour alternately with milk.
2 Spoon mixture into a lightly greased and lined 10 x 12 in/25 x 30 cm shallow jelly roll pan and bake for 12-15 minutes or until firm. Turn out onto a sheet of parchment paper, remove lining paper and trim edges of cake. Roll up from the narrow end, using paper to lift and guide roll. Stand for 5 minutes, then unroll and allow to cool.
3 To make filling, place ricotta cheese, IOX (confectioners') sugar, vanilla and crème de cacao in a mixing bowl and beat until well combined. Fold chocolate and candied fruit through mixture and spread over cake. Reroll and transfer to a serving platter. Spread with cream and decorate with shaved chocolate.

Cassata Siciliana, Sicilian Roll, Coffee Sponge Puffs

APRICOT ALMOND SHORTCAKE

Serves 8
Oven temperature 350°F, 180°C

- ☐ ¹/₂ **cup/1 stick/125 g butter**
- ☐ ¹/₂ **cup/125 g sugar**
- ☐ **1 egg**
- ☐ ³/₄ **cup/90 g self-rising flour, sifted**
- ☐ ³/₄ **cup/90 g all-purpose flour, sifted**

ALMOND APRICOT FILLING

- ☐ **3 tablespoons/45 g butter**
- ☐ **2 tablespoons superfine sugar**
- ☐ **1 egg yolk**
- ☐ ³/₄ **cup/90 g ground almonds**
- ☐ **2 teaspoons all-purpose flour**
- ☐ **14 oz/440 g canned apricots, drained**

ALMOND TOPPING

- ☐ **3¹/₂ cups/410 g ground almonds**
- ☐ ¹/₃ **cup/90 g superfine sugar**
- ☐ **6 eggs, separated**
- ☐ **2 tablespoons almond-flavored liqueur**
- ☐ **1 cup/250 g apricot jam, warmed and sieved**
- ☐ ¹/₃ **cup/60 g sliced almonds, toasted**

1   Place butter and sugar in a large mixing bowl and beat until light and creamy. Add egg and beat well, stir in self-rising and plain flours. Turn out onto a lightly floured surface and knead lightly until smooth. Divide mixture into two equal portions and wrap and chill for 30 minutes.

2   Roll out each portion between sheets of plastic food wrap or waxed paper to an 8 in/20 cm circle. Press one circle dough into a greased and lined deep 8 in/20 cm cake pan or springform pan.

3   To make filling, place butter, sugar and egg yolk in a small bowl and beat until light and fluffy. Stir in almonds and flour. Place apricots in a food processor or blender and process until smooth. Swirl apricots through almond mixture. Take care not to overmix. Spread mixture over dough in cake pan, leaving a small border around edge. Place second circle of dough over apricot mixture and press edges together. Brush with water and bake for 35-40 minutes. Stand 15 minutes before turning out on a wire rack to cool.

4   To make topping, place almonds and sugar in a mixing bowl. Combine egg yolks and liqueur in a small bowl, then gradually stir into almond mixture. Remove one-third of mixture and set aside. Add 1 tablespoon of unbeaten egg white to remaining mixture and spread over sides and top of shortcake. Add a little more egg white if mixture is difficult to spread.

5   Add 2 tablespoons of unbeaten egg white to reserved almond mixture and spoon into a pastry bag fitted with a large star nozzle. Pipe lines in a zigzag pattern over top and pipe small rosettes around the edge. Place cake on a cookie sheet and bake at 500°F/250°C for 8-10 minutes or until top is lightly browned. Spoon two-thirds of jam between zigzag piping and set aside for 10 minutes to cool slightly. Spread sides with remaining jam and coat with toasted almonds. Cool cake completely before cutting.

Apricot Almond Shortcake

SUMMER WINE JELLY

Almost any fresh fruit can be used to make this dessert. You should avoid pineapple, papaya and kiwifruit (Chinese gooseberry) as they contain an enzyme which prevents the gelatin from setting.

Serves 8

- ☐ **4 apricots, pitted and halved**
- ☐ **6¹/₂ oz/200 g green grapes**
- ☐ **8 oz/250 g strawberries, hulled and halved**
- ☐ **8 oz/250 g fresh or drained canned cherries, pitted**
- ☐ **¹/₃ cup/60 g gelatin dissolved in ¹/₂ cup/125 mL hot water, cooled**
- ☐ **2 cups/500 mL sweet white wine**
- ☐ **2 cups/500 mL apple juice**
- ☐ **¹/₃ cup/90 mL melon liqueur or additional apple juice**

1   Place apricots, grapes, strawberries and cherries in a bowl and toss to combine.

2   Place gelatin mixture, wine, apple juice and melon liqueur or additional apple juice in a bowl and mix to combine. Pour one-quarter of the wine mixture into a lightly oiled 1 quart/1 liter capacity mold and top with one-quarter of the fruit. Place in refrigerator to set.

3   Repeat with remaining liquid and fruit. When jelly is set, unmold and serve garnished with extra fruit if desired.

Unmolding a gelatin dessert: Molded gelatin desserts need to be loosened before you try to turn them out. This is easily done by placing the mold in warm water for a few seconds. After removing mold from water dry the base and tip the mold sideways, while at the same time gently pulling the mixture away from the edge of the mold. This breaks the airlock. Rinse a serving plate with cold water and place upside down on top of the mold. Then, holding firmly, quickly turn over both mold and plate and give a sharp shake. The dessert should fall onto the plate. If it refuses to move, place a hot, wet cloth over the base of the mold for 10-20 seconds. Wetting the plate means that you can easily move the dessert if it does not land in the center when you unmold it.

Summer Wine Jelly

TURKISH SYLLABUB

Serve this tangy dessert on its own in pretty glass dishes, or as a topping for fruit salad.

Serves 4

- ☐ **1 cup/250 mL thick cream**
- ☐ **1 tablespoon honey**
- ☐ **1cup/250 g plain yogurt**
- ☐ **1 tablespoon brown sugar**

Place cream and honey in a bowl and whip until thick. Fold in yogurt, spoon into individual serving glasses and sprinkle with sugar. Chill for 2-3 hours before serving.

BANANA ICE CREAM

Serves 4

- ☐ **6 large ripe bananas, chopped**
- ☐ **1 cup/250 mL vegetable oil**
- ☐ **2 tablespoons honey**
- ☐ **¹/₂ cup full cream milk powder**
- ☐ **1 cup/250 mL water**
- ☐ **2 tablespoons fine carob powder**

Place bananas, oil, honey, milk powder, water and carob powder in a food processor or blender and process until smooth. Pour into a freezerproof container, cover and freeze until firm.

MASTER CLASS

STRIPED ROULADE WITH APRICOT MOUSSE FILLING

This impressive roulade may look very grand but it is in fact easy to make. Follow our step-by-step recipe and see just how easy it really is.

Serves 6
Oven temperature 400°F, 200°C

- ☐ ¹/₂ cup/60 g self-rising flour, sifted
- ☐ 2 tablespoons cocoa, sifted
- ☐ 4 eggs
- ☐ ¹/₂ cup/5 tablespoons superfine sugar

APRICOT MOUSSE FILLING
- ☐ 4 teaspoons/1 tablespoon plain gelatin
- ☐ ¹/₄ cup/60 mL apricot nectar
- ☐ 14 oz/440 g canned apricots, drained and ¹/₄ cup/60 mL liquid reserved
- ☐ 3 eggs, separated
- ☐ ¹/₃ cup/90 g superfine sugar
- ☐ 1 tablespoon brandy
- ☐ 1 tablespoon Cointreau
- ☐ ¹/₂ cup/125 mL thick cream

1   Place 2 tablespoons flour and cocoa in a mixing bowl and the remaining flour in another.
2   Beat eggs and sugar until thick and creamy. Divide mixture evenly between two bowls. Fold cocoa mixture through egg mixture in one bowl and fold flour mixture through the remaining egg mixture.
3   Place chocolate and plain cake batters into two separate pastry bags fitted with ³/₄ in/2 cm plain nozzles. Pipe lines of chocolate mixture, ³/₄ in/2 cm apart, diagonally across a greased and lined 10 x 12 in/25 x 30 cm shallow Jelly roll tin. Then pipe plain mixture in lines between chocolate strips. Bake for 8-10 minutes, or until cake is cooked through and springy to touch.
4   Turn roulade out onto a damp teatowel sprinkled with superfine sugar. Roll up with teatowel from short end and allow to cool.
5   To make filling, sprinkle gelatin over apricot nectar in a small bowl, place it over a small saucepan of simmering water and stir until gelatin dissolves. Set aside to cool at room temperature. Place apricots and reserved liquid in a food processor or

blender and process until smooth. Beat egg yolks and sugar in a bowl until thick and creamy. Stir in apricot purée, gelatin mixture, brandy and Cointreau. Beat cream until soft peaks form, fold into apricot mixture. Beat egg whites until soft peaks form, fold into apricot mixture. Refrigerate for 2-3 hours, or until mixture is almost set. Unroll roulade and spread with filling. Reroll and refrigerate until filling is set.

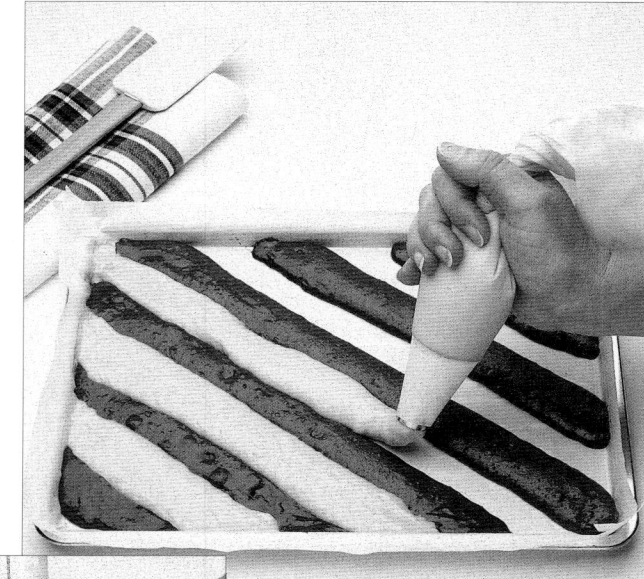

Pipe lines of chocolate mixture ³/₄ in /2 cm apart diagonally across a greased and lined Jelly roll tin. Then pipe plain mixture between chocolate stripes.

Turn roulade onto a damp teatowel sprinkled with superfine sugar, and roll up from short end.

Unroll roulade, spread with filling, and reroll. Refrigerate until filling is set.

RHUBARB FOOL WITH ORANGE COOKIES

Serves 8
Oven temperature 375°F, 190°C

- [ ] 1½ lb/750 g rhubarb, trimmed and cut into ½ in/1 cm pieces
- [ ] 1½ cups/250 g packed brown sugar
- [ ] ¼ teaspoon ground cloves
- [ ] ½ teaspoon vanilla extract
- [ ] 2 tablespoons lemon juice
- [ ] 2 tablespoons orange juice
- [ ] ¾ cup/185 mL thick cream
- [ ] ½ cup/100 g plain yogurt

ORANGE BISCUITS
- [ ] ¼ cup plus 1 tablespoon/75 g unsalted butter
- [ ] ¼ cup/60 g superfine sugar
- [ ] 1 egg
- [ ] 1½ teaspoons finely grated orange rind
- [ ] ¾ cup/90 g all-purpose flour

1   Place rhubarb, sugar, cloves, vanilla extract and lemon and orange juices in a saucepan. Bring to the boil, then reduce heat and simmer, stirring occasionally, for 15 minutes or until rhubarb is soft and mixture thick. Spoon rhubarb mixture into a bowl, cover and chill.

2   Place cream in a bowl and beat until soft peaks form. Fold yogurt into cream, then fold in chilled rhubarb mixture to give a marbled effect. Spoon into individual serving glasses and chill.

3   To make cookies, place butter and sugar in a mixing bowl and beat until light and creamy. Add egg and orange rind and beat well to combine. Stir in flour.

4   Place teaspoons of mixture, 2 in/5 cm apart, on lightly greased cookie sheets and bake for 10 minutes or until golden. Cool cookies on sheets for 1 minute before removing to wire racks to cool completely. Accompany each fool with two or three cookies.

APPLE COMPOTE WITH RICOTTA CREAM

The Ricotta Cream served with this dessert is a delicious alternative to cream. You might like to try it as an accompaniment to other desserts.

Serves 4
Oven temperature 400°F, 200°C

- [ ] 6 green apples, cored, peeled and cut into 1 cm/½ in slices
- [ ] ⅓ cup/100 g golden raisins
- [ ] ¼ cup/60 g pine nuts (pignola), toasted
- [ ] 1 cup/250 mL orange juice

INDIVIDUAL SUMMER PUDDINGS

Fresh or frozen berries can be used to make this dessert.

Serves 4

- ☐ ¹/₃ cup/100 g superfine sugar
- ☐ 2 cups/500 mL water
- ☐ 1³/₄ lb/875 g mixed berries, such as raspberries, strawberries, blueberries or blackberries
- ☐ 14 slices bread, crusts removed

BERRY SAUCE
- ☐ 5 oz/155 g mixed berries, such as raspberries, strawberries, blueberries or blackberries
- ☐ 2 tablespoons IOX (confectioners') sugar
- ☐ 1 tablespoon fresh lemon juice
- ☐ 2 tablespoons water

1   Place sugar and water in a saucepan and cook over a low heat, stirring constantly, until sugar dissolves. Bring to the boil, reduce heat, add berries and simmer for 4-5 minutes or until fruit is soft, but still retains its shape. Remove from heat. Drain, reserving liquid, and set aside to cool.

2   Cut 8 circles of bread with a pastry cutter. Line the base of four ¹/₂ cup/125 mL soufflé dishes or custard cups with 4 rounds of the bread. Cut remaining bread slices into fingers and line the sides of dishes, trimming bread to fit if necessary. Spoon fruit into dishes and enough reserved liquid to moisten bread well, then cover with remaining bread circles. Reserve any remaining liquid. Cover tops of dishes with aluminum foil, top with a weight, and refrigerate overnight.

3   To make sauce, place berries, IOX sugar, lemon juice and water in a food processor or blender and process until puréed. Push mixture through a sieve to remove seeds and chill until required.

4   Turn puddings onto individual serving plates, spoon sauce over or pass separately.

Serving suggestion: Garnish with additional berries and plain yogurt.

- ☐ ¹/₃ cup/90 g honey
- ☐ ¹/₂ teaspoon ground cinnamon
- ☐ 6 whole cloves
- ☐ 1 tablespoon finely grated orange rind
- ☐ ¹/₂ cup/60 g ground almonds

RICOTTA CREAM
- ☐ ¹/₂ cup/125 g fresh ricotta cheese
- ☐ ¹/₂ cup/125 g cottage cheese
- ☐ 1-2 tablespoons milk
- ☐ 1-2 tablespoons superfine sugar

1   Layer apples, raisins and pine nuts in a shallow baking dish. Pour over orange juice, drizzle with honey, then sprinkle with cinnamon, cloves, orange rind and almonds. Cover dish with aluminum foil and bake for 35-40 minutes or until apples are tender.

2   To make cream, place ricotta and cottage cheese in a food processor or blender and process until smooth. Add a little milk if the mixture is too thick and sweeten with sugar to taste.

Serving suggestion: Serve this dessert hot or cold with a little Ricotta Cream.

Left: Individual Summer Puddings
Above: Apple Compote with Ricotta Cream, Rhubarb Fool with Orange Biscuits

BANANA FRITTERS WITH CARAMEL SAUCE

Fruit fritters are always popular, especially with children. You might like to make these using other fruits, such as apples, peaches or canned pineapple rings.

Serves 4

- [ ] **4 large firm bananas, cut in half then split lengthwise**
- [ ] **2 tablespoons lime juice**
- [ ] **oil for cooking**

BATTER
- [ ] **1 cup/125 g self-rising flour, sifted**
- [ ] **1 egg, lightly beaten**
- [ ] **$^1/_2$ cup/125 mL milk**
- [ ] **2 tablespoons superfine sugar**
- [ ] **1 egg white**

CARAMEL SAUCE
- [ ] **$^1/_2$ cup/125 g sugar**
- [ ] **$^1/_2$ cup/125 mL water**
- [ ] **$^1/_2$ cup/125 mL thick cream**
- [ ] **2 teaspoons whiskey (optional)**

1   To make batter, place flour in a mixing bowl and make a well in the center. Combine egg, milk and superfine sugar and mix into flour mixture to make a batter of a smooth consistency. Set aside to stand for 10 minutes.

2   To make sauce, place sugar and water in a saucepan and cook over a low heat, stirring constantly, until sugar dissolves. Bring to the boil, then reduce heat and simmer, without stirring, for 5 minutes or until mixture is golden.

3   Remove pan from heat and carefully stir in cream and whiskey, if using. Return pan to a low heat and cook, stirring carefully, until combined. Remove pan from heat and set aside to cool.

4   Beat egg white until soft peaks form, then fold into batter.

5   Heat oil in a large saucepan. Brush bananas with lime juice and dip in batter to coat. Drain off excess batter and cook bananas in hot oil for 2-3 minutes or until golden. Drain on paper. Serve immediately with sauce.

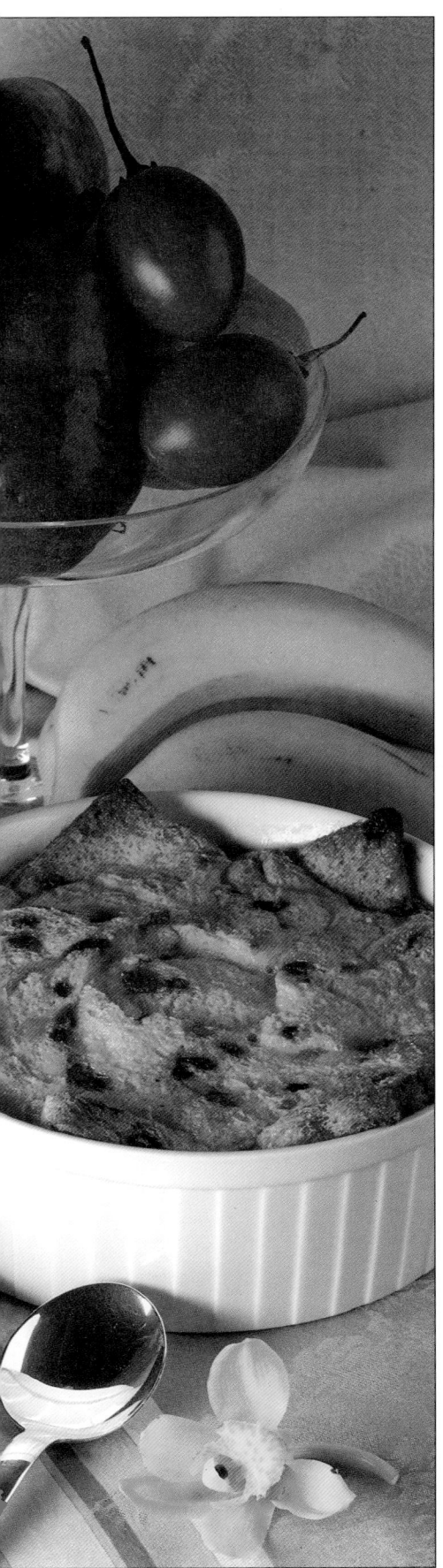

FRUITY BREAD AND BUTTER PUDDING

The fruitiest bread and butter pudding you will ever have. This version of the traditional English dessert uses golden raisins, apples and raisin bread to make it extra fruity.

Serves 8
Oven temperature 350°F, 180°C

- ☐ ¹/₄ cup/¹/₂ stick/60 g butter
- ☐ ¹/₂ cup/90 g packed brown sugar
- ☐ ¹/₂ cup/90 g golden raisins
- ☐ ¹/₂ teaspoon ground cinnamon
- ☐ 14 oz/440 g canned sliced apples (not pie filling)
- ☐ 12 thick slices raisin bread, buttered and crusts removed
- ☐ 3 eggs
- ☐ 1¹/₄ cups/10 mL milk
- ☐ ³/₄ cup/185 mL thick cream
- ☐ ¹/₂ teaspoon vanilla extract

1 Melt butter in a skillet and add sugar and cook over a medium heat, stirring constantly, until sugar dissolves. Stir in raisins, cinnamon and apples, toss to combine and cook for 1-2 minutes longer. Remove pan from heat and set aside to cool.
2 Cut bread slices into triangles and arrange one-third, buttered side up, in the base of a greased casserole. Top with half the apple mixture and another layer of bread triangles. Spoon over remaining apple mixture and top with bread triangles and arrange remaining slices around the edges.
3 Place eggs, milk, cream and vanilla extract in a mixing bowl and beat until well combined. Pour carefully over bread and apples in dish. Place casserole in a baking dish with enough water to come halfway up the sides of the casserole. Bake for 45-50 minutes or until pudding is firm and top is golden.

Fruity Bread and Butter Pudding, Banana Fritters with Caramel Sauce, Jaffa Pudding Cake

JAFFA PUDDING CAKE

Chocolate and orange combine in this recipe to make the most wonderful self-saucing dessert you will ever taste.

Serves 8
Oven temperature 350°F, 180°C

- ☐ ¹/₂ cup/1stick/125 g butter
- ☐ 2 teaspoons finely grated orange rind
- ☐ ²/₃ cup/170 g superfine sugar
- ☐ 2 eggs
- ☐ ¹/₃ cup/100 g semi-sweet chocolate chips
- ☐ 1¹/₂ cups/185 g self-rising flour, sifted
- ☐ ¹/₂ cup/125 mL orange juice

CHOCOLATE SAUCE
- ☐ ¹/₄ cup/30 g cocoa powder
- ☐ ¹/₃ cup/100 g superfine sugar
- ☐ 1¹/₂ cups/375 mL boiling water

1 Place butter and orange rind in a large mixing bowl and beat until light and fluffy. Gradually add sugar, beating well after each addition until mixture is creamy.
2 Beat in eggs one at a time. Toss chocolate chips in flour, then fold flour mixture and orange juice, alternately, into batter. Spoon batter into a greased casserole.
3 Sift together cocoa powder and sugar over batter in casserole, then carefully add boiling water, pouring evenly. Bake for 40 minutes or until pudding is firm. Serve warm.

PEAR AND WALNUT UPSIDE-DOWN CAKE

Serves 8
Oven temperature 350°F, 180°C

- ☐ ¹/₄ **cup/60 g granulated brown (raw) sugar**
- ☐ **2 x 14 oz/440 g canned pear halves, drained and 1cup/ 250 mL syrup reserved**
- ☐ **8 red candied cherries, halved**
- ☐ **1 cup/2 sticks/250 g butter, softened**
- ☐ **4 eggs**
- ☐ **2 cups/250 g self-rising flour**
- ☐ **1 cup/200 g superfine sugar**
- ☐ **1 cup/125 g chopped walnuts**
- ☐ ¹/₄ **cup/60 mL maple syrup**

1 Sprinkle base of a greased and parchment-paper lined, deep 9 in/23 cm round cake pan or springform pan with brown sugar. Arrange pears and cherries over base.

2 Place butter, eggs, flour and superfine sugar in food processor and process until smooth. Stir in walnuts. Carefully spoon batter over pears and cherries in pan and bake for 1-1¹/₄ hours, or until cooked when tested with a skewer.

3 Place maple syrup and reserved pear juice in a small saucepan and cook over a medium heat until syrup is reduced by half.

4 Turn cake onto a serving plate and pour syrup over. Serve hot or warm with cream or ice cream if desired.

Sprinkle base of cake pan with raw sugar. Arrange pears and cherries over base.

Carefully spoon batter over pears and cherries in pan.

ALMOND CHEESECAKE

Serves 8
Oven temperature 300°F, 150°C

- ☐ ²/₃ cup/170 g superfine sugar
- ☐ ¹/₄ cup/¹/₂ stick/60 g butter, softened
- ☐ 1 lb/500 g cream cheese
- ☐ ¹/₄ cup/30 g all-purpose flour, sifted
- ☐ 2 tablespoons honey
- ☐ 5 eggs, separated
- ☐ ¹/₂ cup/125 mL thick cream
- ☐ 1 teaspoon vanilla extract
- ☐ ¹/₃ cup/75 g blanched almonds, finely chopped

BROWN SUGAR TOPPING
- ☐ ¹/₄ cup/45 g packed brown sugar
- ☐ ¹/₄ cup/30 g finely chopped blanched almonds
- ☐ 1 teaspoon ground cinnamon

1   To make topping, place brown sugar, almonds and cinnamon in a bowl and mix to combine. Set aside.
2   Place superfine sugar and butter in a bowl and beat until light and fluffy. Add cream cheese and beat until mixture is creamy. Add flour, honey and egg yolks and beat well to combine, then fold in cream and vanilla. Place egg whites in a bowl and beat until stiff peaks form. Fold egg whites and almonds into cream cheese mixture.
3   Spoon into a greased and lined 10 in/ 25 cm springform pan. Sprinkle with topping and cook for 1¹/₂ hours or until just firm. Leave cheesecake to cool in turned off oven, with door closed.

Cook's note: This cheesecake will sink a little on cooling.

APPLE AND RHUBARB CRUMBLE

Serves 4
Oven temperature 350°F, 180°C

- ☐ 8 stalks rhubarb, cut into 2 in/ 5 cm pieces
- ☐ 4 cooking apples, cored, peeled and sliced
- ☐ ¹/₃ cup/100 g superfine sugar
- ☐ ¹/₂ cup/125 mL water
- ☐ ¹/₄ cup/60 mL orange juice

HAZELNUT CRUMBLE
- ☐ ³/₄ cup/100 g ground hazelnuts (filberts)

- ☐ ¹/₂ cup/45 g rolled oats
- ☐ ¹/₄ cup/30 g flaked coconut
- ☐ ¹/₃ cup/45 g all-purpose flour
- ☐ ¹/₄ cup/45 g packed brown sugar
- ☐ ¹/₄ teaspoon ground cinnamon
- ☐ 3 oz/90 g butter, chopped into small pieces

1   Place rhubarb, apples, superfine sugar, water and orange juice in a saucepan and cook over a medium heat, stirring constantly, until sugar dissolves. Bring to the boil, then reduce heat, cover and simmer for 10 minutes or until fruit is tender. Spoon fruit mixture into a 3 cups/750 mL casserole.
2   To make crumble, combine hazelnuts, oats, coconut, flour, brown sugar and cinnamon in a bowl. Rub in butter using fingertips until mixture resembles coarse bread crumbs. Sprinkle crumble over fruit mixture and bake for 20-25 minutes.

COLLEGE PUDDING

Serves 4

- ☐ ¹/₄ cup/60 g strawberry jam
- ☐ ¹/₄ cup/¹/₂ stick/60 g butter, softened
- ☐ ¹/₄ cup/60 g superfine sugar
- ☐ 1 egg, lightly beaten
- ☐ ¹/₂ teaspoon vanilla extract
- ☐ 1 cup/125 g all-purpose flour
- ☐ 1 teaspoon baking powder
- ☐ ¹/₃ cup/90 mL milk

1   Line bottom of greased 4 cup/1 liter pudding basin, mold or heatproof mixer bowl with parchment paper. Place jam in bottom of container.
2   Place butter and sugar in mixing bowl and beat until creamy. Add egg and vanilla extract and beat until light and fluffy.
3   Sift together flour and baking powder. Fold flour mixture and milk, alternately, into egg mixture. Spoon batter into prepared container.
4   Cover top of pudding with a greased round of parchment paper, then seal with lid. (If using mold or bowl, cover paper with aluminum foil and tie securely to rim with string.)
5   Place basin in large saucepan or kettle with enough boiling water to come halfway up sides of basin. Simmer over medium heat 1¹/₂ hours or until cooked when tested with a skewer. Add more boiling water to kettle during cooking, if necessary. Serve warm.

CREAMY BERRY RICE

Serves 4

- ☐ ¹/₂ cup/100 g short grain rice
- ☐ 4 oz/125 g blueberries
- ☐ 4 oz/125 g raspberries
- ☐ ¹/₃ cup/90 g plain yogurt
- ☐ ¹/₄ cup/60 g berry fruit yogurt
- ☐ ³/₄ cup/185 mL evaporated milk
- ☐ 1 tablespoon honey
- ☐ ¹/₂ teaspoon pumpkin pie spice

1   Cook rice in a large saucepan of boiling water for 10-12 minutes, or until tender. Drain and rinse under cold running water.
2   Place rice, blueberries, raspberries, plain yogurt, berry yogurt, evaporated milk, honey and spice in a bowl and mix to combine. Spoon into individual serving dishes and chill.

Variation: You might like to use chopped drained, canned fruits such peaches, pears or apricots in place of the berries and a complementary-flavored fruit yogurt in place of the berry yogurt.

CHERRY PEACH CRUMBLES

Serves 4
Oven temperature 350°F, 180°C

- ☐ 14 oz/440 g canned pitted black (Bing) cherries, drained and ¹/₂ cup/125 mL juice reserved
- ☐ 14 oz/440 g canned sliced peaches, drained and ¹/₂ cup/ 125 mL juice reserved
- ☐ 2 teaspoons cornstarch blended with 2 tablespoons cherry brandy

ALMOND TOPPING
- ☐ ¹/₂ cup/60 g crushed macaroons
- ☐ 1 tablespoon brown sugar
- ☐ 2 tablespoons chopped sliced almonds

1   Spoon cherries and peaches into four soufflé or custard cups. Place reserved cherry and peach juices and cornstarch mixture into a saucepan and cook over a medium heat, stirring constantly, until mixture thickens slightly. Pour over fruit.
2   To make topping, place macaroons, sugar and almonds in a bowl and mix to combine. Sprinkle topping over fruit and bake for 10-15 minutes or until topping is golden and fruit is heated through.

Almond Cheesecake, Apple and Rhubarb Crumble, College Pudding

TRIPLE-CHOCOLATE TERRINE

This wonderful dessert fulfils every chocoholic's dream. It takes a little time to prepare, but is well worth the effort.

Serves 10
Oven temperature 350°F, 180°C

BUTTER CAKE
- ☐ ¹/₂ cup/1 stick/125 g butter
- ☐ 1 teaspoon vanilla extract
- ☐ ¹/₃ cup/90 g superfine sugar
- ☐ 2 eggs
- ☐ 1 cup/125 g self-rising flour, sifted
- ☐ ¹/₃ cup/90 mL milk

DARK CHOCOLATE FUDGE FILLING
- ☐ ¹/₂ cup/1 stick/125 g unsalted (sweet) butter
- ☐ 2 tablespoons IOX (confectioners') sugar
- ☐ 90 g/3 oz semi-sweet dark chocolate, melted and cooled
- ☐ 1 cup/250 mL thick cream, chilled

MILK CHOCOLATE MOUSSE
- ☐ 6 oz/185 g sweet milk chocolate, chopped
- ☐ ¹/₂ cup/1 stick/125 g unsalted (sweet) butter
- ☐ 2 eggs
- ☐ 2 tablespoons superfine sugar
- ☐ 1 cup/250 mL thick cream
- ☐ 1 tablespoon dark rum
- ☐ 2 tablespoons plain gelatin dissolved in 2 tablespoons hot water, cooled

WHITE CHOCOLATE GLAZE
- ☐ 8 oz/250 g white chocolate, chopped
- ☐ 3 oz/100 g unsalted (sweet) butter

1   To make cake, place butter and vanilla extract in a mixing bowl and beat until light and fluffy. Gradually add sugar, beating well after each addition, until mixture is creamy. Beat in eggs one at a time. Fold flour and milk, alternately, into butter mixture. Spoon mixture into a greased and parchment paper-lined 4¹/₂ x 8¹/₂ in/11 x 21 cm loaf tin and bake for 20-25 minutes

or until cooked when tested with a skewer. Stand in pan for 5 minutes, then turn onto a wire rack to cool.

2   To make fudge filling, beat butter and IOX sugar until creamy. Fold in chocolate, then cream. Refrigerate until required.

3   To make mousse, place chocolate and butter in a saucepan and cook over a low heat, stirring constantly, until well blended. Remove from heat and set aside to cool. Place eggs and sugar in a bowl and beat until thick and creamy. Fold in chocolate mixture, cream, rum and gelatin mixture.

4   To assemble terrine, cut cake horizontally into three layers. Spread 2 layers with fudge filling and place one of

these layers, filling side upwards, in the base of an 4¹/₂ x 8¹/₂ in/11 x 21 cm loaf pan lined with plastic food wrap. Top with half the chocolate mousse and refrigerate for 10 minutes or until almost set. Place the second layer of filling-topped cake over the mousse with filling facing upwards. Top with remaining mousse and refrigerate until almost set. Place remaining cake layer on top and refrigerate until set.

5   To make glaze, place white chocolate and butter in a small saucepan and cook over a low heat, stirring constantly, until well blended. Set aside and cool slightly. Turn terrine onto a wire rack, trim edges, pour glaze over to cover and allow to set.

Spread 2 layers of cake with fudge filling and place one of these layers, filling side upwards, in the base of a loaf pan lined with plastic food wrap. Top with half the chocolate mousse and refrigerate.

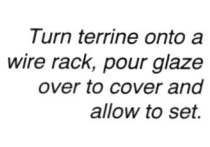

Turn terrine onto a wire rack, pour glaze over to cover and allow to set.

RHUBARB AND APPLE TART

Rhubarb and apple combine to give a new twist to a traditional recipe.

Serves 10
Oven temperature 400°F, 200°C

PASTRY
- ☐ **1 cup/125 g all-purpose flour, sifted**
- ☐ **2 teaspoons IOX (confectioners') sugar, sifted**
- ☐ **3 oz/90 g butter, cubed**
- ☐ **1 tablespoon iced water**

RHUBARB AND APPLE FILLING
- ☐ **6 stalks rhubarb, chopped**
- ☐ **2 tablespoons granulated sugar**
- ☐ **3 green apples, cored, peeled and sliced**
- ☐ **2 tablespoons/30 g butter**
- ☐ **4 oz/125 g cream cheese**
- ☐ **1/3 cup/90 g granulated sugar**
- ☐ **1 teaspoon vanilla extract**
- ☐ **1 egg**

1   To make pastry, place flour and IOX sugar in a bowl and cut in butter, using two knives or a pastry blender, until mixture resembles coarse bread crumbs. Add water and knead to a smooth dough. Wrap in plastic wrap and refrigerate for 30 minutes.
2   Roll out pastry on a lightly floured surface and line a greased 9 in/23 cm tart pan fluted with removable base. Line pastry shell with parchment paper and weigh down with uncooked rice. Bake for 15 minutes. Remove rice and paper and cook for 5 minutes longer.
3   To make filling, poach or microwave rhubarb until tender. Drain well, stir in sugar and set aside to cool. Melt butter in a skillet and cook apples for 3-4 minutes. Remove apples from pan and set aside to cool.
4   Place cream cheese, sugar, vanilla extract and egg in a bowl and beat until smooth. Spoon rhubarb into pastry shell, then top with cream cheese mixture and arrange apple slices attractively on the top. Reduce oven temperature to 350°F/180°C and cook for 40-45 minutes or until filling is firm.

Cook's tip: The pastry for this tart can be made in the food processor if you wish. Place flour, IOX sugar and butter in a food processor and process until mixture resembles coarse bread crumbs. With machine running, add water and continue to process until a smooth dough forms.

COFFEE NUT PIE

This version of the traditional Mississippi Mud Pie is sure to be popular as a dessert.

Serves 6

- ☐ **7 oz/220 g chocolate wafer cookies**
- ☐ **1/2 cup/1 stick/125 g butter, melted**

COFFEE FILLING
- ☐ **1 quart/1 liter vanilla ice cream, softened**
- ☐ **2 teaspoons instant coffee powder dissolved in 1 1/2 tablespoons hot water and cooled**

CHOC-NUT TOPPING
- ☐ **1/2 cup/125 mL evaporated milk**
- ☐ **1/3 cup/90 g superfine sugar**
- ☐ **7 oz/220 g semi-sweet dark chocolate, chopped**
- ☐ **1/2 cup/60 g chopped pecans or walnuts**

1   Place cookie crumbs and butter in a bowl and mix well to combine. Press mixture into a 9 in/23 cm pie plate.
2   To make filling, place ice cream and coffee mixture in a bowl and mix to combine. Spoon over cookie crust and place in freezer.
3   To make topping, place evaporated milk, sugar and chocolate in a saucepan and cook over a low heat, stirring, until chocolate is melted and mixture is smooth. Stir in pecans or walnuts, allow to cool, then pour topping over filling and freeze until firm.

Decorating suggestion: Top with chocolate curls and whipped cream.

Coffee Nut Pie, Rhubarb and Apple Tart

FRENCH CHRISTMAS LOG

Serves 10
Oven temperature 350°F, 180°C

- [ ] **5 eggs**
- [ ] **¹/₃ cup/90 g superfine sugar**
- [ ] **2 oz/60 g semi-sweet dark chocolate, melted and cooled**
- [ ] **¹/₂ cup/60 g self-rising flour**
- [ ] **2 tablespoons cocoa powder**
- [ ] **IOX (confectioners') sugar**

RUM FILLING
- [ ] **³/₄ cup/185 mL thick cream**
- [ ] **1 tablespoon IOX (confectioners') sugar**
- [ ] **1 tablespoon dark rum**

GANACH FROSTING
- [ ] **6 oz/185 g semi-sweet dark chocolate**
- [ ] **5 oz/155 mL thick cream**
- [ ] **2 tablespoons/30 g unsalted (sweet) butter**

CHOCOLATE MUSHROOMS
- [ ] **1 egg white**
- [ ] **¹/₂ teaspoon white vinegar**
- [ ] **¹/₃ cup/90 g superfine sugar**
- [ ] **1 teaspoon cornstarch**
- [ ] **1 oz/30 g semi-sweet dark chocolate**
- [ ] **1 teaspoon cocoa powder**

1   Place eggs in a mixing bowl and beat until fluffy. Gradually add sugar, beating well after each addition, until thick and creamy. Beat in chocolate. Sift together flour and cocoa powder and fold into egg mixture. Pour mixture into a greased and parchment paper-lined 10¹/₂ x 12³/₄ in/26 x 32 cm Jelly roll pan and bake for 10-12 minutes or until just firm. Turn cake onto a damp teatowel dusted with cocoa powder, remove paper and roll up cake from short end. Allow to stand for 2-3 minutes, then unroll, cover with a second damp teatowel and set aside to cool.
2   To make filling, place cream, IOX sugar and rum in a mixing bowl and beat until soft peaks form. Cover and chill until required.
3   To make frosting, place chocolate, cream and butter in a saucepan and cook over a low heat, stirring constantly, until mixture is well combined. Remove from heat and chill until mixture is almost set, but of a spreadable consistency. Beat mixture until thick, then chill until required.
4   To make mushrooms, place egg white and vinegar in a small mixing bowl and beat until soft peaks form. Gradually add sugar, beating well after each addition,

until stiff peaks form and mixture is thick and glossy. Fold in cornstarch. Spoon mixture into a pastry bag fitted with a plain nozzle and pipe seven button shapes for the tops of the mushrooms and small knobs for the stems onto a greased and parchment paper-lined cookie sheet. Reduce oven temperature to 250°F/120°C and bake for 30 minutes or until meringues are crisp and dry. Allow to cool on sheet, then join tops and stems, using a little melted chocolate, to make mushrooms. Sprinkle with cocoa powder.
5   To assemble log, spread cake with filling and roll up. Spread log with frosting and mark with a spatula to show textured bark. Decorate with mushrooms and dust with IOX sugar.

Serving suggestion: Decorate serving plate with any remaining mushrooms. Cut into slices and serve with vanilla ice cream, if desired.

ICED CHRISTMAS BOMBE

This dessert is also delicious made with chocolate ice cream in place of the vanilla.

Serves 10-12

- [ ] **¹/₃ cup/60 g golden raisins**
- [ ] **¹/₃ cup/60 g currants**
- [ ] **¹/₃ cup/60 g seeded raisins, chopped**
- [ ] **3 tablespoons/30 g chopped red candied cherries**
- [ ] **3 tablespoons/30 g chopped green candied cherries**
- [ ] **1 oz/30 g mixed candied citrus peel**
- [ ] **¹/₄ cup/60 mL brandy**
- [ ] **1 quart/1 liter vanilla ice cream, softened**
- [ ] **¹/₂ cup/125 mL thick cream**
- [ ] **¹/₂ cup/60 g sliced almonds, toasted**
- [ ] **¹/₄ cup/30 g semi-sweet chocolate chips**

1   Place golden raisins, currants, seeded raisins, red and green cherries, peel and brandy in a bowl and mix to combine. Cover and set aside to macerate overnight.
2   Place ice cream and cream in a large bowl, stir in fruit mixture, almonds and chocolate chips and mix well to combine.
3   Spoon ice cream mixture into an 8 cup/ 2 liter round bottomed bowl lined with plastic wrap, cover and freeze until required.
4   To serve, remove covering, immerse

in hot water and turn bombe onto a chilled serving plate. Serve immediately.

ENGLISH CHRISTMAS STEAMED PUDDING

Serves 10-12

- [ ] **1 lb/500 g golden raisins**
- [ ] **1¹/₂ cups/250 g seeded raisins**
- [ ] **¹/₃ cup/60 g mixed candied citrus peels**
- [ ] **4 oz/125 g candied apricots, chopped**
- [ ] **4 oz/125 g candied cherries, halved**
- [ ] **4 oz/125 g blanched slivered almonds**
- [ ] **³/₄ cup/185 mL brandy**
- [ ] **1 cup/2 sticks/250 g butter, softened**
- [ ] **¹/₂ cup/90 g packed brown sugar**
- [ ] **1 tablespoon finely grated orange rind**
- [ ] **4 eggs**
- [ ] **4 teaspoons orange juice**
- [ ] **1 cup/125 g all-purpose flour**
- [ ] **1 teaspoon ground cinnamon**
- [ ] **¹/₂ teaspoon pumpkin pie spice**
- [ ] **¹/₂ teaspoon ground nutmeg**
- [ ] **4 cups/240 g soft bread crumbs made from stale bread**

1   Combine golden and seeded raisins, mixed peel, apricots, cherries, almonds and brandy in a bowl and set aside.
2   Place butter, sugar and orange rind in a large mixing bowl and beat until creamy. Add eggs one at a time, beating well after each addition. Mix in orange juice.
3   Sift together flour, cinnamon, pie spice and nutmeg. Fold flour mixture, fruit mixture and bread crumbs into butter mixture.
4   Spoon pudding mixture into an 8 cup/ 2 liter pudding basin, mold or heatproof mixer bowl lined with a plastic oven bag. Seal oven bag with string, place a piece of aluminum foil over pudding and seal with pudding basin lid. (If using mold or bowl, tie foil securely to rim with kitchen string.)
5   Place basin in a large saucepan or kettle with enough water to come halfway up the side of the basin. Boil 4¹/₂-5¹/₂ hours or until pudding is cooked through. Serve hot, warm or cold with whipped cream or vanilla ice cream.

English Christmas Steamed Pudding, French Christmas Log

RASPBERRY CHOCOLATE TRUFFLE CAKES

These rich little chocolate cakes filled with a raspberry cream and served with a bittersweet chocolate sauce are a perfect finale to any dinner party. Follow the step-by-step instructions and you will see just how easy this spectacular dessert is.

Serves 8
Oven temperature 350°F, 180°C

- [ ] **¹/₂ cup/60 g cocoa powder, sifted**
- [ ] **1 cup/250 mL boiling water**
- [ ] **¹/₂ cup/1 stick/125 g butter**
- [ ] **1³/₄ cups/375 g superfine sugar**
- [ ] **1¹/₂ tablespoons raspberry jam**
- [ ] **2 eggs**
- [ ] **1¹/₂ cups/220 g self-rising flour, sifted**
- [ ] **13 oz/410 g semi-sweet dark chocolate, melted**
- [ ] **raspberries for garnishing**

RASPBERRY CREAM
- [ ] **4 oz/125 g raspberries, puréed and sieved**
- [ ] **¹/₂ cup/125 mL thick cream, whipped**

CHOCOLATE SAUCE
- [ ] **4 oz/125 g bitter sweet dark chocolate**
- [ ] **¹/₂ cup/125 mL water**
- [ ] **¹/₄ cup/60 g superfine sugar**
- [ ] **1 teaspoon brandy (optional)**

1   Combine cocoa powder and boiling water. Mix to dissolve and set aside to cool.
2   Place butter, sugar and jam in a bowl and beat until light and fluffy. Beat in eggs one at a time, adding a little flour with each egg. Fold remaining flour and cocoa mixture, alternately, into creamed mixture.
3   Spoon mixture into eight lightly greased ¹/₂ cup/125 mL soufflé/custard cups or use a muffin pan. Bake for 20-25 minutes or until cakes are cooked when tested with a skewer. Cool for 5 minutes then turn onto wire racks to cool. Turn cakes upside down and scoop out center leaving a ¹/₂ in/1 cm shell. Spread each cake with melted chocolate to cover top and sides, then place right way up on a wire rack.

4   To make cream, fold raspberry purée into cream. Spoon cream into a pastry fitted with a large nozzle. Carefully turn cakes upside down and pipe in cream to fill cavity. Place right way up on individual serving plates.
5   To make sauce, place chocolate and water in a small saucepan and cook over a low heat for 4-5 minutes or until chocolate melts. Add sugar and continue cooking, stirring constantly, until sugar dissolves. Bring just to the boil, then reduce heat and simmer, stirring, for 2 minutes. Set aside to cool for 5 minutes, then stir in brandy, if using. Cool sauce to room temperature.

To serve: Decorate plates with sauce.

Turn cakes upside down and scoop out center of each cake leaving a ¹/₂ in/1 cm shell.

Carefully turn chocolate-coated cakes upside down and pipe in cream to fill cavity.

PEACH AND BLACKBERRY COBBLER

Serves 6
Oven temperature 350°F, 180°C

- [ ] **2 x 14 oz/440 g cans sliced peaches, drained**
- [ ] **14 oz/440 g canned blackberries, drained**
- [ ] **4 teaspoons cornstarch blended with 1/4 cup/60 mL water**
- [ ] **1 tablespoon brown sugar**

TOPPING
- [ ] **1/4 cup/30 g all-purpose flour**
- [ ] **1/2 cup/60 g self-rising flour**
- [ ] **2 tablespoons superfine sugar**
- [ ] **1/4 cup/1/2 stick/60 g butter**
- [ ] **1 egg, lightly beaten**
- [ ] **2 teaspoons milk**

1 To make topping, sift together all-purpose and self-rising flours into a mixing bowl. Stir in superfine sugar. Rub in butter, using fingertips, until mixture resembles fine bread crumbs. Make a well in the center of the flour mixture and mix in egg and milk to form a soft dough.

2 Arrange peaches and blackberries in a greased, shallow casserole and pour over cornstarch mixture. Drop heaped spoonfuls of batter around edge of fruit mixture and sprinkle with brown sugar. Bake for 30-35 minutes or until topping is golden.

Serving suggestion: Delicious served with fresh berries and whipped cream.

CHOCOLATE MALTED PUDDING CAKE

This wonderful dessert makes enough for everyone to enjoy second helpings.

Serves 8
Oven temperature 350°F, 180°C

- [ ] **1 cup/125 g all-purpose flour**
- [ ] **1 cup/125 g self-rising flour**
- [ ] **1 teaspoon baking powder**
- [ ] **1/4 cup/30 g cocoa powder**
- [ ] **1/4 cup/30 g malted milk powder**
- [ ] **1 cup/220 g superfine sugar**
- [ ] **1 cup/250 mL milk**
- [ ] **2 eggs, beaten**

CHOCOLATE SAUCE
- [ ] **4 oz/125 g semi-sweet dark chocolate, chopped chips**
- [ ] **2 cups/500 mL hot water**

- [ ] **2 tablespoons/30 g butter**
- [ ] **1 cup/170 g packed brown sugar**
- [ ] **1/4 cup/30 g cocoa powder, sifted**
- [ ] **2 tablespoons cornstarch**
- [ ] **malted milk powder**

1 Sift together all-purpose and self-rising flours, baking powder, cocoa and malt into a large bowl. Stir in superfine sugar. Place milk and eggs in a separate bowl and whisk to combine. Stir milk mixture into flour mixture and mix well to combine. Spoon batter into a greased deep 8 cup/2 liter casserole.

2 To make sauce, place chocolate, water and butter in a saucepan and cook over a low heat, stirring constantly until chocolate melts.

3 Place brown sugar, cocoa powder and cornstarch in a mixing bowl, pour in chocolate mixture and mix well to combine. Spoon sauce evenly over batter and bake for 45-50 minutes or until firm. Just prior to serving dust top of dessert with malted milk powder. Serve warm.

RUM CHERRY CREAM

Serves 6

- [ ] **6 oz/185 g fresh Bing cherries, pitted and halved**
- [ ] **1/4 cup/60 mL dark rum**
- [ ] **1/2 cup/125 g sugar**
- [ ] **5 oz/155 g ricotta cheese**
- [ ] **12 oz/375 g cream cheese, softened**
- [ ] **1/3 cup/90 g dairy sour cream**

PLUM SAUCE
- [ ] **4 large dark plums, skinned, pitted and halved**
- [ ] **7 oz/220 g loganberries or blackberries**
- [ ] **2 tablespoons IOX (confectioners') sugar**

1 Place cherries, half the rum and 1 tablespoon sugar in a bowl and set aside to macerate for 1 hour. Drain and dry cherries on paper towels.

2 Press ricotta cheese through a sieve and set aside. Place cream cheese in a bowl and beat until soft and creamy. Beat in ricotta cheese, sour cream and remaining sugar and rum. Continue to beat until well combined.

3 Line six soufflé or custard cups with damp cheesecloth and half fill with cheese

mixture. Arrange cherries over the mixture and top with remaining mixture. Cover and refrigerate overnight.

4 To make sauce, place plums, berries and IOX sugar in a food processor or blender and process until smooth. Push purée through a sieve and refrigerate. To serve, spoon sauce onto serving plates. Turn out creams, remove cheesecloth and place in center of plates.

APPLE AND BERRY CRUMBLE

Blueberries have been used to make this delicious crumble, but you might like to try blackberries, raspberries or strawberries instead.

Serves 6
Oven temperature 350°F, 180°C

- [ ] **1/4 cup/60 g superfine sugar**
- [ ] **1/2 cup/125 mL water**
- [ ] **4 green apples, cored, peeled and sliced**
- [ ] **14 oz/440 g canned blueberries, drained**

CRUMBLE TOPPING
- [ ] **8 oz/250 g crushed cookies**
- [ ] **3 tablespoons/45 g unsalted (sweet) butter, softened**
- [ ] **1/3 cup/45 g ground almonds**
- [ ] **2 tablespoons granulated brown (raw) sugar**
- [ ] **1/2 teaspoon ground cinnamon**
- [ ] **1 egg yolk**
- [ ] **1 1/2 tablespoons thick cream**

1 Place sugar and water in a saucepan and cook over a medium heat, stirring constantly, until sugar dissolves. Bring to the boil, then add apples and cook over a low heat for 8-10 minutes or until apples are tender. Remove from heat and set aside to cool.

2 Drain apples and combine with blueberries. Spoon apple mixture into a greased, shallow baking dish.

3 To make topping, place cookie crumbs butter, almonds, brown sugar, cinnamon, egg yolk and cream in a mixing bowl and mix until just combined. Sprinkle topping over apple mixture and bake for 20-25 minutes or until golden.

Serving suggestion: This crumble is delicious served with plain yogurt or fruited yogurt.

*Apple and Berry Crumble,
Peach and Blackberry Cobbler*

chapter ten

THE FRESH OUTDOORS

Barbecues and picnics
are a great way for family
and friends to spend time together
and enjoy each other's company
in an informal atmosphere. These
recipes are sure to make your
next outdoor meal a
great success.

Garlic Grilled Potatoes,
Seafood Kabobs,
Curried Chicken Kabobs

CURRIED CHICKEN KABOBS

Serves 6

- ☐ 1¹/₂ lb/750 g boned skinned chicken breasts, cut into 1 in/ 2.5 cm cubes
- ☐ 12 skewers, lightly oiled

LIME CURRY GLAZE
- ☐ 1¹/₄ cups/315 g lime marmalade
- ☐ 2 tablespoons Dijon mustard
- ☐ 2 teaspoons curry powder
- ☐ 1 tablespoon lime juice

1 To make glaze, place marmalade, mustard, curry powder and lime juice in a small saucepan and cook over a medium heat, stirring, for 3 minutes or until ingredients are combined. Remove from heat and set aside to cool.
2 Thread chicken cubes onto skewers. Place skewers in a shallow glass or ceramic dish, spoon glaze over, cover and set aside to marinate at room temperature for 1 hour.
3 Remove chicken from glaze and reserve any remaining glaze. Cook kabobs on a lightly oiled preheated barbecue, brushing kabobs with reserved glaze and turning frequently, for 8-10 minutes or until cooked.

GARLIC GRILLED POTATOES

These potatoes are the perfect accompaniment to any barbecue.

Serves 6

- ☐ 6 large potatoes, scrubbed
- ☐ 1 tablespoon olive oil
- ☐ 1 tablespoon finely chopped fresh rosemary
- ☐ freshly ground black pepper
- ☐ 6 cloves garlic, halved

1 Using an apple corer, carefully remove a plug from each potato, making sure not to go right through the potato. Reserve the plugs.
2 Combine oil, rosemary and black pepper to taste. Fill hole in each potato with two garlic halves and a little oil mixture. Cut off two-thirds of each plug and discard. Replace remaining plug in potato and wrap potatoes in aluminum foil. Cook potatoes on a preheated barbecue for 1 hour or until tender, turning occasionally.

SEAFOOD KABOBS

Serves 4

- ☐ 8 mussels, removed from shells
- ☐ 1 large white fish fillet, cut into 8 x ³/₄ in/2 cm cubes
- ☐ 8 large uncooked shrimp, shelled and deveined, tails left intact
- ☐ 8 scallops
- ☐ 1 salmon fillet, cut into 8 x ³/₄ in/2 cm cubes
- ☐ 8 skewers, lightly oiled

CHILI LIME GLAZE
- ☐ ¹/₄ cup/60 mL olive oil
- ☐ 2 fresh red chilies, seeds removed and finely chopped
- ☐ 1 clove garlic, crushed
- ☐ ¹/₄ cup/60 mL lime juice

1 Alternately thread a mussel, a piece of white fish, a shrimp, a scallop and a piece of salmon onto a skewer. Repeat with remaining seafood and skewers.
2 To make glaze, place oil, chilies, garlic and lime juice in a small bowl and mix to combine. Brush kabobs with glaze and cook on a lightly oiled preheated barbecue, turning frequently and brushing with remaining glaze, until seafood changes color and is cooked through. Serve immediately.

GRILLED TROUT WITH APPLE STUFFING

Serves 4

- ☐ 4 small trout, cleaned with head and tail intact
- ☐ olive oil

APPLE STUFFING
- ☐ 2 tablespoons/30 g butter
- ☐ 1 small onion, chopped
- ☐ 1 apple, cored and finely chopped
- ☐ ¹/₂ cup/30 g soft bread crumbs, made from stale bread
- ☐ 1 teaspoon lemon juice
- ☐ 1 tablespoon finely chopped fresh mint
- ☐ 2 teaspoons finely chopped fresh parsley
- ☐ freshly ground black pepper

1 To make stuffing, melt butter in a skillet, add onion and cook for 5 minutes or until transparent. Place apple and bread crumbs in a bowl, add onion, lemon juice, mint, parsley and black pepper to taste and mix to combine.
2 Fill cavity of each trout with stuffing. Secure openings using toothpicks and lightly brush outside of each trout with oil. Cook trout on a preheated medium barbecue for 5-8 minutes each side or until flesh flakes when tested with a fork.

SAVORY BREAD

Garlic and herb breads are easy to make and can be prepared in advance and frozen if you wish.

Serves 8

- ☐ 1 large French bread stick (baguette)

FLAVORED BUTTER
- ☐ ¹/₂ cup/1 stick/125 g butter, softened
- ☐ 2 cloves garlic crushed; or 2 tablespoons finely chopped fresh herbs – choose from rosemary, parsley, thyme, chives
- ☐ freshly ground black pepper

1 Slice bread on a slight diagonal at ³/₄ in/ 2 cm intervals almost all the way through so that the slices remain joined at the base.
2 To make Flavored Butter, place butter, garlic or herbs, and black pepper to taste in a food processor and process to combine.
3 Spread one side of each slice of bread with Flavored Butter. Wrap loaf in a double thickness of aluminium foil and heat on a preheated barbecue for 15-20 minutes or until bread is hot.

MARSHMALLOW SURPRISES

Eat with care – these delicious morsels are very hot when first assembled.

Serves 10

- ☐ **20 large, wafer cookies or halved graham crackers**
- ☐ **40 white marshmallows**
- ☐ **20 pieces semi-sweet eating chocolate**

1 Top 10 cookies or crackers with a chocolate piece.

2 Thread 2 marshmallows onto a long-handled fork or skewer and toast slowly over a preheated low barbecue so that the marshmallow is hot and gooey in the center. Using a spoon, push marshmallows onto chocolate-topped cookies and top with remaining cookies. Press together and eat!

PUFF TOMATO AND MUSHROOM PIZZA

This easy pizza will keep hunger pangs at bay while your food is cooking on the barbecue.

Serves 8
Oven temperature 400°F, 200°C

- ☐ **2 sheets/500 g frozen pre-rolled puff pastry, thawed**
- ☐ **¹/₂ cup/60 g grated Parmesan cheese**
- ☐ **4 oz/125 g mozzarella cheese, shredded**
- ☐ **1 onion, finely sliced**
- ☐ **7 oz/220 g button mushrooms, sliced**
- ☐ **3 tomatoes, cut into ¹/₂ in/1 cm slices**
- ☐ **10 black olives, pitted**
- ☐ **2 teaspoons chopped fresh oregano or ¹/₂ teaspoon dried oregano**
- ☐ **2 teaspoons chopped fresh thyme, or ¹/₂ teaspoon dried thyme**

1 Line a greased 10¹/₂ x 12³/₄ in/26 x 32 cm jelly roll pan with a single layer of pastry, cutting sheets to fit and overlapping slightly where they join. Sprinkle pastry with Parmesan and mozzarella cheeses, then top with onion, mushrooms, tomatoes and olives. Sprinkle with oregano and thyme.

2 Bake for 30 minutes or until pastry is puffed and golden. Serve hot, warm or cold.

Puff Tomato and Mushroom Pizza

FOIL-WRAPPED CHICKEN BREASTS

Serves 6

- [ ] **6 boned, skinned chicken breast halves, pounded flat**
- [ ] **¹/₄ cup/¹/₂ stick/60 g butter**
- [ ] **1 small onion, chopped**
- [ ] **1 clove garlic, crushed**
- [ ] **2 cups/125 g soft bread crumbs, made from stale bread**
- [ ] **¹/₄ cup finely chopped fresh parsley**
- [ ] **freshly ground black pepper**

1 Melt 1 tablespoon/15 g butter in a small skillet, add onion and garlic and cook over a medium heat for 3-4 minutes or until onion is soft.
2 Place bread crumbs in a bowl, add onion mixture and parsley. Melt remaining butter and mix into bread crumb mixture. Season to taste with black pepper.
3 Cut six pieces of heavy-duty aluminum foil large enough to enclose chicken breasts. Brush foil lightly with oil and place a breast half on each piece of foil. Top one half of each breast with some stuffing and fold other half over to enclose. Wrap foil around chicken to form a tight parcel so that juice will not escape during cooking.
4 Place foil parcels on a preheated medium barbecue and cook, turning halfway through cooking, for 10-15 minutes or until chicken is cooked and tender.

Cook's tip: If you do not have heavy-duty aluminum foil, use a double thickness of ordinary foil instead.

VEGETABLE AND SALAD ROLL-UPS

Serves 4

- [ ] **4 wholewheat pita bread rounds**
- [ ] **4 tablespoons mayonnaise**
- [ ] **8 lettuce leaves, shredded**
- [ ] **2 tomatoes, sliced**
- [ ] **1 beet, shredded**

SOYA PATTIES
- [ ] **1 cup/60 g wholewheat bread crumbs, made from stale bread**
- [ ] **14 oz/440 g canned soy beans, drained and coarsely mashed**
- [ ] **1 carrot, shredded**
- [ ] **1 zucchini, shredded**
- [ ] **2 tablespoons tomato paste**
- [ ] **¹/₂ teaspoon ground cumin**
- [ ] **1 egg white**

1 To make patties, place bread crumbs, soy beans, carrot, zucchini, tomato paste cumin and egg white in a bowl and mix to combine. Shape mixture into 12 small patties and cook in a nonstick skillet, for 3 minutes each side or until golden brown. Set aside and keep warm.
2 Spread bread rounds with mayonnaise. Top with lettuce, tomato, beet and patties. Roll up bread to form a cylinder and serve immediately.

TORTELLINI SALAD

Serves 4

- [ ] **1¹/₂ lb/750 g fresh mixed-colored tortellini**
- [ ] **8 oz/250 g asparagus, cut into 2 in/5 cm pieces**
- [ ] **7 oz/220 g snow peas, trimmed**
- [ ] **1 lettuce**
- [ ] **1 red pepper, sliced**
- [ ] **8 oz/250 g yellow or red cherry tomatoes**
- [ ] **¹/₂ cup/125 mL bottled Italian dressing**

1 Cook tortellini in boiling water in a large saucepan, following packet directions. Drain, rinse under cold water and set aside to cool.
2 Boil, steam or microwave asparagus and snow peas separately until tender. Refresh under cold running water and set aside to cool.
3 Arrange lettuce, red pepper, tomatoes, tortellini, asparagus and snow peas in a large serving bowl. Pour dressing over and serve immediately.

Do ahead: Cook the pasta and vegetables for this salad in advance and store in the refrigerator for up to 2 days. The salad then only takes minutes to assemble.

FRESH HERB AND CHICKEN BURGERS

Serves 4

- [ ] **1 teaspoon butter or oil**
- [ ] **4 boned, skinned chicken breast halves, approximately 4 oz/125 g each**
- [ ] **4 round, wholewheat bread rolls, halved and toasted**
- [ ] **12 cherry tomatoes, sliced**
- [ ] **8 lettuce leaves**

HERB MAYONNAISE
- [ ] **¹/₃ cup/90 g mayonnaise**
- [ ] **2 teaspoons snipped fresh chives**
- [ ] **2 teaspoons chopped fresh parsley**

1 To make mayonnaise, place mayonnaise, chives and parsley in a bowl and mix to combine.
2 Heat butter in a large nonstick skillet and cook chicken for 4-5 minutes each side or until golden and tender. Place a chicken breast on base of each roll. Top with tomato and lettuce. Spoon mayonnaise over and top with remaining roll halves.

Serving suggestion: Serve with coleslaw and fresh fruit.

TRI-POTATO SALAD

Serves 4

- [ ] **12 baby new potatoes**
- [ ] **1 lb/500 g sweet potato, cubed**
- [ ] **1 lb/500 g white potato, cubed**
- [ ] **1 small onion, chopped**
- [ ] **8 oz/250 g smoked ham, chopped**

MUSTARD HERB DRESSING
- [ ] **1 cup/250 g mayonnaise**
- [ ] **¹/₄ cup/60 g plain yogurt**
- [ ] **2 teaspoons coarse grain mustard**
- [ ] **2 tablespoons snipped fresh chives**

1 Boil, steam or microwave new potatoes, sweet potatoes and white potatoes separately, until tender. Drain, set aside and keep warm.
2 Heat a nonstick skillet and cook onion and ham for 3 minutes or until onion is soft.
3 Place potatoes in a large serving bowl and toss onion mixture through.
4 To make dressing, place mayonnaise, yogurt, mustard and chives in a bowl and mix to combine. Spoon over warm salad and serve.

Serving suggestion: A salad of oranges and onions tossed in French Dressing is a good accompaniment for this salad.

Tortellini Salad, Tri-Potato Salad, Fresh Herb and Chicken Burgers, Vegetable and Salad Roll-Ups

BLUE CHEESE CAESAR SALAD

If romaine lettuce is unavailable iceberg lettuce can be used instead.

Serves 10

- ☐ ⅓ cup/90 mL olive oil
- ☐ 2 slices bread, crusts removed and cut into ½ in/1 cm cubes
- ☐ 2 slices bacon, chopped
- ☐ 1 romaine lettuce, washed, leaves separated, torn into large pieces
- ☐ ½ cup/60 g pine nuts (pignola), toasted
- ☐ ½ cup/125 g grated Parmesan cheese

BLUE CHEESE DRESSING
- ☐ 3 oz/90 g Stilton or blue cheese
- ☐ 2 tablespoons plain yogurt
- ☐ 2 tablespoons dairy sour cream
- ☐ ⅓ cup/90 mL thick cream
- ☐ 2 tablespoons lemon juice
- ☐ freshly ground black pepper

1   To make croutons, heat oil in a skillet and cook bread over a medium-high heat, tossing frequently, for 1-2 minutes or until golden on all sides. Remove from pan and drain on paper towels.

2   Place bacon in a nonstick skillet and cook over a medium heat for 3-4 minutes or until crisp. Remove from pan and drain on paper towels.

3   To make dressing, place Stilton or blue cheese, yogurt, sour cream, cream, lemon juice and black pepper to taste in a food processor or blender and process until smooth.

4   Place lettuce, bacon, croutons and pine nuts in a serving bowl, pour dressing over and toss. Sprinkle with Parmesan cheese and serve immediately.

CHICKEN WITH CREAMY PESTO STUFFING

Serves 10

- ☐ 3 x 3 lb/1.5 kg chickens

CREAMY PESTO STUFFING
- ☐ 3 oz/90 g basil leaves
- ☐ ½ cup/60 g pine nuts (pignola)
- ☐ ½ cup/60 g finely grated Parmesan cheese
- ☐ 8 oz/250 g cream cheese, softened

1   To make stuffing, place basil leaves, pine nuts and Parmesan cheese in a food processor and process to finely chopped. Stir basil mixture into cream cheese.

2   Cut through backbone of each chicken. Remove both halves of backbone, then turn chicken over and press to flatten.

3   Using your fingers or the handle of a wooden spoon, loosen skin over breasts, thighs and legs of chicken. Push stuffing under loosened skin, then thread skewers through wings and legs of chickens.

4   Cook chicken on a lightly oiled preheated medium barbecue for 15-20 minutes each side or until chicken is cooked through.

When is the chicken cooked? To test your chicken for doneness pierce the thickest part of the chicken at the thigh joint and when the juices run clear the bird is cooked.

BROWN ALE DAMPER

An Australian version of simple Soda Bread

Makes an 8 in/20 cm loaf

- ☐ 2 cups/250 g self-rising flour
- ☐ 2½ cups/315 g wholewheat self-rising flour
- ☐ 1 teaspoon salt
- ☐ 3 tablespoons/45 g butter
- ☐ 2 cups/500 mL beer

1   Sift together flours and salt into a bowl. Return grits to bowl. Cut in butter with a pastry blender until mixture resembles coarse bread crumbs. Make a well in the center of the flour mixture and pour in beer. Using a fork, mix to form a soft dough.

2   Turn dough onto a lightly floured surface and knead until smooth. Shape dough into an 8 in/20 cm round and place on a double thickness of oiled aluminum foil large enough to completely encase damper. Score dough into wedges using a sharp knife. Lightly dust with flour and wrap foil loosely around damper to completely enclose. Cook on a preheated barbecue, turning several times, for 1 hour or until cooked through. Serve warm, broken into pieces, with butter if desired.

Cook's Tip: If wholewheat self-rising flour is not available, use all-purpose wholewheat flour and 2½ teaspoons baking powder.

Brown Ale Damper, Chicken with Creamy Pesto Stuffing, Blue Cheese Caesar Salad

EGG SALAD WITH HERB DRESSING

Serves 6

- ☐ lettuce leaves
- ☐ 6 hard-boiled eggs, quartered
- ☐ 12 cherry tomatoes
- ☐ 1 avocado, pitted, peeled and sliced
- ☐ 24 black olives

FRESH HERB DRESSING

- ☐ 1 cup/250 g plain yogurt
- ☐ 2 tablespoons chopped fresh parsley
- ☐ 1 tablespoon chopped fresh mint
- ☐ 1 tablespoon snipped fresh chives
- ☐ 2 tablespoons apple juice
- ☐ freshly ground black pepper

1 To make dressing, place yogurt, parsley, mint, chives and apple juice in a food processor or blender, and process until dressing is combined and green in color. Season to taste with black pepper.

2 Arrange lettuce leaves, eggs, tomatoes, avocado slices and olives attractively on a serving platter and just prior to serving spoon over dressing.

COUSCOUS SALAD

This salad would be perfect for your next 'al fresco' meal.

Serves 4

- ☐ 1 cup/250 mL vegetable stock or water
- ☐ 7 oz/220 g couscous
- ☐ 1 carrot, thinly sliced
- ☐ 1 red pepper, chopped
- ☐ 1 tomato, chopped
- ☐ 1 small cucumber, cubed
- ☐ 1 avocado, pitted, peeled and cubed
- ☐ 1/4 cup/30 g sliced almonds, toasted

DRESSING

- ☐ 1 tablespoon olive oil
- ☐ 1 teaspoon grated lime rind
- ☐ 2 tablespoons lime juice
- ☐ 1 teaspoon coarse grain mustard
- ☐ 1 tablespoon honey
- ☐ 1 tablespoon chopped fresh basil

1 Bring vegetable stock to the boil and pour over couscous. Set aside to stand for 10 minutes, then drain.

2 Combine couscous, carrot, pepper, tomato, cucumber and avocado in a bowl.

3 To make dressing, place oil, rind, juice, mustard, honey and basil in a screwtop jar. Shake well to combine. Pour over salad and toss. Just prior to serving, sprinkle with almonds.

Couscous: Couscous is a fine semolina made from wheat that originated in North Africa, however variations on the traditional dish can be found in Sicily, France and even Brazil, where it is 'cuscuz' rather than couscous.

It is readily available in packages, much the same as rice, and is served as an accompaniment to a meal.

SPICY PEA PARATHAS

Serves 4

- ☐ 2 cups/250 g wholewheat all-purpose flour
- ☐ 8 oz/250 g white all-purpose flour
- ☐ 2 tablespoons/30 g butter
- ☐ 1 cup/250 mL warm water, approximately

POTATO AND PEA FILLING

- ☐ 1 large potato, cooked and mashed
- ☐ 1/4 cup/45 g split peas, cooked and mashed
- ☐ 1/2 cup/125 g ricotta cheese
- ☐ 2 teaspoons coriander seeds
- ☐ 2 teaspoons cumin seeds
- ☐ 1 1/2 tablespoons sweet fruit chutney

1 Sift wholewheat and white flours into a large bowl. Rub in butter, make a well in the center and gradually add enough water to form a soft dough. Knead on a lightly floured surface until smooth.

2 To make filling, place potato, split peas, ricotta cheese, coriander and cumin seeds, and chutney in a bowl. Mix well to combine.

3 Divide dough into eight portions and roll into small flat rounds. Place a spoonful of filling in the center of each round. Mold dough around filling to enclose.

4 Cook parathas on a lightly greased preheated barbecue griddle, or in a skillet, for 4 minutes each side or until golden.

Couscous Salad

234

MARINATED EGGPLANT AND TOMATO SALAD

Using basil, garlic and balsamic vinegar, this salad combines the flavors of Italy. Serve as a starter, as part of an antipasto platter or take it on a picnic. It is delicious served with pita bread and yogurt.

Serves 6

- ☐ **6 baby eggplant, cut lengthwise into $1/2$ in/1 cm slices**
- ☐ **olive oil**
- ☐ **3 tomatoes, peeled and thinly sliced**
- ☐ **$1/3$ cup/90 mL finely chopped fresh basil**
- ☐ **freshly ground black pepper**

DRESSING
- ☐ **$1/4$ cup/60 mL balsamic vinegar**
- ☐ **1 tablespoon olive oil**
- ☐ **2 cloves garlic, crushed**

1   Brush each eggplant slice generously with oil and cook under a preheated broiler for 4-5 minutes each side or until golden and tender.

2   To make dressing, place vinegar, oil and garlic in a screwtop jar. Shake well to combine.

3   Place a layer of warm eggplant slices in a shallow ceramic or glass serving dish. Top with a layer of tomato slices. Sprinkle with a tablespoon of dressing, a tablespoon of basil and season with black pepper to taste. Repeat layers until all eggplant and tomatoes are used. Cover and refrigerate for at least 2 hours.

Cook's tip: If the eggplant appears to be drying out during cooking, brush with a little more olive oil. This salad is even better if left to marinate overnight.

MARINATED LEG OF LAMB

Your butcher will butterfly the leg in minutes for you. Otherwise, refer to instructions in the Glossary.

Serves 6

- ☐ **3-4 lb/1.5-2 kg leg of lamb, boned and butterflied**
- ☐ **freshly ground black pepper**

LEMON HERB MARINADE
- ☐ **2 cloves garlic, crushed**
- ☐ **$1/4$ cup/60 mL olive oil**
- ☐ **$1/4$ cup/60 mL lemon juice**
- ☐ **1 tablespoon finely chopped fresh marjoram or 1 teaspoon dried marjoram**
- ☐ **1 tablespoon finely chopped fresh thyme or 1 teaspoon dried thyme**

1   Lay lamb out flat and season well with black pepper. Place in a shallow glass or ceramic dish.

2   To make marinade, place garlic, oil, lemon juice, marjoram and thyme in a small bowl and mix to combine. Pour marinade over lamb, cover and allow to marinate for 3-4 hours or overnight.

3   Remove lamb from marinade and reserve marinade. Place lamb on a lightly oiled preheated medium barbecue grill and cook, turning several times and basting with reserved marinade for 15-25 minutes or until cooked to your liking.

Spicy Pea Parathas,
Marinated Eggplant and Tomato Salad

MIXED SAUSAGE AND ONION GRILL

Buy a selection of your favorite sausages for this mixed grill. Mild or hot Italian sausages, bratwurst, knackwurst, fresh pork or beef sausages or frankfurters.

Serves 6

- [ ] **12 sausages and franks of different varieties**
- [ ] **12 baby new potatoes, scrubbed**
- [ ] **3 red onions, cut into quarters**
- [ ] **12 skewers, lightly oiled**
- [ ] **olive oil**

1 Parboil fresh sausages, if necessary. Drain and set aside to cool, then refrigerate.
2 Boil, steam or microwave potatoes until just tender.
3 Thread 2 onion quarters onto 6 of the skewers, then brush with oil. Cook on a preheated lightly oiled barbecue, turning halfway through cooking, for 15-20 minutes or until onions are golden and tender.
4 Thread 2 potatoes onto each of the remaining skewers and brush with oil. Cook on barbecue, turning halfway through cooking, for 10-15 minutes or until potatoes are golden and heated through.
5 Cook sausages and franks on lightly oiled barbecue for 10-15 minutes or until sausages are golden and crisp on the outside and heated through.

Serving suggestion: Serve with a selection of mustards and sauces.

CHAR-GRILLED VEGETABLE SLICES

Serves 6

- [ ] **$\frac{1}{2}$ cup/125 mL olive oil**
- [ ] **1 clove garlic, crushed**
- [ ] **1 large eggplant, cut lengthwise into thick slices**
- [ ] **3 large zucchini, cut lengthwise into thick slices**
- [ ] **2 red peppers, cut into quarters, seeds removed and sliced**
- [ ] **3 large firm tomatoes, cut into thick slices**
- [ ] **freshly ground black pepper**

1 Place oil and garlic in a small bowl and whisk to combine. Brush eggplant slices, zucchini slices, red pepper slices and tomato slices with oil mixture.
2 Cook eggplant, zucchini and red pepper slices on a lightly oiled preheated barbecue, turning frequently, for 4-5 minutes or until almost cooked. Add tomato slices to barbecue and cook all vegetables for 2-3 minutes longer.

BARBECUE A SAUSAGE

Children and adults alike love fresh sausages cooked on a barbecue. Here's a simple way to ensure perfectly cooked sausages every time.

- [ ] **required number of fresh pork or beef sausages**

1 To cook perfect barbecued sausages they should be parboiled first. This ensures that they will be cooked on the inside and golden on the outside and that some of the fat will be removed.
2 To parboil sausages, place them in a saucepan, cover with water and bring slowly to the boil, then reduce heat and simmer for 5 minutes. Drain and set aside to cool. When cool, cover and refrigerate for several hours or overnight.
3 Cook sausages on a lightly oiled pre-heated grill barbecue, turning several times, for 10 minutes or until golden and heated through.

Mixed Sausage and Onion Grill, Char-grilled Vegetable Slices

PITA CRISPS

These easy-to-make snacks are great to nibble on while waiting for the barbecue food to cook.

Serves 10
Oven temperature 400°F, 200°C

- [ ] **6 pita bread rounds**
- [ ] **$^1/_3$ cup/90 mL vegetable oil**
- [ ] **$^1/_2$ cup/60 g grated Parmesan cheese**
- [ ] **2 teaspoons paprika**
- [ ] **$^1/_2$ teaspoon chili powder**

1 Split each pita bread in half, horizontally, brush with oil and place on cookie sheets.
2 Place Parmesan cheese, paprika and chili in a small bowl and mix to combine. Sprinkle bread with cheese mixture and bake for 15 minutes or until bread is crisp. Allow bread to cool, then break into pieces.

HAM AND CHEESE SKEWERS

Grilled ham and cheese sandwiches on a skewer!

Makes 10 skewers

- [ ] **8 oz/250 g sliced packaged ham, cut into strips $1^1/_4$ in/3 cm wide**
- [ ] **12 oz/375 g mature Cheddar cheese, cut into $^1/_2$ in/1 cm cubes**
- [ ] **1 loaf wholewheat bread, cut into $^1/_2$ in/1 cm cubes**
- [ ] **10 skewers, lightly oiled**

1 Wrap ham strips around cheese cubes. Thread ham-wrapped cheese cubes and bread cubes, alternately, on to skewers.
2 Cook on a lightly oiled preheated barbecue grill, turning frequently, for 4-5 minutes or until bread is toasted and cheese just starts to melt.

BEST EVER HAMBURGERS

Serve the patties and rolls separately and allow people to make their own hamburger using the salad bar ingredients.

Makes 10 burgers

- [ ] **10 wholewheat rolls, split in half**

MEAT PATTIES
- [ ] **2 lb/1 kg lean ground beef**
- [ ] **1 onion, finely chopped**
- [ ] **1 carrot, shredded**
- [ ] **1 cup/60 g bread crumbs, made from stale bread**
- [ ] **1 tablespoon Worcestershire sauce**
- [ ] **1 tablespoon tomato paste**
- [ ] **dash chili sauce, according to taste**
- [ ] **2 tablespoons finely chopped fresh parsley**
- [ ] **freshly ground black pepper**

1 To make patties, place beef, onion, carrot, bread crumbs, Worcestershire sauce, tomato paste, chili sauce, parsley and black pepper to taste in a bowl, and mix to combine.
2 Wet hands and shape meat mixture into ten patties. Place patties on a tray, cover and refrigerate until ready to cook.
3 Cook patties on a lightly oiled preheated barbecue griddle, or in a lightly oiled skillet on the barbecue, for 4-5 minutes each side or until cooked to your liking, pressing down with a spatula during cooking. Toast rolls on the grill.

Burgers with onions: Onions can be cooked at the same time as the burgers. Allowing 1 onion for every 2 people, slice onions and cook with a little oil on barbecue plate griddle or in a skillet.

Hamburgers with hidden fillings: It is fun and easy to make hamburgers that hold a surprise. Cheese is always a popular hidden ingredient – you might like to try Cheddar, mozzarella or blue cheese. Simply cut cheese into 1 in/2.5 cm cubes and, when shaping your pattie, place cheese in center of pattie and shape meat around it.

CHILI HONEY DRUMSTICKS

Serves 10

- [ ] **10 chicken drumsticks**

CHILI HONEY MARINADE
- [ ] **$^1/_2$ cup/125 mL lemon juice**
- [ ] **$^1/_2$ cup/155 g honey**
- [ ] **1 clove garlic, crushed**
- [ ] **pinch chili powder**

1 To make marinade, place lemon juice, honey, garlic and chili powder in a bowl and mix to combine.

2 Place drumsticks in a shallow glass or ceramic dish, pour marinade over and toss to coat. Cover and marinate in the refrigerator for at least 2 hours, or overnight, turning several times during marinating.

3 Drain drumsticks and reserve marinade. Cook drumsticks on a lightly oiled preheated barbecue, brushing frequently with marinade for 10-15 minutes or until chicken is tender.

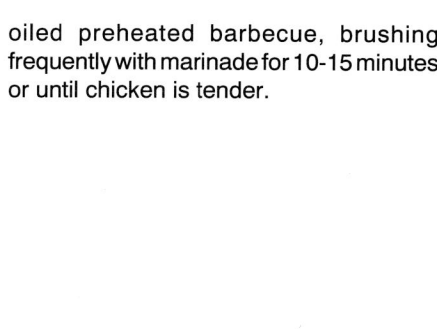

Chili Honey Drumsticks, Ham and Cheese Skewers, Pita Crisps

SALAD BAR

Arranging a salad bar that includes bowls of salad ingredients and toppings for potatoes is a great way of allowing people to assemble their own hamburgers, make their own salads and choose their favorite toppings for baked potatoes.
Quantities will vary depending on who you are feeding, but remember that appetites seem to increase outdoors.

SALAD BOWLS
- ☐ **mixed lettuce leaves**
- ☐ **tomato slices or halved cherry tomatoes**
- ☐ **cooked beet slices**
- ☐ **sliced cucumbers**
- ☐ **Cheddar cheese slices**
- ☐ **sliced red and green peppers**
- ☐ **hard-boiled eggs, sliced**
- ☐ **chopped spring onions**
- ☐ **sliced raw mushrooms**
- ☐ **shredded raw carrot**

POTATO TOPPERS
- ☐ **snipped chives**
- ☐ **dairy sour cream**
- ☐ **crisp-cooked bacon pieces**
- ☐ **shredded Cheddar cheese**

PICKLES AND SAUCES
- ☐ **tomato catsup**
- ☐ **mustard pickles**
- ☐ **barbecue sauce**
- ☐ **Worcestershire sauce**
- ☐ **selection of mustards**

FRUIT AND NUTS
Fruit and nuts provide a healthy and delicious snack to eat while waiting for the barbecued food and make a good alternative for dessert.

- ☐ **melon slices**
- ☐ **orange segments**
- ☐ **kiwifruit slices**
- ☐ **fresh pineapple wedges or slices**
- ☐ **bananas, whole or sliced and tossed in lemon juice**
- ☐ **apples, whole or cubed and tossed in lemon juice**
- ☐ **selection dried fruit and nuts**

MARINATED MUSHROOM SALAD

Serves 10

- [ ] $^1/_3$ **cup/90 mL olive oil**
- [ ] **2 cloves garlic, crushed**
- [ ] **$1^1/_2$ lb/750 g small button mushrooms, trimmed**
- [ ] **2 tablespoons red wine vinegar**
- [ ] **1 tablespoon lemon juice**
- [ ] **$^1/_4$ cup/60 mL chicken stock**
- [ ] **1 tablespoon chopped fresh basil**
- [ ] **2 tablespoons chopped fresh parsley**

1 Heat oil in a skillet and cook garlic and mushrooms for 2-3 minutes. Reduce heat, add vinegar, lemon juice and stock, and simmer for 1 minute.

2 Stir in basil and parsley and set aside to cool. Cover cooled mushroom mixture and refrigerate until required.

BARBECUED CHIPS

Serves 10

- [ ] **1 lb/500 g potatoes, cut crosswise into $^1/_4$ in/5 mm slices**
- [ ] **1 lb/500 g parsnips, cut lengthwise into $^1/_4$ in/5 mm slices**
- [ ] **1 lb/500 g sweet potatoes, cut crosswise into $^1/_4$ in/5 mm slices**
- [ ] **$^1/_4$ cup/60 mL olive oil**
- [ ] **4 onions, chopped**

1 Blanch potato, parsnip and sweet potato slices in a large saucepan of boiling water for 2 minutes. Drain, rinse under cold running water and drain on paper towels.

2 Heat oil in a large skillet on a preheated barbecue and cook onions for 15-20 minutes or until golden and crisp. Add potato, parsnip and sweet potato slices and cook for 10 minutes or until chips are tender.

Barbecued Chips, Marinated Mushroom Salad, Vegetable Burgers

VEGETABLE BURGERS

Makes 10 burgers

- ☐ **10 wholewheat rolls, split**
- ☐ **10 lettuce leaves**

MIXED VEGETABLE PATTIES
- ☐ **1 lb/500 g broccoli, chopped**
- ☐ **1 lb/500 g zucchini, chopped**
- ☐ **8 oz/250 g carrots, chopped**
- ☐ **2 onions, finely chopped**
- ☐ **2 cloves garlic, crushed**
- ☐ **3 tablespoons chopped fresh parsley**
- ☐ **1¹/₂ cups/185 g dried bread crumbs**
- ☐ **¹/₂ cup/60 g all-purpose flour, sifted**
- ☐ **freshly ground black pepper**

SPICY TOMATO SAUCE
- ☐ **1 tablespoon olive oil**
- ☐ **1 onion, finely chopped**
- ☐ **1 clove garlic, crushed**
- ☐ **1 fresh red chili, seeded and finely chopped**
- ☐ **1 green pepper, finely chopped**
- ☐ **14 oz/440 g canned tomatoes, undrained and mashed**
- ☐ **freshly ground black pepper**

1   To make patties, boil, steam or microwave broccoli, zucchini and carrots until tender. Drain, rinse under cold running water and pat dry.

2   Place broccoli, zucchini, carrots, onions, garlic and parsley in a food processor and process until puréed. Transfer vegetable mixture to a mixing bowl, add bread crumbs and flour, season to taste with black pepper and mix to combine. Cover and refrigerate for 30 minutes.

3   Shape mixture into ten patties. Place on a tray lined with parchment paper, cover and refrigerate until required.

4   To make sauce, heat oil in a saucepan and cook onion, garlic, chili and green pepper for 5 minutes or until onion and green pepper are soft. Add tomatoes, bring mixture to the boil, then reduce heat and simmer for 15-20 minutes or until sauce thickens. Season to taste with black pepper.

5   Cook patties on a lightly oiled preheated medium barbecue griddle or in a lightly oiled skillet on a preheated barbecue for 3-4 minutes each side. Toast rolls on the grill. Place a lettuce leaf, a pattie and a spoonful of sauce on the bottom half of each roll, top with remaining roll half and serve immediately.

SMOKED CHICKEN SALAD WITH GINGER DRESSING

A pretty salad with a fresh taste that is easy to make and travels well. Put the salad in the serving bowl to marinate on the way to your picnic.

Serves 6

- [ ] **1 x 2-3 lb/1-1.5 kg smoked chicken, meat removed and broken into bite-sized pieces**
- [ ] **4 spring onions, finely chopped**
- [ ] **1 small red pepper, thinly sliced**
- [ ] **1 small fresh red chili, seeded and thinly sliced**
- [ ] **1 tablespoon chopped fresh coriander (cilantro)**
- [ ] **1 tablespoon chopped fresh mint**
- [ ] **freshly ground black pepper**

ORANGE AND GINGER DRESSING
- [ ] **$1/4$ cup/60 mL olive oil**
- [ ] **2 tablespoons white wine vinegar**
- [ ] **2 tablespoons orange juice**
- [ ] **1 teaspoon coarse grain mustard**
- [ ] **1 teaspoon brown sugar**
- [ ] **1 teaspoon finely grated fresh ginger**

1   Place chicken, spring onions, red pepper, chili, coriander and mint in a serving bowl. Season to taste with black pepper.
2   To make dressing, place oil, vinegar, orange juice, mustard, sugar and ginger in a screwtop jar and shake well to combine. Pour over chicken mixture and toss to combine. Cover and refrigerate.

BAKED CAMEMBERT AND GORGONZOLA LOAF

Bake this loaf within the hour before you leave for your picnic. It is wrapped in foil and will stay warm.

Serves 6
Oven temperature 350°F, 180°C

- [ ] **9 in/23 cm round loaf of bread**
- [ ] **12 oz/375 g Camembert cheese, thinly sliced**
- [ ] **7 oz/220 g Gorgonzola cheese, thinly sliced**
- [ ] **3 pears, cored, peeled and thinly sliced**
- [ ] **3 fresh dates, thinly sliced**

1   Slice top from bread and scoop out center, leaving a 1 in/2.5 cm shell. Top and center of bread can be reserved and made into bread crumbs for use later.
2   Place a layer of Camembert cheese slices over base of bread and top loaf with a layer of Gorgonzola cheese and a layer of pear slices. Repeat layers, finishing with a layer of pears. Wrap loaf in a sheet of aluminum foil and bake for 30 minutes.
3   Remove from oven, open foil and top loaf with dates. While still hot, rewrap for transportation to picnic. Serve directly from the foil.

BROWNIES

Makes 24
Oven temperature 350°F, 180°C

- [ ] **2 oz/60 g unsweetened chocolate, coarsely chopped**
- [ ] **$1/2$ cup/1 stick/125 g unsalted (sweet) butter, cut up**
- [ ] **1 teaspoon vanilla extract**
- [ ] **2 eggs**
- [ ] **1 cup/220 g superfine sugar**
- [ ] **1 cup/125 g all-purpose flour**
- [ ] **$1/2$ cup/125 g chopped walnuts**

CHOCOLATE FUDGE ICING
- [ ] **7 oz/220 g semi-sweet dark chocolate, melted**
- [ ] **$1/4$ cup/$1/2$ stick/60 g butter, melted**

1   Melt chocolate and butter in a saucepan over a low heat, taking care not to overheat. Remove from heat and stir in vanilla.
2   Beat eggs and sugar together until just combined. Fold through chocolate mixture. Sift flour over chocolate mixture. Sprinkle walnuts over chocolate mixture, then fold in using a spatula.
3   Spoon mixture into a greased and parchment paper-lined 8 in/20 cm square cake pan. Smooth top using a spatula. Bake for 25-30 minutes, or until only just set. Cool in pan on a wire rack.
4   To make glaze, combine chocolate and butter in a mixing bowl and beat until well blended. Spread over brownie and set aside to firm. Cut into squares to serve.

Baked Camembert and Gorgonzola Loaf, Brownies, Smoked Chicken Salad with Ginger Dressing

BARBECUED LEG OF LAMB WITH LEMON HERB BUTTER

Ask your butcher to butterfly the lamb, or follow our instructions in the glossary.

Serves 8

- [ ] **1 leg of lamb, boned and butterflied**
- [ ] **2 cloves garlic, cut into slivers**
- [ ] **2 sprigs fresh rosemary**
- [ ] **freshly ground black pepper**

LEMON HERB BUTTER
- [ ] **¹/₂ cup/1 stick/125 g butter, softened**
- [ ] **2 teaspoons grated lemon rind**
- [ ] **1 tablespoon chopped fresh basil**
- [ ] **1 tablespoon chopped fresh parsley**
- [ ] **1 tablespoon lemon juice**
- [ ] **1 teaspoon sweet chili sauce**

1 Trim meat of excess fat. Make three deep slashes on top of meat with a sharp knife and tuck slivers of garlic and rosemary leaves into each. Sprinkle liberally with black pepper.
2 To make herb butter, combine butter, rind, basil, parsley, lemon juice and sauce and mix well.
3 Barbecue lamb over a gentle heat, basting with herb butter until tender.

POTATO SALAD AND AVOCADO DRESSING

Serves 6

- [ ] **2 lb/1 kg baby new potatoes, scrubbed**
- [ ] **2 tablespoons chopped fresh parsley**
- [ ] **6 hard-boiled eggs, quartered**
- [ ] **1 onion, sliced**

AVOCADO DRESSING
- [ ] **1 avocado, peeled and pitted**
- [ ] **1 clove garlic, crushed**
- [ ] **1 tablespoon lemon juice**
- [ ] **¹/₂ cup/125 g dairy sour cream**
- [ ] **2 drops hot red pepper sauce**
- [ ] **1 teaspoon honey**

1 Boil or steam potatoes until tender. Drain and place potatoes in a salad bowl with parsley, eggs and onion.
2 To make dressing, process avocado, garlic, lemon juice, sour cream, pepper sauce and honey in a food processor or blender until smooth.

Nutrition tip: Try plain yogurt in recipes instead of sour cream. If using in hot food, stir through at the end of cooking and do not allow to boil or it will go grainy.

GLAZED FRUIT KABOBS

Serves 4

- [ ] **7 oz/220 g canned pineapple chunks**
- [ ] **1 cooking apple, cored, peeled and cubed**
- [ ] **2 large bananas, thickly sliced**
- [ ] **8 oz/250 g strawberries, washed and hulled**
- [ ] **2 kiwifruit, cubed**
- [ ] **1 orange, segmented**

ORANGE GLAZE
- [ ] **¹/₂ cup/125 mL orange juice**
- [ ] **1 tablespoon honey**
- [ ] **1 tablespoon orange-flavored liqueur**
- [ ] **2 teaspoons cornstarch**

1 Thread fruit pieces onto eight oiled wooden skewers, alternating the pieces attractively.
2 To make the glaze, combine ingredients in a saucepan. Cook over a medium heat for 2-3 minutes until glaze boils and thickens.
3 Barbecue kabobs over a gentle heat, turning and brushing frequently with glaze.

Barbecued Leg of Lamb with Lemon Herb Butter, Potato Salad and Avocado Dressing, Glazed Fruit Kabobs

COOK'S TIP

When using wooden skewers, don't forget to soak them in cold water for at least an hour before using under grill or over a barbecue, as they can burn.

BARBECUED STEAK SANDWICHES

Marinated steak, barbecued and placed between slices of grilled bread makes the best steak sandwiches you will ever taste.

Serves 6

- ☐ **6 ribeye (Delmonico) steaks, cut $^1/_2$ in/1 cm thick**
- ☐ **3 onions, thinly sliced**
- ☐ **12 thick slices wholewheat or grain bread**
- ☐ **olive oil**

GINGER WINE MARINADE
- ☐ **1 cup/250 mL red wine**
- ☐ **$^1/_2$ cup/125 mL olive oil**
- ☐ **1 clove garlic, crushed**
- ☐ **2 teaspoons grated fresh ginger**

1 To make marinade, place wine, oil, garlic and ginger in a bowl and mix to combine. Place steaks in a shallow glass or ceramic dish. Pour marinade over, cover, and marinate at room temperature for 2-3 hours or overnight in the refrigerator.

2 Cook onions on a lightly oiled preheated barbecue griddle or in a lightly oiled skillet on a preheated grill for 10-15 minutes or until golden. Drain steaks and cook on lightly oiled grill for 3-5 minutes each side or until cooked to your liking.

3 Lightly brush bread slices with oil and cook on a preheated grill for 1-2 minutes each side or until lightly toasted. To assemble sandwiches, top 6 toasted bread slices with steak, onions and remaining bread slices.

Cook's tip: You may like to add some salad ingredients to your sandwiches. Mustard or relish is also a tasty addition.

Left: Barbecued Steak Sandwiches
Above: Caribbean Poussin

CARIBBEAN POUSSIN

Serves 6

- ☐ **3 poussins (small spatchcocks), halved**
- ☐ **2 tablespoons cracked black peppercorns**
- ☐ **1 teaspoon ground coriander (cilantro)**

LIME MARINADE
- ☐ **$^1/_4$ cup/60 mL white rum**
- ☐ **2 teaspoons finely grated lime rind**
- ☐ **1 tablespoon lime juice**
- ☐ **2 tablespoons honey**
- ☐ **2 cloves garlic, crushed**
- ☐ **1 teaspoon grated fresh ginger**

1 To make marinade, place rum, lime rind, lime juice, honey, garlic and ginger in a bowl and mix to combine. Place poussin halves in a shallow glass or ceramic dish and rub marinade into them. Cover and set aside to marinate for 1 hour.

2 Thread a skewer through wings and legs of each poussin half and brush with any remaining marinade. Combine black peppercorns and coriander and press onto skin of birds. Cook on a lightly oiled preheated barbecue grill, turning frequently for 15-20 minutes or until birds are cooked through.

Cook's tip: This is also a delicious way to prepare and cook chicken pieces. Instead of using poussins, simply use chicken pieces and prepare and marinate as in this recipe – the cooking time for the chicken pieces will be about the same as for the poussins. You should cook them until the juices run clear.

chapter eleven

BAKED TO
PERFECTION

Chocolate Cake, Brownies
and Dundee Cake are all family
favorites and are just three of the
sumptuous recipes you will find in
this chapter. When you cook these
and the other delicious home-
baked goodies you are sure
to draw compliments from
family and friends.

Chocolate Shortbread, Quick Brownies,
White Choc-Chip Chocolate Cake

QUICK NUT FUDGE CAKE

Makes an 8 in/20 cm round cake
Oven temperature 350°F, 180°C

- ☐ ¹/₂ cup/1stick/125 g butter, melted
- ☐ 1¹/₂ cups/250 g packed brown sugar
- ☐ 2 eggs, lightly beaten
- ☐ 1 teaspoon vanilla extract
- ☐ ¹/₄ cup/30 g cocoa powder, sifted
- ☐ 2 cups/250 g self-rising flour, sifted
- ☐ ¹/₂ cup/60 g chopped walnuts

CHOCOLATE BUTTER FROSTING
- ☐ ¹/₂ cup/1stick/125 g butter, softened
- ☐ 4 oz/125 g semi-sweet dark chocolate, melted and cooled
- ☐ 2 egg yolks
- ☐ ¹/₂ cup/90 g IOX (confectioners') sugar, sifted

1   Place butter, brown sugar, eggs and vanilla extract in a large mixing bowl and mix to combine. Stir in cocoa powder, flour and walnuts. Mix well to combine.
2   Spoon batter into a deep greased and parchment-paper lined 8 in/20 cm round cake pan or springform and tin bake for 35-40 minutes or until cake is cooked when tested with a skewer. Stand cake in pan for 5 minutes before turning onto a wire rack to cool.
3   To make frosting, place butter in a mixing bowl and beat until light and fluffy. Add chocolate, egg yolks and IOX sugar and beat until smooth. Spread frosting over cold cake.

CHOCOLATE SHORTBREAD

Makes 30
Oven temperature 325°F, 160°C

- ☐ 1 cup/2 sticks/250 g butter, softened
- ☐ ¹/₂ cup/90 g IOX (confectioners') icing sugar
- ☐ 1 cup/125 g all-purpose flour
- ☐ 1 cup/125 g cornstarch
- ☐ ¹/₄ cup/30 g cocoa powder

1   Place butter and IOX sugar in a mixing bowl and beat until mixture is creamy. Sift together flour, cornstarch and cocoa powder. Stir flour mixture into butter mixture.
2   Turn dough onto a floured surface and knead lightly until smooth. Roll spoonfuls of mixture into balls, place on greased cookie sheets and flatten slightly with a fork. Bake for 20-25 minutes or until firm. Allow to cool on cookie sheets.

WHITE CHOC-CHIP CHOCOLATE CAKE

Makes a 9 in/23 cm round cake
Oven temperature 350°F, 180°C

- ☐ ¹/₂ cup/1 stick/125 g butter, softened
- ☐ 1 cup/220 g superfine sugar
- ☐ 1 teaspoon vanilla extract
- ☐ 2 eggs
- ☐ 1¹/₄ cups/170 g self-rising flour
- ☐ ¹/₄ cup/30 g cocoa powder
- ☐ ¹/₂ teaspoon baking powder
- ☐ 1 cup/250 mL milk
- ☐ 7 oz/220 g white chocolate, chopped

WHITE CHOCOLATE FROSTING
- ☐ ¹/₂ cup/1 stick/125 g butter, softened
- ☐ 3 oz/90 g white chocolate, melted and cooled
- ☐ 2 egg yolks
- ☐ ¹/₂ cup/90 g IOX (confectioners') sugar, sifted

1   Place butter, sugar and vanilla extract in a mixing bowl and beat until mixture is creamy. Add eggs one at a time beating well after each addition.
2   Sift together flour, cocoa powder and baking powder. Fold flour mixture and milk, alternately, into butter mixture, then fold in chocolate.
3   Spoon batter into a greased and parchment-paper lined 9 in/23 cm round cake pan or springform and bake for 30-35 minutes or until cooked when tested with a skewer. Stand in pan for 5 minutes before turning onto a wire rack to cool completely.
4   To make frosting, place butter in a mixing bowl and beat until light and fluffy. Add chocolate, egg yolks and IOX sugar and beat until smooth. Spread frosting over top and sides of cold cake.

QUICK BROWNIES

Makes 25
Oven temperature 350°F, 180°C

- ☐ 5 oz/155 g butter, softened
- ☐ ¹/₂ cup/170 g honey, warmed
- ☐ 4 teaspoons water
- ☐ 2 eggs, lightly beaten
- ☐ 1³/₄ cups/220 g self-rising flour, sifted
- ☐ ³/₄ cup/125 g packed brown sugar
- ☐ 4 oz/125 g semi-sweet dark chocolate, melted and cooled
- ☐ IOX (confectioners') sugar

1   Place butter, honey, water, eggs, flour, sugar and chocolate in a food processor and process until ingredients are combined.
2   Spoon batter into a greased and parchment-paper lined 9 in/23 cm square cake pan and bake for 30-35 minutes or until cooked when tested with a skewer. Stand cake in pan for 5 minutes before turning onto a wire rack to cool. Dust cold cake with IOX sugar and cut into squares.

MELTING CHOCOLATE

🞜 Chocolate melts more rapidly if broken into small pieces.

🞜 Keep the container in which the chocolate is being melted, uncovered and completely dry. Covering can cause condensation and just one drop of water will ruin the chocolate.

🞜 The melting process should occur slowly, as chocolate scorches if overheated.

🞜 Chocolate 'seizes' if it is overheated or if it comes in contact with water or steam. Seizing results in the chocolate tightening and becoming a thick mass that will not melt.

🞜 To rescue seized chocolate stir in a little cream or vegetable oil until the chocolate becomes smooth again.

🞜 To melt chocolate, place in the top of a double boiler and set aside. Fill bottom of boiler with enough water to come just under the top; the water should not touch the insert when it is placed in the saucepan. Bring water to the boil, then remove from heat and place chocolate over the hot water. Stand off the heat, stirring chocolate occasionally until it melts and is of a smooth consistency. Cool at room temperature.

🞜 Chocolate can be melted quickly and easily in the microwave. Place chocolate in a microwave-safe glass or ceramic dish and cook on HIGH (100%) for 2 minutes per 12 oz/375 g chocolate. When melting chocolate in the microwave oven you will find that it tends to hold its shape, so always stir it before additional heating. If the chocolate is not completely melted, cook for an extra 30 seconds, then stir again.

BASIC COOKIES

Makes 40
Oven temperature 350°F, 180°C

- ☐ ¹/₂ **cup/1 stick/125 g butter**
- ☐ **1 teaspoon vanilla extract**
- ☐ ³/₄ **cup/185 g sugar**
- ☐ **1 egg**
- ☐ **1 cup/125 g all-purpose flour, sifted**
- ☐ **1 cup/125 g self-rising flour, sifted**

1 Cream butter, sugar and vanilla extract until light and fluffy. Add egg and beat well. Fold in all-purpose flour and self-rising flours, cover and refrigerate for 2 hours.
2 Roll heaped teaspoonfuls of mixture into balls. Place onto a greased cookie sheet, spacing well apart to allow for spreading. Flatten each cookie slightly with a fork and bake for 12-15 minutes or until golden brown. Allow to cool on sheet for a few minutes then transfer to a wire rack to finish cooling.

Variations

Spicy Fruit Cookies: Replace ¹/₃ cup of the sugar with ¹/₃ cup packed brown sugar. Sift 2 teaspoons of cinnamon, 1 teaspoon pumpkin pie spice and 1 teaspoon of ginger with the flour. Roll out mixture and cut 16 rounds with a cookie cutter. Place teaspoonfuls of bottled fruit mince meat on half the rounds and cover with remaining rounds. Press the edges lightly to seal and bake for 20-25 minutes, or until golden brown.

Three-Chocolate Cookies: Add 1¹/₂ oz/ 45 g finely chopped semi-sweet dark chocolate, 1¹/₂ oz/45 g finely chopped sweet milk chocolate and 1¹/₂ oz/45 g finely chopped white chocolate to the cookie mixture after beating in the egg. Place spoonfuls of mixture on a greased cookie sheet and bake for 12-15 minutes or until golden brown.

Creamy Jam Drops: Roll mixture into balls and flatten slightly. Make indents in the center of each round and fill with a small amount of cream cheese and top with a teaspoon of raspberry jam, or a jam of your choice. Be careful not to fill the holes too much, or the jam will overflow during cooking. Bake for 12-15 minutes, or until golden brown.

DATE WRAPS

Makes 20
Oven temperature 325°F, 160°C

- ☐ **20 dried dates, pitted**
- ☐ ¹/₃ **cup/90 mL brandy**
- ☐ **1 quantity Basic Cookies**

1 Soak dates in brandy for 30 minutes, then drain.
2 Divide cookie dough into 20 equal portions. Mold each portion around a date.

Place on a greased cookie sheet and bake for 20-25 minutes, or until golden brown.

Basic Cookies, Spicy Fruit Cookies, Three-Chocolate Cookies, Creamy Jam Drops, Date Wraps

COFFEE LAYER CAKE

Layers of light cake sandwiched together with a liqueur cream and topped with a coffee frosting. All this cake needs is a wonderful cup of coffee to accompany it.

Makes an 8 in/20 cm two layer cake
Oven temperature 325°F, 160°C

- [ ] **1 cup/2 sticks/250 g butter, softened**
- [ ] **1 cup/220 g superfine sugar**
- [ ] **6 eggs, lightly beaten**
- [ ] **2 cups/250 g self-rising flour, sifted**
- [ ] **4 teaspoons baking powder**

COFFEE FROSTING
- [ ] **¹/₄ cup/¹/₂ stick/60 g butter, softened**
- [ ] **³/₄ cup/125 g IOX (confectioners') sugar, sifted**
- [ ] **¹/₂ teaspoon ground cinnamon**
- [ ] **2 teaspoons instant coffee powder dissolved in 2 teaspoons hot water, cooled**

LIQUEUR CREAM
- [ ] **1 tablespoon coffee-flavored liqueur**
- [ ] **¹/₂ cup/125 mL thick cream whipped**

1 Place butter and sugar in a food processor and process until creamy. Add eggs, flour and baking powder and process until all ingredients are combined. Spoon batter into two greased and parchment paper-lined 8 in/20 cm round cake pans and bake for 30-35 minutes or until golden. Turn onto a wire rack to cool.

2 To make frosting, place butter, IOX sugar, cinnamon and coffee mixture in a food processor and process until fluffy.

3 To make filling, fold liqueur into whipped cream. Spread frosting over one layer and top with remaining cake. Spread frosting over top of cake.

Cook's tip: To make a nonalcoholic version of this dessert dissolve 1 teaspoon instant coffee powder in 1 teaspoon hot water, cool, then fold into cream in place of the liqueur.

Sponge Cake, Crunchy Caramel Cake

SPICED GINGER DROPS

Ginger lovers won't be able to get enough of these spicy cookies.

Makes 30
Oven temperature 350°F, 180°C

- ☐ **1 cup/125 g all-purpose flour, sifted**
- ☐ **¹/₄ teaspoon ground ginger**
- ☐ **¹/₄ teaspoon ground pumpkin pie spice**
- ☐ **¹/₄ teaspoon ground cinnamon**
- ☐ **¹/₂ teaspoon baking soda**
- ☐ **¹/₄ cup/¹/₂ stick/60 g butter, cut into pieces**
- ☐ **¹/₂ cup/90 g packed brown sugar**
- ☐ **2¹/₂ tablespoons honey or light molasses, warmed**
- ☐ **1¹/₂ tablespoons finely chopped candied ginger or preserved ginger in syrup**

1   Place flour, ground ginger, spice, cinnamon and baking soda in a large mixing bowl. Rub in butter until mixture resembles fine bread crumbs. Stir in sugar, honey and candied or preserved ginger.

2   Turn dough onto a lightly floured surface and knead to form a soft dough. Roll rounded teaspoons of mixture into balls and place 1¹/₄ in/3 cm apart on greased cookie sheets. Bake for 10-15 minutes or until golden. Transfer cookies to wire racks to cool.

Spiced Ginger Drops

DUNDEE CAKE

This traditional Scottish recipe, dating right back to the eighteenth century, is characterized by the almonds that decorate the top of the cake.

Makes an 8 in/20 cm round cake
Oven temperature 300°F, 150°C,

- ☐ **1 cup/2 sticks/250 g butter, softened**
- ☐ **1 teaspoon rum extract**
- ☐ **1 cup/220 g superfine sugar**
- ☐ **4 eggs, lightly beaten**
- ☐ **2 cups/250 g all-purpose flour**
- ☐ **1 teaspoon baking powder**
- ☐ **$^{1}/_{4}$ cup/30 g cornstarch**
- ☐ **$1^{1}/_{2}$ cups/250 g golden raisins**
- ☐ **$1^{2}/_{3}$ cups/250 g currants**
- ☐ **$^{3}/_{4}$ cup/125 g mixed candied citrus peel**
- ☐ **1 cup/125 g slivered almonds**
- ☐ **$^{1}/_{3}$ cup/60 g candied cherries, halved**
- ☐ **2 teaspoons finely grated orange rind**
- ☐ **1 tablespoon orange juice**
- ☐ **$^{1}/_{3}$ cup/45 g blanched whole almonds**

1   Place butter and rum extract into a large mixing bowl and beat until light and fluffy. Gradually add sugar, beating well after each addition until mixture is creamy.
2   Add eggs one at a time, beating well after each addition. Sift together flour, baking powder and cornstarch, then fold into butter mixture.
3   Stir in raisins, currants, mixed peel, slivered almonds, cherries, orange rind and orange juice. Spoon mixture into a greased and parchment paper-lined deep 8 in/20 cm round cake pan or springform. Decorate top of cake with almonds, arranged in circles, and bake for $2^{1}/_{2}$-3 hours, or until cooked when tested with a skewer. Set aside to cool in pan before turning out.

Spoon mixture into a greased and lined deep 8 in/20 cm round cake tin.

Decorate the top of the cake with almonds, arranged in circles.

TANGY APPLE AND APRICOT LOAF

An easily prepared moist loaf that is great for picnics and lunch boxes.

Makes an 4¹/₂ x 8¹/₂ in/11 x 21 cm loaf
Oven temperature 350°F, 180°C

- ☐ 1¹/₄ cups/155 g dried apricots, chopped
- ☐ 2 cups/125 g dried apples, chopped
- ☐ 2 teaspoons finely grated lemon rind
- ☐ 2 tablespoons lemon juice
- ☐ 5 oz/155 mL water
- ☐ 1 cup/185 g packed brown sugar
- ☐ ¹/₄ cup/¹/₂ stick/60 g butter
- ☐ 1¹/₂ cups/185 g wholewheat all-purpose flour, sifted
- ☐ ¹/₂ cup/60 g white self-rising flour, sifted
- ☐ 1¹/₂ teaspoons baking powder

1 Place apricots, apples, lemon rind, lemon juice, water, sugar and butter in a saucepan, bring to the boil and simmer for 5 minutes. Remove pan from heat and set aside to cool for 5 minutes.

2 Stir wholewheat, white self-rising flours and baking powder into fruit mixture. Spoon batter into greased and parchment paper-lined 4¹/₂ x 8¹/₂ in/11 x 21 cm loaf pan and bake for 1 hour or until cooked when tested with a skewer. Cool loaf in pan for 15 minutes before turning onto a wire rack to cool completely.

ORANGE AND LIME YOGURT SYRUP CAKE

Serves 10
Oven temperature 350°F, 180°C

- ☐ ¹/₂ cup/1 stick/125 g butter
- ☐ 1 teaspoon grated lime rind
- ☐ 1 tablespoon grated orange rind
- ☐ 1 cup/220 g superfine sugar
- ☐ 3 eggs
- ☐ 1¹/₂ cups/200 g self-rising flour, sifted
- ☐ ¹/₂ cup/125 g plain yogurt

LIME AND ORANGE SYRUP
- ☐ 2 tablespoons lime juice
- ☐ ¹/₄ cup/60 mL orange juice
- ☐ ¹/₄ cup/60 g sugar

1 Place butter, and lime and orange rinds in a large mixing bowl and beat until light and creamy. Add sugar a little at a time, beating well after each addition.

2 Beat in eggs one at a time and mix well. Fold through flour alternately with yogurt. Spoon mixture into a greased 8 in/20 cm ring cake pan and bake for 30-35 minutes or until cooked. Stand in cake pan for 5 minutes, then turn out onto a wire rack with a cookie sheet underneath.

3 To make syrup, place lime juice, orange juice and sugar in a saucepan. Cook over a medium heat, stirring constantly, until sugar dissolves. Bring mixture to the boil without stirring, and boil for 3 minutes. Remove from heat and pour hot syrup over hot cake. Set aside to cool.

WHOLEWHEAT CHERRY AND ALMOND BREAD

An eye-catching, tasty bread that can be served while still warm. Great to serve with coffee in place of dessert.

Makes 30 slices
Oven temperature 350°F, 180°C

- ☐ 2 eggs
- ☐ ¹/₂ cup/125 g superfine sugar
- ☐ 1 cup/155 g whole blanched almonds
- ☐ ³/₄ cup/125 g whole red candied cherries
- ☐ 1 cup/125 g self-rising flour, sifted
- ☐ 1 cup/125 g wholewheat all-purpose flour, sifted

1 Place eggs and sugar in a bowl and beat with an electric mixer for 6 minutes or until mixture is thick and creamy. Stir in almonds, cherries, self-rising and wholewheat flours.

2 Spread mixture into a greased and parchment paper-lined standard loaf pan and bake for 30-35 minutes or until firm and browned. Cool bread in pan for 15 minutes before turning onto a wire rack to cool completely. Wrap in foil and leave overnight.

3 Cut bread into ¹/₈ in/3 mm slices using a sharp knife. Place slices on cookie sheets in single layers and bake for 10 minutes or until bread is lightly browned.

Cook's tip: If you have an electric knife, it is ideal for cutting this loaf.

STRAWBERRY TARTS

The wicked jam and moreish topping will make these tarts disappear in no time.

Makes 24
Oven temperature 400°F, 200°C

- ☐ ¹/₂ **cup/1 stick/125 g butter**
- ☐ ¹/₄ **cup/60 g sugar**
- ☐ **1 egg**
- ☐ **2 teaspoons milk**
- ☐ **2 cups/250 g self-rising flour, sifted**
- ☐ ³/₄ **cup/185 g strawberry jam**

COCONUT TOPPING
- ☐ ¹/₄ **cup/60 g sugar**
- ☐ ²/₃ **cup/60 g flaked coconut**
- ☐ **1 egg**

1 Place butter and sugar in a bowl and beat until light and fluffy. Mix in egg and milk, then flour, mixing to form a dough. Turn out onto a lightly floured surface and roll out thinly, cut into rounds using a 3 in/ 7.5 cm cutter and place in lightly greased small muffin pans. Top with a spoonful of jam.
2 To make topping, place sugar, coconut and egg in a bowl and mix well. Place a spoonful of topping on each tart and bake for 10-15 minutes, or until tops are golden and pastry is cooked.

Variations
You might like to change the filling and/or topping for the Strawberry Tarts.
Lemon Tarts: Replace strawberry jam with lemon curd (recipe page 300). Top with topping and cook as for Strawberry Tarts.
Orange Tarts: Remove rind and pith from 2 oranges and chop orange flesh. Use in place of strawberry jam. Top with topping and cook as for Strawberry Tarts.
Marmalade Tarts: Replace strawberry jam with marmalade. Top with a rolled oats topping. To make rolled oats topping, place ²/₃ cup/60 g rolled oats, ¹/₃ cup/60 g packed brown sugar, ¹/₂ cup/60 g wholewheat self-rising flour in a bowl and stir in 3 oz/90 g butter, melted. Sprinkle over tarts and cook as for Strawberry Tarts.
Jam Tarts: To make plain jam tarts, fill the tarts with a jam of your choice and omit topping. Cook as for Strawberry Tarts.

Wholewheat Cherry and Almond Bread, Strawberry Tarts, Orange and Lime Yogurt Syrup Cake

CHILI SOUP BISCUITS

Makes 16 biscuits
Oven temperature 425°F, 220°C

- [ ] **2 slices bacon, finely chopped**
- [ ] **2 cups/250 g flour**
- [ ] **1 tablespoon baking powder**
- [ ] **$^1/_2$ teaspoon salt**
- [ ] **3 oz/90 g butter**
- [ ] **$^3/_4$ cup/90 g shredded Cheddar cheese**
- [ ] **2 small fresh red chilies, seeded and finely chopped**
- [ ] **$^3/_4$ cup/185 mL milk**
- [ ] **2 tablespoons/30 g butter, melted**

1   Cook bacon in a nonstick skillet over a medium high heat for 3-4 minutes or until crisp. Remove from pan and drain on absorbent paper towels.
2   Sift together flour, baking powder and salt into a mixing bowl. Rub in butter with fingertips until mixture resembles coarse bread crumbs.
3   Stir bacon, cheese and chilies into flour mixture. Add milk and mix to form a soft dough. Turn onto a floured surface and knead lightly with fingertips until smooth.
4   Using heel of hand, gently press dough out to $^1/_2$ in/1 cm thick. Cut out rounds using a 2 in/5 cm pastry cutter. Place on a greased cookie sheet and brush with melted butter. Bake for 12-15 minutes or until golden brown. Remove from sheet and cool on a wire rack or serve warm spread with butter.

HERB BISCUIT BALLS

Spring onions and herbs have been added to this soda bread recipe.

Makes 12 rolls
Oven temperature 350°F, 180°C

- [ ] **3 oz/90 g butter**
- [ ] **8 spring onions, finely chopped**
- [ ] **$2^1/_2$ cups/315 g all-purpose flour**
- [ ] **1 cup/125 g self-rising flour**
- [ ] **1 tablespoon baking powder**
- [ ] **$^1/_2$ teaspoon baking soda**
- [ ] **4 teaspoons sugar**
- [ ] **1 tablespoon finely chopped fresh parsley**
- [ ] **1 tablespoon finely chopped fresh basil**
- [ ] **$^1/_2$ cup/125 mL buttermilk or milk**
- [ ] **3 eggs, lightly beaten**
- [ ] **1 egg, beaten with $1^1/_2$ teaspoons olive oil**

1   Melt butter in a skillet and cook spring onions over a medium heat for 2-3 minutes or until onions are soft. Remove from heat and set aside.
2   Sift together all-purpose and self-rising flours, baking powder and baking soda into a large mixing bowl. Stir in sugar, parsley and basil. Combine milk, eggs and onion mixture and mix into flour mixture to form a firm dough.
3   Turn onto a floured surface and knead lightly until smooth. Divide dough into twelve portions and roll each into a ball then place on greased and floured cookie sheets. Brush each roll with egg and oil mixture and bake for 30-35 minutes or until cooked through.

SODA BREAD

A loaf for when you need bread unexpectedly. Soda bread is made with baking soda rather than yeast so requires no rising. It is best eaten slightly warm.

Serves 8
Oven temperature 400°F, 200°C

- [ ] **4 cups/500 g all-purpose flour**
- [ ] **1 teaspoon baking soda**
- [ ] **1 teaspoon salt**
- [ ] **3 tablespoons/45 g butter**
- [ ] **2 cups/500 mL buttermilk or milk**

1   Sift together flour, baking soda and salt into a mixing bowl. Rub in butter using fingertips until mixture resembles coarse bread crumbs. Make a well in the center of the flour mixture and pour in milk. Using a round-ended knife, mix to form a soft dough.
2   Turn dough onto a floured surface and knead lightly until smooth. Shape into a 7 in/18 cm round and place on a greased and floured cookie sheet. Score dough into eighths using a sharp knife. Dust lightly with flour and bake for 35-40 minutes or until loaf sounds hollow when tapped on the base.

Serving suggestion: Wonderful spread with butter and honey.

Herb Biscuit Balls, Soda Bread, Chili Soup Biscuits

GINGERBREAD UPSIDE-DOWN CAKE

Makes an 8 in/20 cm ring cake
Oven temperature 350°F, 180°C

- ☐ ¹/₂ **cup/60 g dried apricots**
- ☐ ¹/₄ **cup/¹/₂ stick/60 g butter, softened**
- ☐ ¹/₂ **cup/90 g packed brown sugar**
- ☐ ¹/₃ **cup/45 g chopped pecans**

GINGERBREAD CAKE
- ☐ **1 cup/125 g all-purpose flour, sifted**
- ☐ ¹/₂ **cup/60 g self-rising flour, sifted**
- ☐ ¹/₂ **teaspoon baking soda**
- ☐ **1 tablespoon ground ginger**
- ☐ ¹/₂ **teaspoon ground nutmeg**
- ☐ ¹/₂ **cup/90 g packed brown sugar**
- ☐ ¹/₃ **cup/125 g light molasses or honey**
- ☐ ¹/₂ **cup/125 mL water**
- ☐ ¹/₂ **cup/1 stick/125 g butter**

1 Place apricots in a bowl, cover with boiling water, cover bowl and set aside to soak for 30 minutes. Drain and set aside. Place butter and sugar in a small bowl and beat until smooth. Spread butter mixture over the base of a greased and parchment paper-lined 8 in/20 cm ring tin. Sprinkle with pecans and top with apricots, cut side up.

2 To make gingerbread, place all-purpose and self-rising flours, baking soda, ginger, nutmeg and sugar in a large bowl and mix to combine. Place molasses, water and butter in a saucepan and cook over a low heat, stirring, until butter is melted and ingredients are combined. Remove pan from heat and set aside to cool for 5 minutes. Pour molasses mixture into dry ingredients and mix well to combine. Spoon gingerbread into prepared pan and bake for 35-40 minutes or until cake is cooked when tested with a skewer. Allow cake to stand for 15 minutes before turning out.

MASTER CLASS

COFFEE KISSES *double*

The dough for these coffee-flavored cookies is similar to a shortbread — making it perfect for piping. Follow the step-by-step instructions and see just how easy these cookies are to make.

Makes 25
Oven temperature 350°F, 180°C

- [ ] **1 cup/2 sticks/250 g butter, softened**
- [ ] **¹/₂ cup/90 g IOX (confectioners') sugar, sifted**
- [ ] **2 teaspoons instant coffee powder dissolved in 1 tablespoon hot water, cooled**
- [ ] **2 cups/250 g all-purpose flour, sifted**
- [ ] **1¹/₂ ozs/45 g dark chocolate, melted**
- [ ] **IOX (confectioners') sugar**

1 Place butter and IOX sugar in a large mixing bowl and beat until light and fluffy. Stir in coffee mixture and flour.

2 Spoon mixture into a pastry bag fitted with a medium star nozzle and pipe ³/₄ in/2 cm rounds of mixture ³/₄ in/2 cm apart on greased cookie sheets. Bake for 10-12 minutes or until lightly browned. Stand on sheets for 5 minutes before removing to wire racks to cool completely.

3 Join cookies with a little melted chocolate, then dust with IOX sugar.

Spoon mixture into a pastry bag fitted with a medium star nozzle.

Pipe ³/₄ in/2 cm rounds of mixture ³/₄ in/2 cm apart on greased cookie sheets.

Join cookies with a little melted chocolate, then dust with IOX sugar.

GRANOLA BARS

Makes 24
Oven temperature 325°F, 160°C

- ☐ ¹/₄ cup/¹/₂ stick/60 g butter
- ☐ ¹/₄ cup/60 g honey
- ☐ 2 eggs, lightly beaten
- ☐ 1 cup/250 g plain yogurt
- ☐ 1 cup/250 g ricotta cheese
- ☐ ¹/₂ cup/45 g flaked coconut
- ☐ ¹/₃ cup/45 g sliced almonds
- ☐ ³/₄ cup/125 g chopped raisins
- ☐ 1¹/₄ cups/155 g wholewheat all-purpose flour, sifted and grits returned
- ☐ ¹/₄ cup/60 mL sesame seeds

1   Place butter and honey in a mixing bowl and beat to combine. Gradually mix in eggs and yogurt, then stir in ricotta cheese, coconut, almonds, raisins, flour and sesame seeds.
2   Pour mixture into a lightly greased and parchment paper-lined shallow 7 x 11 in/ 18 x 28 cm cake pan and bake for 35-40 minutes, or until firm and golden brown. Cool in pan. Cut into bars or squares.

SPEEDY DATE BARS

Makes 24
Oven temperature 350°F, 180°C

- ☐ 3 oz/90 g butter
- ☐ ³/₄ cup/185 g raw (brown granulated) sugar
- ☐ 1 egg
- ☐ 1 cup/155 g chopped dried dates
- ☐ 1 cup/125 g self-rising flour
- ☐ 2 oz/60 g granola
- ☐ 2 tablespoons sunflower seeds
- ☐ 1 tablespoon poppy seeds
- ☐ 2 tablespoons chopped pumpkin seeds
- ☐ ¹/₂ cup/125 g plain yogurt

LEMON GLAZE
- ☐ 2 teaspoons butter
- ☐ 2 tablespoons hot water
- ☐ ¹/₄ cup/60 mL lemon juice
- ☐ 2 cups/350 g IOX (confectioners') sugar, sifted

1   Place butter and raw sugar in a small mixing bowl and beat until light and fluffy. Beat in egg, then stir in dates, flour, granola, sunflower seeds, poppy seeds, pumpkin seeds and yogurt.

2   Spoon mixture into a lightly greased and parchment paper-lined shallow 7 x 11 in/18 x 28 cm cake pan and bake for 25 minutes, or until firm and golden brown. Cool in pan.
3   To make glaze, melt butter in hot water and combine with lemon juice. Add icing sugar and beat until smooth. Spread evenly over cooled layer. Allow glaze to set then cut into bars or squares.

OATY COOKIES

Makes 15
Oven temperature 350°F, 180°C

- ☐ ¹/₄ cup/¹/₂ stick/60 g butter
- ☐ ¹/₄ cup/60 g packed brown sugar
- ☐ 1 teaspoon vanilla extract
- ☐ 1 egg
- ☐ 1 cup/90 g rolled oats
- ☐ ¹/₄ cup wheat germ
- ☐ ²/₃ cup/75 g wholewheat all-purpose flour, sifted and grits returned
- ☐ 1 teaspoon baking powder
- ☐ ¹/₄ cup/30 g chopped pecans
- ☐ ¹/₄ cup/45 g chopped dates

GLAZE
- ☐ 2 teaspoons butter
- ☐ ¹/₄ cup/60 mL hot water
- ☐ 1cup/155 g IOX (confectioners') sugar, sifted
- ☐ few drops red food coloring

1   Place butter in a small mixing bowl and beat until light and fluffy. Add brown sugar and vanilla extract and beat to combine. Add egg and beat to combine.
2   Stir in oats, wheat germ, flour, baking powder, pecans and dates and mix well.
3   Place spoonfuls of mixture onto lightly greased cookie sheets and bake for 10 minutes or until golden brown. Remove cookies from sheets and cool on a wire rack.
4   To make glaze, melt butter in hot water. Combine with IOX sugar and beat until smooth. Color with food coloring and place a drop of glaze on each cookie.

WHOLEHEARTED ROCKCAKES

Makes 20
Oven temperature 350°F, 180°C

- ☐ 2¹/₂ cups/315 g wholewheat all-purpose flour, sifted and grits returned

- ☐ ¹/₂ teaspoon ground cinnamon
- ☐ ¹/₃ cup/90 g raw (brown granulated) sugar
- ☐ ¹/₂ cup/1 stick/125 g butter
- ☐ ³/₄ cup/125 g seeded raisins, chopped
- ☐ ¹/₂ cup/30 g dried apples, chopped
- ☐ 1 egg, lightly beaten
- ☐ ¹/₃ cup/90 mL milk

1   Place flour, baking powder, cinnamon and sugar in a large mixing bowl. Rub in butter with fingertips. Stir in raisins and apples, then gradually add egg and enough milk to make a thick dough.
2   Place large spoonfuls of mixture onto greased cookie sheets and bake for 12-15 minutes, or until cooked through and golden brown.

MINCEMEAT SHORTCAKE

Serves 8
Oven temperature 350°F, 180°C

- ☐ 2 cups/250 g self-rising flour
- ☐ ¹/₂ cup/1 stick/125 g butter
- ☐ ¹/₂ cup/125 g superfine sugar
- ☐ 1 egg, beaten
- ☐ 1 tablespoon lemon juice
- ☐ 1 cup/220 g bottled fruit mincemeat
- ☐ 1 egg white, lightly beaten
- ☐ extra superfine sugar

1   Place flour in a food processor and process to sift. Add butter and process until mixture resembles fine bread crumbs. Add sugar, egg and lemon juice and process to make a firm dough. Turn dough onto a lightly floured surface and knead briefly. Wrap dough in plastic food wrap and refrigerate for 30 minutes.
2   Divide dough into two equal portions. Roll one portion out to line the bottom and sides of a lightly greased 8 in/20 cm round shallow cake pan. Spread mincemeat over dough.
3   Roll out remaining dough to make a 8¹/₂ in/21 cm circle and place over mincemeat. Press edges together, brush with egg white, sprinkle with extra sugar and bake for 30-35 minutes or until cooked. Stand for 10 minutes before turning out onto a wire rack to cool.

Wholehearted Rockcakes, Speedy Date Bars, Oaty Cookies, Granola Bars

BASIC FRUIT MIXTURE

This recipe is sufficient to make a Christmas fruit cake, a steamed pudding and twenty-four mince meat pies.

- ☐ 2 lb/1 kg golden raisins, chopped
- ☐ 12 oz/375 g dried currants
- ☐ 6 oz/185 g seeded raisins, chopped
- ☐ 2 tablespoons/30 g chopped mixed candied citrus peels
- ☐ 6 oz/185 g pitted dried dates, chopped
- ☐ 5 oz/155 g dried apricots, chopped
- ☐ 5 oz/155 g pitted prunes, chopped
- ☐ 8 oz/250 g candied cherries, quartered
- ☐ 5 oz/155 g candied pineapple, chopped
- ☐ 1/2 honeydew melon or canteloupe, peeled, seeded and chopped
- ☐ 2 oz/60 g candied angelica, chopped (optional)
- ☐ 1 cup/350 g honey or light molasses
- ☐ 1 cup/250 mL melon-flavored liqueur, brandy or sherry

Place golden raisins, currants, seeded raisins, mixed peels, dates, apricots, prunes, cherries, pineapple, honeydew and angelica in a large mixing bowl. Stir in honey or molasses and liqueur, brandy or sherry and mix well to combine. Cover tightly with plastic food wrap and stand overnight, or transfer to an airtight container and store in the refrigerator until required.

MINCEMEAT PIES

Makes 24
Oven temperature 350°F, 180°C

FRUIT FILLING
- ☐ 2 tablespoons honey or light molasses
- ☐ 1/2 cup/1 stick/125 g butter, frozen and shredded
- ☐ 1/4 quantity Basic Fruit Mixture

ALMOND PASTRY
- ☐ 2 cups/250 g all-purpose flour
- ☐ 1/2 cup/1 stick/125 g butter, chilled and cut into small pieces
- ☐ 2/3 cup/155 g oz superfine sugar
- ☐ 1/2 cup/60 g ground almonds
- ☐ 3 drops almond extract
- ☐ 5-6 tablespoons iced water

1   To make filling, place honey or molasses, butter and fruit mixture in a bowl and mix to combine. Set aside.

2   To make pastry, sift flour into a bowl. Cut in butter with pastry blender until mixture resembles fine bread crumbs. Stir in sugar, almonds, almond extract and enough water to mix to a firm dough. Wrap pastry in plastic food wrap and refrigerate for 30 minutes.

3   Roll out pastry to 1/8 in/3 mm thick and cut twenty-four 3 in/7 cm rounds and twenty-four 2 1/2 in/6 cm rounds, using biscuit cutters. Place large pastry rounds in lightly greased small muffin pans. Spoon in filling and top with smaller pastry rounds. Press edges together and bake for 15-20 minutes or until pastry is golden and crisp. Stand in pans for 10 minutes before removing to a wire rack to cool.

SPICY SYRUP CHRISTMAS CAKE

Makes a 9 in/23 cm square cake
Oven temperature 325°F, 160°C

- ☐ 1 cup/2 sticks/250 g butter
- ☐ 2 1/2 cups/425 g semolina
- ☐ 5 eggs, lightly beaten
- ☐ 1 cup/220 g superfine sugar
- ☐ 2 teaspoons pumpkin pie spice
- ☐ 1 teaspoon grated orange rind
- ☐ 1/2 quantity Basic Fruit Mixture

ORANGE SYRUP
- ☐ 1 orange
- ☐ 1 1/2 cups/375 mL water
- ☐ 1 1/2 cups/375 g sugar
- ☐ 1 cinnamon stick

1   Place butter in a large bowl and beat until light and creamy. Add semolina and beat in eggs one at a time, beating well after each addition.

2   Add superfine sugar a little at a time, beating well after each addition. Stir in spice, orange rind and fruit mixture. Mix well to combine. Spoon into a paper-lined 4-5 in/10-12 cm deep, 9 in/23 cm square cake pan. Bake for 2 1/2-3 hours or until cooked when tested with a skewer.

3   To make syrup, cut 2-3 thin slices of rind from the orange using a vegetable peeler. Place water, sugar, cinnamon stick and orange peel in a saucepan and cook over a medium heat, stirring constantly until sugar dissolves. Bring syrup to the boil without stirring, then reduce heat and simmer for 10 minutes. Set aside to cool slightly, then strain.

4   Pour syrup over cooked hot cake and set aside. Allow cake to completely cool in cake pan.

Preparing the cake pan: To achieve a good, evenly shaped cake, line your cake with heavy-duty aluminum foil, placing the shiny side against the tin. Cut three strips of newspaper or brown paper 2.5 cm/1 in wider than the depth of the cake tin. Position these strips around the outside of the tin and secure in place with string. The paper acts as an insulator and prevents the outside of the cake from burning.

STEAMED CHRISTMAS PUDDING

Serves 8

- ☐ 1 cup/2 sticks/250 g butter, softened
- ☐ 1/2 cup/100 g semolina
- ☐ 3 eggs, lightly beaten
- ☐ 1/3 cup/90 g honey or light molasses
- ☐ 2 1/4 cups/140 g rye bread crumbs, made from stale bread
- ☐ 7 oz/220 g ground hazelnuts (filberts) or almonds
- ☐ 1/4 quantity Basic Fruit Mixture

1   Place butter in a bowl and beat until light and fluffy. Add semolina, eggs and honey or molasses and beat well to combine. Fold in bread crumbs, hazelnuts or almonds and fruit mixture.

2   Spoon batter into a well-greased 8 cup/2 liter heatproof mold, round bottomed mixer bowl or steamed pudding basin. Cover with a large piece of greased aluminum foil. If using mold or bowl, place the lid over the foil and bring surplus foil up over it. If using a mold or bowl, tie the foil securely in position, using string. Lower pudding into a large saucepan or kettle containing sufficient boiling water to come halfway up the side of the basin and cook for 4 hours. Add more boiling water as required during the cooking. On completion of cooking remove and set aside to cool to room temperature. Refrigerate in basin for up to six weeks. On the day of serving steam for 1 hour then turn out and serve warm.

Cook's tip: Christmas pudding is delicious served with Hard Brandy Sauce. This can be made up to 3 months in advance and frozen, or it will keep in the refrigerator for up to a week. To make, place 1/2 cup/1 stick/125 g softened butter in a bowl and beat until light and fluffy. Add 2 cups/350 g sifted IOX (confectioners') sugar a little at a time, beating well after each addition until mixture is light and fluffy. Beat in 2 tablespoons brandy. Store and use as required.

SPONGE LAYER CAKE

Makes an 8 in/20 cm round cake
Oven temperature 350°F, 180°C

- ☐ **4 eggs**
- ☐ **²/₃ cup/155 g superfine sugar**
- ☐ **1 cup/125 g self-rising flour**
- ☐ **1 tablespoon cornstarch**
- ☐ **¹/₃ cup/90 mL warm water**
- ☐ **2 tablespoons melted butter**
- ☐ **1 tablespoon IOX (confectioners') sugar, sifted**

JAM AND CREAM FILLING
- ☐ **¹/₂ cup/155 g strawberry or raspberry jam**
- ☐ **¹/₂ cup/125 mL thick cream (double), whipped**
- ☐ **1 tablespoon IOX (confectioners') sugar**

1 Place eggs in a bowl and beat until thick and creamy. Gradually add sugar, beating well after each addition. Continue beating until mixture becomes thick. This will take about 10 minutes.

2 Sift together flour and cornstarch over egg mixture and fold in. Light fold in water and melted butter.

3 Divide mixture evenly between two greased parchment paper-lined 8 in/20 cm round cake layer pans and bake for 20-25 minutes or until cake shrinks away slightly from sides of pan and springs back when touched with the fingertips. Stand in cake pan for 5 minutes before turning onto wire racks to cool completely.

4 To assemble, spread one sponge layer with jam, then top with whipped cream and remaining sponge cake. Sprinkle top of cake with IOX sugar and serve.

ENGLISH TEA SCONES

Scones are a sweetened version of Baking Powder Biscuits. They are traditionally served warm, split in half and toppped with strawberry jam and whipped cream. Accompany with a cup of tea.

Makes 12
Oven temperature 425°F, 220°C

- ☐ **2 cups/250 g self-raising flour**
- ☐ **1 teaspoon baking powder**

- ☐ **2 teaspoons sugar**
- ☐ **3 tablespoons/45 g butter**
- ☐ **1 egg**
- ☐ **¹/₂ cup/125 mL milk**

1 Sift together flour and baking powder into a large mixing bowl. Stir in sugar, then rub in butter using fingertips until mixture resembles coarse bread crumbs.

2 Whisk together egg and milk. Make a well in center of flour mixture and pour in egg mixture. Mix to form a soft dough, turn onto a floured surface and knead lightly.

3 Press dough out to a 1³/₄ in/2 cm thickness, using palm of hand. Cut out rounds using a floured 2 in/5 cm cutter.

Avoid twisting the cutter or the scones will rise unevenly.

4 Arrange close together on a greased and lightly floured cookie sheet. Brush with a little milk and bake for 12-15 minutes or until golden brown.

English Tea Scones

FIG PINWHEEL COOKIES

Pinwheel Cookies always look impressive and are very easy to make. Just follow the step-by-step instructions for making these delicious cookies that wrap a spiced dough around a wonderful fig and almond filling.

Makes 50
Oven temperature 350°F, 180°C

- ☐ ²/₃ **cup/155 g butter**
- ☐ **1 cup/155 g packed brown sugar**
- ☐ **1 egg**
- ☐ ¹/₂ **teaspoon vanilla extract**
- ☐ **3 cups/375 g all-purpose flour**
- ☐ ¹/₂ **teaspoon baking soda**
- ☐ ¹/₄ **teaspoon ground cinnamon**
- ☐ ¹/₄ **teaspoon ground nutmeg**
- ☐ **2 tablespoons milk**

FIG AND ALMOND FILLING
- ☐ **1¹/₂ cups/250 g finely chopped dried figs**
- ☐ ¹/₄ **cup/60 g sugar**
- ☐ ¹/₂ **cup/125 mL water**
- ☐ ¹/₂ **teaspoon pumpkin pie spice**
- ☐ ¹/₂ **cup/30 g almonds, finely chopped**

1   To make filling, place figs, sugar, water and spice in a saucepan and bring to the boil. Reduce heat and cook, stirring, for 2-3 minutes or until mixture is thick. Remove from heat and stir in almonds. Set aside to cool.

2   Place butter in a large mixing bowl and beat until light and fluffy. Gradually add sugar, beating well after each addition until mixture is creamy. Beat in egg and vanilla.

3   Sift together flour, baking soda, cinnamon and nutmeg. Beat milk and half the flour mixture into butter mixture. Stir in remaining flour mixture. Turn dough onto a lightly floured surface and knead lightly. Roll into a ball, wrap in plastic food wrap and refrigerate for 30 minutes.

4   Divide dough into two portions. Roll out one portion to an 8 x 11 in/20 x 28 cm rectangle and spread with filling. Roll up from the long side, like a jelly roll. Repeat with remaining dough and filling. Wrap rolls in plastic food wrap and refrigerate for 15 minutes or until you are ready to cook the cookies.

5   Cut rolls into ¹/₂ in/1 cm slices. Place slices on greased cookie sheets and cook for 10-12 minutes. Stand cookies on sheets for 1 minute before removing to a wire rack to cool completely.

Freeze it: The uncooked rolls can be frozen if you wish. When you have unexpected guests or the cookie barrel is empty, these cookies are great standbys.

Divide dough into two portions. Roll out one portion to an 8 x 11 in/20 x 28 cm rectangle and spread with filling.

Roll up dough from the long side, like a jelly roll. Wrap rolls in plastic food wrap.

Cut rolls into ¹/₂ in/1 cm slices and place on greased cookie sheets.

BASIC BUTTER CAKE

The following recipe works perfectly using the cake pans and cooking times we have given in the chart.

- ☐ ¹/₂ cup/1 stick/125 g butter
- ☐ 1 teaspoon vanilla extract
- ☐ ³/₄ cup/185 g superfine sugar
- ☐ 2 eggs
- ☐ 1¹/₂ cups/185 g all-purpose flour, sifted
- ☐ 1¹/₂ teaspoons baking powder
- ☐ ¹/₂ cup/125 mL milk

1 Cream butter and vanilla extract in a small mixing bowl until light and fluffy. Add sugar gradually, beating well after each addition.

2 Beat in eggs one at a time and fold in. Combine flour and baking powder alternately with milk. Spoon mixture into prepared cake pan.

3 Bake according to size of cake pan you have chosen. Stand for 5 minutes before turning onto a wire rack to cool completely. When cooked, decorate with frosting or glaze of your choice.

Variations

Apple cake: Spread two-thirds of the cake mixture into the prepared cake pan. Top with ³/₄ cup/185 g stewed apple, then remaining cake mixture. Bake according to cake pan size. Stand 10 minutes before turning out.

Orange cake: Replace vanilla extract with 2 teaspoons grated orange rind when creaming butter. Substitute ¹/₃ cup/90 mL orange juice for milk. Bake according to cake pan size. Stand 5 minutes before turning out.

Coffee cake: Replace vanilla extract with 1 tablespoon instant coffee dissolved in 1 tablespoon boiling water. Cool then cream with butter. Bake according to cake pan size. Stand 5 minutes before turning out.

Coconut cake: Replace vanilla extract with ¹/₂ teaspoon coconut extract and add ¹/₂ cup/45 g flaked coconut with flour and baking powder. Bake according to cake pan size. Stand 5 minutes before turning out.

Banana cake: Omit milk and add 3 small very ripe mashed bananas to creamed butter and egg mixture. Combine flour, baking powder and 1 teaspoon baking soda and fold into butter and egg mixture. Bake according to cake pan size. Stand 5 minutes before turning out.

Basic Butter Cake, Apple Cake, Coffee Cake

Cook's tip: Test your cake just before the end of cooking time. Insert a skewer into the thickest part of the cake. If it comes away clean, your cake is cooked. If there is still cake mixture on the skewer, cook 5 minutes more then test again.

Alternatively, you can gently press the top of cake with your fingertips. When cooked, the depression will spring back quickly. When the cake starts to leave the sides of the pan, it is also a good indication that the cake is cooked.

PREPARATION
AND COOKING TIMES

TIN SIZE	PREPARATION	TEMPERATURE	COOKING TIME (minutes)
8 in/20 cm shallow ring pan	Grease and line with parchment paper	350°F, 180°C	40
4 in/10 cm deep, 8 in/20 cm round pan	Grease and line with parchment paper	350°F, 180°C	50
8 in/20 cm baba or kugelhopf pan	Lightly grease	350°F, 180°C	40
4$^1/_2$ x 8 in/11 x 21 cm loaf pan	Grease and line with parchment paper	350°F, 180°C	60
24 small cupcake pans	Paper cup cake liners	400°F, 200°C	15-20

LEMON CREAM CHEESE FROSTING

- ☐ 4 oz/125 g cream cheese, softened
- ☐ 1 teaspoon grated lemon rind
- ☐ 1½ cups/250 g IOX (confectioners') sugar, sifted
- ☐ 2 teaspooons lemon juice

Beat cream cheese in a small mixing bowl until creamy. Add lemon rind, IOX sugar and lemon juice and mix well.

Cook's tip: To soften cream cheese, leave at room temperature. To soften in the microwave, remove foil wrap, place in a microwave-safe dish and cook on HIGH (100%) for 20 seconds.

CHOCOLATE FROSTING

- ☐ 3 oz/90 g butter
- ☐ 1½ cups/250 g IOX (confectioners') sugar, sifted
- ☐ 1 tablespoon cocoa powder, sifted
- ☐ 2 tablespoons cream

Beat butter in a small bowl until creamy. Add IOX sugar, cocoa powder and cream. Beat until frosting is of a spreadable consistency.

Coconut Cake, Banana Cake, Orange Cake

COFFEE FROSTING

- ☐ ¼ cup/½ stick/60 g butter
- ☐ 1½ cups/250 g IOX (confectioners') sugar, sifted
- ☐ 2 teaspoons instant coffee powder, dissolved in 4 teaspoons boiling water

Beat butter in a small mixing bowl until creamy. Add IOX sugar and cooled coffee mixture and beat until frosting is of a spreadable consistency.

ORANGE CREAM FROSTING

- ☐ 2 oz/60 g cream cheese
- ☐ 2 tablespoons cream
- ☐ 1 teaspoon grated orange rind
- ☐ 1½ cups/250 g IOX (confectioners') sugar, sifted

Beat cream cheese, cream and orange rind in a small mixing bowl until creamy. Add IOX sugar and beat until smooth.

Cook's Tip: Butter frosting can be used as a filling for cakes or made to a thicker consistency for piping.

EASY BERRY BREAD

Finding an ingredient hidden inside a quickbread or a cake is always fun. To make sure the berries stay hidden in this Easy Berry Bread during cooking do not overfill the dough. Follow these simple step-by-step instructions and make this Easy Berry Bread.

Makes a 7 in/18 cm round
Oven temperature 425°F, 220°C

- ☐ **3 cups/375 g self-rising flour**
- ☐ **1 teaspoon baking powder**
- ☐ **1½ teaspoons pumpkin pie spice**
- ☐ **1½ tablespoons sugar**
- ☐ **2 tablespoons/30 g butter**
- ☐ **½ cup/125 mL milk**
- ☐ **⅔ cup/155 mL water**
- ☐ **7 oz/220 g raspberries**
- ☐ **1 tablespoon extra sugar**
- ☐ **4 teaspoons milk**

1   Sift together flour, baking powder and spice into a mixing bowl. Add sugar and cut in butter with two knives or a pastry blender until mixture resembles coarse bread crumbs.

2   Make a well in the center of flour mixture and, using a fork, mix in milk and water. Mix to form a soft dough.

3   Turn dough onto a floured surface and knead lightly until smooth. Divide dough into two portions and flatten each into an 8 in/20 cm round. Sprinkle raspberries and sugar over surface of one round leaving 1 in/2.5 cm around edge. Brush edge with a little milk and place remaining round on top. Seal edges securely using fingertips.

4   Place on a greased and lightly floured cookie sheet. Brush surface with milk and bake for 10 minutes. Reduce oven temperature to 350°F/180°C and bake for 20-25 minutes longer or until cooked through.

Make a well in the center of flour mixture and, using a round-ended knife, mix in milk and water to form a soft dough.

Divide dough into two portions and flatten each into an 8 in/20 cm round. Sprinkle raspberries and sugar over one round leaving 1 in/2.5 cm around edge.

Place remaining round on top and seal edges securely using fingertips.

COCONUT CAKE

Makes a 9 in/23 cm round 2 layer cake
Oven temperature 350°F, 180°C

- [ ] $^1/_2$ cup/1 stick/125 g butter, softened
- [ ] 1 teaspoon vanilla extract
- [ ] 1 cup/220 g superfine sugar
- [ ] 3 egg whites
- [ ] 2 cups/250 g self-rising flour, sifted
- [ ] $^3/_4$ cup/185 mL milk
- [ ] 3 oz/90 g flaked coconut

FLUFFY FROSTING
- [ ] $^1/_2$ cup/125 mL water
- [ ] 1$^1/_4$ cups/315 g sugar
- [ ] 3 egg whites
- [ ] 1 teaspoon lemon juice

1   Place butter and vanilla extract in a mixing bowl and beat until light and fluffy. Gradually add superfine sugar, beating well after each addition until mixture is creamy.
2   Beat in egg whites, one at a time. Fold flour and milk, alternately, into creamed mixture. Divide batter evenly between two greased and parchment paper-lined 9 in/ 23 cm layer pans and bake for 25-30 minutes or until cakes are cooked when tested with a skewer. Stand in pans for 5 minutes before turning onto a wire rack to cool.
3   To make frosting, place water and sugar in a saucepan and cook over a medium heat, without boiling, stirring constantly until sugar dissolves. Brush any sugar from sides of pan using a pastry brush dipped in water. Bring syrup to the boil and boil rapidly for 3-5 minutes, without stirring, or until syrup reaches the soft ball stage (239°F/115°C on a candy thermometer). Place egg whites in a mixing bowl and beat until soft peaks form. Continue beating while pouring in syrup in a thin stream a little at a time. Continue beating until all syrup is used and frosting will stand in stiff peaks. Beat in lemon juice.
4   Spread one cake with a little frosting and sprinkle with 2 tablespoons coconut, then top with remaining cake. Spread remaining frosting over top and sides of cake and sprinkle with remaining coconut.

Cook's tip: This cake looks pretty when decorated with edible flowers such as violets, rose petals or borage.

OATY CHOC-CHIP COOKIES

Makes 25
Oven temperature 375°F, 190°C

- [ ] $^1/_2$ cup/1 stick/125 g butter, softened
- [ ] $^1/_2$ teaspoon vanilla extract
- [ ] $^3/_4$ cup/125 g brown sugar
- [ ] 1 egg
- [ ] $^1/_2$ teaspoon baking soda dissolved in 4 teaspoons warm water
- [ ] $^3/_4$ cup/90 g all-purpose flour, sifted
- [ ] 1$^1/_2$ cups/140 g rolled oats
- [ ] $^1/_2$ cup/45 g flaked coconut
- [ ] 6 oz/185 g semi-sweet chocolate chips
- [ ] $^1/_2$ cup/75 g seeded raisins, chopped

1   Place butter, vanilla extract and sugar in a bowl and beat until light and creamy. Beat in egg, baking soda mixture and flour.
2   Stir in oats, coconut, chocolate chips and chopped raisins. Place rounded tablespoons of mixture 4 in/10 cm apart on greased cookie sheets. Using a knife, spread out each mound of mixture to form a thin round, 3 in/7.5 cm in diameter. Bake for 8-10 minutes or until golden. Transfer to wire racks to cool.

ORANGE COCONUT LOAF

Makes a 4$^1/_2$ x 8$^1/_2$ in/11 x 21 cm loaf
Oven temperature 350°F, 180°C

- [ ] 1 cup/220 g superfine sugar
- [ ] 3 oz/90 g butter, softened
- [ ] 1 teaspoon vanilla extract
- [ ] 1 tablespoon finely grated orange rind
- [ ] $^3/_4$ cup/185 mL canned coconut milk
- [ ] 3 egg whites
- [ ] 1$^1/_2$ cups/200 g self-rising flour, sifted
- [ ] 1 teaspoon baking powder

1   Place sugar, butter, vanilla and orange rind in a food processor and process until combined. Add coconut milk, egg whites, flour and baking powder and process until just combined and smooth.
2   Pour batter into a greased and parchment paper-lined standard 4$^1/_2$ x 8$^1/_2$ in/11 x 21 cm loaf pan and bake for 35-40 minutes or until cooked when tested with a skewer. Stand for 5 minutes in pan. Turn out and cool on a wire rack.

LIME AND COCONUT COOKIES

The tang of lime and the unique flavor and texture of coconut combine to make these wonderful cookies.

Makes 35
Oven temperature 350°F, 180°C

- [ ] $^1/_2$ cup/1 stick/125 g butter, chopped
- [ ] 1 cup/170 g packed brown sugar
- [ ] 1 teaspoon vanilla extract
- [ ] 1 egg
- [ ] 1 cup/125 g all-purpose flour
- [ ] $^1/_2$ cup/60 g self-rising flour
- [ ] 1 cup/90 g rolled oats
- [ ] $^1/_2$ cup/45 g flaked coconut
- [ ] 2 teaspoons finely grated lime rind
- [ ] 2 tablespoons lime juice

1   Place butter, sugar, vanilla extract, egg, flour and self-rising flour, rolled oats, coconut, lime rind and lime juice in a food processor and process until well combined.
2   Place heaped spoonfuls of mixture on greased cookie sheets and bake for 12-15 minutes or until lightly browned. Cool on wire racks.

GOLDEN OAT COOKIES

Makes 30
Oven temperature 350°F, 180°C

- [ ] 1 cup/90 g rolled oats
- [ ] 1 cup/125 g flour, sifted
- [ ] 1 cup/90 g flaked coconut
- [ ] 1 cup/250 g sugar
- [ ] 4 teaspoons honey or light molasses, warmed
- [ ] $^1/_2$ cup/1 stick/125 g butter, melted
- [ ] 3 tablespoons boiling water
- [ ] 1 teaspoon baking soda

1   Place oats, flour, coconut and sugar in a large mixing bowl. Combine honey, butter, water and baking soda.
2   Pour honey mixture into dry ingredients and mix well to combine. Place spoonfuls of mixture 1$^1/_4$ in/3 cm apart on greased cookie sheets and bake for 10-15 minutes or until cookies are just firm. Stand on sheets for 3 minutes before transferring to wire racks to cool.

Golden Oat Biscuits,
Lime and Coconut Cookies

APRICOT DANISH PASTRIES

Makes 8
Oven temperature 425°F, 220°C

- [ ] **2 sheets/500 g frozen pre-rolled puff pastry sheets, thawed**
- [ ] **8 canned apricot halves, drained**
- [ ] **1 quantity Apricot Glaze (below)**

1 Cut each pastry sheet into four 4$\frac{1}{4}$ in/11 cm squares. Make four 2$\frac{1}{4}$ in/5.5 cm cuts, starting from each corner and cutting towards the center of each pastry square.
2 Fold one half of each corner to center and place an apricot over the top. Repeat with remaining pastry squares and apricots.
3 Place pastries on greased cookie sheets and bake for 15-20 minutes or until puffed and golden. Brush hot pastries with glaze. Cool pastries on a wire rack.

SWEET CHEESE PASTRIES

Makes 8
Oven temperature 425°F, 220°C

- [ ] **2 sheets/500 g frozen pre-rolled puff pastry sheets, thawed**
- [ ] **1 tablespoon water**
- [ ] **1 quantity Apricot Glaze**

CREAM CHEESE FILLING
- [ ] **6 oz/185 g cream cheese**
- [ ] **1 egg yolk**
- [ ] **2 tablespoons superfine sugar**

1 To make filling, place cream cheese, egg yolk and sugar in a food processor or blender and process until smooth.
2 Cut each pastry sheet into four 4$\frac{1}{2}$ in/11 cm squares. Spread filling over half of each pastry rectangle leaving a $\frac{1}{2}$ in/1 cm border. Brush edge with a little water and fold pastry over to enclose filling. Press edges firmly together to seal. Cut six slits 1$\frac{1}{4}$ in/3 cm in length along joined edges of pastry. Repeat with remaining pastry rectangles and filling.
3 Place pastries on greased cookie sheets and bake for 15-20 minutes or until puffed and golden. Brush hot pastries with glaze. Cool pastries on a wire rack.

CHERRY SQUARES

Makes 8
Oven temperature 425°F, 220°C

- [ ] **2 sheets/500 g frozen pre-rolled puff pastry sheets, thawed**
- [ ] **1 quantity Apricot Glaze**

CHERRY FILLING
- [ ] **3 cups/750 g bottled, pitted morello (sour) cherries, drained**
- [ ] **$\frac{1}{4}$ cup/60 g superfine sugar**
- [ ] **1 teaspoon ground cinnamon**

1 To make filling, combine cherries, sugar and cinnamon in a bowl. Set aside.
2 Cut each pastry sheet into four 4$\frac{1}{2}$ in/11 cm squares. Roll in edges to form a narrow rim, then place a spoonful of filling in center of each pastry square.
3 Place pastries on greased cookie sheets and bake for 15-20 minutes or until puffed and golden. Brush hot pastries with glaze. Cool pastries on a wire rack.

APRICOT GLAZE

- [ ] **$\frac{1}{2}$ cup/155 g apricot jam**
- [ ] **4 teaspoons water**

Place jam and water in a small saucepan and cook over a high heat until mixture boils. Remove from heat and use as required.

From top: Sweet Cheese Pastries, Apricot Danish Pastries, Cherry Squares

MASTER CLASS

BEST EVER COCOA CAKE

Makes an 8 in/20 cm round cake
Oven temperature 350°F, 180°C

- ☐ ³/₄ cup/90 g **cocoa powder**
- ☐ 1¹/₂ cups/375 mL **boiling water**
- ☐ ³/₄ cup/1¹/₂ sticks/185 g **butter**
- ☐ 1³/₄ cups/440 g **superfine sugar**
- ☐ 2 tablespoons **raspberry jam**
- ☐ 3 **eggs**
- ☐ 2¹/₄ cups/300 g **self-rising flour**

CHOCOLATE MOCHA FROSTING
- ☐ ¹/₂ cup/1 stick/125 g **butter**
- ☐ 2 cups/330 g **IOX (confectioners') sugar, sifted**
- ☐ 2 tablespoons **cocoa powder, sifted**
- ☐ 2 teaspoons **instant coffee**
- ☐ 2 tablespoons **milk**

DECORATION
- ☐ **candied cherries**
- ☐ **silver dragees**

1 Combine cocoa powder and boiling water, and mix to dissolve. Allow to cool completely.

2 Cream butter, sugar and jam until light and fluffy. Beat in eggs one at a time, adding a little flour with each egg. Fold in remaining flour and cocoa mixture alternately.

3 Spoon mixture into two greased and parchment paper-lined 8 in/20 cm cake layer pans and bake for 35 minutes or until cooked.

4 To make frosting, place butter in a small mixing bowl. Beat until creamy. Add IOX sugar a little at a time, beating well after each addition. Combine cocoa powder and coffee and mix to a smooth paste with milk, then beat into frosting.

5 Frost cake when cold and decorate with candied cherries and silver dragees.

Spread one layer of cake with frosting.

Top with second cake layer. Cover top and sides of cake with frosting.

Decorate cake with candied cherries and silver dragees.

chapter twelve

JUST A SNACK

A *little taste of something*
delicious is 'good for the soul' . . .
not to mention children's morning
break at school, mid-afternoon
in a frantic office, or whenever
time is short and food
is needed.

Fruity Banana and Camembert Muffins,
Chili Bean Tacos, French Onion Rolls

FRENCH ONION ROLLS

Serves 4
Oven temperature 400°F, 200°C

- [ ] **4 wholewheat rolls**
- [ ] **1 tablespoon/15 g butter**
- [ ] **1 large onion, sliced**
- [ ] **2 eggs, lightly beaten**
- [ ] **$1/2$ cup/125 g dairy sour cream**
- [ ] **$1/4$ cup/60 mL evaporated milk**
- [ ] **$1/2$ teaspoon ground nutmeg**
- [ ] **1 teaspoon bottled horseradish**
- [ ] **freshly ground black pepper**
- [ ] **1 cup/125 g shredded Cheddar cheese**

1   Cut tops from rolls and scoop out centers, leaving about $1/2$ in/1 cm thick shell. Place rolls on a baking sheet and set aside.
2   Melt butter in a skillet and cook onion for 4-5 minutes or until golden. Divide onion between rolls.
3   Place eggs, sour cream, milk, nutmeg and horseradish in a bowl. Mix to combine and season to taste with black pepper. Spoon egg mixture into rolls, top with cheese and bake for 20-25 minutes or until firm.

TOMATO AND MOZZARELLA PIZZA SUBS

Serves 2

- [ ] **2 long wholewheat rolls, split and toasted**
- [ ] **2 tablespoons tomato paste**
- [ ] **1 small onion, chopped**
- [ ] **1 tablespoon finely chopped fresh basil**
- [ ] **4 olives, pitted and sliced**
- [ ] **1 tablespoon pine nuts (pignola)**
- [ ] **$1/4$ cup/30 g shredded mozzarella cheese**
- [ ] **freshly ground black pepper**

1   Spread each roll half with tomato paste. Top with onion, then sprinkle with basil, olives, pine nuts and cheese. Season to taste with black pepper.
2   Cook under a preheated broiler for 4-5 minutes or until cheese melts and topping is golden.

PITA PIZZA ROLL-UPS

Makes 6
Oven temperature 425°F, 220°C

- [ ] **$1/4$ cup/60 mL tomato paste**
- [ ] **2 tablespoons chopped fresh basil**
- [ ] **$1/4$ cup/60 mL chopped pitted olives**
- [ ] **6 large pita bread rounds**
- [ ] **6 oz/185 g button mushrooms, chopped**
- [ ] **1 small red pepper, sliced**
- [ ] **1 onion, chopped**
- [ ] **$3/4$ cup/200 g ricotta cheese**
- [ ] **$1^1/2$ cups/200 g shredded mozzarella cheese**

1   Place tomato paste, basil and olives in a bowl and mix to combine. Divide mixture into six portions and spread over pitta bread rounds. Top with mushrooms, red pepper, onion and ricotta cheese. Roll up tightly and secure with a toothpick.
2   Place rolls on a cookie sheet, sprinkle with mozzarella cheese and bake for 15-20 minutes or until cheese melts and rolls are heated through.

CHILI BEAN TACOS

Serves 4
Oven temperature 350°F, 180°C

- [ ] **14 oz/440 g canned red kidney beans, drained and rinsed**
- [ ] **1 teaspoon ground cumin**
- [ ] **1 tomato, peeled and chopped**
- [ ] **1 teaspoon chili sauce**
- [ ] **8 taco shells**
- [ ] **4 lettuce leaves, shredded**
- [ ] **shredded Cheddar cheese**

1   Place kidney beans, cumin, tomato and chili sauce in a saucepan and cook over a medium heat for 3-4 minutes or until heated through.
2   Arrange taco shells on a baking sheet and heat for 5 minutes or until heated through. Fill taco shells with bean mixture. Top with shredded lettuce and cheese. Serve immediately.

CHEESY CHICKEN PASTIES

Makes 10 pasties
Oven temperature 400°F, 200°C

- [ ] **12 oz/375 g prepared short (flaky) pastry**
- [ ] **2 tablespoons milk**

CHICKEN FILLING
- [ ] **2 tablespoons/30 g butter**
- [ ] **1 clove garlic, crushed**
- [ ] **2 boned skinned chicken breast halves, chopped**
- [ ] **8 button mushrooms, sliced**
- [ ] **6 stalks asparagus, chopped**
- [ ] **2 tablespoons dairy sour cream**
- [ ] **$1/2$ cup/60 g shredded Cheddar cheese**
- [ ] **2 tablespoons grated Parmesan cheese**
- [ ] **1 tablespoon chopped fresh parsley**
- [ ] **freshly ground black pepper**

1   Roll out pastry to $1/8$ in/3 mm thick and, using an upturned saucer as a guide, cut out ten $5^1/4$ in/13 cm circles.
2   To make filling, melt 1 tablespoon/15 g butter in a skillet, add garlic and chicken and cook for 3-4 minutes or until chicken is just cooked. Remove chicken mixture from pan and set aside to cool. Melt remaining butter in pan, add mushrooms and asparagus and cook over a high heat for 3-4 minutes or until asparagus is tender crisp. Remove vegetable mixture from pan and set aside to cool.
3   Combine chicken mixture, vegetable mixture, sour cream, Cheddar, Parmesan cheese, parsley and black pepper to taste. Place a spoonful of mixture in the center of each pastry round and brush edges of pastry with a little water. Draw edges together over top of filling, press to seal and crimp edges with fingertips to form a fluted pattern.
4   Brush pastry parcels with a little milk, place on a greased baking sheet and bake for 20-25 minutes or until golden and heated through.

MIDDLE EASTERN POCKET SANDWICHES

Pita bread makes a wonderful container for holding all kinds of your favorite fillings. We have filled our pocket bread with refreshing cucumber salad, exotic lettuce leaves and succulent chunks of lean roast lamb.

Serves 4

- [ ] **4 wholewheat pita breads**
- [ ] **lettuce leaves**
- [ ] **1 lb/500 g lean roast lamb, cut into $^1/_2$ in/1 cm chunks**
- [ ] **fresh mint sprigs for garnish**

CUCUMBER AND YOGURT SALAD
- [ ] **1 cucumber, chopped**
- [ ] **3 spring onions, finely chopped**
- [ ] **$^1/_4$ cup/60 g finely chopped fresh mint leaves**
- [ ] **1$^1/_4$ cups/300 g plain yogurt**
- [ ] **1 tablespoon lemon juice**
- [ ] **$^1/_2$ teaspoon chili sauce, or according to taste**
- [ ] **freshly ground black pepper**

1   Cut pita breads in half and carefully open. Line each half with lettuce leaves.
2   To make salad, place cucumber, spring onions and mint in a bowl. Mix together yogurt, lemon juice and chili sauce. Pour over cucumber salad and fold gently to combine. Season to taste with black pepper.
3   Spoon salad and lamb into pita pockets. Serve with fresh mint sprigs.

SMOKED SALMON ON RYE

Makes 4 sandwiches

- [ ] **5 oz/155 g thinly sliced smoked salmon**
- [ ] **4 slices rye bread**
- [ ] **juice $^1/_2$ lemon**
- [ ] **$^1/_2$ red onion, cut into thin slices**
- [ ] **8 thin slices cucumber**
- [ ] **4 teaspoons drained capers**
- [ ] **4 thin slices lemon**
- [ ] **freshly ground black pepper**
- [ ] **fresh dill sprigs for garnish**

1   Arrange salmon on bread slices and sprinkle with a little lemon juice.
2   Place onion on salmon. Arrange cucumber, capers and lemon slices attractively on top. Season with plenty of freshly ground black pepper and garnish with dill sprigs. Serve with a tossed green salad.

AVOCADO AND CHICKEN ON PUMPERNICKEL

Makes 4 open sandwiches

- [ ] **1 large avocado, pitted and peeled**
- [ ] **juice 1 lemon**
- [ ] **4 slices pumpernickel bread**
- [ ] **5 oz/155 g watercress**
- [ ] **fresh mint sprigs for garnish**

CHICKEN SALAD
- [ ] **1$^1/_2$ /300 g chopped cooked chicken**
- [ ] **2 spring onions, finely chopped**
- [ ] **1 tablespoon pine nuts (pignola)**
- [ ] **1 teaspoon finely chopped fresh mint**
- [ ] **2 tablespoons mayonnaise**

1   Cut avocado into 12 slices and sprinkle with lemon juice.
2   To make chicken salad, combine chicken, spring onions, pine nuts, mint and mayonnaise in a bowl.
3   Divide watercress between bread slices and top with chicken salad. Arrange three avocado slices on top of chicken salad and garnish with mint sprigs.

FRUITY BANANA AND CAMEMBERT MUFFINS

Serves 4

- [ ] **1 large banana, sliced**
- [ ] **$^1/_2$ green apple, chopped**
- [ ] **$^1/_2$ stalk celery, sliced**
- [ ] **$^1/_4$ cup/30 g pecans**
- [ ] **2 teaspoons flaked coconut**
- [ ] **2 tablespoons mayonnaise**
- [ ] **4 English muffins, halved, lightly toasted and buttered**
- [ ] **4 oz/125 g Camembert cheese, sliced**

Combine banana, apple, celery, pecans, coconut and mayonnaise. Spoon onto toasted muffin halves and top with Camembert slices. Broil under a medium heat until cheese melts. Serve immediately.

Smoked Salmon on Rye,
Avocado and Chicken on Pumpernickel,
Middle Eastern Pocket Sandwiches

SALMON TOASTIES

This easy snack uses pantry ingredients and is just as delicious made with canned tuna.

Makes 2 toasties
Oven temperature 400°F, 200°C

- ☐ ²/₃ cup/155 g drained canned salmon
- ☐ ¹/₄ cup/60 g dairy sour cream
- ☐ 2 teaspoons lemon juice
- ☐ 2 teaspoons chopped fresh dill weed or parsley
- ☐ freshly ground black pepper
- ☐ 1 tablespoon/15 g butter
- ☐ 4 slices bread, crusts removed

1 Place salmon, sour cream, lemon juice, dill or parsley and black pepper to taste in a small bowl and mix to combine. Lightly butter bread on one side.
2 Spread half of the salmon mixture over unbuttered side of 2 slices of bread. Cover with remaining bread slices, buttered side up. Secure sides with toothpicks.
3 Place on a greased baking sheet and bake for 10 minutes or until bread is crisp and golden.

Cook's tip: If you do not have any sour cream or mayonnaise, plain yogurt can be used instead.

NACHOS

Serves 4
Oven temperature 400°F, 200°C

- ☐ 5 oz/155 g corn chips
- ☐ 2 tomatoes, peeled and finely chopped
- ☐ 1 cup/125 g shredded mozzarella cheese
- ☐ 1 cup/125 g shredded monterey jack cheese

AVOCADO TOPPING
- ☐ 2 small avocados, peeled and chopped
- ☐ 2 teaspoons lemon juice
- ☐ 1 small onion, grated
- ☐ 2 cloves garlic, crushed
- ☐ 1 teaspoon chili sauce

1 Layer corn chips, tomatoes, mozzarella and jack cheese in an ovenproof dish, finishing with a layer of jack cheese and bake for 10-15 minutes or until cheese melts and is golden.
2 To make topping, place avocados, lemon juice, onion, garlic and chili sauce in a food processor or blender and process until smooth. Spoon into center of hot corn chips and serve immediately.

HAM AND CORN TRIANGLES

Makes 4 triangles
Oven temperature 350°F, 180°C

- ☐ 2 slices bread
- ☐ 1 tablespoon/15 g butter, melted

CORN TOPPING
- ☐ ¹/₄ cup/60 g canned creamed corn
- ☐ 1 spring onion, finely chopped
- ☐ 1 slice canned pineapple, chopped
- ☐ 1 slice packaged ham, finely chopped
- ☐ ¹/₄ cup/60 g shredded Cheddar cheese

1 Cut each slice of bread in half diagonally and brush both sides with butter. Place bread triangles on a baking sheet and bake for 5 minutes or until crisp on both sides.
2 Top toasted triangles with corn, spring onion, pineapple, ham and cheese. Bake for 5 minutes or until cheese is melted and golden.

From left: Open Focaccia Sandwich, Ham and Corn Triangles, Salmon Toasties

OPEN FOCACCIA SANDWICH

For something different use any of your favorite breads, spreads, meats and vegetables to make this sandwich.

Makes 1 serving

- ☐ 1 piece focaccia bread, halved and buttered
- ☐ 4 slices roast beef or lamb
- ☐ ¼ avocado, peeled and sliced
- ☐ 4 cherry tomatoes, sliced
- ☐ 1 teaspoon finely chopped fresh rosemary (optional)
- ☐ 4 slices Swiss cheese
- ☐ freshly ground black pepper

To assemble sandwiches, top focaccia with beef or lamb, avocado and tomatoes then sprinkle with rosemary (if used) and top with Swiss cheese. Season to taste with black pepper.

Toasted Focaccia Sandwich: Toasted, this sandwich is a wonderful light evening meal. Toast focaccia slices under a preheated broiler on both sides before buttering. Prepare as in recipe then place under a preheated medium broiler and cook for 3-4 minutes or until heated and cheese is melted.

Cook's tip: Why not use a bread that you have not tried before to make this sandwich. There are many breads available from bread shops, supermarkets and delicatessens. You might try using white bread, wholewheat bread, multigrain bread, rye bread, sandwich rolls, baguettes/French rolls, pita bread, crispbread or bagels. Remember that bread freezes well so you can buy a whole loaf and any leftover can be frozen to use at a later date.

SALMON SCROLLS

Smoked salmon with a tasty filling makes a perfect treat. Or you might like to serve these scrolls with a mixed lettuce and fresh herb salad as a first course or light meal.

Serves 2

- ☐ **4 slices smoked salmon**
- ☐ **1 tablespoon chopped fresh parsley**
- ☐ **2 teaspoons chopped fresh dill weed**

CREAM CHEESE FILLING
- ☐ **4 oz/125 g cream cheese**
- ☐ **2 tablespoons dairy sour cream**
- ☐ **2 teaspoons coarse grain mustard**
- ☐ **2 teaspoons lemon juice**
- ☐ **freshly ground black pepper**

1 Place salmon in a rectangle shape on a piece of plastic food wrap.
2 To make filling, beat together cream cheese, sour cream, mustard, lemon juice and black pepper to taste. Spread evenly over salmon slices and sprinkle with parsley and dill.
3 Roll up salmon widthwise, like a jelly roll, cover and refrigerate until firm. To serve, cut into $^1/_2$ in/1 cm rounds.

EGGPLANT DIP WITH FRESH VEGETABLES

Serves 4
Oven temperature 400°F, 200°C

- ☐ **1 large eggplant**
- ☐ **$^1/_3$ cup/90 mL plain yogurt**
- ☐ **2 tablespoons lemon juice**
- ☐ **$^1/_4$ cup/30 g chopped fresh parsley**
- ☐ **2 cloves garlic, crushed**
- ☐ **2 tablespoons olive oil**
- ☐ **1 tablespoon tahini (sesame seed) paste**
- ☐ **fresh parsley sprigs**
- ☐ **paprika**
- ☐ **selection crisp vegetables such as snow peas, carrot sticks, cauliflower florets and radishes**

1 Prick eggplant in several places with a fork and place in an ovenproof dish. Bake for 40-45 minutes or until tender. Set aside until cool enough to handle.
2 Peel skin off eggplant and coarsely chop flesh. Place eggplant flesh, yogurt, lemon juice, parsley, garlic, oil and tahini paste in a food processor or blender and process until smooth. Transfer to a bowl and garnish with parsley sprigs and paprika. Serve with vegetables.

FRUITY APRICOT COOKIES

Makes 25
Oven temperature 350°F, 180°C

- ☐ **$^1/_2$ cup/1 stick/125 g butter**
- ☐ **$^3/_4$ cup/125 g packed brown sugar**
- ☐ **$^1/_2$ teaspoon ground cinnamon**
- ☐ **1 egg**
- ☐ **$^1/_2$ cup/60 g self-rising flour**
- ☐ **$^2/_3$ cup/75 g wholewheat all-purpose flour**
- ☐ **1 teaspoon baking powder**
- ☐ **2 tablespoons/15 g wheat germ**
- ☐ **$^1/_3$ cup/30 g flaked coconut**
- ☐ **$^1/_2$ cup/45 g rolled oats**
- ☐ **$^3/_4$ cup/90 g dried apricots, chopped**
- ☐ **1cup/60 g dried apples, chopped**
- ☐ **$^1/_4$ cup/45 g currants**

1 Place butter and sugar in a mixing bowl and beat until light and fluffy. Stir in egg, then fold in flours, baking powder, wheat germ, coconut, rolled oats, apricots, apples and currants. Mix to combine ingredients.
2 Roll spoonfuls of mixture into balls, place on lightly greased cookie sheets and flatten slightly with a fork. Bake for 10-12 minutes, or until cookies are firm. Remove from oven and cool on sheets.

ENERGY BARS

Great to have on hand as after work or school snacks, or tuck them into your bag for a quick boost of energy during the day.

Makes 20

- ☐ **2 cups/60 g crisp rice cereal**
- ☐ **$^2/_3$ cup/75 g bran flake cereal, lightly crushed**
- ☐ **$^3/_4$ cup/75 g flaked coconut**
- ☐ **$^1/_2$ cup/60 g dried apricots, chopped**
- ☐ **$^1/_2$ cup/30 g dried apples, chopped**
- ☐ **$^1/_2$ cup/60 g candied pineapple, chopped**
- ☐ **$^1/_2$ cup/90 g golden raisins**
- ☐ **1 teaspoon ground cinnamon**
- ☐ **$^1/_2$ cup/90 g packed brown sugar**
- ☐ **3 oz/90 g butter**
- ☐ **$^1/_2$ cup/185 g honey**
- ☐ **$^1/_2$ cup/125 mL coconut milk**

1 Place rice cereal, bran flakes, coconut, apricots, apples, pineapple, raisins and cinnamon in a bowl and mix to combine.
2 Place brown sugar, butter, honey and coconut milk in a small saucepan and cook over a low heat, stirring, until sugar and honey melt and all ingredients combine. Bring to the boil, reduce heat and simmer for 5 minutes or until mixture is thick and syrupy. Pour over dry ingredients and mix well. Press into a greased and parchment paper-lined 6 x 10 in/15 x 25 cm shallow cake pan and refrigerate until set. Cut into bars and store in an airtight container.

RICE CAKES WITH THREE TOPPINGS

Each topping is enough for 4 rice cakes

- ☐ **4 rice cakes**

FRUITY TOPPING
- ☐ **$^1/_4$ cup/90 g strawberry jam**
- ☐ **2 bananas, sliced**
- ☐ **2 tablespoons sunflower seeds**

Spread rice cakes with jam, top with banana slices and sprinkle with sunflower seeds.

NUTTY CHEESE TOPPING
- ☐ **2 tablespoons peanut butter**
- ☐ **$^1/_2$ cup/125 g cottage cheese**
- ☐ **1 apple, cored and sliced**

Spread rice cakes with peanut butter, top with cottage cheese and apple slices.

SALMON TOPPING
- ☐ **7 oz/220 g canned salmon, drained**
- ☐ **$^1/_4$ cup/60 mL plain yogurt or dairy sour cream**
- ☐ **2 teaspoons lemon juice**
- ☐ **2 teaspoons Dijon mustard**
- ☐ **freshly ground black pepper**
- ☐ **1 oz/30 g bean sprouts**

Mix together salmon, yogurt or sour cream, lemon juice, mustard and black pepper to taste. Place sprouts on rice cakes and top with salmon mixture.

Top shelf from left: Fruity Apricot Cookies, Energy Bars, Rice Cakes with Three Toppings.
Bottom shelf from left: Salmon Scrolls, Eggplant Dip with Fresh Vegetables

CROSTINI

This super-quick snack can be topped with olives and red pepper just before serving if you wish.

Serves 2

- ☐ **1 clove garlic, crushed**
- ☐ **8 black olives, pitted and finely chopped**
- ☐ **1 tablespoon capers, finely chopped**
- ☐ **1/3 cup/90 mL olive oil**
- ☐ **4 slices wholewheat bread, crusts removed and slices cut in half**
- ☐ **3 oz/90 g mozzarella cheese, thinly sliced**

1   Place garlic, olives, capers and 1 tablespoon oil in a food processor or blender and process until smooth. Spread garlic mixture over half the bread slices. Top with cheese and remaining bread slices.

2   Brush top of each sandwich with oil and cook under a preheated broiler until lightly browned. Turn over, brush with remaining oil and broil until brown.

EGG AND MUSTARD HAM ROLLS

In this recipe the eggs are baked in the oven. These rolls make a great snack or a delicious brunch.

Serves 4
Oven temperature 350°F, 180°C

- ☐ **4 wholewheat rolls**
- ☐ **2 tablespoons coarse grain mustard**
- ☐ **1 tablespoon/15 g butter**
- ☐ **1 1/2 oz/45 g button mushrooms, sliced**
- ☐ **1 onion, chopped**
- ☐ **1 1/2 oz/45 g packaged sliced ham, cut into strips**
- ☐ **freshly ground black pepper**
- ☐ **4 eggs**
- ☐ **1/2 cup/60 g shredded Cheddar cheese**

1   Cut a slice from the top of each bread roll, set aside and reserve. Scoop out the center, leaving a thin shell and reserve crumbs for another use. Spread inside of each roll with mustard.

2   Melt butter in a skillet and cook mushrooms and onion for 2-3 minutes over a medium heat. Add ham and cook for 2 minutes longer. Divide the mixture between the rolls and sprinkle with black pepper to taste.

3   Break an egg into a small bowl, then slide it into a roll. Repeat with remaining eggs and rolls. Sprinkle with cheese and replace the tops.

4   Place rolls on a baking sheet and bake for 25 minutes or until egg whites are firm.

Variations

Egg and Spinach Rolls: Replace coarse grain mustard with tomato paste, and mushrooms and onion with 2 chopped spinach leaves. Prepare as directed. You may also like to sprinkle the cheese with chopped fresh oregano before baking.

Egg and Mustard Ham Rolls

TURKEY TRIANGLES

Makes 4 triangles
Oven temperature 425°F, 220°C

- ☐ **1 sheet/250 g frozen pre-rolled puff pastry, thawed**

TURKEY FILLING
- ☐ **4 slices smoked turkey, chopped**
- ☐ **2 tablespoons dairy sour cream**
- ☐ **1 tablespoon cranberry sauce**
- ☐ **2 teaspoons snipped fresh chives**
- ☐ **freshly ground black pepper**

1 Cut pastry sheet into four 4¹/₂ in/11 cm squares.
2 To make filling, place turkey, sour cream, cranberry sauce and chives in a small bowl and mix to combine. Place a spoonful of filling in the center of each pastry square. Fold opposite pastry corners together to form a triangle. Brush edges with a little water and press together, using a fork to seal and make a decorative edge. Place on a greased baking sheet and bake for 15 minutes or until pastry is puffed and golden.

PEANUT DIP

This peanut dip is great served with vegetable crudités.

Makes 8 oz/250 g

- ☐ **1 tablespoon peanut oil**
- ☐ **1 clove garlic, crushed**
- ☐ **1 onion, chopped**
- ☐ **1 teaspoon chili sauce**
- ☐ **¹/₃ cup/90 g crunchy peanut butter**
- ☐ **¹/₂ cup/125 mL water**
- ☐ **¹/₂ cup/125 g plain yogurt**
- ☐ **freshly ground black pepper**

Heat oil in a skillet, add garlic and onion and cook for 4-5 minutes or until onion is soft. Add chili sauce, peanut butter and water and mix well to combine. Bring to the boil, then remove pan from heat, stir in yogurt and season to taste with black pepper. Serve hot, warm or at room temperature.

SPICED ALMONDS

Serves 6

- ☐ **¹/₂ teaspoon chili powder**
- ☐ **¹/₄ teaspoon ground cumin**
- ☐ **¹/₂ teaspoon ground coriander**
- ☐ **1¹/₄ cups/185 g blanched almonds**

1 Place chili, cumin and coriander in a small nonstick skillet and cook over a low heat for 1 minute. Add almonds, toss with spices and cook for 3-5 minutes longer or until almonds are golden.
2 Remove pan from heat and set aside to cool. Serve warm or at room temperature as a snack or with drinks.

Peanut Dip, Spiced Almonds

MELON CUPS WITH YOGURT DRESSING

Serves 4

- [ ] **2 small melons, halved and seeds removed**
- [ ] **2 nectarines, pitted and sliced**
- [ ] **5 oz/155 g strawberries, hulled and sliced**
- [ ] **5 oz/155 g black grapes**

YOGURT DRESSING
- [ ] **³/₄ cup/185 g plain yogurt**
- [ ] **1 tablespoon honey**
- [ ] **1 kiwifruit, coarsely chopped**

1 To make dressing, place yogurt, honey and kiwifruit in a bowl and mix to combine.
2 Place melon halves on individual serving plates. Fill with nectarines, strawberries and grapes. Spoon dressing over fruit in melon halves and chill.

FRENCH TOASTED SANDWICHES

Serves 4

- [ ] **8 slices wholewheat bread, crusts removed**
- [ ] **4 slices packaged ham, finely chopped**
- [ ] **10 oz/315 g canned asparagus tips, drained and mashed**
- [ ] **1 cup/125 g shredded Swiss cheese**
- [ ] **3 eggs, well beaten**
- [ ] **³/₄ cup/90 mL milk**

1 Roll bread slices out flat using a rolling pin. Layer half of each slice, diagonally, with ham, asparagus and cheese. Fold uncovered half over filling and press flat. Secure with toothpicks to enclose filling.
2 Combine egg and milk in a shallow dish. Dip each filled bread triangle in egg mixture and cook in a preheated nonstick skillet until golden brown on both sides. Serve immediately.

FRUIT AND NUT MUFFINS

Serves 2

- [ ] **2 English muffins, halved and toasted**

FRUIT AND NUT TOPPING
- [ ] **¹/₃ cup/90 g ricotta cheese**
- [ ] **1 tablespoon currants**
- [ ] **1 tablespoon chopped seeded raisins**
- [ ] **1 teaspoon grated orange rind**
- [ ] **2 tablespoons chopped pecans**

Place ricotta cheese, currants, raisins and orange rind in a bowl. Mix to combine and spread over muffin halves. Sprinkle with pecans and serve.

PEACHES AND CREAM MUFFINS

Serves 2

- [ ] **2 English muffins, halved and toasted**

PEACHES AND CREAM TOPPING
- [ ] **¹/₃ cup/90 g cottage cheese**
- [ ] **pulp of 1 passion fruit**
- [ ] **2 peaches, pitted and sliced**

Combine cottage cheese and passion fruit pulp in a bowl. Spread mixture over muffin halves, top with peach slices and serve.

TURKEY MUFFINS

Serves 2

- [ ] **2 English muffins, halved and toasted**

TURKEY TOPPING
- [ ] **1 tomato, sliced**
- [ ] **2 slices cooked turkey breast**
- [ ] **¹/₄ cup/30 g shredded Cheddar cheese**
- [ ] **freshly ground black pepper**

Place tomato slices on muffin halves. Top with turkey slices, cheese and black pepper to taste. Place under a preheated broiler until heated through.

Melon Cups with Yogurt Dressing

SPRING OMELET

Serves 2

- ☐ **2 tablespoons/15 g butter**
- ☐ **4 eggs, lightly beaten**
- ☐ **¹/₄ cup/60 mL milk**
- ☐ **freshly ground black pepper**
- ☐ **¹/₄ cup/30 g shredded Cheddar cheese**

VEGETABLE FILLING
- ☐ **1 tablespoon/15 g butter**
- ☐ **2 spring onions, finely chopped**
- ☐ **6 button mushrooms, sliced**
- ☐ **¹/₂ small red pepper, sliced**
- ☐ **1 teaspoon chopped fresh coriander (cilantro)**

1 To make filling, melt butter in a nonstick skillet and cook spring onions, mushrooms, red pepper and coriander for 2 minutes or until tender. Remove vege-tables from pan, set aside and keep warm.

2 To make omelet, melt butter in a clean nonstick skillet. Combine eggs, milk and black pepper to taste in a bowl. Pour into pan and cook over a low heat until almost set. Top half the omelet with filling, then sprinkle with cheese. Fold omelet over, cut into half, slide onto serving plates and serve immediately.

Turkey Muffins, Fruit and Nut Muffins, Peaches and Cream Muffins

PRESERVED FOR FLAVOR

I*f you have never ventured
into preserving, why not start by
trying some of these mouthwatering
recipes. Preserves are not only a great
way of storing excess produce, but
they also make wonderful gifts
for family and friends.*

Top shelf; Spicy Apple Chutney,
Cinnamon Pears in Brandy, Corn and
Mustard Seed Relish
Bottom shelf; Mini Dill Pickles,
Pickled Onions

CINNAMON PEARS IN BRANDY

Makes 8 servings

- [ ] **8 small pears, peeled, halved and cored with stems left intact**
- [ ] **¼ cup/60 mL lemon juice**
- [ ] **1 cup/250 g sugar**
- [ ] **1½ cups/375 mL water**
- [ ] **1 cinnamon stick, broken into pieces**
- [ ] **2 teaspoons finely grated lime rind**
- [ ] **1½ cups/375 mL brandy**

1 Place pears in a large bowl, add lemon juice and just enough water to cover pears.
2 Place sugar and water in a large heavy-based saucepan and cook over a low heat, stirring until sugar dissolves. Bring to the boil without stirring.
3 Drain pears and add to pan with cinnamon stick and lime rind. Cook over a low heat until pears are just tender.
4 Arrange pears in hot sterilized jars. Stir brandy into sugar syrup, then pour over pears to completely cover. Seal and store in refrigerator.

MINI DILL PICKLES

akes 20-24 cups

- [ ] lb/3 kg (about 100) small ucumbers, trimmed
- [ ] cup granulated pickling salt
- [ ] ps boiling water
- [ ] ps/2.5 liters white wine ar
- [ ] spoon black mustard
- [ ] on whole black ns
- [ ] ves
- [ ] h dill weed

rs in large bowl.
ng water and pour for 2-3 hours. Rinse r and pat dry on mbers in a large

ard seeds, in another boil. Pour d stand

edium rs are

293

just tender. Pack cucumbers and liquid into hot sterilized jars, leaving ½ in/1 cm headspace. Adjust lids. Process in boiling water bath for 5 minutes (after water returns to boil).

PICKLED ONIONS

Makes 16 cups/4 liters

- [ ] **4 lb/2 kg pickling onions, unpeeled**
- [ ] **1½ lb/750 g granulated pickling salt**

PICKLING VINEGAR
- [ ] **6 cups/1.5 liters white wine vinegar**
- [ ] **4 teaspoons salt**
- [ ] **2 teaspoons ground ginger**
- [ ] **6 whole cloves**
- [ ] **2 fresh red chilies, cut in half**
- [ ] **2 teaspoons yellow mustard seeds**
- [ ] **6 whole black peppercorns**
- [ ] **2 bay leaves**

1 Place onions and salt in a bowl. Add enough water to cover onions and set aside to stand for 2 days. Stir occasionally during standing time.
2 Drain onions and discard liquid. Peel onions and cover with boiling water. Set aside to stand for 3 minutes, then drain and repeat twice more using additional boiling water. Pack onions into hot sterilized jars and set aside.
3 To make vinegar, place white wine vinegar, salt, ginger, cloves, chilies, mustard seeds, peppercorns and bay leaves in a large saucepan. Bring to the boil, then reduce heat and simmer for 10 minutes. Cool slightly, then pour liquid over onions in jars, leaving ½ in/1 cm headspace. Adjust lids. Process in boiling water bath for 15 minutes (after water returns to boil).

SPICY APPLE CHUTNEY

Makes 2 x 8 oz/250 g jars (2 cups)

- [ ] **2 tablespoons vegetable oil**
- [ ] **1 clove garlic, crushed**
- [ ] **1 teaspoon grated fresh ginger**
- [ ] **2 fresh red chilies, seeded and chopped**
- [ ] **2 tablespoons mustard seeds**
- [ ] **1 teaspoon pumpkin pie spice**
- [ ] **1 teaspoon ground turmeric**
- [ ] **15 whole black peppercorns**

- [ ] **2 teaspoons ground cumin**
- [ ] **8 large cooking apples, cored, peeled and sliced**
- [ ] **⅔ cup/170 mL white vinegar**
- [ ] **½ cup/125 g sugar**

1 Heat oil in a large saucepan and cook garlic, ginger and chilies over a medium heat for 2-3 minutes. Combine mustard seeds, spice, tumeric, peppercorns and cumin, add to pan and cook for 3-4 minutes longer.
2 Add apples, vinegar and sugar to pan and simmer, uncovered, for 1 hour or until thick. Pour chutney into hot sterilized jars and seal when cold. Store in a cool dark place.

CORN AND MUSTARD SEED RELISH

Makes 3 x 1 lb/500 g jars (about 6 cups)

- [ ] **1 large onion, finely chopped**
- [ ] **2 cups/500 mL white wine vinegar**
- [ ] **½ cup/100 g sugar**
- [ ] **1 tablespoon curry powder**
- [ ] **1 teaspoon ground turmeric**
- [ ] **2 teaspoons yellow mustard seeds**
- [ ] **2 tablespoons grated fresh ginger**
- [ ] **2 x 14 oz/440 g cans corn kernels, drained**
- [ ] **1 carrot, finely chopped**
- [ ] **2 stalks celery, chopped**
- [ ] **1 red pepper, chopped**
- [ ] **2 tablespoons cornstarch, blended with ⅓ cup/90 mL water**
- [ ] **freshly ground black pepper**

1 Place onion in a saucepan and add enough water to cover onion. Bring to the boil, remove from heat, drain and set aside.
2 Place vinegar, sugar, curry powder, turmeric, mustard seeds and ginger in a clean saucepan. Bring to the boil, then reduce heat and simmer for 3-4 minutes.
3 Add corn kernels, carrot, celery, red pepper and onion to pan. Bring to the boil, then reduce heat and simmer for 15 minutes.
4 Stir in cornstarch mixture and cook over a medium heat, stirring constantly, for 5 minutes or until mixture boils and thickens. Season to taste with black pepper. Spoon hot relish into hot sterilized jars, leaving ½ in/1 cm headspace. Adjust lids. Process in boiling water bath for 15 minutes (after water returns to boil).

PRESERVED FOR FLAVOR

*If you have never ventured
into preserving, why not start by
trying some of these mouthwatering
recipes. Preserves are not only a great
way of storing excess produce, but
they also make wonderful gifts
for family and friends.*

*Top shelf; Spicy Apple Chutney,
Cinnamon Pears in Brandy, Corn and
Mustard Seed Relish
Bottom shelf; Mini Dill Pickles,
Pickled Onions*

CINNAMON PEARS IN BRANDY

Makes 8 servings

- [ ] **8 small pears, peeled, halved and cored with stems left intact**
- [ ] **1/4 cup/60 mL lemon juice**
- [ ] **1 cup/250 g sugar**
- [ ] **1 1/2 cups/375 mL water**
- [ ] **1 cinnamon stick, broken into pieces**
- [ ] **2 teaspoons finely grated lime rind**
- [ ] **1 1/2 cups/375 mL brandy**

1 Place pears in a large bowl, add lemon juice and just enough water to cover pears.
2 Place sugar and water in a large heavy-based saucepan and cook over a low heat, stirring until sugar dissolves. Bring to the boil without stirring.
3 Drain pears and add to pan with cinnamon stick and lime rind. Cook over a low heat until pears are just tender.
4 Arrange pears in hot sterilized jars. Stir brandy into sugar syrup, then pour over pears to completely cover. Seal and store in refrigerator.

MINI DILL PICKLES

Makes 20-24 cups

- [ ] **6 lb/3 kg (about 100) small cucumbers, trimmed**
- [ ] **1/2 cup granulated pickling salt**
- [ ] **8 cups boiling water**
- [ ] **10 cups/2.5 liters white wine vinegar**
- [ ] **1 tablespoon black mustard seeds**
- [ ] **1/2 teaspoon whole black peppercorns**
- [ ] **4 whole cloves**
- [ ] **4 sprigs fresh dill weed**

1 Place cucumbers in large bowl. Dissolve salt in boiling water and pour over cucumbers. Stand for 2-3 hours. Rinse under cold running water and pat dry on paper towels. Place cucumbers in a large saucepan.
2 Place vinegar, mustard seeds, peppercorns, cloves and dill in another large saucepan and bring to the boil. Pour mixture over cucumbers and stand overnight.
3 Remove cloves. Cook over a medium heat until liquid boils and cucumbers are just tender. Pack cucumbers and liquid into hot sterilized jars, leaving 1/2 in/1 cm headspace. Adjust lids. Process in boiling water bath for 5 minutes (after water returns to boil).

PICKLED ONIONS

Makes 16 cups/4 liters

- [ ] **4 lb/2 kg pickling onions, unpeeled**
- [ ] **1 1/2 lb/750 g granulated pickling salt**

PICKLING VINEGAR
- [ ] **6 cups/1.5 liters white wine vinegar**
- [ ] **4 teaspoons salt**
- [ ] **2 teaspoons ground ginger**
- [ ] **6 whole cloves**
- [ ] **2 fresh red chilies, cut in half**
- [ ] **2 teaspoons yellow mustard seeds**
- [ ] **6 whole black peppercorns**
- [ ] **2 bay leaves**

1 Place onions and salt in a bowl. Add enough water to cover onions and set aside to stand for 2 days. Stir occasionally during standing time.
2 Drain onions and discard liquid. Peel onions and cover with boiling water. Set aside to stand for 3 minutes, then drain and repeat twice more using additional boiling water. Pack onions into hot sterilized jars and set aside.
3 To make vinegar, place white wine vinegar, salt, ginger, cloves, chilies, mustard seeds, peppercorns and bay leaves in a large saucepan. Bring to the boil, then reduce heat and simmer for 10 minutes. Cool slightly, then pour liquid over onions in jars, leaving 1/2 in/1cm headspace. Adjust lids. Process in boiling water bath for 15 minutes (after water returns to boil).

SPICY APPLE CHUTNEY

Makes 2 x 8 oz/250 g jars (2 cups)

- [ ] **2 tablespoons vegetable oil**
- [ ] **1 clove garlic, crushed**
- [ ] **1 teaspoon grated fresh ginger**
- [ ] **2 fresh red chilies, seeded and chopped**
- [ ] **2 tablespoons mustard seeds**
- [ ] **1 teaspoon pumpkin pie spice**
- [ ] **1 teaspoon ground turmeric**
- [ ] **15 whole black peppercorns**
- [ ] **2 teaspoons ground cumin**
- [ ] **8 large cooking apples, cored, peeled and sliced**
- [ ] **2/3 cup/170 mL white vinegar**
- [ ] **1/2 cup/125 g sugar**

1 Heat oil in a large saucepan and cook garlic, ginger and chilies over a medium heat for 2-3 minutes. Combine mustard seeds, spice, tumeric, peppercorns and cumin, add to pan and cook for 3-4 minutes longer.
2 Add apples, vinegar and sugar to pan and simmer, uncovered, for 1 hour or until thick. Pour chutney into hot sterilized jars and seal when cold. Store in a cool dark place.

CORN AND MUSTARD SEED RELISH

Makes 3 x 1 lb/500 g jars (about 6 cups)

- [ ] **1 large onion, finely chopped**
- [ ] **2 cups/500 mL white wine vinegar**
- [ ] **1/2 cup/100 g sugar**
- [ ] **1 tablespoon curry powder**
- [ ] **1 teaspoon ground turmeric**
- [ ] **2 teaspoons yellow mustard seeds**
- [ ] **2 tablespoons grated fresh ginger**
- [ ] **2 x 14 oz/440 g cans corn kernels, drained**
- [ ] **1 carrot, finely chopped**
- [ ] **2 stalks celery, chopped**
- [ ] **1 red pepper, chopped**
- [ ] **2 tablespoons cornstarch, blended with 1/3 cup/90 mL water**
- [ ] **freshly ground black pepper**

1 Place onion in a saucepan and add enough water to cover onion. Bring to the boil, remove from heat, drain and set aside.
2 Place vinegar, sugar, curry powder, turmeric, mustard seeds and ginger in a clean saucepan. Bring to the boil, then reduce heat and simmer for 3-4 minutes.
3 Add corn kernels, carrot, celery, red pepper and onion to pan. Bring to the boil, then reduce heat and simmer for 15 minutes.
4 Stir in cornstarch mixture and cook over a medium heat, stirring constantly, for 5 minutes or until mixture boils and thickens. Season to taste with black pepper. Spoon hot relish into hot sterilized jars, leaving 1/2 in/1 cm headspace. Adjust lids. Process in boiling water bath for 15 minutes (after water returns to boil).

HERB VINEGARS

Flavored vinegars add extra zest to any savory dish, pickle or salad that calls for vinegar. Use fresh herbs such as basil, tarragon, thyme or rosemary. For something different, you might like to use red or white wine vinegar. Homemade flavored vinegars make wonderful gifts.

Makes 4 cups/1 liter

- ☐ **4 oz/125 g fresh herbs of your choice**
- ☐ **4 cups/1 liter vinegar**

1 Wash herbs and pat dry. Crush slightly.
2 Place herbs in a bottle and add vinegar. Seal and leave in a warm place, like a sunny windowsill, for 3-4 weeks.
3 Strain vinegar through cheesecloth. Place a fresh herb sprig in a clean, pretty bottle and add vinegar. Seal and label.

PICKLED PEPPPERS

Makes 2 cups/500 g

- ☐ **2 onions, sliced**
- ☐ **2 red peppers, sliced**
- ☐ **2 green peppers, sliced**
- ☐ **2 yellow peppers, sliced**
- ☐ **2 tablespoons granulated pickling salt**
- ☐ **1 fresh red chili, finely chopped**
- ☐ **2 bay leaves**
- ☐ **1¹/₂ cups /375 mL white wine vinegar**
- ☐ **1 teaspoon black mustard seeds**
- ☐ **2 teaspoons pink peppercorns**
- ☐ **³/₄ cup/185 g sugar**

1 Combine onions, red, green and yellow peppers and salt in large bowl. Cover and let stand overnight.
2 Rinse vegetables under cold running water. Drain and pat dry on paper towels. Arrange attractively in a sterilized jar with the red chili and bay leaves.
3 Combine vinegar, mustard seeds, peppercorns and sugar in a saucepan. Cook over a medium heat without boiling, stirring constantly until sugar dissolves. Bring to the boil, then reduce heat and simmer, uncovered, for 3 minutes. Pour over vegetables to completely cover. Seal and store in refrigerator.

BEET, ORANGE AND APPLE CHUTNEY

This chutney is delicious with cheese and cold lamb.

Makes 4 x 12 oz/375 g jars

- ☐ **2 lb/1 kg beets, stems and leaves removed**
- ☐ **1 cup/250 g sugar**
- ☐ **1 onion, finely chopped**
- ☐ **2 cups/500 mL red wine vinegar**
- ☐ **1 teaspoon ground allspice**
- ☐ **2 large Granny Smith apples, cored, peeled and chopped**
- ☐ **1 orange, segmented**

1 Place beets in a large saucepan and cover with water. Cover pan, bring to the boil, then reduce heat and simmer for 1 hour or until beets are tender. Drain and set aside until cool enough to handle. Peel beets and dice.
2 Place sugar, onion, vinegar and allspice in a saucepan and cook over a medium heat, without boiling, stirring constantly until sugar dissolves.
3 Bring sugar mixture to the boil, reduce heat, add apples and simmer for 15-20 minutes or until apples pulp. Stir in beets and orange and cook for 5 minutes longer. Spoon chutney into hot sterilized jars. Cover and label when cold.

A selection of Herb Vinegars

BOCCONCINI MARINATED WITH HERBS

Serve bocconcini sliced with assorted salad leaves and a little of the marinade spooned over.

Serves 8

- ☐ **1 lb/500 g fresh bocconcini, drained and dried**
- ☐ **3 cloves garlic, peeled**
- ☐ **2 sprigs fresh oregano**
- ☐ **2 sprigs fresh thyme**
- ☐ **1 sprig fresh parsley**
- ☐ **1 bay leaf**
- ☐ **3 small fresh red chilies**
- ☐ **³⁄₄ cup/185 mL extra virgin olive oil**

Place bocconcini, garlic, oregano, thyme, parsley, bay leaf and chilies in a sterilized jar. Cover with olive oil. Seal jar and refrigerate for up to 2 weeks.

Cook's tip: Bocconcini are small balls of fresh mozzarella cheese. If they are unavailable you can use fresh mozzarella cut into cubes instead.

CHICK PEAS IN GARLIC OIL

Makes 2 cups/500 mL

- ☐ **1 cup/185 g dried chick peas (garbanzo beans)**
- ☐ **1¹⁄₄ cups/300 mL olive oil**
- ☐ **4 cloves garlic, crushed**

- ☐ **freshly ground black pepper**
- ☐ **¹⁄₄ cup/60 mL lemon juice**
- ☐ **¹⁄₄ cup/30 g chopped fresh parsley**

1   Place chick peas in a small saucepan and cover with cold water. Bring to the boil, then turn off heat, cover and soak for 1 hour. Drain and cover with fresh cold water. Cover pan and cook over a low heat for 2-3 hours or until chick peas are tender. Drain well.

2   Heat oil in a skillet, add garlic and chick peas and cook, stirring constantly, until chick peas are lightly browned. Season to taste with black pepper and mix in lemon juice and parsley. Pack into a warm sterilized jar, seal and refrigerate until required.

SICILIAN PRESERVED EGGPLANT

*Serve preserved eggplant as part of an antipasto selection,
or as a vegetable accompaniment
to cooked meats.*

Makes 4 cups/1 liter

- ☐ **2 lb/1 kg baby eggplant, cut lengthwise into thin strips**
- ☐ **¹/₄ cup/60 g salt**
- ☐ **2 tablespoons finely chopped fresh mint**
- ☐ **3 cloves garlic, crushed**
- ☐ **1 teaspoon finely chopped fresh oregano**
- ☐ **2 tablespoons red wine vinegar**
- ☐ **3 small fresh red chilies, seeded and sliced**
- ☐ **1³/₄ cups/410 mL extra virgin olive oil**

1   Sprinkle eggplant slices with salt and set aside to stand for 2 hours. Rinse and pat dry.
2   Combine eggplant, mint, garlic, oregano and 1 tablespoon vinegar. Layer eggplant and chilies in a warm sterilized jar. Press down firmly and add remaining vinegar and enough olive oil to cover. Seal and refrigerate until required.

ROASTED PEPPERS IN OLIVE OIL

Roasting peppers gives them a succulent, sweet taste. This can be done over coals, a gas flame or under the broiler.

Makes 2 cups/500 g

- ☐ **4 red peppers, roasted until black**
- ☐ **4 yellow peppers, roasted until black**
- ☐ **2 teaspoons salt**
- ☐ **3 cloves garlic, peeled**
- ☐ **³/₄ cup/185 mL extra virgin olive oil**

1   Cut peppers in half, remove seeds and skin. Slice into large pieces.
2   Sprinkle peppers with salt and pack into a warm sterilized jar. Add garlic cloves and cover with oil. Allow to settle, cover and refrigerate until required.

SPICED OLIVES

Serve these olives as part of an antipasto platter, to top pizzas, or in salads for an extra-special flavor.

Makes 2 cups/500 g

- ☐ **1 lb/500 g black Greek olives**
- ☐ **2 cloves garlic, chopped**
- ☐ **3 small fresh red chilies, chopped**
- ☐ **2 tablespoons chopped fresh parsley**
- ☐ **3 bay leaves**
- ☐ **³/₄ cup/200 mL extra virgin olive oil**

Combine olives, garlic, chilies and parsley. Place olive mixture and bay leaves in a warm sterilized jar. Cover with olive oil, seal and refrigerate until required.

Spiced Olives, Roasted Peppers in Olive Oil, Bocconcini Marinated with Herbs, Sicilian Preserved Eggplant

CHILI SAMBAL

Use this sambal as a dipping sauce or keep in a jar in the refrigerator to add some quick flavor to your recipes.

Makes $\frac{1}{2}$ cup/125 mL

- [ ] **25 small fresh red chilies, stalks removed**
- [ ] **2 cloves garlic**
- [ ] **1 small onion, chopped**
- [ ] **2 tablespoons brown sugar**
- [ ] **$\frac{3}{4}$ cup/185 mL water**
- [ ] **1 teaspoon cornstarch**
- [ ] **2 tablespoons white vinegar**

1 Place whole chilies, garlic and onion in a food processor or blender and process to make a paste. Transfer to a small saucepan and stir in sugar, water, cornstarch and vinegar. Bring to the boil, reduce heat and simmer until thickened.

2 Remove from heat and set aside to cool. Transfer to a warm sterilized jar. Seal and label when cold. Store in the refrigerator until required.

Preserving tips: Always use clean unchipped jars.

Remove any old labels by soaking.

The jars must be sterilized before filling or the preserve will go moldy. To sterilize jars, wash in hot water then warm in the oven at a low temperature until dry. Remember that the lids must also be sterilized.

Jars should be warm when adding the hot preserve. Cold jars will crack or break if a hot mixture is suddenly added to them.

MINT CHUTNEY

A food processor makes the preparation of this chutney very easy. The chutney will keep for up to a week in the refrigerator, however it will lose its color after the first day

Makes $\frac{1}{2}$ cup/125 mL

- [ ] **4 oz/125 g fresh mint sprigs**
- [ ] **3 fresh green chilies, seeds removed and chopped**
- [ ] **3 spring onions, chopped**
- [ ] **2 teaspoons sugar**
- [ ] **$\frac{1}{2}$ teaspoon salt**
- [ ] **1 tablespoon vinegar**

1 Remove mint leaves from stalks. Wash and dry.

2 Place mint leaves, chilies, spring onions, sugar, salt and vinegar in a food processor or blender and process until smooth.

3 Transfer to a warm sterilized jar. Seal and store in the refrigerator until required.

DATE AND ORANGE CHUTNEY

A delicious sweet chutney that can also be made using fresh figs rather than dates if you wish.

Makes 2 cups/500 g

- [ ] **8 oz/250 g fresh dates, pitted and chopped**
- [ ] **1 orange, chopped**
- [ ] **1 teaspoon grated fresh ginger**
- [ ] **$\frac{1}{3}$ cup/60 g seeded raisins**
- [ ] **1 tablespoon brown sugar**
- [ ] **$\frac{1}{3}$ cup/90 mL cider vinegar**
- [ ] **$\frac{1}{4}$ cup/60 mL water**

1 Place dates, orange, ginger, raisins, sugar, vinegar and water in a saucepan and cook, stirring occasionally, over a low heat for 20 minutes.

2 Transfer to warm sterilized jars, seal and label when cold. Store in the refrigerator until required.

Date and Orange Chutney, Chili Sambal, Mint Chutney, Chili Pickled Cabbage

CHILI PICKLED CABBAGE

Traditional Kim Chee is made months in advance and is placed in large stone jars to mature. This simplified version is ready after one week.

Makes about 5 cups/1.2 liters

- [ ] **2 lb/1 kg Chinese cabbage, coarsely chopped**
- [ ] **1 tablespoon salt**
- [ ] **2 spring onions, chopped**
- [ ] **2 cloves garlic, crushed**
- [ ] **1 tablespoon sambal oelek (chili paste)**
- [ ] **2 teaspoons grated fresh ginger**
- [ ] **$^1/_2$ cup/125 mL light soy sauce**
- [ ] **$^1/_2$ cup/125 mL white vinegar**
- [ ] **$^1/_2$ teaspoon sesame oil**

1 Sprinkle cabbage with salt and set aside for 4 hours.
2 Press cabbage to remove excess liquid. Add spring onions, garlic, sambal oelek (chili paste), ginger, soy sauce and vinegar, and stir to combine.
3 Place into a large, warm, sterilized jar, seal and store in refrigerator for at least 1 day before using to allow flavors to develop.
4 Sprinkle with the sesame oil to serve.

MIDDLE EASTERN PEACH

An exotic pickle that combines the flavors of lush peaches with spices of the Middle East.

Makes 12 oz/375 g

- [ ] **$1^1/_2$ teaspoons tamarind paste**
- [ ] **$1^1/_2$ cups/375 mL white wine vinegar**
- [ ] **1 lb/500 g fresh peaches, peeled and sliced**
- [ ] **1 tablespoon grated fresh ginger**
- [ ] **1 tablespoon ground coriander**
- [ ] **3 cloves garlic, crushed**
- [ ] **$^1/_2$ cup/125 g sugar**
- [ ] **2 small fresh red chilies**

1 Dissolve tamarind paste in $^1/_2$ cup/ 125 mL vinegar. Place peaches, ginger, coriander, garlic, tamarind mixture, remaining vinegar, sugar and chilies in a saucepan. Bring to the boil, stirring, until sugar is dissolved.
2 Reduce heat and simmer without stirring for 20 minutes. Transfer to warm, sterilized jars. Seal and label when cold. Store in refrigerator.

CURRIED EGGPLANT PICKLE

Blend your own spices to create this perky pickle. Adjust the amount of chili according to the degree of hotness you desire.

Makes about 6 cups/1.5 liters

- [ ] **4 small fresh red chilies, seeded and chopped**
- [ ] **5 cloves garlic**
- [ ] **1 tablespoon grated fresh ginger**
- [ ] **$1^1/_2$ tablespoons mustard seeds**
- [ ] **2 teaspoons ground turmeric**
- [ ] **2 teaspoons garam masala**
- [ ] **1 cup/250 mL vegetable oil**
- [ ] **3 lb/1.5 kg eggplant, cut into $^3/_4$ in/2 cm cubes**
- [ ] **$^1/_2$ teaspoon salt**
- [ ] **$^3/_4$ cup/125 g packed brown sugar**
- [ ] **$^3/_4$ cup/185 mL white vinegar**

1 Blend chilies, garlic, ginger, mustard seeds, turmeric and garam masala to a paste in a food processor or blender.
2 Heat oil in a skillet and cook spice paste for 1 minute. Add eggplant, toss to coat with spice paste. Reduce heat, cover and cook until eggplant are tender. Add salt, sugar and vinegar and simmer, uncovered, until thickened.
3 Transfer to warm sterilized jars. Allow to cool and skim off any oil that rises to the surface. Seal and label when cold. Store in refrigerator.

*Curried Eggplant Pickle,
Middle Eastern Peach*

THREE-FRUIT MARMALADE

The name 'marmalade' comes from the Portuguese word for quince. The original marmalade was a quince jelly from Portugal which was taken to England in the fourteenth century.

Makes 6 x 8 oz/250 mL jars

- ☐ **2 large oranges**
- ☐ **2 limes**
- ☐ **1 large grapefruit**
- ☐ **4 cups/1 liter water**
- ☐ **3¹/₂ lb/1.75 kg sugar**

1   Cut oranges, limes and grapefruit in half, then slice thinly, discarding seeds. Place fruit in a large bowl and add water. Cover and stand overnight.
2   Transfer fruit and water to a large saucepan and bring to the boil, then reduce heat and simmer, uncovered, for 1 hour or until fruit is soft.
3   Add sugar, stirring constantly without boiling, until sugar dissolves. Bring to the boil and cook, uncovered, without stirring, for 45 minutes or until marmalade gels when tested.
4   Stand 10 minutes before pouring marmalade into hot sterilized jars. Seal when cold.

MIXED-BERRY JAM

Makes 4 x 8 oz/250 g jars

- ☐ **1¹/₂ lb/750 g mixed fresh berries**
- ☐ **1 cup/250 mL water**
- ☐ **3 cups/750 g sugar**
- ☐ **¹/₄ cup/60 mL lemon juice**

1   Place berries, water, sugar and lemon juice in a large saucepan and cook over a low heat, stirring until sugar dissolves.
2   Bring to the boil, then reduce heat and simmer for 30-35 minutes or until jam gels when tested.
3   Stand for 10 minutes, then pour into hot sterilized jars. Seal when cold.

PLUM JAM

This jam is delicious as a cake or tart filling.

Makes 4 x 8 oz/250 g jars

- ☐ **2 lb/1 kg blood plums halved and pitted**
- ☐ **1 cup/250 mL water**
- ☐ **2 lb/1 kg sugar**
- ☐ **1 tablespoon/15 g butter**

1   Place plums and water in a large saucepan and bring to the boil. Reduce heat, cover and simmer for 15-20 minutes or until fruit is soft and pulpy.
2   Add sugar and cook, stirring constantly without boiling, until sugar dissolves. Bring jam to the boil and cook, uncovered, for 20-30 minutes or until jam gels when tested. Stir in butter.
3   Stand jam for 10 minutes, before spooning into hot sterilized jars. Seal and label when cold.

Setting test: To test the set or gel of a jam, remove the pan from heat and allow the bubbles to subside. Drop a spoonful of jam onto a chilled saucer and set aside at room temperature to cool. The jam should form a skin that will wrinkle when pushed with your finger. If the jam does not pass the setting test, return to heat and boil for a few minutes longer, then retest. Remember to remove the pan from the heat while testing the jam or it will continue to cook.

STRAWBERRY JAM

Makes 4 x 8 oz/250 g jars

- ☐ **2 lb/1 kg strawberries, washed and hulled**
- ☐ **2 lb/1 kg sugar**
- ☐ **¹/₂ cup/125 mL lemon juice**
- ☐ **³/₄ cup/185 mL water**

1   Place strawberries, sugar, lemon juice and water in a large saucepan and cook over a low heat, stirring until sugar dissolves.
2   Bring to the boil and cook, without stirring, for 40-45 minutes or until jam gels when tested.
3   Pour jam into hot sterilized jars. Seal and label when cold.

Sealing and labeling preserves: Preserves should be covered immediately after potting or when completely cold. Never cover when just warm as that creates conditions ideal for the growth of mold. If you are going to allow the jam to cool before covering, place a clean cloth over the jars to prevent dust falling on the surface of the jam.

LEMON CURD

Lemon curd, butter or honey seems to have originated from the curd tarts, known as cheesecakes, of the seventeeth century. Use it as a tart or cake filling, or as a spread on toast.

Makes 1 x 8 oz/250 g jar

- ☐ **2 eggs**
- ☐ **¹/₂ cup/125 g sugar**
- ☐ **¹/₃ cup/90 mL lemon juice**
- ☐ **1 tablespoon finely grated lemon rind**
- ☐ **2 tablespoons/30 g butter**

1   Place eggs and sugar in a heatproof bowl or in top of double boiler and beat lightly. Stir in lemon juice, lemon rind and butter.
2   Place over a saucepan of simmering water and cook, stirring constantly, for 15 minutes or until mixture thickens.
3   Pour into hot sterilized jars. Seal and label when cold.

BRANDIED APRICOTS

Makes 3 x 8 oz/250 g jars

- ☐ **2 cups/500 g sugar**
- ☐ **1 cup/250 mL water**
- ☐ **2 lb/1 kg apricots, halved and pitted**
- ☐ **¹/₄ teaspoon ground nutmeg**
- ☐ **1 cup/250 mL brandy**

1   Place sugar and water in a large saucepan and cook over a medium heat, stirring constantly, until sugar dissolves. Add apricots and nutmeg, bring to simmering and simmer until apricots are just tender.
2   Using a slotted spoon remove apricots from liquid and pack tightly into hot sterilized jars. Bring syrup to the boil and boil for 8 minutes or until reduced by half and golden.
3   Half fill each jar with brandy, then add syrup to within ³/₄ in/2 cm of the top. Seal and label when cold.

Lemon Curd, Mixed-Berry Jam, Plum Jam, Three-Fruit Marmalade, Strawberry Jam

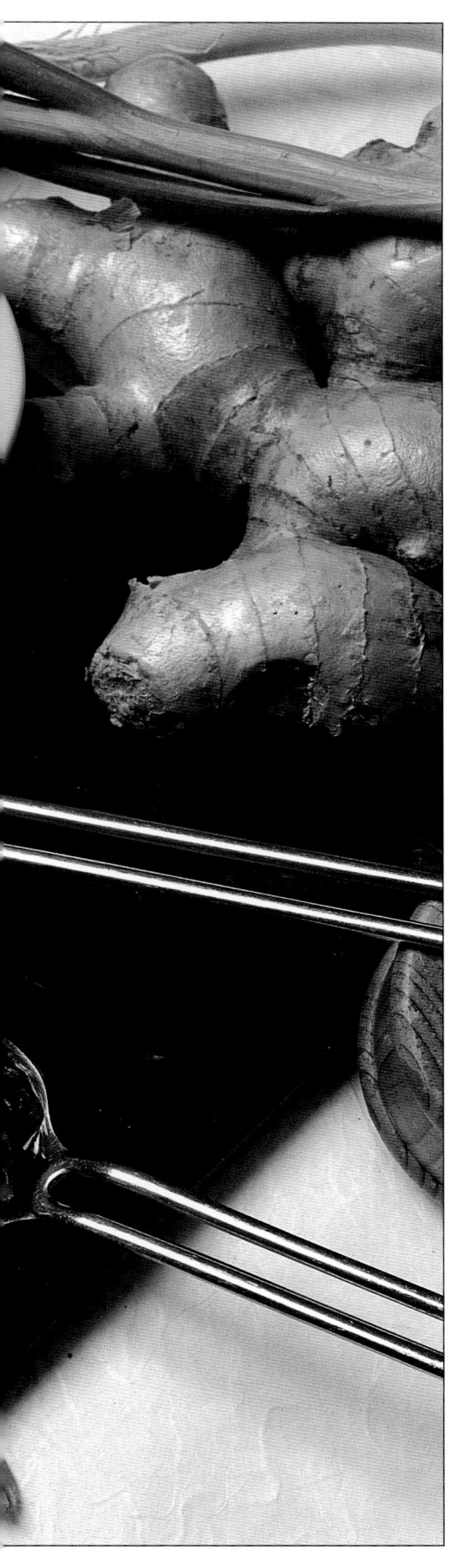

chapter fourteen

•

BASIC
RECIPES

In this chapter you will find
recipes for stocks, sauces and
dressings that will add that special
something to your cooking. Many of the
sauces are delicious spooned over
steamed vegetables, while the stocks
provide the basis for tasty
homemade soups.

Italian Green Sauce with Basil,
Creamy Mustard Sauce,
Mexican Chili Sauce,
Spicy Peanut Satay Sauce

CORIANDER PESTO

A delicious sauce for pasta, an excellent addition to soup, or just serve it as a dip.

Makes about 8 fl oz/250 mL

- ☐ **3 large bunches fresh coriander (cilantro)**
- ☐ **2 cloves garlic, crushed**
- ☐ **¹/₂ cup/60 g pine nuts (pignola)**
- ☐ **¹/₂ cup/125 mL olive oil**
- ☐ **¹/₂ cup/60 g grated Parmesan cheese**

Place coriander leaves, garlic and pine nuts in a food processor or blender and process until finely chopped. With machine running, slowly pour in the oil and process until smooth. Add cheese and process to blend.

ITALIAN GREEN SAUCE WITH BASIL

Wonderful with hot pasta!

Makes 8 fl oz/250 mL

- ☐ **2 small bunches fresh basil**
- ☐ **3 spring onions, finely chopped**
- ☐ **2 cloves garlic, crushed**
- ☐ **1 tablespoon capers, drained and rinsed**
- ☐ **²/₃ cup/155 mL olive oil**
- ☐ **1 tablespoon lemon juice**
- ☐ **freshly ground black pepper.**

Place basil leaves, spring onions, garlic and capers in a food processor or blender and process until smooth. With machine running, slowly pour in oil, then lemon juice, and continue to process until well blended. Season to taste with black pepper.

SPICY PEANUT SATAY SAUCE

Makes 12 fl oz/375 mL

- ☐ **2 tablespoons peanut oil**
- ☐ **2 cups/315 g roasted peanuts, finely chopped**
- ☐ **2 cloves garlic, crushed**
- ☐ **1 onion, finely chopped**
- ☐ **¹/₂ teaspoon chili powder**
- ☐ **1 tablespoon brown sugar**
- ☐ **2 tablespoons soy sauce**
- ☐ **¹/₄ teaspoon five spice powder**
- ☐ **2 cups/500 mL coconut milk**

1 Heat oil in a saucepan and cook peanuts, garlic, onion and chili powder, stirring for 3-4 minutes.
2 Add sugar, soy sauce and five spice powder, reduce heat and pour in coconut milk. Simmer for 5-10 minutes, stirring occasionally. If sauce becomes too thick, thin with a little milk.

CREAMY MUSTARD SAUCE

Best made just before serving, this superbly tangy sauce is great poured over steamed vegetables.

Makes about 8 fl oz/250 mL

- ☐ **1¹/₄ cups/315 mL thin cream**
- ☐ **1¹/₂ tablespoons coarse grain mustard**
- ☐ **1 clove garlic, crushed**
- ☐ **¹/₄ cup/60 mL vegetable stock**
- ☐ **1 tablespoon finely snipped fresh chives or finely chopped parsley**
- ☐ **freshly ground black pepper**

Place cream in a small saucepan and bring to the boil. Boil rapidly until reduced by a quarter. Stir in mustard, garlic and vegetable stock. Simmer for 5-10 minutes, stirring frequently, until sauce reduces and thickens a little. Stir in chives or parsley and season to taste with pepper. Serve immediately.

MEXICAN CHILI SAUCE

Makes about 16 fl oz/500 mL

- ☐ **2 tablespoons sesame oil**
- ☐ **3 small fresh red chilies, seeded and finely chopped**
- ☐ **3 small fresh green chilies, seeded and finely chopped**
- ☐ **3 cloves garlic, crushed**
- ☐ **2 onions, finely chopped**
- ☐ **1 tablespoon finely chopped fresh coriander (cilantro)**
- ☐ **14 fl oz/440 g canned tomatoes, undrained and mashed**
- ☐ **1 teaspoon brown sugar**
- ☐ **¹/₂ teaspoon ground cinnamon**
- ☐ **¹/₄ teaspoon ground cloves**
- ☐ **¹/₄ teaspoon ground ginger**
- ☐ **2 tablespoons lemon juice**
- ☐ **¹/₄ cup/60 mL water**

Heat oil in a skillet and cook red and green chilies, garlic, onions and coriander for 2-3 minutes. Stir in tomatoes, sugar, cinnamon, cloves, ginger, lemon juice and water and simmer for 10-15 minutes or until sauce reduces and thickens.

LIME AND LEMON SAUCE

Serve this sauce spooned over grilled fish or chicken or steamed vegetables.

Makes 16 fl oz/500 mL

- ☐ **¹/₄ cup/¹/₂ stick/60 g butter**
- ☐ **1 clove garlic, crushed**
- ☐ **1¹/₂ tablespoons cornstarch blended with ¹/₄ cup/60 mL water**
- ☐ **2 cups/500 mL vegetable stock**
- ☐ **1 tablespoon lemon juice**
- ☐ **1 tablespoon lime juice**
- ☐ **¹/₂ teaspoon grated lime rind**
- ☐ **¹/₂ teaspoon grated lemon rind**
- ☐ **¹/₄ teaspoon ground turmeric**

Melt butter in a saucepan, add garlic and cook over a medium heat for 1 minute. Stir in cornstarch mixture, stock, lemon juice, lime juice, lemon rind, lime rind and turmeric and cook, stirring constantly, for 4-5 minutes or until sauce boils and thickens.

BARBECUE SAUCE

This sauce can be served hot, warm or cold and is the perfect accompaniment for any barbecued or grilled foods.

Makes 8 fl oz/250 mL

- ☐ **1 tablespoon vegetable oil**
- ☐ **1 onion, chopped**
- ☐ **1 clove garlic, crushed**
- ☐ **1 teaspoon dry mustard**
- ☐ **1 tablespoon Worcestershire sauce**
- ☐ **1 tablespoon brown sugar**
- ☐ **¹/₄ cup/60 mL tomato catsup**
- ☐ **1 teaspoon chili sauce**
- ☐ **³/₄ cup/185 mL beef stock**
- ☐ **freshly ground black pepper**

Heat oil in a saucepan, add onion and garlic and cook for 3-4 minutes or until onion is soft. Stir in mustard, Worcestershire sauce, sugar, tomato catsup, chili sauce and stock and bring to the boil. Reduce heat and simmer for 8-10 minutes or until sauce reduces and thickens slightly. Season to taste with black pepper.

SWEET AND SOUR BARBECUE SAUCE

A sweet and sour sauce is always a popular accompaniment for chicken and pork, but is also delicious served with sausages and fish.

Makes 2 cups/500 mL

- [ ] 1 tablespoon vegetable oil
- [ ] 1 small onion, chopped
- [ ] 1 red pepper, chopped
- [ ] 1 tablespoon soy sauce
- [ ] 2 tablespoons honey
- [ ] 1 tablespoon tomato paste
- [ ] 2 tablespoons cornstarch
- [ ] 1/2 cup/125 mL cider vinegar
- [ ] 1/2 cup/125 mL chicken stock or water
- [ ] 14 oz/440 g canned pineapple chunks, drained

1 Heat oil in a saucepan, add onion and red pepper and cook for 4-5 minutes or until soft. Place soy sauce, honey, tomato paste, cornstarch and vinegar in a small bowl and mix to combine.
2 Stir cornstarch mixture into vegetables, then stir in stock or water and cook over a medium heat, stirring constantly, for 2-3 minutes or until sauce boils and thickens. Stir in pineapple chunks and cook for 2-3 minutes longer.

APPLE AND HORSERADISH SAUCE

Delicious served with beef and sausages, this condiment also makes an interesting accompaniment for barbecued or grilled fish.

Makes 1 cup/250 mL

- [ ] 1/2 cup/125 mL thick cream
- [ ] 1 green apple, cored and grated
- [ ] 1/4 cup bottled horseradish
- [ ] freshly ground black pepper

Place cream in a bowl and whip until soft peaks form. Fold in apple and horseradish and season to taste with black pepper.

EASY HOLLANDAISE SAUCE

Hollandaise sauce is normally made in the top of a double boiler by slowly adding the melted butter to the egg mixture. In this easy version no cooking is required if you make sure that the butter is hot and bubbling when you add it to the egg mixture.

Makes 1 cup/250 mL

- [ ] 3 egg yolks
- [ ] 2 tablespoons lemon juice
- [ ] 1/2 cup/1 stick/125 g butter
- [ ] freshly ground black pepper

Place egg yolks and lemon juice in a food processor or blender and process until light and frothy. Melt butter until it is hot and bubbling. With food processor running, slowly pour in hot, melted butter and process until thick. Season to taste with black pepper and serve immediately.

Microwave it: Hollandaise sauce can be quickly and easily made in the microwave. Place egg yolks and lemon juice in a small pitcher and whisk to combine. Melt butter in a separate pitcher, then whisk into egg yolk mixture and cook on MEDIUM (50%), stirring every minute, for 1 1/2 minutes or until sauce thickens.

TARTARE SAUCE

Makes 1 cup/250 mL

- [ ] 1 cup/250 mL mayonnaise
- [ ] 2 tablespoons finely chopped sweet pickles
- [ ] 1 tablespoon finely chopped fresh parsley
- [ ] 1 tablespoon chopped fresh dill weed
- [ ] freshly ground black pepper

Place mayonnaise, pickle, capers, parsley, dill and black pepper to taste in a bowl and mix well to combine.

STIRRED EGG CUSTARD

Makes 1 1/2 cups/375 mL

- [ ] 3/4 cup/185 mL milk, scalded
- [ ] 1 tablespoon sugar
- [ ] 3 eggs, lightly beaten
- [ ] 3/4 cup/185 mL thin cream
- [ ] 1/2 teaspoon vanilla extract

1 Place milk and sugar in a small saucepan and cook over a low heat, stirring constantly, for 3-4 minutes or until sugar dissolves.
2 Place eggs in a top of double boiler, place over a saucepan of simmering water and gradually stir in milk mixture, then cream. Cook, stirring constantly, until custard evenly coats the back of a wooden spoon.
3 Remove insert from saucepan and place in iced water to stop the cooking process. Stir in vanilla extract and use custard warm or chilled as desired.

CREME ANGLAISE

Crème Anglaise is a light custard sauce which is great served warm or chilled with fruit desserts and puddings.

Makes 1 cup/250 mL

- [ ] 3 egg yolks
- [ ] 2 tablespoons sugar
- [ ] 1 1/4 cups/300 mL milk, scalded
- [ ] 1/2 teaspoon vanilla extract

1 Place egg yolks and sugar in top of a double boiler and mix to combine. Place over a saucepan of simmering water and beat with electric mixer or whisk until a ribbon trail forms.
2 Gradually stir in milk and vanilla extract, then cook over a low heat, stirring in a figure-eight pattern, until custard thickens and coats the back of a wooden spoon. Do not allow the custard to boil.
3 Remove insert from heat, place in a bowl of ice, and stir until custard cools a little. Strain through a fine sieve if necessary and use as desired.

WHITE SAUCE

This classic sauce is the base for many sauces. Add ¹/₂ cup/60 g shredded cheese for a cheese sauce or 2 tablespoons finely chopped fresh parsley to make parsley sauce. Or make a curry sauce with 2 teaspoons curry powder and ¹/₂ onion, chopped. For mushroom sauce, simply add 2 oz/60 g sliced mushrooms cooked for about 5 minutes in butter.

Makes 1 cup/250 mL

- ☐ **2 tablespoons/30 g butter**
- ☐ **2 tablespoons all-purpose flour**
- ☐ **1 cup/250 mL milk**

1   Melt butter in a saucepan. Stir in flour and cook for 1 minute, stirring constantly.
2   Gradually stir in milk and cook over a medium heat until sauce boils and thickens. Season to taste if desired.

Microwave it: To make White Sauce, melt butter in a microwave-safe pitcher, mix in flour, gradually add milk and cook on HIGH (100%) for 3-4 minutes or until thickened. Stir after 1¹/₂ minutes.

ONION AND HERB YOGURT SAUCE

Serve this low-calorie (kilojoule) sauce poured over vegetables as a delicious alternative to white sauce.

Makes 1¹/₄ cups/315 mL

- ☐ **1 tablespoon olive oil**
- ☐ **1 onion, finely chopped**
- ☐ **¹/₄ teaspoon ground coriander**
- ☐ **2 tablespoons all-purpose flour**
- ☐ **¹/₂ cup/125 mL low-fat milk**
- ☐ **³/₄ cup/185 g plain yogurt**
- ☐ **1 tablespoon finely chopped fresh basil**
- ☐ **1 tablespoon finely chopped fresh parsley**
- ☐ **1 tablespoon finely snipped fresh chives**
- ☐ **freshly ground black pepper**

1   Heat oil in a saucepan and cook onion and coriander for 4-5 minutes or until onion is soft. Stir in flour and gradually mix in milk. Reduce heat and cook until sauce thickens.
2   Mix in yogurt, basil, parsley and chives and stir over a low heat until heated through. Season to taste with black pepper.

GREEN SAUCE

This sauce is a colorful addition to meals that seem to be a little bland in color. Try it with vegetables such as cauliflower. It is also delicious served with poultry or fish.

Makes 1 cup/250 mL

- ☐ **1 oz/30 g fresh parsley, chopped**
- ☐ **2 tablespoons chopped fresh basil**
- ☐ **¹/₃ cup/30 g snipped fresh chives**
- ☐ **1 cup/250 mL milk**
- ☐ **1 tablespoon/15 g butter**
- ☐ **2 tablespoons all-purpose flour**
- ☐ **1 tablespoon grated Parmesan cheese**
- ☐ **freshly ground black pepper**

1   In a food processor or blender, purée parsley, basil and chives with a little of the milk to make a green paste. Mix in remaining milk.
2   Melt butter in saucepan, stir in flour and cook for 1 minute. Blend in milk mixture and cook until sauce boils and thickens, stirring frequently during cooking.
3   Stir in cheese and season to taste with black pepper.

COCKTAIL SAUCE

This sauce is delicious served with seafood. It will keep in the refrigerator for up to 2 days.

Makes 1 cup/250 mL

- ☐ **1 cup/250 mL tomato catsup**
- ☐ **1 tablespoon Worcestershire sauce**
- ☐ **1 teaspoon bottled horseradish**
- ☐ **1 teaspoon cider vinegar**
- ☐ **1 teaspoon prepared mustard**
- ☐ **1 tablespoon lemon juice**
- ☐ **3-4 drops hot red pepper sauce or to taste**
- ☐ **2 tablespoons thick cream**

1   Place catsup sauce, Worcestershire sauce, horseradish, vinegar, mustard and lemon juice in a bowl and whisk to combine.
2   Season to taste with pepper sauce and stir in cream. Cover and chill until required.

FRESH TOMATO SAUCE

Serve this sauce with any boiled, steamed or microwaved vegetables. Top with bread crumbs and Parmesan cheese and place under a hot broiler to create a tomato-flavored gratin. Use six fresh large tomatoes in summer when they are plentiful. You may need to add a tablespoon of tomato paste for extra flavor.

Makes 1¹/₂ cups/375 mL

- ☐ **1 tablespoon olive oil**
- ☐ **1 onion, sliced**
- ☐ **1 clove garlic, crushed**
- ☐ **¹/₂ green pepper, sliced**
- ☐ **14 oz/440 g canned, peeled tomatoes, mashed**
- ☐ **¹/₂ cup/125 mL white wine**
- ☐ **1 teaspoon dried mixed herbs**
- ☐ **freshly ground black pepper**

1   Heat oil in a saucepan and cook onion, garlic and green pepper for 4-5 minutes until onion is soft. Stir in tomatoes and wine and simmer for 5 minutes.
2   Add herbs and season to taste with black pepper. Simmer for a further 20 minutes or until sauce reduces.

Microwave it: Fresh Tomato Sauce is made in about 15 minutes in the microwave. In a large microwave-safe pitcher, cook onion and garlic in oil on HIGH (100%) for 2-3 minutes Add remaining ingredients. Cook on HIGH (100%) for a further 10-15 minutes or until sauce reduces and thickens.

HOT CURRY SAUCE

As a topping for baked potatoes or as an accompaniment to steamed vegetables, this easy-to-prepare sauce makes a tasty change.

Makes 2 cups/500 mL

- ☐ **6 zucchini, peeled and chopped**
- ☐ **1 tablespoon vegetable oil**
- ☐ **1 onion, chopped**
- ☐ **1 teaspoon curry powder**
- ☐ **¹/₂ teaspoon chili sauce**
- ☐ **1 tablespoon fruit chutney**

Boil, steam or microwave zucchini until tender. Drain and set aside.

2   Heat oil in a skillet, add onion and curry powder and cook for 4-5 minutes or until onion is soft.

3   Place zucchini, onion mixture, chili sauce and chutney in a food processor or blender and process until smooth. Pour into a saucepan and cook over a low heat, stirring, for 4-5 minutes or until sauce is heated through.

CAMEMBERT SAUCE

This creamy fondue-like sauce will dress up the plainest vegetable. Try it poured over zucchini, broccoli, potatoes or butternut squash. It is also a great way to use up that odd piece of Camembert or Brie left in the fridge.

Makes ³/₄ cup/185 mL

- [ ] **1 tablespoon/15 g butter**
- [ ] **1 tablespoon flour**
- [ ] **¹/₂ cup/125 mL milk**
- [ ] **¹/₄ cup/60 mL white wine**
- [ ] **3 oz/90 g Camembert or Brie cheese, rind removed**
- [ ] **freshly ground black pepper**

1   Melt butter in a small saucepan. Stir in flour and cook for 1 minute. Blend in milk and cook until sauce boils and thickens, stirring frequently during cooking.

2   Stir in wine and cheese. Season to taste with black pepper, and cook over a low heat until cheese melts.

Microwave it: In a microwave-safe pitcher, melt butter. Stir in flour and milk. Cook on HIGH (100%) for 2 minutes or until sauce thickens. Stir after 1 minute. Mix in wine and cheese. Cook 1 minute on MEDIUM (50%) or until cheese melts.

From top: Camembert Sauce, Fresh Tomato Sauce, White Sauce, Green Sauce, Onion and Herb Yogurt Sauce

YOGURT DRESSING

This dressing makes a great lower calorie (kilojoule) alternative to mayonnaise. Try it on potato salad or coleslaw.

Makes 1 cup/250 mL

- [ ] ³/₄ cup/185 g plain yogurt
- [ ] 1 clove garlic, crushed (optional)
- [ ] 2 tablespoons white wine vinegar
- [ ] 2 tablespoons snipped fresh chives

Combine yogurt, garlic, vinegar and chives in a bowl. Whisk well to combine.

Variations

Mint Yogurt Dressing: Prepare Yogurt Dressing as directed. Mix in 2 tablespoons finely chopped fresh mint.
Curried Yogurt Dressing: Prepare Yogurt Dressing. Blend in a teaspoon of curry powder and a dash of chili sauce.
Thousand Island Yogurt Dressing: Prepare Yogurt Dressing, omitting garlic. Mix in 2 tablespoons chopped green olives, 2 finely sliced spring onions, 1 finely chopped hard-boiled egg, 1 tablespoon finely chopped green pepper, 1 tablespoon tomato paste and ¹/₂ teaspoon chili sauce.

VINAIGRETTE

Makes 1 cup/250 mL

- [ ] ³/₄ cup/185 mL olive oil
- [ ] ¹/₄ cup/60 mL cider vinegar
- [ ] 1 tablespoon Dijon mustard
- [ ] freshly ground black pepper

Place oil, vinegar and mustard in a screwtop jar. Season to taste with black pepper. Shake well to combine.

Variations

Walnut or Hazelnut Dressing: Replace olive oil with ¹/₃ cup/90 mL walnut or hazelnut oil and ¹/₃ cup/90 mL vegetable oil.
Lemon Herb Vinaigrette: Replace vinegar with ¹/₄ cup/60 mL lemon juice, add 2 oz/60 g mixed chopped fresh herbs. Suggested herbs include basil, parsley, chives, rosemary, thyme or tarragon.

GINGER AND SOY DRESSING

If possible, make earlier in the day to allow the flavors to develop.

Makes 1 cup/250 mL

- [ ] 1 tablespoon sesame oil
- [ ] 1 tablespoon grated fresh ginger
- [ ] ¹/₂ cup/125 mL soy sauce
- [ ] ¹/₂ cup/125 mL water
- [ ] 1 tablespoon cider vinegar
- [ ] 1 clove garlic, crushed (optional)

Combine sesame oil, ginger, soy, water, vinegar and garlic in a screwtop jar. Shake well to combine. Stand 15 minutes before using.

ORIENTAL MAYONNAISE

Serve as a dipping sauce for lightly cooked fresh vegetables such as asparagus spears, celery and carrot sticks, or spoon over hot vegetables.

Makes 1¹/₂ cups/375 mL

- [ ] 1 clove garlic, crushed
- [ ] 2 teaspoons grated fresh ginger
- [ ] ¹/₃ cup/90 mL soy sauce
- [ ] 2 tablespoons cider vinegar
- [ ] 2 tablespoons brown sugar
- [ ] 1 teaspoon fennel seeds
- [ ] 2 egg yolks
- [ ] ¹/₂ teaspoon dry mustard powder
- [ ] ³/₄ cup/185 mL vegetable oil
- [ ] 2 teaspoons sesame oil
- [ ] ¹/₂ teaspoon hot chili sauce

1 Place garlic, ginger, soy sauce, vinegar, sugar and fennel seeds in a small saucepan and bring to the boil. Reduce heat and simmer, uncovered, for 10 minutes or until mixture reduces by half. Remove from heat and strain to remove fennel seeds. Set aside to cool.
2 Combine egg yolks and mustard in food processor or blender. Process until just combined. With the machine running, pour in vegetable and sesame oils in a steady stream. Process until mayonnaise thickens.
3 Add soy mixture and process to combine. Mix in chili sauce to taste.

APPLE AND HERB DRESSIN

Use this dressing as a low-fat, low-calorie (kilojoule) alternative to traditional French dressing or try it as a tasty dressing on rice salad.

Makes 1¹/₂ cups/375 mL

- [ ] 1 cup/250 mL unsweetened apple juice
- [ ] ¹/₄ cup/60 mL apple cider vinegar
- [ ] 1 clove garlic, crushed
- [ ] 1 tablespoon finely snipped fresh chives
- [ ] 2 tablespoons finely chopped fresh parsley
- [ ] freshly ground black pepper

Place apple juice, vinegar, garlic, chives, parsley and black pepper to taste in a screwtop jar and shake well to combine.

TOFU MAYONNAISE

This delicious mayonnaise made from tofu is a cholesterol-free alternative to traditional mayonnaise.

Makes 1¹/₂ cups/375 mL

- [ ] 1 cup/250 g tofu (soft or silken)
- [ ] 1 teaspoon Dijon mustard
- [ ] ¹/₄ cup/60 mL cider vinegar
- [ ] ¹/₂ cup/125 mL olive oil
- [ ] freshly ground black pepper

1 Place tofu, mustard and 1 tablespoon vinegar in food processor or blender and process until smooth.
2 With machine running, slowly add 2 tablespoons oil then 1 tablespoon vinegar. Continue in this way until all the oil and vinegar are used. Season to taste with black pepper.

LOW-OIL VINAIGRETTE

Makes 1 cup/250 mL

- [ ] $^1/_3$ **cup/90 mL olive oil**
- [ ] $^2/_3$ **cup/170 mL cider vinegar**
- [ ] $^1/_2$ **teaspoon dry mustard**
- [ ] **cayenne pepper**
- [ ] **freshly ground black pepper**

Combine oil, vinegar and mustard in a screwtop jar. Season to taste with cayenne and black pepper. Shake well to combine.

MAYONNAISE

Makes $1^1/_2$ cups/375 mL

- [ ] **2 egg yolks**
- [ ] $^1/_4$ **teaspoon dry mustard**
- [ ] **1 cup/250 mL olive oil**
- [ ] **2 tablespoons lemon juice or white wine vinegar**
- [ ] **freshly ground black pepper**

1   Place egg yolks and mustard in a food processor.
2   With machine running, slowly pour in olive oil, and process until mixture thickens. Blend in lemon juice or vinegar and season to taste with black pepper.

Variations
Green Herbed Mayonnaise: Purée 1 oz/ 30 g basil leaves, 2 tablespoons fresh parsley, 12 chives and 1 clove garlic. Prepare as above using vinegar, not lemon juice.
Blue Cheese Mayonnaise: Blend 3 oz/ 90 g blue cheese into prepared mayonnaise.

From top: Mayonnaise, Oriental Mayonnaise, Yogurt Dressing, Vinaigrette, Low-Oil Vinaigrette, Ginger and Soy Dressing

BEEF STOCK

This recipe will make a rich stock. If you wish, the meat can be omitted and just the bones used.

Makes 8 cups/2 liters

- [ ] **1 lb/500 g boneless shank beef, diced**
- [ ] **1 lb/500 g beef marrow bones, cut into pieces**
- [ ] **1 onion, quartered**
- [ ] **2 carrots, coarsely chopped**
- [ ] **4 stalks celery, coarsely chopped**
- [ ] **fresh herbs of your choice**
- [ ] **1/2 teaspoon whole black peppercorns**
- [ ] **12 cups/3 liters cold water**

1 Place beef, bones, onion, carrots, celery, herbs, peppercorns and water in a large saucepan and bring to the boil. Reduce heat and simmer, stirring occasionally, for 2 hours
2 Strain stock and refrigerate overnight.
3 Skim fat from the surface and use as required.

Keeping stock: Stock will keep in the refrigerator for 3-4 days or in the freezer for 12 months. As stock really does not keep very well, except in the freezer, it is better to freeze it even if you are only keeping it for a few days.

CHICKEN STOCK

Makes 8 cups/2 liters

- [ ] **1 chicken carcass, skin removed and trimmed of all visible fat**
- [ ] **1 onion, quartered**
- [ ] **2 carrots, coarsely chopped**
- [ ] **4 stalks celery, coarsely chopped**
- [ ] **fresh herbs of your choice**
- [ ] **1/2 teaspoon whole black peppercorns**
- [ ] **12 cups/3 liters cold water**

1 Place chicken carcass, onion, carrots, celery, herbs, peppercorns and water in a large saucepan and bring to the boil. Reduce heat and simmer, stirring occasionally, for 2 hours.
2 Strain stock and refrigerate overnight.
3 Skim fat from the surface and use stock as required.

Freeze it: Freeze stock in 1/2 cup/125 mL or 1 cup/250 mL portions for easy use at a later date. It is also a good idea to freeze some stock in ice cube trays for those times when you require only one or two tablespoons of stock. Remember to remove the stock from the trays once frozen and place it in a freezer bag or it will evaporate and you will be left with nothing. The plastic trays in which the stock has been frozen are no longer suitable for ice as the stock taints the trays and the flavor will be absorbed by the ice cubes.

FISH STOCK

Fish stock is even better if you can include the shells of lobster, shrimp or crab in it. When making fish stock it is important that the cooking time is no longer than 20 minutes as the bones and trimming become bitter and impart an unpleasant taste.

Makes 8 cups/2 liters

- [ ] **fish bones, skin and seafood shells, the quantity and type used is not important**
- [ ] **1 large onion, quartered**
- [ ] **1 large carrot, coarsely chopped**
- [ ] **4 stalks celery, coarsely chopped**
- [ ] **1 bay leaf**
- [ ] **1 sprig fresh thyme**
- [ ] **1/2 teaspoon whole black peppercorns**
- [ ] **12 cups/3 liters cold water**

1 Place fish trimmings, onion, carrot, celery, bay leaf, thyme, peppercorns and water in a large saucepan and bring to the boil. Reduce heat and simmer for 20 minutes.
2 Strain stock and use as required.

VEGETABLE STOCK

This is a wonderful vegetable stock and well worth the effort. It will add a delicious flavor to any dish, and is a must for any vegetarian cook.

Makes 8 cups/2 liters

- [ ] **2 large onions, quartered**
- [ ] **2 large carrots, coarsely chopped**
- [ ] **1 head celery, leaves included, coarsely chopped**
- [ ] **1 bunch parsley, stalks included**
- [ ] **1/2 teaspoon whole black peppercorns**
- [ ] **10 cups/2.5 liters cold water**

1 Place onions, carrots, celery, parsley, peppercorns and water in a large saucepan. Bring to the boil, reduce heat and simmer, stirring occasionally, for 30 minutes.
2 Remove stock from heat and allow to cool. Place stock in a food processor or blender and process to purée. Push vegetable mixture through a sieve. Discard solids and use liquid as required.

Cook's tip: Do not add salt when making stock, especially if you do not know how it is to be used. Salting stock can lead to a dish that is too salty if you reduce the stock or if you are using other salty ingredients.

MICROWAVE CHICKEN STOCK

The microwave is particularly good for making small quantities of stock. The chicken carcass remaining after a roast is ideal for making stock.

Makes 6 cups/1.5 liters

- [ ] **1 chicken carcass**
- [ ] **1 onion, chopped**
- [ ] **1 carrot, chopped**
- [ ] **2 stalks celery, chopped**
- [ ] **1 tablespoon chopped fresh parsley**
- [ ] **1 teaspoon chopped fresh thyme or 1/2 teaspoon dried thyme**
- [ ] **1/2 teaspoon whole black peppercorns**
- [ ] **cold water**

1 Place chicken carcass, onion, carrot, celery, parsley, thyme and peppercorns in a large microwave-safe casserole. Cover with water and cook, uncovered, on HIGH (100%) for 45 minutes.
2 Strain stock and refrigerate overnight.
3 Skim fat from the surface and use as required.

Cook's tip: Beef, fish and vegetable stock can be made in the microwave in much the same way as chicken stock. Just remember that beef stock requires a little longer cooking and fish stock should not be cooked for more than 20 minutes.

RICH SHORT (FLAKY) PASTRY

Rich short pastry can be used for both sweet and savory pies.

- [ ] **2 cups/250 g all-purpose flour, sifted**
- [ ] **³/₄ cup/1¹/₂ sticks/185 g butter or shortening, chilled and cut into small pieces**
- [ ] **1 egg yolk, lightly beaten**
- [ ] **4-5 tablespoons chilled water**

1 Place flour in a bowl and cut in butter or shortening using two knives or a pastry blender until mixture resembles coarse bread crumbs.
2 Mix in egg yolk and enough water to form a soft dough with a fork.
3 Turn dough onto a lightly floured surface and knead gently until smooth. Wrap in plastic food wrap and refrigerate for 30 minutes. Roll out and use as desired.

ALMOND PASTRY SHELLS

Bake these pastry shells and serve filled with lemon curd or your favorite jam or fresh fruit.

Oven temperature 400°F, 200°C

- [ ] **2 cups/250 g all-purpose flour, sifted**
- [ ] **¹/₄ cup/60 g superfine sugar**
- [ ] **³/₄ cup/1¹/₂ sticks/185 g butter or shortening, chilled and cut into small pieces**
- [ ] **1 egg yolk, lightly beaten with a few drops vanilla extract**
- [ ] **4-5 tablespoons chilled water**
- [ ] **¹/₄ cup/30 g ground almonds**

1 Place flour and sugar in a bowl and mix to combine. Cut in butter using two knives or a pastry blender until mixture resembles coarse bread crumbs.
2 Mix in egg yolk mixture and enough water to form a soft dough with a fork. Turn onto a lightly floured surface and knead gently until smooth. Wrap in plastic food wrap and refrigerate for 30 minutes.
3 On a lightly floured surface roll pastry out to ¹/₈ in/3 mm thickness. Sprinkle with almonds. Cut into 4-6 in/10-15 cm circles to fit lightly greased tartlet pans, small cupcake pans or muffin cups.
4 Prick bases with a fork and bake for 15-20 minutes or until golden. Remove shells from pans and cool on a wire rack.

CHEESE PASTRY

Cheese pastry makes a tasty pastry for savory tarts. Omit the mustard and pepper and this pastry is perfect with apples and pears.

- [ ] **3 oz/90 g mature Cheddar cheese, shredded**
- [ ] **1¹/₂ teaspoons dry mustard**
- [ ] **¹/₂ teaspoon cayenne pepper**
- [ ] **2 cups/250 g all-purpose flour, sifted**
- [ ] **³/₄ cup/1¹/₂ sticks/185 g butter, chilled and cut into small cubes**
- [ ] **1 egg yolk, lightly beaten**
- [ ] **4-5 tablespoons chilled water**

1 Place cheese, mustard, cayenne pepper and flour in a bowl and mix to combine. Cut butter in using two knives or a pastry blender until mixture resembles coarse bread crumbs.
2 Mix in egg yolk and enough water to form a soft dough with a fork.
3 Turn dough onto a lightly floured surface and knead gently until smooth. Wrap in plastic food wrap and refrigerate for 30 minutes. Roll out and use as desired.

FOOD PROCESSOR PASTRY

The food processor is great for making pastry. Place the flour and butter or shortening in a food processor and, using the pulse button, process to cut the fat until the mixture resembles coarse bread crumbs. Add egg yolk and water and process until a dough is just formed. Turn dough onto a lightly floured surface and knead until smooth. Wrap in plastic food wrap and refrigerate for 30 minutes before using. When making pastry in the food processor you may not require as much water as when making it by hand. Use sufficient water to bind the ingredients together.

TIPS FOR PERFECT PASTRY MAKING

Practice makes perfect pastry so they say. To some, the thought of making pastry can be intimidating. Pastry is in fact easy to make and handle if a few ground rules are followed.

❦ Crisp flaky pastry is best made using chilled butter or shortening and water. It also helps to have cool utensils, so in hot weather it is a good idea to place them in the refrigerator for 10-15 minutes before making your pastry.

❦ Handle pastry quickly and lightly, as overhandling will result in tough pastry that will be difficult to roll.

❦ The amount of liquid used to bind the ingredients together will vary depending on the quality of the flour. If the dough is too soft the pastry will shrink on cooking.

❦ Kneading the pastry should be done using the coolest part of your hands, the fingertips. After kneading, wrap the pastry in plastic food wrap and refrigerate for 30 minutes before rolling out.

❦ Always roll pastry out in light, short strokes, starting from the middle of the pastry, rolling away from you and lifting the rolling pin off the edge of the pastry. This ensures even thickness.

❦ Lift and turn the pastry on a floured surface as you roll.

❦ Line the pie plate, trim the edges and rest the pastry in the refrigerator for 10 minutes longer before baking.

BAKING BLIND

Baking blind means to precook the pastry shell without a filling. This is done if the filling you are using requires little or no cooking. It is also used when a liquid filling, such as a quiche filling, is being put into the pastry shell. The precooking prevents the pastry becoming soggy.

To bake blind, line the pastry shell with parchment paper, then cover the paper with uncooked rice, pasta or dried beans. This keeps the base of the pastry shell flat during cooking. Bake the pastry shell at 400°F/200°C for 10 minutes or as directed in the recipe. Remove rice, pasta or beans and paper and bake for 7-10 minutes longer. Allow pastry shell to cool before filling.

GLOSSARY

Al dente: Just firm to the bite, the correct texture for pasta and some vegetables.

Au gratin: A cheese and bread crumb topping, browned under the broiler or in the oven.

Baste: To moisten meat or vegetables during cooking.

Blending: Mixing a liquid such as water with a dry ingredient such as cornstarch. The mixture should be smooth and well combined.

Bind: To hold dry ingredients together with egg or liquid.

Bouillon: Broth or uncleared stock.

Bouquet garni: A small bunch of herbs, usually parsley, thyme and bay leaf. A bouquet garni is added to stews, soups or stocks for flavoring. Commercially prepared sachets of dried herbs are also available from most supermarkets.

Buttermilk: This is a cultured dairy product that has the same food value as skim milk. It is a useful low-fat ingredient that is sometimes used in baked goods.

CHICKEN

To disjoint a chicken:

1 Using a sharp knife, cut through the skin where the leg joins the body, then cut through the bone joint between the leg and the body. This section consists of the leg and thigh and is sometimes called a 'maryland'. Separate the thigh from the leg by cutting through the joint.

2 Cut a small amount of breast meat down through the wing section, bending the wing away from the body to reveal the joint. Cut through the joint bone.

3 Cut through the rib bones, along each side of the body between the breast and back to separate the two pieces. The back portion can be frozen and used at a later date for the stockpot.

4 Divide the breast section into two pieces by cutting through the center of the breast bone. Trim all pieces of excess fat and skin.

Trussing a chicken: Trussing a chicken helps it maintain its shape during cooking. Insert a metal skewer widthwise, just below the thigh bone, right through the body of the chicken. The ends of the skewer should be exposed either side. Place the chicken, breast side down, on a work surface. Take a length of string and catch the wing tips, then pass the string under the ends of the skewer and cross over the back. Turn the chicken breast side up and tie in the legs and the tail.

To test when a bird is cooked: Place a skewer into the thickest part of the thigh and when the skewer is removed the juices should run clear. If the juices are tinged pink, return the bird to the oven and cook for 15 minutes longer, then test again. On completion of cooking, allow whole birds to stand in a warm place for 10-20 minutes before carving. This tenderizes the meat by allowing the juices to settle into the flesh.

CHOCOLATE

To melt chocolate: Place chocolate in a heatproof bowl or top of a double boiler, and set aside. Partly fill a saucepan with water so that when the bowl or insert is placed over it the water comes just below its bottom. Bring water to the boil, then remove the pan from the heat and place the bowl or insert with the chocolate in it over the saucepan. Stand off the heat, stirring occasionally until the chocolate melts and is smooth. Use as required.

Melting chocolate in the microwave: Place 12 oz/375 g chocolate in a microwave-safe glass or ceramic dish and cook on HIGH (100%) for 2 minutes. When melting chocolate in the microwave you will find that it tends to hold its shape, so always stir it before additional heating. If the chocolate is not completely melted, cook for 30 seconds longer, then stir again.

Seized chocolate: Chocolate 'seizes' if it is overheated or if it comes in contact with water or steam. Seizing results in the chocolate tightening and becoming a thick mass that will not melt. To rescue seized chocolate stir in a little cream or vegetable oil until the chocolate becomes smooth again.

CHOCOLATE DECORATIONS

Chocolate curls: Pour melted chocolate over a cool work surface such as marble, ceramic or granite. Spread the chocolate as smoothly as possible using a flexible metal spatula, in a layer about $1/16$ in/ 1.5 mm thick; do not leave any holes. If the chocolate is too thick it will not roll. Allow the chocolate to set at room temperature. Holding a long sharp knife at a 45° angle, pull gently over the surface of the chocolate to form large curls.

Chocolate shavings: Chocolate shavings are made from chocolate that is at room temperature. To make shavings, chill the chocolate first. Using a vegetable peeler, shave the sides of the chocolate. Shavings or larger curls will fall depending on the temperature of the chocolate.

Chocolate leaves: Use stiff, fresh, nonpoisonous leaves such as rose, ivy or lemon leaves, with as much stem as possible for holding on to. Wash and dry leaves, brush the shiny surface of the leaf with a thin layer of melted, cooled chocolate. Allow to set to room temperature then carefully peel away the leaf.

Piping chocolate: Chocolate can be piped into fancy shapes for decorating desserts or cakes. Trace a simple design on a thin piece of paper. Tape a sheet of parchment paper to the work surface and slide the drawing under the parchment paper. Pipe around the design outline with melted chocolate. Allow to set at room temperature, then remove carefully with a metal spatula.

Clarify: To remove milk solids and impurities from butter. It also means to clear stocks and jellies by filtering.

The process of clarifying butter separates it into three layers; a top layer of foam, a middle layer of pure butterfat and a bottom layer of milky-white solids. It is the middle layer that is used for sautéing; the other two layers contain water, milk proteins and carbohydrates.

To clarify butter, place it in a small saucepan and melt it over a low heat. Skim the foam from the surface of the butter, then slowly pour the butter into a bowl, leaving behind the milky-white solids. Ghee, which is used in Indian cooking, is a type of clarified butter.

Coconut milk: Coconut milk can be purchased canned, or as a long-life product in cartons, or as a powder to which you add water. These products have a short life once opened and should be used within a day or so.

You can make coconut milk using either grated fresh or un-sweetened flaked or shredded coconut and water: Place 1 lb/ 500 g prepared coconut in a bowl and pour over 3 cups/750 mL boiling water. Leave to stand for 30 minutes, then strain, squeezing the coconut to extract as much liquid as possible. This will make a thick coconut milk. The coconut can be used again to make a weaker coconut milk.

EGGS

Separating eggs: To separate an egg, crack the shell by tapping with the back of a knife to break cleanly in half. Carefully pass the yolk from one half of the shell to the other, so that the white of the egg passes into a bowl. Then place the yolk in a separate bowl. If separating more than one egg, break into separate bowls to ensure freshness before adding to the other eggs. If the egg white is to be beaten to the soft- or stiff-peak stage, it is vital that not a speck of yolk goes into the white, as the white will not beat up.

Beating egg whites: To beat egg whites to 'soft peaks' or 'stiff peaks' requires a little care. Firstly, all utensils being used must be free of grease and very clean. The smallest amount of grease, or even the smallest amount of egg yolk, will spoil the end result. If the whites are overbeaten, they become difficult to fold through and the mixture could collapse during cooking. For the best volume have the egg whites at room temperature before beating.

Soft peaks: Round mounds form when beaters are lifted from the egg whites after beating for a short time at a high speed (if using an electric mixer).

Stiff peaks: Slightly dryer and more peaked in shape than soft peaks. Use beaten egg whites immediately; if left to stand they will collapse.

Leftover eggs: Keep leftover yolks and whites in airtight containers in the refrigerator. Place 1 tablespoon of water over yolks to prevent a skin forming. Yolks will keep for up to 3 days and whites for up to 10 days. You can freeze whites for up to a month.

Flake: To separate cooked or canned fish flesh into small pieces.

Folding in: To combine ingredients quickly and gently, without deflating what is usually a light mixture. A large metal spoon or pancake turner is ideal for doing this. When folding egg whites into a mixture, first mix in 2-3 tablespoons of the egg whites to loosen the mixture. Then add the remaining egg whites and gently fold them in, using a metal spoon or pancake turner.

GARNISHES

Avocado fans: Using a small sharp knife and starting at the pointed end of the avocado, cut through the skin and flesh until you reach the pit. Run the knife around the avocado then, holding it in both hands, twist to separate the halves. Remove the seed and cut each half into two, lengthwise. Starting at the broad end, make 3-4 lengthwise cuts in each avocado quarter, leaving about a quarter of the avocado uncut at the narrow end. Peel away the skin, fan out slices and place on serving plate.

Celery curls: Cut the celery into even lengths, then split each piece of celery in half lengthwise. Using a small sharp knife, make thin parallel lengthwise cuts in celery, cutting almost to the end. Drop the celery pieces into a bowl of iced water and refrigerate for several hours or overnight, until the celery pieces curl and open out.

Chili flowers: Choose small chilies or trim the ends from long chilies, keeping the stem ends intact. Using a small pair of scissors cut around each chili to form petals, taking care not to cut all the way to the stem. Remove the seeds, drop the chilies into a bowl of iced water and refrigerate until the 'flowers' open out.

Lemon and lime twists: Cut thin slices of lemon or lime, then cut each slice through to the center. Twist the two bottom halves in opposite directions and place in position.

Omelet shreds: One of the classic Asian garnishes, omelet shreds are quick and easy to make when you know how. Use as a garnish for soups, fried rice and noodle dishes and in salads. To make, place 3 eggs, 1 tablespoon cold water, 1 tablespoon finely chopped fresh herbs and black pepper to taste in a bowl and whisk to combine. Heat a lightly greased skillet. Add enough egg mixture to thinly coat the bottom of the skillet and cook until the underside is set. Flip omelet and cook the second side for 10 seconds. Remove and set aside to cool. Use the remaining egg mixture to make more omelets. To make shreds, place cold omelets in a stack, roll up and cut into fine shreds. The omelet can also be cut into 1 in/2.5 cm squares.

Spring onion whisks: Wash spring onions and trim off some of the green top. Trim the bulb end to where the white starts to turn green. Using a small pair of kitchen scissors, cut the onions from the top into fine strips, stopping about halfway down. Drop the onions into a bowl of cold water and leave until the strips curl. This takes only a few minutes at the most.

Hull: To remove green calyx from fruit such as strawberries.

Knead: This is usually done on a lightly floured surface. The hands or fingertips are used to turn the outside edge of a mixture into the center. Do this to either shape a mixture into a ball (pastry) or alter the nature of the mixture by working it with your hands (bread dough).

Leeks: To clean and prepare, cut down lengthwise and dunk upside down in a bowl of cold water to remove dirt.

Lettuce: To wash and separate the lettuce leaves, remove the stem of the lettuce using a twisting motion with the hand until the stem comes free. For firmer, tighter stems, cut free from the lettuce using the point of a sharp knife. Place lettuce, stem side up, under cold running water. The weight of the continually running water will cause the leaves to separate. For crisp leaves, shake off excess water and place in a plastic food bag, tie and refrigerate for 30 minutes or until required.

Mangoes: Cutting a mango is easy once you know how. The waste from around the pit can be used to make mango ice cream, or cut into cubes, tossed in lime or lemon juice and served as a side dish to a main meal. Allow half a mango per person for dessert.

1 Place the mango on a chopping board and, cutting as close as possible to the pit, cut a large slice from either side.

2 Taking one slice, cut the flesh into cubes, with the tip of a knife being careful not to cut the skin. Repeat with the other slice.

3 Turn the skin inside out. The flesh can now be easily removed.

MEAT

Boning a leg of lamb: Boning a leg of lamb is not nearly as daunting as you may think, as long as you remember that a sharp knife is essential and that the knife should always stay as close as possible to the bone.

1 Turn the leg of lamb so that the skin side is lying flat on your work surface and the thick end of the leg is facing you. Using a sharp knife, cut around the edges of the pelvic bone at the thick end (the pelvic bone is the one that you can see). This will loosen the bone.

2 Now cut deep around the pelvic bone, until you have freed it at the joint and through the tendons that connect it to the leg bone (the leg bone is the middle bone in the joint). Remember to keep your knife as close as possible to the bone so that you do not cut into

the meat.

3 The next step is to remove the shank bone. Hold on to this bone at the tip and cut close to the bone to free tendons and meat. Continue cutting down the bone until you reach the joint that connects it to the leg bone, cut through the tendons at this joint and remove the shank bone.

4 The leg bone is now removed in a tunnel fashion by gently loosening the meat at either end of the bone then cutting the meat from the bone and easing it out as you work. The leg of lamb is now boned and can be used as desired.

Butterflying a leg of lamb: First bone the leg of lamb as described above, then butterfly it by placing your knife horizontally in the cavity left by the leg bone and partially splitting the meat open. The flap is then turned outwards and the meat spread flat. Now make a similar horizontal cut into the thick muscle opposite so that it too can be opened out flat.

To roll and secure a loin: Place seasoning along the flap, roll loin up firmly and hold in position with skewers or poultry pins. Cut a long piece of string, place under the meat at one end, bringing the two ends – one long length, one short length – to the top of the meat. Twist the ends and knot. Then, working with the long length of string, extend out along the top of the meat 1 in/2.5 cm, hold in position with a finger at that point while passing the remaining length down the side, under and up the other side of meat. Loop under the finger position and pull long length to tighten. Continue in this manner along the loin, knotting at the other end.

Parboil: To boil for part of the cooking time before finishing by another method.

Pasta: The secret to cooking pasta is to use lots of water and a large saucepan so the pasta does not stick together.

To cook pasta, bring a large saucepan of water to the boil. As a general rule allow 4 cups/1 liter water to $3^{1}/_{2}$ oz/100 g pasta. Stir in the pasta and salt to taste, bring back to the boil and begin timing.

The pasta is done when it is 'al dente' – that is, tender, but with resistance to the bite. Remove the pasta from the water by straining through a colander or lifting out of the saucepan with tongs or fork. Use the packet directions as a guide to the cooking time, but generally fresh pasta will take 3-5 minutes and dried pasta 12-15 minutes.

PASTRY DECORATIONS

Give a professional finish to your pies with simple pastry decorations.

Pastry leaves: Cut leftover pastry scraps into 1 in/2.5 cm strips then diagonally across to form diamond shapes. Mark with the back of a knife to resemble veins of leaves. Arrange decoratively in the center of a glazed pie or overlap leaves and use as a decorative edging.

To make a lattice pattern: Cut the pastry into $^{1}/_{2}$ in/1 cm wide strips, long enough to cover the pie. Moisten the edges with water and lay half the strips over the filling, about 1 in/2.5 cm apart. Then lay remaining strips diagonally across these. Trim off excess and press edges together.

Poach: To cook by simmering very gently in liquid.

PORK

Butterfly pork steaks: These steaks are cut from the mid loin area, boned, cut almost in half and opened out flat. Try placing a fruit or savory filling on one side of the steak, then folding it over and securing with toothpicks. You can then pan fry or bake these steaks.

Pork tenderloins: Pork tenderloins are lean pieces of meat taken from the loin ribs. Tenderloins are quick and easy to cook and they have no waste. You can roast or pan fry pork tenderloins, then serve, sliced, with a sauce.

Reduce: To concentrate or thicken a liquid by rapid boiling.

Refresh: To rinse freshly cooked food in cold water to stop the cooking process and set the color, usually with green vegetables.

Rest: To allow the protein in flour

(gluten) to contract after kneading and rolling pastry. To allow the starch cells in batter to expand, for example when making crêpes.

RICE

The time that rice takes to cook depends on the type of rice and the method you choose to use. The following are the most common methods used for cooking rice.

Rapid boil: Place 8 cups/2 liters water in a large saucepan and bring to the boil. Stir in 1 cup/ 220 g rice and return to the boil. Boil rapidly for 12-15 minutes for white rice or 30-40 minutes for brown rice or until rice is tender. Drain through a sieve or colander and serve.

Absorption method: An easy way to cook rice and the grains stay separate and fluffy. For white rice, place $1^1/_2$ cups/375 mL water in a large saucepan, stir in 1 cup/220 g rice, cover and simmer for 20-25 minutes or until the water is absorbed and the rice is tender. Uncover, toss with a fork and stand for a few minutes before serving. For brown rice, use 2 cups/500 mL of water and cook for 55 minutes.

Steaming: This is a popular Chinese method of cooking rice. Wash 1 cup/220 g rice, then drain and set aside to dry. Place the rice in a heavy-based saucepan and add enough water to cover the rice by 1 in/2.5 cm. Bring to the boil and boil rapidly until steam holes appear on the surface of the rice. Reduce heat to as low as possible, cover with a tight-fitting lid, or foil, and steam for 10 minutes for white rice or 25-30 minutes for brown rice. Remove lid, or foil, toss the rice with a fork and stand for 5 minutes before serving.

Microwave: Cooking rice in the microwave does not save time but it does guarantee a perfect result and there is no messy saucepan at the end of the cooking time. To cook white rice in the microwave, place 1 cup/220 g rice and 2 cups/500 mL water in a large microwave-safe container. Cook, uncovered, on HIGH (100%) for 12-15 minutes or until the liquid is absorbed. Toss the rice with a fork,

cover and stand for 5 minutes before serving. For brown rice use 3 cups/750 mL water and cook for 30-35 minutes.

Roux: A blend of melted butter and flour, cooked as a base for thickening sauces and soups.

Scald: To heat liquid, usually milk, to just below boiling point. To scald milk or cream, rinse a small heavy-based saucepan with cold water, add milk or cream and bring almost to the boil over a low heat, stirring occasionally. Scalding helps prevent curdling during cooking.

Sear: To brown meat quickly on a hot surface to retain juices.

Segment: To cut the peel and all the white pith from citrus fruit, then cut between membranes joining segments.

Skim: To remove scum or fat from the surface of liquid.

Spatchcocking: To spatchcock a bird means to split and flatten it. The easiest way to cut the bird is to use a pair of poultry shears. First cut off the wing tips then cut the bird along each side of the backbone to remove it. Now place the bird breast side up and using the heel of your hand push down sharply to flatten the bird and break the breastbone. To ensure that the bird holds its shape during cooking, thread two skewers through it. One skewer is threaded through the legs, avoiding the bones, and the other through the wings and breast.

Stock: Homemade gives best results (see the Basic Recipes chapter to make your own). For convenience, substitute 1 bouillon cube for every 2 cups/500 mL water.

TURKEY

Carving a turkey: A very sharp, pointed knife with a long flexible blade is best for carving turkey. Before you start carving, remove the string and skewers from the bird and place breast side up on a board or platter. Use a large carving fork to hold the bird steady.

1 Removing the first leg: Cut the skin between the thigh and the breast of the bird. Separate the leg from the body by bending the

thigh outwards to locate the hip joint. Slice down through the joint to remove the leg.

2 Separating the thigh from the drumstick: Hold a knife at an angle between the thigh and drumstick bones and cut firmly through the joint to separate the leg.

3 Slicing the drumstick: Cut a thick slice of meat and skin from each side of the drumstick, keeping the knife close to the bone, then cut these into smaller slices.

4 Slicing the thigh: Holding the thigh steady, cut into four or more pieces, depending on the size of the thigh. Repeat steps 1-4 for the other leg of the turkey.

5 Removing the wing: Slice down through the corner of the breast towards the wing. Push the wing out to show the joint and cut through the joint. Remove the wing with the piece of breast attached.

6 Carving the breast: Holding the breast steady, slice down through the meat. When you reach the incision above the wing joint, the slice will fall free.

Toasting coconut: Coconut can be toasted by spreading the required amount over a cookie sheet, then baking at 350°F/180°C for 5-10 minutes, or until the coconut is lightly and evenly browned. Toss back and forth occasionally with a spoon to ensure even browning. Coconut can also be toasted in the microwave. Place 3 oz/90 g coconut on a microwave-safe ceramic or glass plate or in an oven bag and cook on HIGH (100%), shaking or stirring every minute for 5-6 minutes or until the coconut is golden. The exact length of time can vary considerably depending on the moisture content of the coconut.

Toasting nuts: Nuts can be toasted in much the same way as coconut or placed on a cookie sheet and browned under a broiler on a medium heat. Toss back and forth with a spoon until lightly and evenly browned.

INDEX